A HISTORY OF THE CHRISTIAN CHURCH

A HISTORY OF THE REFORMATION IN GERMANY
TO 1555

A HISTORY OF THE CHRISTIAN CHURCH

APOSTOLIC AND POST-APOSTOLIC TIMES
Leonhard Goppelt

A HISTORY OF THE REFORMATION
IN GERMANY TO 1555
Franz Lau and Ernst Bizer

THE CATHOLIC CHURCH
FROM 1648 TO 1870
Friedrich Heyer

A HISTORY OF
THE REFORMATION IN GERMANY

TO 1555

BY

FRANZ LAU

PROFESSOR OF CHURCH HISTORY, UNIVERSITY OF LEIPZIG

AND

ERNST BIZER

PROFESSOR OF CHURCH HISTORY, UNIVERSITY OF BONN

TRANSLATED BY BRIAN A. HARDY

ADAM & CHARLES BLACK
LONDON

THIS EDITION PUBLISHED 1969
A. AND C. BLACK LTD
4, 5 AND 6 SOHO SQUARE LONDON W.I

© 1964, VANDENHOECK AND RUPRECHT
ENGLISH TRANSLATION © 1969 A. AND C. BLACK LTD
SBN 7136 0905 2

Translated from the German, *Reformationsgeschichte
bis 1532*, by Franz Lau, and *Reformationsgeschichte 1532
bis 1555*, by Ernst Bizer, being Section K of Vol. III of
Die Kirche in ihrer Geschichte: ein Handbuch, edited
by Kurt Dietrich Schmidt and Ernst Wolf (Vandenhoeck and Ruprecht, Göttingen and Zurich).

PRINTED IN GREAT BRITAIN
BY BILLING & SONS LIMITED
GUILDFORD AND LONDON

CONTENTS

PART I

THE HISTORY OF THE REFORMATION TO 1532

BY FRANZ LAU

CONTENTS

PART II

THE REFORMATION FROM 1532 TO 1555

BY ERNST BIZER

ABBREVIATIONS

AELKZ	*Allgemeine ev.-lutherische Kirchenzeitung*, 1868 ff.
AKultG	*Archiv für Kulturgeschichte*, 1903 ff.
AMA	*Abhandlungen der Bayerischen Akademie der Wissenschaften*, 1835 ff.
AÖG	*Archiv für österreichische Geschichte*, Vienna 1865 ff.
ARC	G. Pfeilschifter, *Acta Reformationis Catholicae ecclesiam Germaniae concernentia saeculi XVI*, vol. I 1959, vol. II 1960.
ARG	*Archiv für Reformationsgeschichte*, 1903 ff.
BHR	*Bibliothèque d'Humanisme et Renaissance.*
Brandi	K. Brandi, *Karl V*, 1959⁵. Brandi, *Quellen und Erörterungen*, 1941.
BSLK	*Die Bekenntnisschriften der lutherischen Kirche*, 4th ed. 1959.
BWDG	Rössler and Franz, *Biographisches Wörterbuch zur deutschen Geschichte*, 1958.
BWKG	*Blätter für Württembergische Kirchengeschichte.*
CBG	*Collationes Brugenses et Gandavenses.*
CCath	*Corpus Catholicorum*, begun by J. Greving, 1919 ff.
ChH	*Church History.*
CR	*Corpus Reformatorum*, 1834 ff.
CS	*Corpus Schwenckfeldianorum*, ed. C. Hartranft, 15 vols., 1907–1939.
CThM	*Concordia Theological Monthly.*
CT	*Concilium Tridentinum, Diariorum, Actorum, Epistolarum, Tractatum, Nova collectio*, vol. I, 1901 (ed. by S. Merkle, S. Ehses, T. Freudenberger and B. Buschbell for the Görresgesellschaft).
DThC	*Dictionnaire de Théologie Catholique*, Paris 1909–1937.
DVflG	*Deutsche Vierteljahrsschrift für Literaturwissenschaft und Geistesgeschichte*, 1923 ff.
EC	*Enciclopedia Cattolica*, Rome 1949–1954.

EKL	*Evangelisches Kirchenlexikon.*
Enders	*Dr. Martin Luthers Briefwechsel*, 1884 ff.
FGLP	*Forschungen zur Geschichte und Lehre des Protestantismus*, 1927 ff.

Franz, Wiedertäufer   G. Franz, *Quellen zur Geschichte der Wiedertäufer, Urkundliche Quellen zur hessischen Reformationsgeschichte*, vol. 4, 1951.

Gebhardt-Grundmann   *Handbuch der deutschen Geschichte*, 1954–60.

HJb	*Historisches Jahrbuch*
HJG	*Historisches Jahrbuch der Görresgesellschaft*, 1880 ff.
HKG	*Handbuch der Kirchengeschichte*, ed. G. Krüger, 1923–1931.
HPBl	*Historisch-politische Blätter für das katholische Deutschland*, begun by G. Phillips and G. Görres, 1838–1923.
HV	*Historische Vierteljahresschrift*, 1898–1937.
HZ	*Historische Zeitschrift*, 1859 ff.
JBrKG	*Jahrbuch für brandenburgische Kirchengeschichte*, 1905–1940.
JdTh	*Jahrbücher für deutsche Theologie*, 1856–1878.
Jedin	*Geschichte des Konzils von Trient*, vol. I 1949, vol. II 1957.
JLH	*Jahrbuch für Liturgik und Hymnologie*, 1955 ff.
JpTh	*Jahrbücher für protestantische Theologie*, 1875–1892.
KlT	*Kleine Texte für theologische und philologische Vorlesungen und Übungen*, 1902 ff.
KRA	*Kirchenrechtliche Abhandlungen*, 1902 ff.
Krebs-Rott	= QFRG 7/8, Elsass I/II, 1950–1960.
Lortz	Lortz, *Die Reformation in Deutschland*, 1949³.
LQ	*Lutheran Quarterly.*
LuJ	*Luther-Jahrbuch*, 1919 ff.
MG	*Monumenta Germaniae Historica inde ab a.C. 500 usque ad a. 1500*, 1826 ff.
MIOG	*Mitteilungen des Instituts für Gottesdienst und kirchliche Kunst*, 1896 ff.
Mirbt	C. M. Mirbt, *Quellen zur Geschichte des Papsttums und des römischen Katholizismus*, 5th ed. 1934.
MQR	*Mennonite Quarterly Review.*
NDB	*Neue Deutsche Biographie.*
NKZ	*Neue kirchliche Zeitschrift*, 1890 ff.

v. Pastor L. von Pastor, *Geschichte der Päpste seit dem Ausgang des Mittelalters*, 1885–1933.

Pol. Corr. *Politische Correspondenz der Stadt Strassburg im Zeitalter der Reformation*, ed. H. Virck, O. Winckelmann, H. Gerber and W. Friedensburg, 1882–1928.

QFRG *Quellen und Forschungen zur Reformationsgeschichte*, 1920 ff.

RE *Revue Ecclesiastique.*

Rechtmässigkeit F. Hortleder, Von Rechtmässigkeit, *Anfang, Fort- u. endlichen Ausgang des teutschen Kriegs Kaiser Carls V.*, 2nd ed. by Z. Prüschenck 1645.

RGG *Religion in Geschichte und Gegenwart.*

RHE *Revue d'Histoire Ecclésiastique*, Louvain 1900 ff.

RHPhR *Revue d'Histoire et de Philosophie Religieuses*, Strasbourg 1921 ff.

Ritschl *Dogmengeschichte des Protestantismus* I–IV, 1908–1927.

RQ *Römische Quartalschrift für christliche Altertumskunde und für Kirchengeschichte*, 1889–1942.

SAH *Sitzungsberichte der Akademie der Wissenschaften zu Heidelberg*, Phil.-hist. Klasse, 1910 ff.

SAM *Sitzungsberichte der Bayerischen Akademie der Wissenschaften zu München*, Phil.-hist. Abteilung, 1871 ff.

Schl *Bibliographie zur deutschen Geschichte im Zeitalter der Glaubensspaltung 1517–1585*, ed. K. Schottenloher, 1933–1940.

Seeberg R. Seeberg, *Lehrbuch der Dogmengeschichte*, 1922–1933.

Sehling E. Sehling, *Die evangelischen Kirchenordungen des 16. Jahrhunderts*, vols. 1–5, 1902–1913, vol. 6, 1955 ff.

Sleidan Sleidanus (see Bibliography I).

SVRG *Schriften des Vereins für Reformationsgeschichte*, 1883 ff.

SWDG Rössler and Franz, *Sachwörterbuch zur deutschen Geschichte*, 1958.

ThR *Theologische Rundschau*, 1897 ff.

ThZ *Theologische Zeitschrift.*

ThLZ *Theologische Literaturzeitung*

Ursachen F. Hortleder, *Von den Ursachen des teutschen (=Schmalkaldischen) Kriegs Carls V.*, 1617, 2nd ed. Z. Prüschenck, 1645.

WA   M. Luther, *Werke*. Critical ed. of the complete works,
              Weimar 1833 ff.
              B = Briefwechsel; DB = Die Deutsche Bibel; TR = Tisch-
              reden.

WaG   *Welt als Geschichte.*

ZBKG   *Zeitschrift für bayerische Kirchengeschichte.*

ZKG   *Zeitschrift für Kirchengeschichte*, 1876 ff.

ZRG   *Zeitschrift für Religions- und Geistesgeschichte*, 1948 ff.

ZSavRG   *Zeitschrift der Savigny-Stiftung für Rechtsgeschichte*, 1863 ff.

Zwing   *Zwingliana*, 1897 ff.

PART I

THE HISTORY OF THE REFORMATION TO 1532

Franz Lau

CHAPTER I

THE BACKGROUND OF THE REFORMATION

1. 'REFORMATION' AS AN IDEA AND A SLOGAN IN THE PRE-REFORMATION PERIOD

THE conviction that the Church stood in need of complete renewal was voiced many times during the mediaeval period. In the 15th century, the period of the so-called Reform Councils, it was said that the Church needed to be reformed in head and members.[1] New patterns of monastic life, such as were found within Celtic monasticism, were in effect a means of reforming the Church, and indeed the great Church reform of the 11th and 12th centuries grew out of the monastic reforms of Cluny and Lothringen in the 10th century. Movements based upon the ideal of poverty, like those which sprang up in the heretical churches of the Cathari and the Waldensians, constituted a pressure towards Church reform which was to appear within the Church itself in the mendicant orders. The mendicants' demands for reform were directed against luxury and opulence in the life of the hierarchy, particularly of the Curia. During the period of the Avignon papacy and the papal schism in the 14th and 15th centuries the reform movement specifically singled out the Curia as a target for attack. A major point in the programme of reformers like Ockham, d'Ailli and Marsilius of Padua was the stripping of the power of the papacy in favour of Councils. The demand for a reformation of the Church in these terms could be heard right through to the Council of Trent,[2] and even then it did not die out completely. Mendicants, lawyers,[3] the German estates

---

[1] W. K. Ferguson, *The Renaissance in Historical Thought*, Cambridge, Mass. 1948; W. Maurer, 'Was verstand Luther unter Reformation der Kirche?', *Luther*, 1957, 49–62; Y. Congar, OP, *Vraie et fausse Réforme dans l'Église*, Paris 1950.

[2] J. Huizinga, *Herbst des Mittelalters* (1919), germ. 1953[7]; R. Stadelmann, *Vom Geist des ausgehenden Mittelalters*, 1929; W. Andreas, *Deutschland vor der Reformation* (1932), 1948[5].

[3] E.g. Gregor von Heimburg, cf. *DW* 8679 f.

were among the contrasting groups which joined in demanding reform. In the 15th century it was the last group which became the mouthpiece for complaints about the financial bleeding of Germany caused by the payment of annates, commissions and other imposts to the Curia, and also by the practice of assigning German benefices to foreigners. *Grievances of the German nation* were brought forward repeatedly at German Imperial Diets from 1456 onwards.[1] But the reform movement did not confine itself by any means to ecclesiastical matters in the narrow sense. By this time demands for social reform had come into prominence. The *Reformatio Sigismundi*[2] was not only directed against clerical involvement in secular affairs, but also against usury, the oppression of peasants, and other abuses. In so far as the grievances related to German affairs, the humanists were willing to back the reformers' cause. In theology, too, the prevailing mood was reformist. The Renaissance and humanism were interested in empirical reality and therefore revolted against Scholastic rationalism and its methods. They were looking for a new theology, fighting for a *renovatio Christianismi* and a *simplicitas Christianismi*, or were striving to develop a new kind of scriptural theology, as is evidenced by their interest in the Sermon on the Mount and in the theology of S. Paul.[3] Although it is clear that the Reformation embraced wide-ranging demands for reform (as witnessed by the controversy over indulgences and Luther's *Address to the German Nobility*), it is equally clear that the advocates of 'reform', for their part, did not necessarily go so far as to participate in 'the Reformation'. Indeed, it was possible for the Counter-reformation to link up with a Catholic reform movement in the pre-Reformation period.

2. THE WORLD SITUATION AT THE BEGINNING OF THE REFORMATION PERIOD

It was a unique state of affairs in world politics which made possible, though it did not cause, the spread of the movement for Church reform in the 16th century. It was not a steady progress towards more or less satisfactory realisation of calculated aims, but rather an eruption of elemental spiritual forces, an unprecedented upheaval which led to a real reformation, a reshaping of the Church—though it also occasioned a Counter-reformation and a reinforcing of the old Church. One of the factors which made all this possible was that the European states were in

[1] *Schl* IV, 37534–37543.
[2] Text ed. by K. Beer 1933, and H. Koller 1961. Lit. in *Schl*, 40994–41005, and in L. Graf zu Doh na, *Reformatio Sigismundi*, 1960.
[3] P. Wernle, *Die Renaissance des Christentums in 16. Jahrhundert*, 1904; A. Rich, *Die Anfänge der Theologie H. Zwinglis*, 1949, 9 ff.

process of integration at the beginning of the 16th century.[1] In Western Europe the kings were asserting their power strongly against the feudal powers. This was happening in England,[2] where despite Parliament the feudal system had never quite come to full flowering, and where the struggles between the houses of York and Lancaster threatened to rend the country. It was happening, too, in France,[3] where formerly the more powerful vassals had completely outplayed the crown. On the Iberian peninsula[4] the marriage of Isabella of Castile to Ferdinand of Aragon (1469) led to the creation of a unified Spain, beside which only the kingdom of Portugal remained, for other principalities were absorbed into Spain. In all three countries which we have named the period of absolutism was dawning, and they were able to purchase from the Pope considerable concessions over such matters as making appointments to important ecclesiastical positions, so that in this respect important demands for reform were already being satisfied. Spain, which in the 15th century had put the last Moors to flight, thought of itself as the victorious champion of the Catholic faith. The Burgundian empire was a unique formation[5] consisting of heterogeneous elements (the Netherlands, Franche Comté, and for a time the duchy of Bourgogne, and a number of others). It was exposed to risk from the French side, particularly by the death of Charles the Bold (1477), but its economic strength was great, and it was very open to the influence of the humanist spirit.

By contrast, the situation in the German and Italian territories was one of marked disintegration. Ever since the interregnum (1256–1273) the German Emperor had been merely the president of a college of princes, and in the 15th and 16th centuries the *Movement for reform of the Empire*[6] sought participation by the German estates in the government of the Empire, and it took every opportunity to increase such participation. Yet despite this a few German territories showed a tendency toward integration.

Italy[7] was divided into a large number of individual states, mostly city

[1] H. Rössler, *Europa im Zeitalter der Renaissance, Reformation und Gegenreformation*, 1956; 'Geschichte des europäischen Staatensystems von Maximilian I bis zum Ende des 30 jährigen Krieges', Historia Mundi VII. 1957, 161–226; J. P. Shaw, *Nationality and the Western Church before the Reformation*, 1959.

[2] *Schl* IV, 36681–36699; P. Hughes, *The Reformation in England*, 2 vols., 1950–1953.

[3] *Schl* IV, 36997–3702a; J. Vienot, *Histoire de la Réforme française*, 1926; cf. also I. 6 n. 3.

[4] D. Traver, *Spain's Golden Age 1501–1621*, 1927; Cf. also p. 4 n. 3.

[5] J. Huizinga, *Herbst des Mittelalters*, 1939[5]; W. Reese, *Die Niederlande und das Deutsche Reich I*, 1941.

[6] See p. 6 n 2.

[7] *Schl* IV, 38337–38353; H. Baron, 'Die politische Entwicklung der italienischen Renaissance', *HZ* 174 (1952), 31–56.

states, sometimes constituted as republics, sometimes governed by absolute rulers and defended by *condottieri*. The largest, and therefore the most coveted by France and Aragon, were the duchy of Milan and the kingdom of Naples-Sicily. The latter was conquered in 1503 by Ferdinand of Aragon (or Gonsalvo de Cordoba), and the former was the object of strife throughout the period of the Reformation. Numbered among the Renaissance principalities of Italy was the 'Church-state'.[1]

Habsburg imperialism in particular brought dramatic movement to the European scene in the Reformation period. The archduke Maximilian (b. 1459; Emperor, 1493–1519)[2] as a result of his marriage with Mary, the daughter of Charles the Bold, brought about a union of his Austrian territories (as well as those of so-called Anterior Austria—*Vorderösterreich* —on the Upper Rhine) with Burgundy. His son Philip, who in 1496 married Joanna 'the Mad' (1479–1555), the daughter of Ferdinand of Aragon and Isabella of Castile, thus paved the way for the even wider rule of his son Charles[3] (1516 king of Spain; 1519, as Charles V, German Emperor) over Spain, Burgundy, and (indirectly) Austria. Charles V needed the emperor-concept, the imperial crown, and his role as protector of the Catholic Church to preserve intact his universal dominion. France, therefore, in fear of being enveloped, had to attempt to break through, and did her utmost to get a foothold in Italy, especially in Milan and Naples. In 1519 Francis I (1515–1547) became a contender for the imperial crown.[4] The Pope, as ruler of the Church-state, was in fear of being enveloped, particularly by the Spaniard, the potential occupier of Milan and Naples. Almost always the Pope found himself drawn to the side of Francis I. Thus as a political opponent of the Emperor—despite his ecclesiastical obligations—he became the one who did most to promote the Reformation in Germany.

All Europe lived in terror of the power of the Turks, who since 1463 had surged forward towards the German Empire.[5] Even though they were feared as the enemies of Christendom, they nevertheless sought, and found, allies among the European powers, not least the 'most Christian king' of France, who for his part, when it was to his advantage, had no hesitation in making pacts with Protestants. The Turks compacted even with the Curia.

[1] See previous note.
[2] *Schl* III, 28167–28339; V, 51041–51054c; R. Buchner, *Maximilian I, Kaiser an der Zeitenwende*, 1959.
[3] *Schl* III, 28340–28734; V, 51055–51100; K. Brandi, *Kaiser Karl V*, 2 vols., 1937, 1941; vol. I. 1961[6]; G. von Schwarzenfeld, *Charles V, Father of Europe*, 1957; R. Tyler, *Charles V*, 1959 (dit.); F. Welser, *Charles-Quint et son temps*, Paris 1959; P. Rassow and F. Schalk, *Karl V*, 1960.
[4] H. Lemonnier, 'Les guerres d'Italie', *Histoire de France* (ed. Larisse) V, 1, 1904.
[5] A. Bombaci, 'Das Osmanische Reich', *Hist. Mundi* VII, 1957, 439–485 (Lit. 505); S. N. Fisher, *The Foreign Relations of Turkey 1481–1512*, Urbana, Ill. 1948.

It was obvious that the powers which could not be expected to assist in a reformation of the Church were in a majority. But they were engaged in struggles amongst themselves, and it was this factor which offered to such a reformation unique prospects of success.

3. THE SITUATION IN GERMANY AT THE BEGINNING OF THE 16TH CENTURY[1]

The German Empire was made up of a considerable number of secular and clerical territories (*Länder*) of varying status and importance—electorates, principalities, and territories ruled by counts or by knights—and alongside these there had grown up structures of a distinctive kind, the imperial cities, which were constituted on republican lines.[2] Many of the territories which nominally formed part of the Empire were now only formally members of the Imperial Diet,[3] e.g. the east German bishoprics.[4] Other territorial rulers, particularly the landed nobility in the East, had clearly become feudal lords, while in the West the smallest structures—like the territories belonging to counts or to knights—were in certain circumstances represented corporately at the Imperial Diet. The larger territories, though not always proof against division among heirs (Saxony in 1485, Wittelsbach several times from 1294 onwards), were striving to perfect their administrative organisation (through the creation of administrative districts, for example) and were already in some respects on the way to becoming modern states. Of all the German estates, it was the cities which were economically the strongest and most progressive, though at the Imperial Diets they were not represented as fully as they deserved.[5] Only the imperial cities (85 in 1521) had official representation, though many of the territorial cities (the *Landstädte*) had for all practical purposes won quite extensive freedom from their territorial lords. The knights,[6] who had lost their original function as the result of the growth of mercenary troops (*Landsknechte*), were the most restive element. The distribution of power varied so greatly from one region of Germany to

---

[1] J. von Pflugk-Hartung, *Im Morgenrot der Reformation*, 1912; W. Andreas, *Deutschland vor der Reformation*, 1932, 1948[5]; M. M. Smirin, *Deutschland vor der Reformation*, 1955 (Marxist).

[2] C. W. von Lancizolle, *Übersicht der deutschen Reichs- und Territorialverhältnisse*, 1830.

[3] J. J. Moser, *Von Deutschland und dessen Staatsverfassung überhaupt*, 1766; W. Näf, 'Frühformen des modernen Staates, *HZ* 171 (1951), 225–244.

[4] Cf. the struggles over Meissen: *Schl* III, 31445a; 31446; W. Görnitz, *Staat und Stände unter den Herzogen Albrecht und Georg von Sachsen*, 1928.

[5] W. Andreas, *Deutschland vor der Reformation*, 1948[5], 313–436.

[6] Cf. p. 32 n. 6.

B

another that it is impossible to say in general terms who was actually in a position to effect a reformation of the Church. In one *Land* it would have been the prince, bound to a greater or lesser extent by the representative chamber of his province and also the cities in the territory. In other areas the *Landstäte* were a long way ahead of the territories in which they were situated. In some instances, particularly in the clerical territories, it happened that the estates of the territory[1] seized the initiative from their overlord and claimed for themselves the *ius reformandi* (cf. the so-called *Declaratio Ferdinandea* at the Religious Peace of Augsburg). Since the Emperor and the estates were contending with one another for control of the German Empire—in the movement for reform of the Empire[2] led by Berthold von Henneberg, Archbishop of Mainz,[3] the estates sought participation in the government of the Empire—there was no hope that any reform of the Church would be brought about by the German Empire as whole. But here and there individual territories, including clerical ones, aided by the fact that the various estates vied with one another for power, made it possible for the forces of reform to break through. In the German cities the situation was particularly promising.

4. THE ECONOMIC AND SOCIAL BACKGROUND[4]

The period of the Reformation is at the same time the period of early capitalism.[5] First of all in Italy, then in the cities of South Germany (Nuremberg, Augsburg, etc.) and also on the Rhine, as well as in the cities of the Hanseatic League,[6] vast sums of money accumulated in the hands of individual finance houses (Fugger[7] and Welser in Augsberg, Hochstetter and many others). The mediaeval prohibition of lending at interest had been set aside, and modern forms of commerce came into being. These developments resulted from an increased trade with the distant countries of the Orient and even with the New World (America was discovered in 1492). True, it was a long time before the resources of America had any effect

---

[1] F. L. Carsten, 'Die deutschen Landstände und der Aufstieg der Fürsten', *WaG* 20 (1960), 16–29.
[2] J. Pflugk-Hartung, *Im Morgenrot der Reformation*, 1912, 121–162; F. Hartung, 'Die Reichsreform von 1485–1495', *HV* 16 (1913), 24–53, 181–209.
[3] F. Hartung, *Volk und Staat*, 1940, 48–66.
[4] Pflugk-Hartung, *Morgenrot der Reformation*, 1912, 1–52, 165–206; R. Ehrenberg, *Das Zeitalter der Fugger*, 2 vols. (new impression 1961); H. Bechtel, *Wirtschaftsgeschichte Deutschlands* II, 1952.
[5] H. Barge, *Luther und der Frühkapitalismus*, 1951; H. Lutz, *Conrad Peutinger*, 1958.
[6] F. Rörig, *Vom Werden und Wesen der Hanse*, 1940, 1943³.
[7] G. von Pölnitz, *J. Fugger*, 2 vols., 1949, 1951; *J. Fugger, Kaiser Maximilian und Augsburg* (4 lectures), 1959.

upon the European economy; whereas the production of metals in Germany gave rise to high prices, and finance houses like Fuggers, who were bankers for Emperor and Curia alike, came to exercise an influence on world politics (as, for instance, in the election of the Emperor, 1519, and in the Italian wars). In the cities, of course, other ranks of society struggled against the patriciate and among themselves to establish their rights (e.g. the masters of the guilds and corporations, the journeymen, the so-called commoners who had no possessions); and the decades which mark the transition from the Middle Ages to the modern period are characterised everywhere by struggles within the cities and by the formation of new organs of government.[1] In the cities, the reformation of the Church features regularly as a prominent issue in arguments over the constitution. Sweeping changes take place, too, in the lower orders of the nobility. The knights[2] find themselves without any function, save for those who become 'robber barons'. Young noblemen now attend the universities in great numbers, and alongside educated burghers they appear as lawyers at the courts of princes, very open to humanist influences; and in the various individual territories they become figures of decisive importance for the history of the Reformation (cf. the nobles and lawyers in Albertine and in Ernestine Saxony, in the one case pro-Reformation and in the other case favouring the 'old Church'). For decades there was unrest among the peasants.[3] Almost everywhere they were without freedom, being bound to lords who had control over the land, over justice, and over the peasant's own person and family. The ferment among the peasantry, which manifested itself in the *Bundschuh*[4] and the *Armer Konrad*[5] revolts, was due more to the fact that the peasants were without rights (the only peasant representation was in the *Landstube* in Tirol) than to any actual economic distress, though this was certainly present in the south-west, where it was impossible to divide the plots of land any further. The free peasantry of Switzerland was a model which fanned the flames of revolt.

5. THE RENAISSANCE

Historians, each according to his particular viewpoint, tend to speak either of the period of the Renaissance or of the period of the Refor-

[1] W. Andreas, *Deutschland vor der Reformation*, 1948[5], 316–332; F. Lau, 'Der Bauernkrieg und das angebliche Ende der lutherischen Reformation als spontaner Volksbewegung', *LuJ* 26 (1957), 109–134 (Lit.).
[2] See p. 32 n. 6.
[3] *Schl* IV, 35191–35209; K. S. Bader, 'Bauernrecht und Bauernfreiheit im späten Mittelalter', *HJb* 61 (1941), 51–87.
[4] *Schl* IV, 34885–34896; W. Andreas, *Der Bundschuh*, 1953[2].
[5] H. Oehler, 'Der Aufstand des Armen Konrad 1514', *Württembergisches Jahresheft* 38 (1932), 401–486.

mation.[1] Admittedly the Renaissance, if we look back to its origins,[2] is a great deal earlier than the Reformation. Petrarch, often regarded as the first representative of the Renaissance, died in 1374. The great artists of the Italian Renaissance[3] lived in the 15th century (Giotto, Donatello, Fra Angelico), and only a few in the 16th (Leonardo da Vinci, Raphael, Michelangelo). Most scholars no longer regard the Renaissance merely as a rebirth of classical antiquity. If we give more consideration than has been given in the past to the fact that the Renaissance grew out of the Middle Ages,[4] then we may well have to look back to the High Middle Ages (Dante)[5] for its origins. The new feeling for life, the interest in this present world and a vigorous enthusiasm for Nature, a quest for physical pleasure and a less inhibited style of living; also the desire to examine Nature by means of observation and experiment, or history by means of discovering and studying sources; and enthusiasm for language, whether that of the Greeks or Latins or of one's own people—all this had long been in existence by the time of the Reformation. Of course, the Renaissance movement contained within itself many contradictions and tensions. Strong religious feeling and desire for Church reform were to be found side by side with explicit atheism.[6] Loud and passionate criticism of the traditional Church and of scholastic theology was heard; but at the same time the Roman Curia and the bishops, by their patronage, bound many humanists to the old Church. Alongside the cosmopolitanism of an Erasmus[7] were strong affirmations of national consciousness and of loyalty to the history of one's own people. As the Byzantines driven out of Constantinople by Islam made collections of ancient manuscripts (Bessarion, Plethon), so German humanists collected evidences of Germany's past

[1] On the Renaissance/Reformation problem see P. Wernle, *Die Renaissance der Christenheit im 16. Jahrhundert*, 1904; R. Stupperich, 'Vom Humanismus zur Reformation', *AKultG* 36 (1954), 388–401; W. Dilthey, *Weltanschauung und Analyse des Menschen seit Renaissance und Reformation*, 1957[5].
[2] A survey of the very considerable literature on the Renaissance is given in the *Bibliothèque d'Humanisme et Renaissance*. Important recent works are: A. Renaudet, 'Autour d'une définition de l'Humanisme' *BHR* 6 (1945), 7–49; W. H. Ferguson, *The Renaissance in historical thought*, Cambridge, Mass. 1948; M. P. Gilmore, 'The World of Humanism (1483–1517)', New York 1952; *American Historical Review* 59 (1953), 1–18. H. W. Ferguson, 'The Church in a Changing World'; H. Baron, 'Moot problems of Renaissance Interpretation', *Journal of Historical Ideas* 19 (1958), 26–34; H. A. E. v. Gelder, *The Two Reformations in the 16th Century*, 1961.
[3] A. Chastel, 'Art et religion dans la Renaissance italienne' *BHR* 7 (1945), 7–61; W. Paatz, *Die Kunst der Renaissance in Italien*, 1953 J. Burckhardt, Die Kultur der Renaissance in Italien, 1860 (new ed. 1956).
[4] K. Burdach, *Vom Mittelalter zur Reformation*, 1892; F. Schneider, *Rom und Umgegend im Mittelalter*, 1925[3] (new ed. 1959).
[5] F. Schneider, *Dante*, 1947[4].
[6] C. Angeleri, *Il Problema religioso del Renascimento*, Florence 1952.
[7] On Erasmus, see p. 67 n 9.

(Konrad Celtis).[1] Similarly, among those with strong religious sympathies, there was a new interest in Plato and Aristotle and an attempt to marry ancient philosophy (particularly Stoicism) and the Gospel interpreted as ethic (the Sermon on the Mount; Paul; cf. the Platonic Academy in Florence[2] with Pico della Mirandola[3] and Marsilio Ficino[4]). This interest was reflected, too, in the study of christian antiquity and in discovering afresh the basis of the christian tradition, which meant going back *ad fontes* to the Bible itself. The Renaissance was, at one and the same time, the source from which the Reformation, the Counter-reformation, 'free sectarianism' and finally the Enlightenment all sprang. For the last of these the foundations had already been laid in the Renaissance period, but its development was retarded by the Reformation.

6. GERMAN HUMANSIM

Germany, too, knew the kind of 'Renaissance' which meant a frivolous and extravagant style of living, ostentatious worldliness and moral laxity. The court of cardinal Albert of Magdeburg at Halle was regarded as a German Rome.[5] German humanism[6] as such was primarily an academic movement concerned with scholarship. It did not manifest the Renaissance in all its fullness, and the same is true, to a greater or lesser extent, of the humanist movement in other European countries: France,[7] with Jacques Faber Stapulensis,[8] Tissard, Budé, Briçonnet; England,[9] with John Colet[10] and Thomas More;[11] and Spain, with the school of Alcalá.[12] 'Nat-

On Celtis, see p. 10 n. 8.
[2] C. Baeumcker, 'Mittelalter und Renaissance-Platonismus', *Festgabe für J. Schlecht*, 1917, 1–13; C. Ritter, *Platonismus und Christentum*, 1934.
[3] L. Gautier-Vignal, *Pico della Mirandola*, Paris 1937; J. W. Montgomery, 'Eros and Agape in the Thought of Pico della Mirandola', *CThM* 32 (1961), 733–746.
[4] W. Dress, *Die Mystik des Marsilio Ficino*, 1929; P. O. Kristeller, *The Philosophy of Marsilio Ficino*, New York 1943.
[5] *Schl* III, 31208–31214; G. Hartmann, *Reichserzkanzler, Kurfürst und Kardinal Albrecht II von Brandenburg, der Führer deutscher Renaissance-Kunst*, 1937; W. Delius, *Die Reformations-Geschichte der Stadt Halle*, 1953.
[6] W. Andreas, *Deutschland vor der Reformation*, 1948[5], III/8; H. Rupprich, *Die Frühzeit des Humanismus und der Renaissance in Deutschland*, 1938.
[7] J. Vienot, *Histoire de la Réforme française*, 1926; E. Léonard, *Les origines de la Réforme en France*, 1944; R. Stephan, *Histoire du Protestantisme français*, 1961.
[8] J. Barnaud, *Jean Lefèvre d'Étaples*, 1936; C. L. Salley, *The Ideals of the Devotio Moderna as reflected in the life and writings of Jacques Lefèvre d'Étaples*, Michigan 1953.
[9] F. Caspari, *Humanism and the Social Order in Tudor England*, Chicago 1954; M. Schmidt, *Englische Kirchengeschichte seit dem 16. Jahrhundert* (vol. 3 M in the present series).
[10] E. W. Hunt, *Dean Colet and his Theology*, 1956.
[11] G. Heidingsfelder, *Thomas Morus*, 1950; P. Huber, *Traditionsfestigkeit und Kritik bei Thomas Morus*, 1953.
[12] A. Haupt, *Geschichte der Renaissance in Spanien und Portugal*, 1927.

uralism' in theories of the state and of state-craft (cf. Macchiavelli)[1] certainly had greater effect in the Western European countries than in Germany itself. The history of the Reformation in Poland[2] and Hungary[3] shows how great was the influence of the Renaissance in those countries. In the imperial cities of Germany there were important humanist patrons and scholars—Pirkheimer[4] in Nuremberg, Peutinger[5] in Augsburg, J. Wimpheling[6] in Strasbourg, and others in the Netherlands and West-phalia (R. Agricola)[7]. There were too itinerant scholars like Konrad Celtis, [8] Peter Luder and others.

By far the greatest of all the German humanists were Johann Reuchlin (1455–1522),[9] a Greek scholar and notable Hebraist who in 1506 published his *De rudimentis hebraicis*, influenced by the *cabala*, and Desiderius Erasmus of Rotterdam (1489–1536),[10] who owed much to the *Devotio Moderna*,[11] and who made a great contribution to the Reformation by his Greek edition of the New Testament, his editions of the Patristic writers, his influence on Zwingli, Melanchthon and many other humanists who were siding with the Reformers, and also by his biting satire on monasticism (*Encomium Moriae*, 1509) and superstitious practices, and his rejection of Scholasticism in favour of a much simpler 'lay' Christianity understood primarily as an ethic (cf. the ideal of 'simplicitas christianismi'; *Enchiridion Militis Christiani*). Geographically, the nearest other formative influence upon the Reformation was the Gotha circle, a group which gathered round Conrad Mutianus Rufus (1472–1526).[12] The controversy which raged over Luther was preceded by the so-called *Reuchlinist Feud*,[13] a controversy between Crotus Rubeanus,[14] (with Ulrich von Hutten[15] and

[1] L. von Muralt, *Machiavells Staatsgedanke*, 1945; G. Ritter, *Die Dämonie der Macht*, 1948.
[2] K. Völker, *Kirchengeschichte Polens*, 1930.
[3] M. Bucsay, *Geschichte des Protestantismus in Ungarn*, 1959.
[4] H. Rupperich, 'W. Pirckheimer', *Schweizerische Beiträge zur allgemeinen Geschichte* 15 (1957), 64–110.
[5] H. Lutz, *C. Peutinger*, 1958.   [6] J. Knepper, *J. Wimpheling*, 1902.
[7] P. Joachimsen, 'Loci communes', *LuJ* 8 (1926), 27–97; W. Maurer, 'Melanchthons Loci communes von 1521 als wissenschaftliche Programmschrift', *LuJ* 27 (1960), 1–50.
[8] Selected works of Celtis with the title 'Poeta Laureatus', Vienna 1960.
[9] M. Krebs (ed.), *Festgabe für J. Reuchlin*, 1955; L. W. Spitz, 'Reuchlin's Philosophy', *ARG* 47 (1956), 1–20.
[10] H. Liebing, *Humanismus* (vol. 2 H in the present series); see also p. 67 n. 8 below.
[11] J. Hashagen, 'Die Devotio Moderna in ihrer Einwirkung auf Humanismus, Reformation, usw., *ZKG* 55 (1936), 523–531.
[12] L. W. Spitz, 'The conflict of ideals in Mutianus Rufus', *Journal of the Wartburg and Courtauld Institutes* 16 (1953), 121–143.
[13] W. P. Fuchs, 'Forschungen und Darstellungen zur Geschichte des Reformation-Zeitalters, *Welt als Geschichte* 16 (1956), 124–153.
[14] P. Kalkoff, 'Die Crotuslegende', *ARG* 23 (1926), 113–149.
[15] *Schl* I, 9157–9301; V, 47021–47024; H. Holborn, *Ulrich von Hutten and the German Reformation*, 1937 (German, 1929).

others) and the Dominicans of Cologne. Crotus and von Hutten produced the *Letters of Obscure Men*,[1] a devastating satire on the Scholastic
methods of the day.

7. CHURCH AND STATE AT THE CLOSE OF THE MIDDLE AGES

The result of the Investiture Contest of the 11th and 12th centuries was
that the Curia deprived German royalty of most of its ecclesiastical rights,
and in the 13th century the papacy had managed to make the secular
power largely subordinate.[2] But during the closing centuries of the mediaeval period a remarkable shift took place.[3] In Western Europe state
churches were growing up, and though this by no means involved the
English, French or Spanish churches in any break with Rome or with
the papal primacy, it gave the national authorities considerable influence
over appointments to major ecclesiastical positions, prevented or impeded
appeals to Rome against the decisions of ecclesiastical courts, and assured
the crown of no mean financial income from ecclesiastical institutions
and from the clergy. Reciprocal rights were established by means of con-
cordats (Castile in 1482, France in 1516). The desire to establish Councils,
which persisted for a century after the Councils of reform,[4] made it possible for states to win concessions from the Curia, whilst enabling the
Curia to keep Gallican and Anglican aspirations within bounds. Although
efforts were made (e.g. by Berthold von Henneberg)[5] to establish a
national church in Germany, they proved not to be capable of realisation,
because the tendency in Germany was to develop the power of territorial
rather than imperial authorities. But the territorial princes in Germany,
for their part—especially in East Germany—used their patronage rights
and so-called 'protection'[6] to secure control of the bishoprics by ensuring
that their relatives and landed subordinates sat in cathedral chapters.
Thus they won for themselves in their own territories rights which were
similar to those of the West European monarchs in theirs. They succeeded
in making the bishops feudally subject *de jure*, or at least *de facto*, and in
taxing church properties and the clergy. They also claimed rights of presentation, or at least the right to approve appointments, as well as the

---

[1] Editions by Böcking, 2 vols., 1864, 1870; Stokes, 1925; Bömer 2 vols., 1924.
[2] R. Drögereit, *Sächsische Kaiserzeit* (vol. 2 F in this series).
[3] B. Moeller, *Spätmittelalter* (vol. 2 H in this series); R. Stadelmann, *Vom Geist des
ausgehenden Mittelalters*, 1929, 32–37.
[4] H. Jedin, *Geschichte des Konzils von Trient I* (1949), 1951². (The whole of vol. I
deals almost exclusively with the history of the Council concept from the time of the
Council of Constance (1414–1418) to the Council of Trent (1545).
[5] See p. 6 n. 2.
[6] Hermelink-Maurer, 'Reformation und Gegenreformation, *HKG* III, 1931², 47 f.,
and the literature listed there.

right to act as visitors of the monasteries, making episcopal visitation rights dependent upon their permission or participation.[1] In the cities, the churches were for the most part attached to ecclesiastical bodies corporate (e.g. monasteries), but the city councils in many places were active in promoting a separate body of clergy—the 'preachers'—who subsequently and in various ways were glad to seize reforming initiatives.[2] At the close of the Middle Ages the conditions for the collapse of church organisation, such as was brought on by the Reformation, were already present; though it cannot be denied that where things looked relatively easy, as in West Europe, the Reformation was rendered more difficult.

8. THE INTERNAL LIFE OF THE CHURCH BEFORE THE REFORMATION

Many widely divergent verdicts have been passed on the state of spiritual life in the pre-Reformation period. Traditional Protestant histories have regarded the period which preceded Luther's appearance as a time of total decadence and of hopeless spiritual disintegration and confusion.[3] Johannes Jannssen, in his history of the German people,[4] presents the close of the Middle Ages as a spiritual springtime, full of tender shoots which were attacked and destroyed by Reformation frost. Catholic polemics even in the early Reformation period reproached Luther and his followers for having induced grave moral decadence.[5] It is impossible to deny that there were signs of serious corruption. Indulgences[6] were a blatant abuse of the sacrament of penance. For all practical purposes celibacy had virtually ceased. Indeed, by a kind of episcopal tax the concubines of cathedral canons and country clergy were actually legalised. Italian humanist writers maliciously urged that nunneries be examined for bones of newly born children.[7] Dissolute living was to be found in many German monasteries. Since things were no better at the Roman

[1] P. Kirn, *Friedrich der Weise und die Kirche*, 1926; T. Höss, 'Die Problematic des Spätmittelalterlichen Kirchentums am Beispiel Sachsens', *Geschichte in Wissenschaft und Unterricht* 10 (1959), 352–362.

[2] A. Schultze, 'Stadtgemeinde und Kirche im Mittelalter', *Festgabe für Sohm*, 1914; J. Rauscher, 'Die Prädikaturen in Württemberg vor der Reformation', *Wurtt. Jahrbücher* 1908, 2, 152–211; H. Löscher, 'Gründung und Ausstattung von Kirchen, Pfarren und Hospitälern im Verlaufe der bergmännischen Besiedlung des Erzgebirges', *ZSavRG* 69 Kan. 38 (1952), 297–394.

[3] This view, though somewhat modified, is evident in T. Brieger, *Die Reformation*, 1914.

[4] J. Janssen, *Geschichte des deutschen Volkes seit dem Ausgang des Mittelalters*, 8 vols., 1876–1894.

[5] Cf. Luther's 'Sermon von den guten Werken', *WA* 6 (196) 202–276 and 9 (226) 229–301.

[6] N. Paulus, *Geschichte des Ablasses im Mittelalter*, 3 vols., 1922–1923; H. Karpp, Busse und Ablass im Altertum und Mittelalter', *ThR* 21 (1953), 121–136.

[7] J. Burckhardt, *Die Kultur der Renaissance in Italien*, ed. Kröner 1928[18], 435.

Curia or at the courts of the bishops, there was little hope of improvement. Those who occupied ecclesiastical positions and enjoyed the fruits of them were occasionally not even ordained. Many accumulated such positions, and as they were not capable of discharging the duties attaching to them—many led an entirely secular life—they employed miserably paid vicars to perform them. These latter formed a clerical proletariat, which included also those priests whose sole duty it was to say masses, mostly votive masses.[1] Hardly anywhere were bishops genuine pastors, but were represented by suffragans who spent all their time performing endless ordinations, consecrations and so forth. The Curia was not alone in pursuing a policy of financial exploitation in the grand style.[2] The bishops had no compunction in using their clerical powers of ban and interdict to assist them in the collection of revenue.[3] Even phenomena which at first sight might be judged positively are seen on closer inspection to have their questionable aspects. There is no doubt that at the close of the Middle Ages a great deal of preaching was done.[4] Where new churches were built (as in the Erzgebirge of Saxony) they arose in most cases as preaching stations for the preaching orders. The descriptions of monastic preachers and preaching which we find, for example, in the *Encomium Morias* of Erasmus[5] or even in the ribald literature of the period (e.g. the 'jest-books'; the *Heptameron* of Margaret of Navarre) make disconcerting reading. Series of sermons on biblical texts are presented as a kind of serialised novel. Only a few of the collections of sermons which have come down to us reveal uncompromising spiritual seriousness. The profusion of brotherhoods,[6] the so-called *Kalande*,[7] 'worker' brotherhoods, 'pilgrim' brotherhoods and others served some useful purpose as pastoral tools, but Luther was not the only one to give evidence of the decline of these brotherhoods. In his sermon on the brotherhoods, *Vom hochwürdigen Sakrament des heiligen Leichnams Christi und den Bruder-*

[1] The enormous number of mass and altar priests given in earlier histories is nowadays challenged in various quarters. See, on the one hand, E. Keyser, 'Die Einkünfte der niederen Geistlichkeit an den Hamburger Kirchen am Anfang des 16. Jahrhunderts', *Zeitschrift für Hamburgische Geschichte* 41 (1951), 214–226; and on the other hand H. Hoffmann and K. Engelbert, 'Aufzeichnungen des Breslauer Domherrn Stanislaus Sauer', *Archiv für Schlesische Kirchengeschichte* 14 (1956), 105–140.
[2] Cf. Luther's 'Schrift an den Adel', *WA* 6, 417 ff.; G. von Below, *Die Ursachen der Reformation*, 1917; H. Cellarius, *Die Reichsstadt Frankfurt am Main und die Gravamina der deutschen Nation*, 1938.
[3] Cf. Luther, 'Ein Sermon von dem Bann', *WA* 6, 61 ff.
[4] Celebrated preachers were Johann von Werden in Cologne, Johann Herolt in Basle, Johann Geiler of Keisersberg in Strasbourg or Johann Jenser of Paltz in Erfurt. See article *Predigt* I, RGG³ (1961) by A. Niedergall and the lit. listed there.
[5] English translation, *Praise of Folly* (see p. 67 n. 9).
[6] Literature listed in H. E. Feine, *Kirchliche Rechtsgeschichte* I, 1950, 299.
[7] Full literature in *EKL* II, 512 and *RGG* III, 1099.

schaften (WA 2. 738, 742–758), he said, 'They are named after saints, but a sow would be ashamed to give her name to any of them'. The veneration of saints [1] (S. Anne and S. Joseph were particularly popular at that time) was still a widespread practice, but the veneration of relics which accompanied it, often assuming childish forms, came under the full fire of humanist criticism.[2] Places of pilgrimage, particularly S. Iago di Compostella in Spain and Loreto,[3] were visited by countless numbers of people. German 'holy places'[4] like Wilsnack, Sternberg in Mecklenburg, Grimmenthal near Meiningen, were actively promoted by the territorial princes. The rush to such places assumed epidemic, mass-psychotic proportions.[5] Preoccupation with witchcraft had already begun before the Reformation.[6] Attendance at innumerable masses was very large. There can be no doubt that the Church's life was outwardly wide-ranging. In theology itself some developments had taken plance during the pre-Reformation period. The predominance of Occamism, which had originated in the 14th century, had already been overcome. The *via antiqua* had once more found a place alongside the *via moderna*, Thomism being represented by men like Dionysius Rickel (d. 1471), Tommaso de Vio, Cardinal Cajetan,[7] and Staupitz.[8] A university like Erfurt,[9] in which Occamism dominated almost entirely, was exceptional. There was a future for Scholasticism, too, in Spain, whence it subsequently came to a late flowering in German Protestant orthodoxy. Reform movements in the religious orders (notably in the mendicant orders) were destined to play an important role. The Franciscans, Dominicans and Augustinians had adherents everywhere. To what extent the debate within the religious orders was concerned with clerical interests or with questions of justice is a matter which still remains to be examined.[10] Certain statements to be found in the devotional literature of the period—particularly in the 'books of comfort' for the dying, and also in collections of sermons—clearly

[1] J. Huizinga, *Herbst des Mittelalters*, 1953[7]; K. Lansemann, *Die Heiligentage, besonders die Marien- und Aposteltage*, 1939; L. Pinomaa, 'Luthers Weg zur Verwerfung des Heiligendienstes', *LuJ* 29 (1961), 35–43.
[2] See p. 12 n. 7; Burckhardt pp. 454 ff.
[3] H. J. Hüffer, *Sant' Jago, Entwicklung und Bedeutung des Jakobuskults in Spanien und dem Römisch-deutschen Reich*, 1957;
[4] P. Meier, 'Wilsnack als Spiegel deutscher Vorreformation', *ZRG* 3 (1950), 53–69; K. Schmalz, *Kirchengeschichte Mecklenburgs* I, 1935, esp. 272 ff.
[5] R. Weinjenborg, 'Miraculum a Martino Luthero confictum explicatne eius reformationem?', *Antonianum* (Rome) 31 (1956), 269 f.
[6] *Schl* IV, 37731–37804.
[7] R. Bauer, *Gotteserkenntnis und Gottesbeweis bei Kardinal Cajetan*, 1955.
[8] E. Wolf, *Luther*.
[9] L. Meier, 'Contribution a l'histoire de la théologie a l'université d'Erfurt', *RHE* 50 (1955), 454–479; G. Ritter, *Die Heidelberger Universität* I (1386–1508), 1936.
[10] Cf. Bernd Moeller, *Spätmittelalter*.

point forward to the Reformation. They are aware of the doctrine that men's works are in themselves insufficient for salvation, and they commend the dying solely to the saving grace of Christ.[1]

9. EARLY STAGES OF THE REFORMATION NOT CONNECTED WITH LUTHER

It is important to disentangle the problem of 'origins' correctly. The search for tendencies and personalities (so-called 'pre-Reformers')[2] supposed to have exerted an influence on Luther himself has uncovered precious little. For though Occamism, particularly Gabriel Biel,[3] came to be regarded by Luther as of great importance, and though Luther valued very highly men like Tauler and earlier mystics like S. Bernard,[4] this does not make any of these men precursors of the Reformation. From 1522 onwards Luther was in contact with the Bohemian Brethren (Luke of Prague[5]), and it cannot be denied that there were certain influences from that direction. But the originality of Luther cannot be gainsaid, for he developed everything he found, in such a way that he produced from it something that was new. It has long been recognised that exaggerated claims have been made for the influence upon Luther of such alleged precursors of the Reformation as Johann Ruchrat of Wesel,[6] Johann Wessel Gansfort of Groningen,[7] Johann Pupper of Goch,[8] who waged war on indulgences, advocated a return to Scripture and criticised the structure of the Church. Nor was Johann Staupitz a precursor of the Reformation.[9] A quite different, and very important, question is whether certain areas of population in Germany had been so strongly affected by

[1] H. Appel, *Anfechtung und Trost im Spät-MA und bei Luther*, 1938; A. Zumkeller, 'Das Ungenügen der menschlichen Werke bei den deutschen Predigern des Spätmittelalters', *Zeitschrift für katholische Theologie* 81 (1959), 265–305.

[2] M. Spina, *Advocates of Reform from Wyclif to Erasmus*, Philadelphia, 1953; R. Haubst, 'Der Reformentwurf Pius II', *RQ* 49 (1954), 188–242; K. D. Schmidt, *Katholische Reformation und Gegenreformation*; L. B. Smith, 'The Reformation and the Decay of Mediaeval Ideals', *ChH* 24 (1955), 212–220.

[3] H. A. Oberman, 'Gabriel Biel and Late Mediaeval Mysticism', *ChH* 30 (1961), 259–287.

[4] E. Wolf, *Luther*; K. Wessendorf, 'Ist der Verfasser der "theologia Deutsch" gefunden?', *EvTh* 16 (1956), 188–192.

[5] E. Peschke, 'Der Kirchenbegriff des Bruder Lukas von Prag', *Wissenschaftliche Zeitschrift Rostock* 5 (1955–1956), 273–284; F. Bednau, 'Die erste Abendmahlsagende der böhmischen Bruderunität', *ThZ* 11 (1955), 344–360; K. Bittner, 'Erasmus, Luther und die böhmischen Brüder', *Festschrift Lammert* (1954), 117–129. Cf. also *ARG* 44 (1953), 139 f.

[6] R. Samoray, 'Johann von Wesel', *Phil. Dissertation Münster* 1955.

[7] H. J. J. Wachters, *Wessel Gansfort*, Nijmegen 1940.

[8] O. Clemen, *Johann Pupper von Goch*, 1896.

[9] Cf. E. Wolf, *Luther*.

pre-Reformation sectarianism or other influences that they responded eagerly to Luther's message, though subsequently—indeed after only a short while—being responsible for the introduction of new notes into the 'gospel' of reform, notes which in Luther's own message were absent. The appearance of radical programmes of reform alongside more cautious and 'law-abiding' programmes such as those of the classical reformers might well be explained (as might also the difference in spirit between the reform movement emanating from Luther himself and its rapid development along lines which he had not intended) by the fact that pre-Reformation influences had prepared the soil and were continuing to have their effect. Hussite groups were to be found in various parts of Germany (in Franconia with Friedrich Reiser,[1] and in Mark Brandenburg), and we must take account of the influence which the Waldensians[2] exercised upon them, as also upon the Bohemian Hussites, particularly the *Unitas fratrum*. Attention has been drawn to the *Meistersinger* groups in Southern Germany. In the other European countries the story is similar. The last word has yet to be spoken about Waldensian influence upon Calvinism, and also about the extent to which the Anabaptist movement had been anticipated in the pre-Reformation sects.[3] It is plain that there was Taborite influence on the 'Prophets of Zwickau' and thus on Müntzer. The history of those background events which led to the Peasants' War (e.g. the *Bundschuh* movement and the *Oberrheinischer Revolutionär*), with its slogans about divine justice and christian freedom, is at the same time the history of the off-shoots of the Reformation.[4] A path was prepared for the biblicism of the Reformation period in the first instance by the invention of printing,[5] and subsequently by translations of the Bible into the vernacular (in France, England, Spain and Germany).[6] The spiritualism of the Reformation period, for its part, had its earliest manifestations in the *Devotio moderna*,[7] strongly influenced by the *Imitatio*

---

[1] H. Köpstein, 'Uber den deutschen Hussiten Friedrich Reiser', *Zeitschrift für Geschichtswissenschaft* 7 (1959) 1068–1082.

[2] Bibliography in A. A. Hugon and G. Gonnet, *Bibliografia Valdese*, Torre Pellice 1953.

[3] For the theory that the Anabaptist movement had its precursors in the mediaeval sects, see L. Keller, *Die Reformation und die älteren Reformparteien*, 1885; also F. Roth, 'Der Meistersinger Georg Breunig und die religiösen Bewegungen der Waldenser und Täufer im 15. und 16. Jahrhundert', *Monatsblätter der Comeniusgesellschaft* 13 (1904), 74–93; and H. Böhmer's article 'Die Waldenser', *RE* 20 (1908), 799–840. The theory had been dropped, but appears to be coming into favour again.

[4] See p. 52 notes 4 and 7.

[5] F. Falk, *Die Bibel am Ausgange des Mittelalters, ihre Kenntnis und ihre Verbreitung*, 1905.

[6] F. Maurer, *Studien zur mitteldeutschen Bibelübersetzung vor Luther*, 1929; H. Rost, *Die Bibel im Mittelalter*, 1939.

[7] B. Moeller, *Spätmittelalter*; A. Hyma, *The Brethren of the Common Life*, Grand Rapids/Michigan 1950.

Christi of Thomas á Kempis. The tension between biblicism and spiritualism, as found in the Anabaptist movement, had already been present in the 'majority' and 'minority' parties of the *Unitas fratrum*.[1]

10. THE 'LUTHER CASE'

Luther's posting of his theses on 31 October (or 1 November ?) 1517[2] has traditionally been regarded as the starting point of Reformation history. The attention of all Germany was drawn to the monk of Wittenberg because the proposed academic disputation about the power of indulgences never took place, and because the controversy did not rest merely as a literary controversy between Luther, Tetzel, Eck and Wimpina,[3] but was the cause of the Curia's action against Luther on the grounds of suspected heresy (June 1518). Then on 7 August 1518 Luther was charged with notorious heresy and was summoned to Rome for trial, with a demand that he retract within 60 days. The effect of all this was to give a very wide circulation to Luther's edifying tracts, as can be seen from the number of impressions listed in the Weimar edition of his works. That Luther gained three years, during which his message received sensational publicity, was due to imperial politics. The Emperor Maximilian, ailing in health, sought to get his grandson Charles elected as Roman king at the Diet of Augsburg, but without success. No one had any intention of electing an Emperor, but Maximilian's death on 12 January 1519 made the election of an emperor essential. Contending for election were Charles I[4] of Spain and Burgundy, Francis I of France, and for a time even Henry VIII of England. From Rome's point of view

[1] E. Peschke, 'Der Gegensatz zwischen der kleinen und grossen Partei in der Brüderunität', *Wissenschaftliche Zeitschrift Rostock* 6 (1957), 140–154.

[2] See E. Wolf, *Luther*; H. Bornkamm, 'Der 31. Oktober als Tag des Thesenanschlags', *Deutsches Pfarrerblatt* 61 (1961), 508–509; E. Iserlohn, 'Luthers Thesenanschlag, Tatsache oder Legende?', *Trierer Theologische Zeitschrift* 70 (1961), 303–312.

It is impossible to deal with the history of the Reformation between 1517 and 1532 without referring to Luther. Generally speaking, I have left the task of describing Luther's career in detail to the author of vol. 3 in this series (E. Wolf, *Luther*). However, I have had to say something about the 'Luther case'. Anyone writing a history of the years 1517–1532 without referring to Luther would inevitably be governed by his own conception of the history of the Reformation. The actaul Reformation does not begin until 1521, but it has its roots in the reform movement which Luther began and which is by no means over by 1521, though it develops along rapidly diverging lines. During the period of the 'disorderly growth' of the Reformation (1521–1525) many very loud voices are heard above the general chorus (Karlstadt, Müntzer, Zwingli, etc.) and there is a serious danger that new churches will develop which have little relation to one another. The kind of Protestant church order which develops after 1525 tends, in its broad outlines, towards a certain homogeneity, though it never actually attains a unified structure.

[3] See E. Wolf, *Luther*.

[4] On Charles V and on Francis I see p. 4 notes 3 and 4.

(i.e. Leo X), to give so great an increase in power to Charles I, who was already a menace in his capacity as master of Southern Italy and Sicily and potential ruler of Upper Italy, would have been quite intolerable. But the French king, too, was a possible ruler of Upper Italy and as German Emperor would have been equally dangerous. It was essential for the Curia to maintain good relationships with Frederick the Wise,[1] not only on account of his standing in the college of electors and his position as *Reichsvikar*, but also because Rome regarded him as a serious candidate for the imperial crown. Thus it came about that Frederick was able to have Luther's trial take place in Augsburg under Cajetan (October 1518) and to go on protecting him, albeit somewhat hesitantly. The Curia was grateful for the delay afforded by the efforts of Karl von Miltitz (the Altenburg conversations, 4–6 January, 1519)[2] to get a clarification of the case; indeed, the Curia even gave secret support to such efforts. The case was reopened in January 1520, and even though the work was carried through with all possible haste, it was not until 15 June 1520 that the papal Bull *Exsurge Domine* was published, threatening Luther with excommunication. Even so, Luther had gained three years. The years 1517–1521 represent a period in which decisive steps were taken on the road to the Reformation, for the debate which Luther at first confined to the question of indulgences was now widened to embrace themes which to Rome were more openly provocative. In his *Resolutions* (August 1518) Luther based obedience to the Pope on the principle of obedience to the civil authority and was thus able to assert that a papal ban can have validity only within certain clearly defined limits. At the Leipzig Disputation (27 June to 16 July 1519)[3] he claimed that Councils are capable of error, an assertion which constituted a serious attack on the ecclesiastical system. In the *Letter to the German Nobility* (1520)[4] he attacked the bases of 'Romanist' authority, and even more serious was his attack in *The Babylonian Captivity of the Church* (1520)[5] upon Roman sacramental doctrine. *The Roman Papacy* of 1520[6] developed a new understanding of the Church's nature and structure. It was in 1520 that Luther first described the Pope as Antichrist, and this, together with the burning of the Bull and of the books

---

[1] *Schl* III, 32975–33028, and V, 51421 f.

[2] See my article in *RGG*[3] IV, 954. Historians have tended to minimise Miltitz's efforts, but there is no doubt that the delay suited the Curia's interests.

[3] O. Seitz, *Der authentische Text der Leipziger Disputation*, 1903; J. Eck, *Defensio contra amarulentas D. Andreae Bodenstein Carolstatini invectiones*, ed. J. Greving, 1919; H. Emser, *De disputatione Lipsicensi*, ed. F. Thurnhofer, 1921; H. Barge, *Karlstadt*, 2 vols., 1905; J. Lortz, 'Die Leipziger Disputation', *Bonner Zeitschrift für Theologie und Seelsorge* 3 (1926), 12–37; E. Kähler, *Karlstadt und Augustin*, 1952.

[4] *WA* 6 (381) 404–469, 631.

[5] *WA* 6 (484), 497–632.

[6] *WA* 6 (277), 288–324, 631.

of canon law on 10 December 1520, represented the final break with the existing Church.[1] This made clear to all the world that Luther's interest was not merely in ecclesiastical reform but in a thoroughgoing re-shaping of the Church. It was apparent that many people, both within Germany and outside it, were sympathetic to Luther and were ready to some extent to go along with him. But the actual beginning of the Reformation was the Diet of Worms (1521),[2] when, as a consequence of the formal pronouncement of excommunication on 3 January 1521, Luther was placed under imperial ban and taken in custody to the Wartburg. The effect of this, so far from putting an end to the Lutheran movement, was to unleash the Reformation itself.

[1] E. Bizer, *Luther und der Papst*, 1958.
[2] *Schl* I, 14281–14346; IV, 14534–14542; *Deutsche Reichstagsakten*, Jüngere Reihe II, 1897.

CHAPTER II

THE REFORMATION UNLEASHED

I. THE DIET OF WORMS AND LUTHER'S IMPRISONMENT TRIGGER OFF THE REFORMATION

MAXIMILIAN I died on 12 January 1519, and on 28 June in the same year the electors chose Charles of Ghent to be Emperor Charles V.[1] He was neither a German nor a Spaniard but had been brought up in Burgundy. French was his mother tongue, and his collaborators were Burgundian noblemen – Chièvre, Gattinara and Adrian of Utrecht. The main reason for his election was that he was able to offer larger payments to the electors than any other contestant. The coronation took place at Aachen on 22 and 23 October 1520. How Charles would make out as German Emperor was anyone's guess. For a period of nine years he could find no time to appear in Germany or to take any part in German affairs. The Diet of Worms,[2] arranged to begin on 6 January 1521, which went on until 25 May, gave Charles the opportunity of introducing himself to the German estates and of clarifying his relationship to them. The estates made it clear that they were unwilling to forgo any of their rights or to surrender themselves in 'bovine servitude'; while the Emperor, for his part, made it plain that he did not regard the terms of his election as permanently binding upon himself. The Imperial Governing Council (Reichsregiment)[3] set up by the Imperial Diet became merely a kind of administrative body to serve during the absence of the Emperor. In the discussions relating to the constitution of the Empire (e.g. such institutions as the Imperial Cameral Tribunal and the Imperial Governing Council) it soon became clear that in the contest between Emperor and

[1] On Charles V see p. 4 n. 3, and on Maximilian I see p. 4 n. 2.
[2] Cf. p. 19 n. 2.
[3] Schl III, 27886–27891, *Deutsche Reichstagakten*, Jüngere Reihe, vols. 3 and 7 (1901 and 1903).

Empire the religious question would come into prominence. The fact that against a barrage of protest from the Curia Charles V had invited to Worms the Wittenberg monk who had been formally denounced as a heretic—with the effect that Luther was not placed under imperial ban immediately—was an astonishing novelty.[1] It indicated, too, that Charles found it necessary to be accommodating towards the estates and particularly to popular opinion (note the *Bundschuh* threats at Worms), which a commentator like Aleander[2] judged to be markedly pro-Lutheran. The hearing took place on 17 and 18 April. The discussions with Luther which followed on 24 April give no hint that a single German prince declared himself for Luther, but suggest rather that the estates were extremely anxious to get the 'Luther case' settled peaceably. The Emperor put on record his personal and definite opposition to the heretic,[3] but this was influenced not only by his desire to draw Leo X away from the French king and have him on his side, but also by his own profoundly Catholic conviction. The Edict of Worms,[4] which was not formulated until after the Diet had ended and was then backdated to 8 May, and which contains the ban on Luther, purports to be the decision of the estates of the Empire, but is in fact the work of the Emperor's entourage and of the papal nuncio, Aleander. Whether it was practicable was dubious from the start. But it meant that what had happened in Worms presented every Christian with a choice: either he could acquiesce in the verdict of the Church and of the Empire on Luther and accept all the consequences arising from it, or he could hold that such things were not sufficient to subdue Luther, who had God's Word on his side. From that moment onwards, simple opposition to the Church, however passionate, could not be enough. It had to be a matter of making a breach and turning the Church upside down. Since Luther was now removed from the public sphere, only time would tell whether the influence he exerted was merely his own, or whether it was due to the power of 'God's Word'.

2. EVANGELICAL PREACHING IN GERMAN TERRITORIES

The Reformation, as it burst upon the world in 1521, was above all a preaching movement. It is now recognized that a very considerable number of preachers decided to preach the 'Word of God', and throughout

[1] Cf. Frederick II's 'Privilegium in favorem principum ecclesiasticorum' of 26 April 1220. *MG Leges Lect.* IV, vol. II, 89 ff.; *Mirbt* No. 343 (bibliography).

[2] *Schl* I, 280–304; V, 44745–44746; H. Jedin, *Geschichte des Konzils von Trient* I, 1951², 520 n. 2. Aleander's diplomatic correspondence is an important source for the history of the Reformation. Cf. *Schl* IV, 40505.

[3] Cf. K. Brandi, *Karl V.*, I, 1961⁶, 112 f.; II, 1941, 114.

[4] *Schl* IV, 44534–44542; II, 28591–28594; IV, 45534–45542; V, 52194.

C

Germany men declared their allegiance to the Word of God and to Luther's teachings. The preachers belonged, for the most part, to the urban clergy.[1] It was rare to find preachers of the Word of God among rectors or their chaplains, but very common to find them among monks who had renounced their habit and left their monasteries—Augustinian Eremites like Luther himself, Franciscans, Carmelites and others. It would be an anachronism to speak of 'Evangelical areas' at this period; one can only mention places in which Evangelical preaching was concentrated. In Ernestine Saxony, towns like Altenburg (W. Link),[2] Weimar, Gotha (Fr. Mykonius),[3] Eisenach (J. Strauss),[4] proved receptive to reformers' preaching. The same is true of a number of towns in South Germany, such as Nuremberg (Osiander),[5] Augsburg,[6] Schwäbisch-Hall (J. Brenz),[7] Basle (Oecolampad),[8] Strasbourg (Bucer, Zell, Capito),[9] Constance (A. Blarer, J. Zwick),[10] Nördlingen (Billican, Kantz),[11] Ulm (Kettenbach, Sam),[12] and many others. Where a number of Evangelical preachers were active in any one place, as in Nuremberg and Strasbourg, or where local town officials gave their support (as L. Spengler in Nuremberg and A. Dürer), the Reformation naturally became rather more than merely a preaching movement. But in Augsburg, where for example Oecolampad, J. Frosch and Urbanus Rhegius were active, it was not until 1533–1534 that the Reformation was finally adopted. Reforming initiatives were in evidence very early in Regensburg (1522),[13] but a Reformation in the town as a whole was not possible until 1542. Not even all the early

[1] On the preaching clergy see J. Rauscher, 'Die Prädikaturen in Württ. vor der Reformation', *Württembergische Jahrbüch für Statistik und Landeskunde* 1908, 152–211.
[2] *Schl* II, 23551 f.
[3] G. Hübner, 'Die Reformation in Gotha', *Diss. Leipzig* 1918.
[4] J. Rogge, *Der Beitrag des Predigers Jakob Strauss zur früheren Reformationsgeschichte*, 1957 (bibliography).
[5] *Schl* II, 26154–26164; H. von Schubert, *Lazarus Spengler und die Reformation in Nürnberg*, 1933; K. Schornbaum, 'Beiträge zur Geschichte des Reformations-Zeitalters in Nürnberg', *Mitteilungen des Hist. Vereins Nürnberg* 44 (1933), 286–316.
[6] F. Roth, *Augsburgs Reformationsgeschichte 1517-1527*, 4 vols., 1901-11². Also *Schl* II, 23653–23661.
[7] E. Bizer, *Predigten des Joh. Brenz*, 1955. The Foundation for Reformation Research is to publish a new edition of Brenz's works.
[8] E. Staehelin, *Das Buch der Basler Reformation*, 1929, and *Das theologische Lebenswerk Oecolampads*, 1939; E. Bonjour, *Die Universität Basel von den Anfängen bis zur Gegenwart*, 1960.
[9] N. Paulus, *Die Strassburger Reformatoren und die Gewissensfreiheit*, 1895; H. Strohl, *Le Protestantisme en Alsace*, Oberlin-Strasbourg 1950. Cf. p. 40 n. 1; J. Adam, *Evangelische Kirchengeschichte der Stadt Strassburg*, 1922.
[10] B. Moeller, *Joh. Zwick und die Reformation in Konstanz*, 1961.
[11] M. Simon, *Evangelische Kirchengeschichte Bayerns*, 1952².
[12] P. Kalkoff, 'Die Prädikanten Eberlin und Kettenbach', *ARG* 25 (1928), 128–150.
[13] L. Theobald, *Die Reformationsgeschichte der Reichsstadt Regensburg*, 2 vols., 1936 and 1951; L. Schwab, *Regensburg im Aufruhr*, 1956; R. Dollinger, *Das Evangelium in Regensburg*, 1959.

preachers remained loyal to the Reformation cause (e.g. Billican).[1] Many
of those who sought to bring the Reformation to their own town were
disciples of Luther himself. Only a few of the celebrated 'Reformers' of
the early period had studied at Wittenberg. Martin Bucer, Billican and
Brenz were won over to Luther at the Heidelberg Disputation. But
Balthazar Hubmair[2] in Waldshut and C. Schappeler[3] in Memmingen were
Zwingli students. Others, like Capito,[4] had come direct from the humanist movement. It is quite certain that what was preached as the 'Word
of God' was by no means homogeneous but contained sharp differences and
contrasts.[5] With some preachers, for instance, there is an attention to social
and legal questions which is far stronger than anything we find in Luther
(e.g. J. Strauss),[6] and it needs to be taken into account that the most significant of the reforming preachers each had a theology of his own. What
kind of reformist preaching took place in the country districts is difficult
to assess. We cannot dismiss the possibility that here and there in country
villages it took place or that it was influenced to a certain extent by reformers' preaching elsewhere. But by and large it was with the population of the towns that the Reformation scored its major triumphs.[7]

3. THE EVANGELICAL LORD'S SUPPER

During the early period of the Reformation, that is to say for two or
three years or even longer, it will not have been unusual to find that the
only 'Evangelical' activity in most churches (and by no means all churches)
was preaching. In many places the next logical step of celebrating communion 'Evangelically', i.e. in two kinds, was not taken immediately.
But it soon became apparent that 'right preaching' was giving rise not
only to reflection but also to an actual ecclesiastical upheaval, for priests
began to marry (Bernhardi in Kemberg near Wittenberg,[8] Bucer in

[1] Other 'reformers' returned later to the 'old Church'. See J. Kämmerer, 'Die
Stellung des Ravensburger Humanisten Michael Hummelberg zur Reformation',
Blätter für württembergische Kirchengeschichte 57–58 (1957–1958), 26–34.
[2] Schl I, 9057–9075; G. Franz, Der deutsche Bauernkrieg, 1957⁴.
[3] Schl II, 18977–18980a; V, 49064–49065; G. Franz, 'Die Entstehung der Zwölf
Artikel', ARG 36 (1940), 193–213.
[4] O. E. Strasser, La pensée théologique de W. Capiton, 1938.
[5] This remained true as the Reformation progressed. Cf. E. W. Zeeden, 'Grund-
lagen und Wege der Konfessionsbildung im Zeitalter der Glaubenskämpfe', HZ 185
(1958), 249–299.
[6] See p. 22 n. 4.
[7] G. Kretschmar, Die Reformation in Breslau, 1959; W. Jannasch, Reformationsgeschichte Lübecks 1515–1530, 1958; P. Brunner, 'Die Wormser deutsche Messe',
Kosmos und Ekklesia 1953, 106–162.
[8] Married on 24 August 1521.

Strasbourg[1] and others), monasteries began to empty and escaped monks became preachers. The Reformation became a 'revolutionary' event, not only in Wittenberg, Erfurt and Zwickau, but in many other places. But the most striking break with the previous ecclesiastical structure came with the celebration of communion in both kinds—as opposed to the custom of receiving in only one kind which had begun to appear during the 13th century and had been legalised at the Council of Constance. Naturally it sometimes led to still greater changes in the ordering of the service, such as the removal of prayers containing references to sacrifice and the translation of the service into the vernacular. It is wise to speak of the Reformation being attempted or introduced in any given place only in instances where communion was celebrated in 'Evangelical' style.[2]

4. THE REFORMATION AND THE WRITTEN WORD

The Reformation was the first intellectual movement to further itself by means of the written as well as the spoken word. Johann Gutenberg had invented printing[3] in about 1445, and until the beginnings of the Reformation it had been concentrated on the production of learned volumes in Latin. But then an impressive swing took place in favour of printing more popular writings in German. Obviously the printing presses were at the service of those who championed the new religion as well as those who defended the old.[4] But in fact it was the advocates of reform who were the first to use the new invention and to use it more than others. In the forefront of writers of evangelical pamphlets, whether edifying or polemical in character, was Luther himself, who began with the *Sermon on the Sacrament of Penance*.[5] Several presses in Wittenberg (Grunenberg, Lotter, Lufft) worked for him, and many printing houses elsewhere, both famous ones like Froben and Gengenbach in Basle, Othmar in Augsburg, and others less well known, did reproductions of his leaflets.

---

[1] Bucer married Elizabeth Silbereisen in 1522. Cf. RE 3, 605. It is possible that Jacob Seidel was the first clergyman to marry, even before Bernhardi, cf. F. Gess, *Akten und Briefe zur Kirchenpolitik Herzog Georgs von Sachsen* I, 1905, 172.

[2] It is interesting to examine the instances in which there was a considerable time lag between the first upsurge of the reform movement and the introduction of the Reformation, e.g. Regensburg (1522, 1542), Augsburg (1518, 1533–1534), also Halle/ Saale, Leipzig and many others. See *Schl* II (bibl.).

[3] G. A. Bogeng, *Geschichte der Buchdruckerkunst*, 2 vols., 1931–1941; O Clemen, *Die lutherische Reformation und die Buchdruckerkunst*, 1939.

[4] J. Benzing, *Buchdruckerlexikon des 16. Jahrhunderts*, 1952; J. M. Lenhardt, 'Protestant Latin Bibles of the Reformation', *CBQ* 8 (1946), 416–432; H. Volz, *Bibel und Bibeldruck in Deutschland im 15, u. 16. Jahrhundert*, 1960.

[5] *WA* 1 (239) 243–246; A. Kuczynski, *Thesaurus libellorum historiam reformationis illustrantium*, 1870–1874, reprinted 1960 (it contains an index of over 3,000 pamphlets by Luther and his contemporaries).

Other pamphleteers of the early days were Johann Eberlin of Günzburg,[1] Heinrich von Kettenbach,[2] Erasmus Alber,[3] Martin Bucer and many others. Titles like 'Karsthans', 'Neukarsthans', 'Cuntz and Fritz' indicate that writings of this kind[4] were written for various social groups—peasants, town workmen, and so on. All are fond of addressing themselves to the 'common man'.[5] These literary witnesses reproduce the 'pure doctrine' of Luther himself no more faithfully than did the sermons of reforming preachers. Legalism, summonses to social agitation, demands to go beyond Luther, survivals of mediaeval thinking are all there to be observed. Among the authors were laymen like Spengler[6] in Nuremberg and Gerbel[7] in Strasbourg, later came Manuel[8] in Bern. Even women took part, like Argula von Grumbach[9] and Katharina Zell.[10] A variety of literary forms were used—tracts, dialogues, etc. In many instances these writings reached an even wider public than did the spoken word. Where preaching of the Word was dangerous or aroused strong opposition, it was still possible to meet in small groups to study a written pamphlet. This will prove a factor of some importance when we come to consider the effects of the Reformation movement beyond the frontiers of Germany, particularly in France.

5. ART IN THE SERVICE OF THE EARLY REFORM MOVEMENT

Art was very soon pressed into service in order to assist the spread of the reformers' gospel. Of all the art forms employed, perhaps the most effective was music, particularly song. German religious song had its beginnings in the pre-Reformation period.[11] The first chorale which Luther himself composed ('Ein neues Lied wir heben an') was occasioned by the martyrdoms in Brussels in 1523. Other hymn writers who joined forces

[1] *Schl* I, 5144–5167; E. Deuerlein, 'Joh. Eberlin von Günzburg', *Lebensbilder aus dem Bayerischen Schwaben* 5, 1956, 70–92.

[2] *RGG* III³, 1256.

[3] *RGG* I³, 213.

[4] O. Schade, *Satiren und Pasquille aus der Reformationszeit*, 3 vols., 1863²; O. Clemen, *Flugschriften aus den ersten Jahren der Reformation*, 4 vols., 1907–1911 (which prints the texts).

[5] P. Böckmann, 'Der gemeine Mann in den Flugschriften der Reformationszeit', *DVflG* 22 (1944), 186–230; K. Uhrig, 'Der Bauer in de/ Publizistik der Reformation', *ARG* 33 (1936), 70–125.

[6] *Schl* II, 20362–20372.

[7] *Schl* I, 5219, 7005–7010.

[8] *Schl* I, 14782–14812.

[9] *RGG* II³, 1889; R. Stupperich, 'Die Frau in der Publizistik der Reformation', *AKultG* 37 (1955), 204–233; H. Meyer, *Gewagt auf Gottes Gnad*, 1960, 26–40.

[10] H. Meyer (see previous note), 7–25.

[11] P. Wackernagel, *Das deutsche Kirchenlied von den ältesten Zeiten bis zum Anfang des 17. Jahrhunderts*, vols. 1 and 2, 1864 ff.

with Luther quite early were J. Jonas, L. Spengler, Paul Speratus and others.[1] As early as 1524 the first printed hymn-books containing pieces by Luther and others were published. The *Unitas fratrum* already had hymns and hymn-books in the vernacular (cf. the Czech hymn-book of 1519), and these brothers later joined in composing evangelical hymns. The '*Achtliederbuch*', the '*Erfurter Enchiridion*' and Johann Walther's '*Chorgesangbüchlein*', all published in 1524, were not regular hymn-books in the modern sense, but like their many successors they made hymns widely known, and therefore also the reformers' message.[2]

A work which perhaps had an even greater effect than all his many pamphlets was the *Septembertestament* which Luther produced while at the Wartburg. It appeared with illustrations by Lukas Cranach. From 1523 onwards Hans Holbein junior produced pictures illustrating the New Testament, even though he did not publish them until later.[3] In the *Passionale Christi et Antichristi* of 1521 Cranach (and Luther, who wrote the accompanying text) made pictorial art play its part in the Reformation struggle, and it became a most telling and dangerous weapon in controversy with religious opponents.[4] The attitude of the famous artists towards the Reformation is by no means plain in every case. Dürer's[5] apparently friendly attitude is still the subject of discussion among academics. Historians are perhaps a little clearer about Matthias Grünewald's[6] position, but even with regard to him many questions still remain open.

6. REFORMATION PREACHING 'IN ALL THE WORLD'

Evidence of the elemental force with which Evangelical preaching spread the Word of God (in Luther's sense) throughout the land is that the boundaries of the German Empire could not contain it. The Reformation broke through into Habsburg territories, in Austria and the Netherlands

---

[1] W. Delius, *J. Jonas*, 1952; O. Schlisske, *Handbuch der Lutherlieder*, 1948 and *Handbuch zum evangelischen Kirchengesangbuch* II, I, 1957—on Jonas pp. 37 f., on Spengler pp. 57 f., on Luther pp. 29 ff. (bibliography).

[2] J. Smend, *Das evangelische Lied von 1524*, 1924; T. Knolle, 'Die ersten evangelischen Gesangbücher', *Luther* 6 (1924), 12–15; L. Zscharnack, 'Gesangbücher', *RGG*¹ 3 (1912).

[3] H. Grisar and F. Keege, *Der Bilderkampf in der deutschen Bibel (1522 ff.)*, 1922; A. Schramm, *Die Illustration der Lutherbibel*, 1923; O. Thulin, 'Die Gestalt der Lutherbibel in Druck und Bild', *Luther* 16 (1934), 58–70; H. Volz, *100 Jahre Wittenberger Bibeldruck 1522–1626*, 1954.

[4] S. Scharfe, *Religiöse Bildpropaganda der Reformationszeit*, Göttingen 1951; E. Mühlhaupt, 'Vergängliches und Unvergängliches in Luthers Papstkritik', *LuJ* 26 (1959), 56–74.

[5] R. H. Bainton, 'Albrecht Dürer and Luther as the Man of Sorrows', *The Art Bulletin* 29 (1947), 269–272; E. Panofsky, *Albrecht Dürer*, 2 vols., Princeton 1949.

[6] W. K. Zülch, *Grünewald, Mathis Neithardt genannt Gothart*, 1954; H. Hoffmann, *Das Bekenntnis des Meisters Matthis*, 1961.

alike. In France, humanists and disciples of Faber Stapulensis[1] (Briçonnet, bishop of Meaux, Gérard Roussel and Guillaume Farel) studied Luther's writings, and as early as 1523 Farel was exercising an Evangelical ministry among the Waldensians in his home area (Dauphiné).[2] Proceedings were initiated against the Dominican Aimé Maigret,[3] who in 1524 was preaching the gospel of reform in Lyon and Grenoble. It is likely that translations of Luther's writings into French had already been made in 1524.[4] From 1521 Luther's writings had been studied in England, particularly in Cambridge and Oxford (Barnes, Bolney, Frith, Cranmer, Parker, Latimer, Ridley, Tyndale), and were being disseminated. At the popular level, the English 'Lutheran' movement sounded Erasmian notes as well, and in particular there was a revival of ideas which had gained currency through Wycliff and the Lollards.[5] Tyndale,[6] while he was studying in Wittenberg in 1524–1525, began a translation of the Bible into English. King Henry VIII, who was informed in matters of theology, was of a fundamentally Catholic disposition and wrote against Luther's sacramental teaching.[7] Whereas in France the humanists for the most part lent their support to the Reformation, in England they tended to reinforce the 'old Church'. Lutheran influences reached Scotland[8] at an early date (Patrick Hamilton, Wistcart, Will), even though the social structure there was still quite feudal and Catholic minded. There were some cases of martyrdom, and refugee communities established themselves on the Continent. In the Netherlands[9] the *Devotio moderna*, humanism and Erasmus had all prepared a way for the Reformation. Luther's writings were studied and reprinted from 1520 onwards, even in the Southern Netherlands (later

---

[1] Cf. p. 9 nn. 7, 8; A. Renaudet, *Préréforme et Humanisme à Paris 1494–1517*, Paris 1953; R. J. Lovy, *Les origines de la Réforme française. Meaux 1518–1546*. Paris 1959.

[2] Cf. p. 63 n. 3.

[3] F. Delteil, 'L'enquête sur les documents concernant les débuts de la réforme', *Bulletin de la société de l'histoire du protestantisme français* 105 (1960), 122–137; H. Hours, 'Le procès d'hérésie contre Aimé Maigret', *BHR* 19 (1957), 14–43.

[4] R. Marichet, 'Antoine d'Oraison, premier traducteur français de Luther', *BHR* 9 (1947), 87–106.

[5] See p. 9 n. 9; A. Ogle, *The Tragedy of the Lollards' Tower*, 1949; H. S. Darby, *Hugh Latimer*, 1953; A. G. Chester, *Hugh Latimer*, Philadelphia 1954; E. G. Pearce, 'Luther and the English Reformation', *CThM* 31 (1960) 597–606.

[6] G. Rupp, *Six Makers of English Religion*, 1957—RGG³ VI, 1092.

[7] T. Maynard, *Henry the Eighth*, Milwaukee 1949; E. Doernberg, *Henry VIII and Luther*, 1961.

[8] D. H. Fleming, *Reformation in Scotland*, 1910; J. H. Baxter, 'Luthers Einfluss in Schottland im 16. Jahrhundert', *LuJ* 25 (1958), 99–109; G. Donaldson, *The Scottish Reformation*, 1960; A. M. Renwick, *The Story of the Scottish Reformation*, Grand Rapids/Michigan 1960.

[9] J. P. Dugnoile, 'Quelques recherches récentes sur l'histoire du protestantisme en Belgique', *Revue Belge de philosophie et histoire* 33 (1955), 155–163; E. M. Braekman, 'La réforme à Bruxelles', *Bulletin de la société de l'histoire du Protestantisme français* 102 (1957) 84–112; S. P. Wolfs, *Das Groninger "Religionsgespräch"* (1523), 1959.

Belgium). Particularly strong Lutheran influences ostensibly emanated from the Augustinian monasteries.[1] Since the Edict of Worms was carried out in Charles V's own territories with considerable ferocity, it resulted in the celebrated martyrdom of Henry Voes and John Eschen in Brussels, 1523.[2] The Scandinavian countries, which since the Union of Kalmar (1396) had been dominated by Denmark,[3] were threatening during the reign of Christian II (1513–1522) to fall apart. In 1520 an attempt was made to introduce the Reformation, with the aid of Reinhart and Karlstadt of Wittenberg. But since it was directed against the nobility and the clergy, the latter succeeded in quashing it when Christian II was ousted. The new king, Frederick I of Holstein (1523–1533), had to move very slowly in giving effect to his own Protestant inclinations. (His court chaplain was Hans Tausen.[4]) In Sweden,[5] too, a few Evangelical preachers were active —Olaf Peterson in Strängnas[6] and Lorenz Andersson.[7] The king of independent Sweden, Gustaf Wasa (1523–1560), made use of them in his struggle with the bishops.

In the Habsburgs' Austrian possessions[8] noblemen began to take upon themselves the task of furthering the Reformation (Starhemberg, Tollet). In Iglau (Mähren) Paul Speratus[9] preached the Lutheran message. Noblemen in Mähren were soon offering asylum to persecuted Evangelicals, including those of Anabaptist persuasion. In Hungary[10] (including Slovakia, the Carpathian Ukraine, Transylvania, Banate, Batschka, Sirmia and Croatia) the archbishop of Estergom, presumably not without good reason, had the papal Bull of excommunication read out in 1521 in all the major cities. Reforming movements had begun in Leutschau, Kremnitz and other places before the battle of Mohacz. Reformation influences were felt strongly and early in the Baltic regions,[11] beginning from cities

[1] R. Voeto, 'Hebben de Augustijnen van Enkhuizen invloed gehed op de hervorming',[2] Nederlands Archief for Kerkgeschiedenis 39 (1953), 219–237.

[2] J. Boehmer, 'Die Beschaffenheit der Quellenschriften zu Heinrich Voes und Johann van den Eschen', ARG 28 (1931), 112–133; RGG[3] VI, 1432.

[3] G. Schwaiger, Die Reformation in den nordischen Ländern, 1962.

[4] M. Christensen, Hans Tausen, Copenhagen 1942.

[5] H. Holmquist, Die schwedische Reformation, 1925; I. Svalenius, Gustav Vasa, 1950.

[6] C. Bergendorf, Olavus Petri, New York, 1928.

[7] I. Svalenius, Gustav Vasa, 1950.

[8] G. Mecenseffy, Geschichte des Protestantismus in Osterreich, 1956; H. Wurm, Die Jäger von Tollet, 1955.

[9] P. Gennrich, Die ostpreussischen Kirchenliederdichter, 1938.

[10] M. Bucsay, Geschichte des Protestantismus in Ungarn, 1959; F. Sinowatz, Reformation und katholische Restauration in der Grafschaft Forschtenstein und Herrschaft Eisenstadt, 1957; F. Valjavec, Geschichte der deutschen Kulturbeziehungen zu Südosteuropa 2, 1955[2].

[11] R. Wittram, 'Die Reformation in Livland'. Baltische Kirchengeschichte 1956, 35–36, 309–312; R. Ruttenberg, 'Die Beziehungen Luthers und der anderen Wittenberger Reformatoren zu Livland', Balt. Kirchengeschichte 1956, 55–76; K. Lantee, 'The Beginning of the Reformation in Estonia', ChH 22 (1953), 269–278.

like Danzig[1] (J. Hegge, A. Svennichen; Luther's writings were printed here in 1520), also Thorn, Kulm, Elbing, and above all Riga,[2] where Andreas Knöpke had been active since 1521. Almost everywhere the Reformation met with its first successes among the German burghers in the towns, whence its influence spread to the Latvians and Estonians. It was the Romance countries like Spain[3] and Italy[4] which proved least receptive. Nevertheless, between 1521 and 1525 the reformers' message had inundated practically the whole of Europe, albeit with varying force.

7. THE REFORMATION IN ZWICKAU, ALLSTEDT AND MÜHLHAUSEN

Is it true that from 1521 to 1525 the reform movement expressed itself only in preaching, pamphleteering, and the celebration of communion in both kinds? Or did not more take place, at least in a few places? As early as 1520 certain events took place in Zwickau which seem to suggest this. In May 1520, on Luther's recommendation, a man who was perhaps one of Luther's fellow Augustinians,[5] Thomas Müntzer[6] from Stolberg in the Harz, took the place of the preacher Sylvius Egranus[7] at S. Mary's in Zwickau, and on 1 October 1520 became incumbent of S. Catherine's in the same town. There he came in contact with a group of enthusiasts and seers who clearly had come under Taborite influence (Nikolaus Storch, Markus Thomä, called Stübner) and who appealed to revelations and visions, rejecting the written word and organising themselves in conventicles as a particular community or church.[8] Severe conflict with the Franciscans in Zwickau and with the bishop's official in Zeitz caused Müntzer to go to Prague, in order to join with the

[1] E. Schnaase, *Geschichte der evangelischen Kirche Danzigs*, 1863; E. Keyser, *Danzigs Geschichte*, 1928[2].

[2] P. Johansen, 'Gedruckte deutsche und undeutsche Messen für Riga 1525', *Zeitschrift für Ostforschung* 8 (1959), 523–532; G. Rhode, 'Die Reformation in Osteuropa', *Gestalten und Wege der Kirche im Osten* (ed. H. Kruska) 1958, 133–162; G. Stölk, 'Das Echo von Renaissance und Reformation im Moskauer Russland', *Jahrbuch für die Geschichte Osteuropas* 7 (1959), 413–430.

[3] M. Baraillon, *Erasme et l'Espagne* 1937; J. E. Longhurst, *Erasmus and the Spanish Inquisition. The case of Juan de Valdés*. Albuquerque 1950.

[4] E. Rodocanachi, *La reforme en Italie*, 1900; E. Comba, *Storia dei Valdesi*, 1930.

[5] H. Goebke, 'Neue Forschungen über Thomas Müntzer bis zum Jahre 1520', *Harzzeitschrift* 9 (1957), 1–30.

[6] *Schl* II, 15946–16008; V, 48363–48382; A. Lohmann, *Zur geistigen Entwicklung Müntzers*, 1931; C. Hinrichs, *Luther und Müntzer*, 1952; M. M. Smirin, *Die Volksreformation des Th. Müntzer und der grosse Bauernkrieg*, 1952 (Marxist, and important for Müntzer's theological antecedents); K. Kupisch, *Feinde Luthers*, 1951; W. Ellinger *Thomas Müntzer*, 1960.

[7] *Schl* II, 21037–42; *RGG* II, 313; H. Kirchner, *Johannes Sylvius Egranus*, 1961.

[8] P. Wappler, *Th. Muntzer in Zwickau und die Zwickauer Propheten*, 1908; R. Stadelmann, 'Zeitalter der Reformation', *Handbuch der deutschen Geschichte III*, 1954 (ed. Brandt).

Hussites in establishing the 'New Apostolic Church'.[1] After failure in Prague and subsequently also in Halle,[2] Müntzer took the incumbency of S. John's in Allstedt and tried to carry out his plans there. He became increasingly spiritualist, formed an 'alliance', and in a sermon preached in the presence of Duke Johann[3] on 13 July 1524 he described all who would not receive his gospel as 'godless' and formally issued a summons to fight against them and to set up the kingdom of God by force. A few of his writings[4] like the *Protestation, On artificial faith,* and *The faithless world's false belief exposed*—all in 1524—reveal not only Müntzer's spiritualism but also his departure from Luther's position. This comes to clearest expression in his attack, directed against Luther, on *Spiritless and flabby flesh* in 1524. In Allstedt, too, a reform of the liturgy was undertaken.[5] Müntzer was forced to leave Allstedt and sought employment in Mühlhausen, without success. However, after a journey through Nuremberg to the region in which the Peasants' War took place, where he made contact with Oekolampad and others, he managed to get a post in the imperial city of Mühlhausen. There an Evangelical movement led by Heinrich Pfeiffer[6] had combined with a democratic movement which Müntzer now joined. In 1523 the commoners of Mühlhausen were being drawn into the peasant movement which was surging through the country as far as Thuringia, and both Pfeiffer and Müntzer met their end after the defeat of the peasants at Frankenhausen. The battle of Frankenhausen took place on 15 May 1525, and Müntzer and Pfeiffer were executed in Mühlhausen on 27 May.

In Ernestine Saxony, the region in which the Lutheran Reformation had its origins, there was a radical reforming spirit which drew upon mediaeval movements such as the Joachimists, Taborites and mystics.[7] It was already active even before the Diet of Worms and Luther's stay in the Wartburg, and it certainly went a long way further than anything which Luther envisaged, yet it required Luther's attack on Rome to get it into motion.

---

[1] E. Wolfgramm, 'Der Prager Anschlag des Th. Müntzer', *Wissenschaftliche Zeitschrift Leipzig* V (1956–1957), 295–308. On Müntzer's relation to the Anabaptist movement see below, p. 37 n. 5. It is important to know whether Müntzer first came across adult baptism in Prague or in Zwickau, in order to answer two further questions: (a) Is Müntzer one of the founders of the Anabaptist movement, despite the conviction of Mennonite scholars that he was not ? (b) Or are the roots of the Anabaptist movement to be found within mediaeval sectarianism?

[2] W. Delius, *Die Reformationsgeschichte der Stadt Halle/Saale,* 1953; O. Schiff, 'Thomas Müntzer als Prediger in Halle', *ARG* 23 (1926), 287–293.

[3] C. Hinrichs, *Th. Müntzers Politische Schriften,* 1950, 3.

[4] H. Böhmer and P. Kirn, *Thomas Müntzers Briefwechsel,* 1931. A critical edition of Müntzer's writings is being prepared by G. Franz.

[5] See p. 42 n. 6.

[6] *Schl* II, 17207–11; O. Merx, *Th. Müntzer und Heinrich Pfeiffer 1523–1525,* 1889.

[7] See Smirin (cf. p. 29 n. 6).

Until 1524, when Müntzer preached his sermon before the princes, its particularity and its revolutionary character went unsuspected. It was a contributory factor in the Peasants' Revolt. Infant baptism was rejected by Müntzer at an early date, either during his time at Zwickau or in Prague.[1] He described it as a 'monkeys' game'. Amongst the radicals of Central Germany there was evidently no 'programme' of believers' baptism. It is important to realise that Müntzer's attempts at Reformation, whether in Zwickau or in Mühlhausen, did not in fact issue immediately in any steadily continuing Reformation there.[2]

8. THE REFORMATION IN WITTENBERG

It was even more significant and dangerous that in Wittenberg itself, the seat of the Lutheran Reformation, an attempt at radical Reformation was made—in Luther's absence. It was then suppressed.[3] The leadership at Wittenberg was assumed by Andreas Karlstadt,[4] a former Thomist, who in 1512 had conferred on Luther his doctor's degree. Around 1517, as a result of his own study of Augustine, he came to share many of Luther's ideas, and in 1519 he joined with Luther at Leipzig in disputing against Eck. Karlstadt encouraged priests to marry, monks to 'escape' from their monasteries, services to be held in German, and communion to be administered in both kinds. He had planned a special communion service for the whole parish to take place at New Year 1522, but anticipating its prohibition by the elector he brought it forward to Christmas 1521. Part of his programme was *The abolition of images*,[5] and on 6 February 1522 a destruction of images took place, presumably as a result of Karlstadt's publica-

[1] See p. 30 n. 1.
[2] Johann Forster was a disciple of Luther and taught Hebrew in the local school at Zwickau in 1522, and N. Hausmann was preaching in St. Mary's, Zwickau, from 1521 onwards, but the Lutheran Reformation in Zwichau did not begin until 1525, and Mühlhausen did not adopt the Reformation until 1542. See p. 29 n. 6—Smirin and Hinrich. See also R. Friedmann, 'Thomas Müntzer's Relations to Anabaptism', *MQR* 31 (1957), 75–87.
[3] N. Müller, *Die Wittenberger Bewegung 1521 and 1522*, 1911[2]; K. Bauer, *Die Wittenberger Universität*, 1928 (for the influence of the university and its theology upon the Reformation); E. G. Schwiebert, 'The Reformation from a new Perspective', *ChH* XVII (1947), 3–31.
[4] C. F. Jäger, *Andreas Bodenstein von Karlstadt*, 1856 (includes a great deal of material, including excerpts from Karlstadt's writings); H. Barge, *Andreas Bodenstein von Karlstadt*, 1905; K. Mühler, *Luther und Karlstadt*, 1907; E. Hertzsch, *Karlstadt und seine Bedeutung für das Luthertum*, 1932.
[5] See *Kleine Texte* 74, 1911; H. von Campenhausen, 'Die Bilderfrage in der Reformation', *ZKG* 68 (1957), 96–128; El Freys and H. Barge, 'Verzeichnis der gedruckten Schriften des Andreas Bodenstein von Karlstadt', *Bibliographie für Bibelwesen* 21 (1904), 153–179, 209–243, 305–323; E. Kähler, *Karlstadt und Augustin*, 1952; E. Hertzsch, *Karlstadts Schriften aus den Jahren 1523–1525*, 2 vols., 1956–1957.

tion. In order to carry through a complete transformation of the liturgical services it was necessary to enact a 'Wittenberg ordinance', which was done on 24 January 1522.[1] Such novelties in Wittenberg resulted in a mandate issued by the Imperial Governing Council against them (the novelties in electoral Saxony), and indirectly in a demand by the elector that the old order be restored. Another Augustinian, Gabriel Zwilling, was of a disposition similar to that of Karlstadt. Melanchthon vacillated.

Karlstadt certainly was influenced by the mystics, and he had something of the prophetic in him; but he was far more biblically minded than Müntzer.[2] The 'Zwickau prophets' made a brief appearance in Wittenberg on 27 December 1521, which may be taken as an indication that despite many differences the Reformation in Zwickau was related to the Reformation in Wittenberg. In the ordering of worship, neither Karlstadt in Wittenberg nor Müntzer in Allstedt was completely revolutionary or without consideration for the 'weak'.[3] During Luther's detention in the Wartburg Karlstadt regarded himself as the man who should put Luther's wishes into practice in Wittenberg. On Luther's return he retired, in resentment and bitterness, to Orlamünde, and it was only then that he began the practice of holding conventicles. From Orlamünde he appears to have exercised a considerable influence throughout the Saale region (as Luther himself testified in his detailed and passionate pamphlet against Karlstadt in 1525: *Against the heavenly prophets*[4]); and adopting peasant dress, Karlstadt fostered a 'lay-Christianity'. He was very definite in rejecting the idea that the kingdom of Heaven could be won by force and rebellion, and he resisted revolutionary attitudes towards the ruling powers.[5] This, coupled with the fact that he was driven out of Saxony in 1524, meant that he and his followers were not involved in the catastrophic peasants' movement.

9. THE IMPERIAL KNIGHTS AND THE REFORMATION

Running in some respects parallel to the radical attempts at Reformation in Zwickau, Wittenberg, Allstedt and Mühlhausen were the attempts of the imperial knights to initiate their own kind of Reformation.[6] Ulrich von Hutten,[7] a passionate nationalist and embittered by Roman practices

[1] N. Müller and K. Pallas, 'Die Wittenberger Beutelordnung vom Jahre 1521 und ihr Verhältnis zu der Einrichtung des Gemeinen Kastens im Januar 1522', *Zeitschrift für Kirchengeschichte der Provinz Sachsen* 12 (1915), 1–45, 100–137; 13 (1916), 1–12.
[2] H. Gerdes, *Luthers Streit mit den Schwärmern um das rechte Verständnis des Gesetzes Mose*, 1955, 76 ff. Karlstadt has also been compared to L. Hätzer, see J. F. Goeters, *L. Hätzer*, 1957.   [3] See II. 14.   [4] *WA* 18, 95 ff.
[5] Cf. *WA* 18, 431, 438–445.
[6] K. Schottenloher, *Flugschriften zur Ritterschaftsbewegung des Jahres 1523*, 1929.
[7] See edition of Hutten's works by Böcking, 5 vols. (1859–1862).

and Roman domination, was gripped by Luther and became an adherent
at the Leipzig Disputation of 1519. Hutten's *Vadiscus sive trias Romana*
(1520) is more than the counterpart of Luther's *Address to the Nobility*,
for Hutten himself influenced Luther's writings during the struggles of
1520. The extent of Hutten's influence on the Reformation has been hotly
debated since Kalkoff sought to minimize it.[1] The imperial knights as a
whole took sides with the reformers, and Franz von Sickingen[2] not only
offered asylum to Luther himself but made a 'haven of righteousness'
at the Ebernburg for friends of Luther, such as Bucer and Capito. Knights
like Sickingen planned a reformation of the Empire designed to oust the
clerical overlords and to strip the territorial princes of their power. These
plans went far beyond declaring themselves in favour of evangelical
preaching and purely ecclesiastical reform. Sickingen for his part, and in
his own way, took advanatage of the excitement caused by the Edict of
Worms, and also of the fact that there was no means of enforcing the
Edict. In the hope that Luther and his followers would support him he
made a surprise attack on Trier. Several princes (Richard von Greiffenklau
of Trier, Ludwig V of the Palatinate, and Philip of Hesse) quickly defeated him, and he died on 7 May 1523 at the Ebernburg. The 'Knights'
Reformation' remained a dream. The fact that the dream was shattered
had no abiding effect on the further course of Reformation history. It was
perhaps as well that Luther's attitude to the knights was somewhat reserved. But there were none the less genuine supporters of the Reformation among the knights, of whom Hartmut von Kronberg was[3] one.

10. THE REFORMATION IN SWITZERLAND[4]

Since the Swabian War of 1499 Switzerland's relationship to the German Empire had become a loose one.[5] The Swiss victory at Novara in
1513 gave rise to the short-lived hope that Switzerland might attain the

[1] H. Holborn, *Ulrich von Hutten and the German Reformation*, 1929.
[2] G. Franz, 'Franz von Sickingen', *Saarpfälzische Lebensbilder* I, 1937, 61–74;
K. H. Rendenbach, *Die Fehde Sickingens gegen Trier*, 1933.
[3] E. Kück (ed.), *Die Schriften Harthmuts von Cronberg*, 1899; *WA* 10 II, (42) 53–60;
cf. *WA* 58, 205; F. Kipp, *Sylvester von Schaumberg*, 1911.
[4] Sources: *Eidgenössische Abschiede 1500–1520*, 1869; *1521–1528*, 1873; J. Stumpf,
Schweizer– und Reformationschronik (new ed. 2 vols., 1953–1955); J. Kessler, *Sabbata*
(new ed. by Ehrenzeller 1945); J. Strickler, *Aktensammlung zur Schweizerischen
Reformationsgeschichte 1521–1532*, 5 vols., 1878–1884; H. Bullinger, *Zürcher Chronik*,
3 vols., 1838 ff. Literature: E. Egli, *Schweizerische Reformationsgeschichte* I, 1910;
R. Hauri, *Die Reformation in der Schweiz im Urteil der neueren Geschichtsschreibung*,
1945; A. Bucher and W. Schmid, *Reformation und katholische Reform*, Aarau 1958;
O. Vasella, *Reform und Reformation in der Schweiz*, 1958.
[5] E. Gagliardi, *Geschichte der Schweiz* I, 1932, 288–299. Switzerland formally left
the Empire in 1648.

status of a great power, but such hopes were smashed when the Swiss were defeated at Marignano in 1515.[1] In Switzerland, too, the Reformation gospel gained a hold. A preachers' Reformation[2] made considerable progress in the thirteen regions of the actual Confederacy and also in the associated districts (Wallis, Graubünden, S. Gallen, etc.) and the dependent territories (like Aargau and Waadtland)[3] which for administrative purposes were included in the principal districts. Developments took a course similar to those in Germany, with the difference that the free peasants in Switzerland assumed a role which was more decisive for the future of the Reformation than that of the peasants in the land of the Reformation's origin. It was the peasants who largely determined the fact that in central Switzerland the *Waldstädte* Schwyz, Uri, Unterwalden, and also Lucerne, Zug and Fribourg remained loyal to the old religion,[4] and joined forces with the Habsburg territories against the Cantons in which the new religion was spreading. It is as true of Switzerland as of Germany that the impetus to reform came from Wittenberg. Karlstadt's influence reached Switzerland at an early date and was greater than has so far been generally recognised.[5] Before 1525 the 'Word of God' was being preached in a number of Swiss towns—St. Gallen (Bürgermeister Joachim Watt/Vadianus), Schaffhausen (Sebastian Hofmeister), Graubünden, Glarus, Appenzell, Toggenburg, Bern (Berthold Haller, and the painter and poet Nikolaus Manuel), but above all in Basle (Oecolampad, Konrad Pellikan).[6] In Zürich, under Ulrich Zwingli's[7] influence, the Reformation

[1] Gagliardi, *op. cit.*, 299–312.
[2] A. Moser, 'F. Lamberts Reise durch die Schweiz', *Zwing* 10 (1957), 467–471; E. V. Telle, 'François Lambert d'Avignon et son abbaye de Thelème', *BHR* 11 (1949); 43–55; O. Vasella, 'Zur Biographie des Prädikanten Erasmus Schmid', *Zeitschrift für Schweizerische Kirchengeschichte* 50 (1956), 353–366. See also the literature on Farel p. 63 n. 3 who was travelling around preaching the reformed gospel in 1528. Zwingli claimed to have been preaching the 'gospel' before Luther, about 1515. (Cf. E. Wolf, *Luther*.) Cf. also W. Brändly, *Geschichte des Protestantismus in Stadt und Land Luzern*, 1955; and L. von Muralt, 'Geschichte des Prot. in Stadt und Land Luzern', *Zwing* 10 (1958), 602–613. J. F. Goeters, *L. Hätzer*, 1957, gives a lot of information about the social aspect of early reformed preaching in Switzerland.
[3] On the Swiss constitution cf. H. Nabholz and E. Klätt, *Quellenbuch zur Verfassungsgeschichte der Schweizerischen Eidgenossen*, 1941.
[4] See L. von Muralt (*op. cit.* n. 2) and the literature on Bullinger (note 6 below).
[5] See Vasella, *op. cit.* n. 2 above.
[6] F. Stark, *Die Glaubensspaltung im Lande Appenzell bis 1526*, 1955; *Aktenstücke zur Geschichte der Basler Reformation 1529–1934*, 6 vols., 1921–1950; *Die Amerbach-Korrespondenz*, vols. 1 and 2, 1942–1943; P. Burckhardt, *Geschichte der Stadt Basel von der Zeit der Reformation bis zur Gegenwart*, 1957²; F. Roth, *Durchbruch und Festsetzung der Reformation in Basel*, 1942; A. Stähelin, *Die Einführung der Ehescheidung in Basel zur Zeit der Reformation*, 1957; J. J. Herzog, *Das Leben Johannes Oecolampads und die Reformation der Kirche zu Basel*, 1843; K. R. Hagenbach, *J. Oecolampad und Oswald Myconius, die Reformatoren Basels*, 1859; On Oecolampad see p. 22 n. 8; also p. 72 n. 7; and on Myconius see F. Rudolf, 'Oswald Myconius', *Basler Jahrbuch* 1945, 14–30; K. Guggisberg, *Bernische Kirchengeschichte*, 1958; W. Näf, *Vadian und seine Stadt St.*

had become, since 1522, far more than a preaching movement. Zürich was the most influential Canton of the Confederacy, and although it would be quite false to think of the Reformation in Switzerland as a uniform affair—the history of the Reformation was different in each Canton —the very position of Zürich, coupled with Zwingli's forceful personality, naturally meant that the Reformation in Zürich[1] was a formative influence on the other Cantons,[2] an influence which grew stronger with time. Zwingli was a pupil of Erasmus and had made his own study of Augustine. He was convinced that he had been preaching the gospel at an earlier date than Luther, and independently of Luther. The nationalist character of the Reformation in Switzerland becomes evident in Zwingli's attacks on the commerce in soldiers which was carried on by the Curia, the king of France and other powers, and on the methods by which they were paid.[3] It also becomes evident in the character which Zwingli bestowed on the Gospel, a character which resulted from a fusion of humanism and Reformation. For Zwingli, the exposition of Scripture was 'prophecy', and he made a sharp contrast between the gospel and the superstitious elements to be found in the papal church, particularly in the mass. After the First Zürich Disputation of 29 January 1523[4] the Reformation scored a triumph, for a new church ordinance by the council instructed preachers to preach only what was in the Bible. The Second Zürich Disputation of 26–28 October 1523[5] went much further, for the mass was done away with, together with images, the monasteries were dissolved, a matrimonial court[6] was set up, and between 1523 and 1525 communion celebrated according to Evangelical use was introduced. In Zürich, as also in Bern, Basle and St. Gallen, it was the burghers (cf.

Gallen, 2 vols., 1944 and 1957. Compare with this E. G. Rüsch, *ThZ* 14 (1958), 101–106; J. Staedtke, 'Bullingers Bemühungen um eine Reformation im Kanton Zug', *Zwing* 10 (1957), 24–27. On Bullinger see also p. 83 n. 4. On Geneva before the Reformation see H. Ammann, 'Oberdeutsche Kaufleute und die Anfänge der Reformation in Genf', *Zeitschrift für württembergische Landesgeschichte* 13 (1954), 150–193.

[7] See G. Locher, *Zwingli und die schweizerische Reformation* (3 I in the present series).

[1] E. Egli, *Aktensammlung zur Geschichte der Zürcher Reformation*, 1879; W. Köhler, *Das Buch der Reformation H. Zwinglis*, 1926; O. Farner, 'Leo Jud, Zwinglis treuester Helfer', *Zwing* 10 (1955), 201–209; G. W. Locher, *Im Geist und in der Wahrheit, Die reformatorische Wendung im Gottesdienst in Zürich*, 1957.

[2] A. Moser, 'Die Anfänge der Freundschaft zwischen Zwingli und Oecolampad', *Zwing* 10 (1958), 614–620; W. Koehler, *Zwingli und Bern*, 1928; O. E. Strasser, *Capitos Beziehungen zu Bern*, 1928.

[3] G. Gerig, *Reisläufer und Pensionsherren in Zürich, Ein Beitrag zur Kenntnis der Kräfte, welche der Reformation widerstrebten*, 1947.

[4] See n. 7 above.

[5] See Goeters, *op. cit.*, p. 34 n. 2.

[6] W. Köhler, *Zürcher Ehegericht und Genfer Konsistorium*, 1932.

the great council)[1] who were most influential in establishing the Reformation, whereas the nobility, the patricians, the clergy and (at least in central Switzerland) the peasants opposed the changes, in many cases even after they had been officially introduced.

II. THE BEGINNINGS OF THE ANABAPTIST MOVEMENT

Interesting evidence that Zürich, and then gradually the German-speaking areas of Switzerland, became a second independent centre (beside Wittenberg) of the 'classical' Reformation is provided by a new development which began in Zürich. A second and more radical Reformation grew out of the first, drawing even more strongly on Zwinglian ideas than Müntzer and Karlstadt drew on Luther's, yet subsequently conducting a passionate campaign against Zwingli's 'half-measures'. The Zürich radicals were to begin with Zwinglian and humanist sympathisers like Konrad Grebel,[2] Felix Manz,[3] Simon Stumpf, Wilhelm Röubli, Ludwig Hätzer.[4] Their desire was to establish a new, reformed church, constituted on 'lay' lines, exercising discipline over its members, excluding the 'godless' from its fellowship, and refusing to allow the civil authorities to have any say in the ordering of its life, indeed being so anxious to have nothing to do with public authorities that it forbade public office to any believing Christian. The radicals' campaign against the system of tithes is an indication that social and political themes featured

---

[1] L. von Muralt, 'Stadtgemeinde und Reformation in der Schweiz', *Zeitschrift für Schweizerische Geschichte* 10 (1930), 349–384; C. A. Beerli, *Le peintre poète Nicolaus Manuel et l'évolution sociale de son temps*, 1953; O. Vasella, 'Bauerntum und Reformation in der Eidgenossenschaft', *HJb* 76 (1957), 47–63.

[2] H. S. Bender, *Conrad Grebel, ca 1489–1526*, Goshen/Ind. 1950, and 'The Pacifism of the 16th Century Anabaptists', *ChH* 24 (1955), 119–131; H. Fast, 'The Dependence of the first Anabaptists on Luther, Erasmus and Zwingli', *MQR* 30 (1956), 104–119; R. Kreider, 'Anabaptism and Humanism', *MQR* 26 (1952), 123–141; Heberle, 'Die Anfänge des Anabaptismus in der Schweiz', *JdTh* 3 (1858), 225–280; W. Köhler, 'Die Züricher Täufer', *Gedenkschrift z. 400 jähr. Jub. der Mennoniten*, 1925, 48–64; F. Blanke, 'Zollikon 1525', *ThZ* 8 (1952), 241–262, and *Brüder in Christo*, 1955; J. H. Yoder, 'The Turning in the Zwinglian Reformation', *MQR* 32 (1958), 128–140. For Zwingli's influence on the radicals, see Goeters (p. 34 n. 2), who says that the opponents of infant baptism were applying logically Zwingli's understanding of the sacraments.

[3] E. Krajewski, *Leben und Sterben des Zürcher Täuferführers Felix Manz*, 1958²; J. Yoder, *Täufertum und Reformation in der Schweiz*, 1958.

[4] J. F. G. Goeters, *op. cit.* See also his article, 'Ludwig Hätzer, a Marginal Anabaptist', *MQR* 29 (1955), 251–261. On Hubmair see p. 65 n. 11; also W. Wiswedel, *Balthasar Hubmair*, 1939; W. A. Schulze, 'Neuere Forschungen über B. Hubmair von Landshut', *Alemann. Jahrbuch* 1957, 224–274; G. Westin and T. Bergstein have published an edition of Hubmair's writings (1962); H. Fast, 'Neues zum Leben W. Reublins', *ThZ* 11 (1955), 420–455; J. Schacher, 'Luzerner Akten zur Geschichte der Täufer', *Zeitschrift für Schweizerische Kirchengeschichte* 51 (1951), 1–26.

THE REFORMATION UNLEASHED 37

more prominently in their thinking than was the case with Karlstadt
and Müntzer.[1] For these men, infant baptism was quickly singled out as
evidence of the old church's apostasy, but unlike Müntzer they did not
rest content with merely playing down baptism and the sacraments
generally,[2] but actively promoted a baptism of believers. It appears that
the first such baptism took place at the house of Felix Manz on 21 January
1525. The Lord's Supper was celebrated merely as a remembrance and
love feast. No doubt the Anabaptist movement began as a strongly biblicist one, though Hätzer was one of the early radicals in Zürich and he
quickly developed spiritualist leanings.[3] It is unlikely that Karlstadt exerted much influence over the Zürich Reformation generally or over the
radicals in particular,[4] and any influence of Müntzer on the beginnings of
Anabaptism may be discounted. It is quite another question whether
Müntzer's ideas may have found their way into the Anabaptist movement
at a later date.[5] Historians at first supposed that the Anabaptist movement
was influenced by mediaeval sectarianism, but this was then vigorously
contested. All the same, it cannot be simply dismissed out of hand.[6]
At least some kind of mediated influence is likely, say, from the Taborites
through the Zwickau Prophets to Müntzer and thence to Hut. Denck[7]
was probably influenced by earlier religious undercurrents in Nuremberg.
Before 1525 Anabaptism hardly penetrated beyond Zürich and the boundaries of Switzerland. It has been argued, though quite wrongly, that an

[1] P. Peachey, Die soziale Herkunft der Schweizer Täufer in der Reformationszeit, 1954.
[2] See p. 30 n. 1. Wolfgramm poses the question whether Müntzer merely regarded
infant baptism as a 'fool's game' without necessarily having thought of baptising
adults.
[3] See Goeters, op. cit.
[4] O. Vasella, 'Zur Biographie des Prädikanten Erasmus Schmid', Zeitschrift für
Schweizerische Geschichte 50 (1956), 353–366; also Goeters op. cit., 49.
[5] W. Neuser, Hans Hut, 1913; G. Mecenseffy, 'Die Herkunft des oberösterreichis-
chen Täufertums', ARG 47 (1956), R. Friedman, 'Thomas Muntzer's Relations to
Anabaptism', MQR 31 (1957), 75–87, 252–259; H. Klassen, 'The Life and Teachings
of Hans Hut', MQR 33 (1959), 171–205, 267–304. See p. 38 n. 2 below. Mecenseffy
sees connections between the Anabaptists and Müntzer, but Friedmann and Kievit
(see note 7 below) deny this. Cf. E. G. Rupp, 'Thomas Müntzer, Hans Hut and
the Gospel of all creatures', Bulletin of the John Rylands Library 43 (1961), 492–519.
[6] For the view that the Anabaptist movement goes back to Waldensian influences
see L. Keller, Die Reformation und die älteren Reformparteien, 1885; also H. Böhmer,
'Waldenser', RE³ 20 (1908), 799–840; this view is now rejected by most. However,
G. Franz in ARG 50 (1959), 87, arguing against the conclusions of Mennonite research and F. Blanke, says, 'The Swiss Anabaptist movement cannot be dissociated
from the sectarian movements of the late Middle Ages'.
[7] H. Denck, Schriften (vol. 1, bibliography by G. Baring; vol. 2, Denck's religious
writings, ed. W. Fellmann), 1955–1956; J. Kiewit, H. Denck and his Teaching, 1954;
'The Life of H. Denck', MQR 31 (1957), 277–295; 'The Theology of H. Denck',
MQR 32 (1958), 3–27; For the view that Denck was influenced by the Meistersinger
George Breuning see H. Fast, 'Pilgrim Marbeck und das oberdeutsche Täufertum',
ARG 47 (1956), 212–242.

D

independent Anabaptist movement arose in Bern.[1] The movement gained no foothold in Germany before the Peasants' War.

In the last few decades research into the Anabaptist movement has been conducted more vigorously than into any other branch of Reformation history.[2] Its most valuable fruit has been the publication of a large number of documents which give us a wealth of detailed insight into the life of the Anabaptist congregations.[3] By far the greatest amount of research has been done by the American Mennonites, who regard themselves as the heirs of the Anabaptists of the Reformation period. The achievement of their researchers deserves admiration, even though their work is plainly tendentious. Their assertion that the Anabaptist movement is unique and independent of mediaeval sectarianism is of course one of the points which their research is intended to prove. They try very hard to demon-

[1] J. Staedtke, 'Anfänge des Täufertums in Bern', *ThZ* 11 (1955), 75–78.

[2] It is impossible to give even a partial survey of recent research into the Anabaptist movement. See the periodicals, *Mennonite Life* (with an annual bibliography), *Mennonite Quarterly Review* (with 'bibliographical and research notes'), and the *Mennonitische Geschichtsblatter*. Also the *Mennonite Lexikon* (1913–1960) and the *Mennonite Encyclopedia* (1956–1959). Also H. J. Hillerbrand, *Bibliographie des Taufertums 1525–1630*, 1962. W. Koehle, 'Das Täufertum in der neuren kirchenhistorischen Forschung', *ARG* 37 (1940); 38 (1941); 40 (1943); 41 (1948); H. S. Bender, 'Recent Anabaptist Bibliographies', *MQR* 24 (1950), 88–91; R. Friedmann, 'Recent Interpretations of Anabaptism', *ChH* 24 (1955), 132–151; H. J. Hillerbrand, 'Die gegenwärtige Täuferforschung. Fortschritt oder Dilemma?' *Lebendiger Geist, H. J. Schoeps . . . dargebracht*, 1959, 48–65.

Important studies are: H. Bullinger, *Der Widertäufferen ursprung usw.*, 1560; E. Troeltsch, *The Social Teachings of the Christian Churches* 1923[3]; W. Wiswedel, *Bilder und Führergestalten aus dem Täufertum*, 3 vols., 1928, 1930, 1952; F. Heyer, *Der Kirchenbegriff der Schwärmer*, 1939; R. Friedmann, *Mennonite Piety through the Centuries*, 1949; G. H. Smith, *The Story of the Mennonites*, Newton/Kansas 1950; F. H. Littell, *The Anabaptist View of the Church*, New York 1952; F. J. Wrag, 'The Anabaptist Doctrine of the Restitution of the Church', *MQR* 28 (1954), 186–196; R. Friedmann, 'The Oldest Church Discipline of the Anabaptists', *MQR* 29 (1955), 162–166; P. Peachey, 'Anabaptism and Church Organisation', *MQR* 30 (1956), 213–228; L. H. Zuck, 'Anabaptism: an abortive Counter-Revolt within the Reformation', *ChH* 26 (1957) 211–226; H. S. Bender, 'The Hymnology of the Anabaptists', *MQR* 31 (1957), 5–10; and 'The Historiography of the Anabaptists', *ibid.*, 88–104; H. J. Hillerbrand, 'The Anabaptist View of the State', *MQR* 32 (1958), 83–110; and 'An early Anabaptist Treatise on the Christian and the State', *MQR* 32 (1958), 28–47; and 'Anabaptism and the Reformation—another look', *ChH* 29 (1960), 205–423; J. C. Wenger, *Even unto death. The heroic witness of the sixteenth-century Anabaptists*, 1961; further literature in T. Bergsten, *Balthasar Hubmair*, 1961.

[3] Sources for the History of the Anabaptists (*Quellen zur Geschichte der Täufer*): Württemberg (I. 1930, ed. G. Bossert); South Brandenburg (II.=Bavaria, section 1, ed. K. Schornbaum, 1934); imperial cities now in Bavaria (V.=Bavaria, section 2, ed. K. Schornbaum, 1951); Baden and the Palatinate (IV, ed. M. Krebs, 1951); Alsace (VII, ed. M. Krebs and H. G. Rott, 1959). For Hesse see *Urkundliche Quellen zur hessischen Reformationsgeschichte* IV, Wiedertäuferakten 1527–1626, ed. G. Franz, 1951. See also L. Müller, *Glaubenszeugen oberdeutschen Taufgesinnter*, 1938; and *Quellen zur Geschichte der Täufer in der Schweiz I: Zürich*, ed. L. von Muralt and W. Schmidt, 1951.

strate that there was no connection of any kind between Müntzer (together with the advocates of Reformation by force) and the genuine Anabaptists. Mennonite research runs the risk of reading into the beginnings of the movement the Mennonite insistence on the rejection of force in favour of peaceableness. They are also more ready to emphasise the biblicist element in Anabaptism than the spiritualist element. We have to reckon with the possibility that certain theories about the Anabaptist movement which at first seemed attractive and even today exercise a certain fascination may yet have to be rejected, or at least be reduced to proportions more consistent with historical probability.

12. LUTHER'S RETURN TO WITTENBERG

The beginnings of the Reformation in Zwickau and in Wittenberg took place at a time when Luther was removed from the scene and unable to exert any direct influence on the course of events. At the Wartburg he was kept in touch with developments in Wittenberg.[1] The disturbances in Wittenberg made him leave the Wartburg on his own initiative, and on 6 March 1522 he appeared in Wittenberg again. His celebrated *Invocavit* sermons, preached between 9 and 16 March,[2] succeeded in pacifying everyone and in re-establishing order. Luther was faced with a difficult task, for on the one hand he had to uphold, and if necessary defend, the new order which was the logical outcome of the reformers' message and which in any case had been officially enacted; and on the other hand he had to restrain unclerical zeal and go back on changes which the local churches were not yet ready to assimilate, and which, if insisted on, would amount to neglect of the duty to love and not scandalise the 'weak'. Luther even allowed private masses (without congregation) to be said again, and allowed Latin to be reintroduced in the mass. In September 1523 Luther issued a Latin form of service entitled *Formula Missae et Communionis*.[3] From the canon of the mass those prayers which speak of the sacrificial character of the mass are omitted still. A year after the *Invocavit* sermons the daily mass was discontinued and in its place there were weekday services of the word with preaching.[4] Even these steps meant a considerable transformation in the worship aspect of church life. The first service to be translated into German was the baptism service (*The Manual of Baptism, in German,* 1523).[5] Other reforms which had been

---

[1] Cf. *WAB* 2. Unfortunately in this edition the letters between Luther and his Wittenberg friends are not placed together. For Luther's attitude to the 'Zwickau Prophets' see letter 452, p. 443.

[2] *WA* 10 III, XLVI–LXXXV, 1–64.   [3] *WA* 12 (197) 205–220.

[4] Rietschel-Graff, *Lehrbuch der Liturgik* I, 1951², 342; *WA* 11, 61, 33–62, 5.

[5] *WA* 12, (38) 42–48. For the 1526 revision see *WA* 19, 531, 537–541; 30 I, 339–342.

begun were allowed to remain and new ones were brought in, too. The parochial church in Wittenberg which had previously been incorporated in the collegiate foundation of All Saints' now became the town church. Church finances were completely reorganised. Thus in Wittenberg a Reformation had taken place which involved far more than preaching, for the whole life of the church has been newly ordered. To a very considerable extent, though not fully, the logical consequences of the Reformation gospel had been put into effect. Luther's modification of the Reformation which Karlstadt had begun in Wittenberg now provided a model for others to copy. For a very long time it was a characteristic of the Lutheran Reformation that it proceeded, not by implementing a carefully devised plan, but by modifying and correcting mistaken developments as they arose. The Wittenberg reordering never purported to be anything other than a suggestion which others might care to follow—it was never intended to be binding.

13. THE DISORDERLY GROWTH OF THE REFORMATION

Though Luther's influence in Wittenberg, after his return from the Wartburg, was very powerful, and though the reform movement in Switzerland took its lead from Zwingli, it would be quite mistaken to suppose that in the period before the Peasants' War there was a neatly ordered, doctrinally clear and unified 'Evangelical' church organisation; or even that there were two such organisations, clearly differentiated from one another. Moreover, if it were a matter of making a count, it might almost be necessary to add a third kind of church organisation, for Bucer had begun to establish a pattern of reformed Christianity which was his own.[1] But in reality all that we find in the earliest period is a variety of reformist preaching and forms of church life which roughly corresponded. The relationship between the reformed Christians of Wittenberg and Zwingli soon became clouded, because they considered him a fanatic who despised the sacraments,[2] whereas Oecolampad, whose views were very close to Zwingli's, was regarded for a long time by the Wittenbergers as a Christian brother and partner in dialogue because he was an old friend of Melanchthon and therefore unimpeachable. To describe the many preachers and writers before 1525 as 'Lutherans' would certainly be precipitate. Of

[1] R. Stupperich, 'Bibliographia Bucerana', SVRG 169, 1952; B. Thompson, 'Bucer Study since 1918', ChH 25 (1956), 63–82. The first two volumes of Bucer's German writings have appeared in a new edition by R. Stupperich, i.e. the early writings, 1520–1524. H. Eells, Martin Bucer, New Haven 1931.

[2] Compare the first controversy over the Lord's Supper, which developed from a controversy between Luther and the 'fanatic' Karlstadt into a controversy between Luther and the 'fanatic' Zwingli. See III. 10 below.

course they all preached the 'Word of God' and within varying limits felt a certain solidarity with Luther. For a short while this was true even of Müntzer, and of Zwingli for a longer period. Even a man like Schwenk-feld,[1] active as a reformer in a number of areas in Silesia and the father of the 'spiritualists' who were to become so significant later on, did not de-cide until 1525 that he and Luther had come to the parting of the ways. The reformist preachers prior to 1525 were an assorted company. No norm was set for their preaching; and certainly it would be mistaken to suppose that they shared Luther's docile regard for their rulers. If we bear in mind that the progress of the Reformation varied greatly from place to place, so that in one place Evangelical church services had been introduced while in another place a preacher was perhaps merely making a hesitant attempt to give an Evangelical tinge to his preaching, we shall understand what is meant by the phrase, 'the disorderly growth of the Reformation'. For the period up to 1525 it is only with very careful reser-vations and qualifications that we may speak either of a single Evangelical movement or perhaps of an Evangelical movement which took two, or even three, different forms. At this period even the boundary between the 'classical' Reformation and the fanatics (i.e. Anabaptists, 'Spiritualists') cannot be drawn at all sharply. Indeed, there was little awareness on the part of many that such a boundary existed. The same question might apply to German cities as applies to Paris: Is it possible that some of those engaged in the Reformation were basically humanists with a reformist tinge?[2]

14. NEW FORMS IN WORSHIP

In a very profound sense, the Reformation at Wittenberg in the years following 1522 was essentially a reshaping of worship. The Word of God had to be proclaimed in a setting which was consistent with it, so all other things were regarded as peripheral and therefore had to serve the reshaping of worship. So it is no accident that in other places besides Wittenberg it was worship which came up for revision, and that even at a time when Wittenberg clung cautiously to a Latin mass—albeit a puri-fied one—services elsewhere were being said in German, or at least transla-tions were being prepared for printing and distribution.[3] In other words,

[1] Corpus Schwenckfeldianorum, 19 vols., 1907–1961; E. Ecke, Schwenckfeld, Luther und der Gedanke einer apostolischen Reformation, (1911), 1952²; S. G. Schultz, Caspar Schwenckfeld von Ossig, Norriston/Penn. 1946; H. Urner, 'Die Tauflehre Schwenck-felds', ThLZ 73 (1948), 339–342; P. L. Maier, C. Schwenckfeld and the Person and Work of Christ, 1959; G. Maron, Individualismus und Gemeinschaft bei C. von Schwenck-feld, 1961.
[2] G. Krodel, 'Nürnberger Humanisten am Anfang des Abendmahlsstreites', Zeit-schrift für Bayerischen Kirchengeschichte 25 (1956), 40–50.
[3] Rietschel-Graff, Lehrbuch der Liturgik I, 1951², 346–351.

there were those who in this respect were in greater haste than Luther, and we shall see how Luther had to trail behind them.[1] German service orders appeared in Basle (Wyssenburger) and Pforzheim (J. Schwebel) as early as 1522, but we know nothing more about them. Kaspar Kantz,[2] a preacher in Nördlingen, published a German service book in 1524 entitled, *Of the Evangelical Mass, how it should be held.* We have documentation of German masses in 1524 for Wertheim (Franz Kolb), Wendelstein near Schwabach and Reutlingen (Matthias Alber), for Worms[3] and even for Reval. The new orders of service which appeared in the same year in Strasbourg[4] and Nuremberg are of special importance, particularly in Nuremberg[5], where various efforts appear together (Volbrecht, Dober, Osiander). In Allstedt, Müntzer introduced a *German Office* which in content is still perfectly acceptable, but which Luther, surprisingly, rejected. In recent times Müntzer has gained recognition as a liturgist.[6] It is the reshaping of worship which shows most clearly that it is wrong to regard the Reformation in the period before 1525 as merely a preaching movement. On the other hand it had not yet developed into the new Evangelical Church of the years following the Peasants' War. But in an area of decisive importance, namely worship, conclusions had already been drawn from the new preaching, affecting the form of the Church and its order.[7]

15. NEW ARRANGEMENTS IN THE PARISHES

In addition to the reordering of services, certain other changes soon became a matter of urgency. Whereas it was quite possible for an individual cleric to hold new kinds of church service, including the use of German and communion in two kinds, and succeed in winning approval from his parishioners, there were other reforms which could not be carried

[1] E. Reim, 'The Liturgical Crisis in Wittenberg 1524', *CThM* 20 (1949), 284–292.
[2] See p. 41 n. 3; also W. Jensen, 'Von der evangelischen Messe', *Festgabe für K. Schornbaum*, 1951, 61 f.
[3] P. Brunner, 'Die Wormser deutsche Messe', *Kosmos und Ecclesia. Festschrift für W. Stählin*, 1953, 106–162.
[4] Rietschel-Graff, *op. cit.*, 348 f.
[5] Rietschel-Graff, *op. cit.*, 349 ff; B. Klaus, 'Die Nürnberger deutsche Messe 1524', *JLH* 1 (1958), 1–46; M. Simon, 'Die Nürnberger Spitalmessen der Reformationszeit', *ZBKG* 28 (1959), 143–153.
[6] R. Herrman, 'Thomas Müntzers deutsch-evangelische Messe, Allstedt 1524', *Zeitschrift für die Kirchengeschichte der Provinz Sachsen* 9 (1912), 57–91; K. Schulz, *Th. Müntzers liturgische Bestrebungen*, 1928.
[7] On the beginnings of the so-called 'Upper German' services see the important, and apparently forgotten, work by H. Waldenmaier, *Die Entstehung der lutherischen Gottesdienstordnung in Süddeutschland*, 1916.

through in quite so spontaneous a way. Such reforms included new arrangements for providing for the poor—rendered necessary by reformist preaching against begging[1]; for children's schooling—which the dissolution of the monasteries had made a matter for concern; for removing unqualified holders of benefices, for the appointment of preachers, for the disposal of benefices and new regulations on remuneration, and a host of other reforms such as Luther had demanded in his *Address to the Nobility* (1520),[2] including such things as the closing of brothels and so on. From the time of the late Middle Ages there had already grown up a tendency on the part of the civic authorities[3] to undertake the care of the sick and the poor, to appoint preachers at the authorities' expense, and to make the church life of the town independent of the ecclesiastical foundations into which many of the town churches were incorporated. Thus even in the early days of the Reformation civic ordinances on poverty were enacted (Nuremberg 1522, Strasbourg 1524), so-called 'common chests' were set up, i.e. funds into which were paid the proceeds from all endowed foundations and benefices, and from which preachers were paid and the costs of poor relief were met[4] (cf. the 'Wittenberg Ordinance' of 24 January 1522—passed during Luther's stay at the Wartburg—which owed its origin to Luther's even earlier arrangement for a common purse).[5] All these steps mark the first beginnings of the process by which the organisation of church life within the towns was brought under the control of the civic authorities, who exercised patronage over the churches within their walls and even outside them. Admittedly the congregation in the Reformation period still had the right to make representations to the town council.[6] In his letter to the Bohemian Brethren (1523) Luther wrote 'that a Christian congregation has both the power and the right to judge all doctrine and to appoint its teachers'. He is clearly thinking of congregations appointing their ministers themselves.[7] The fact that Luther felt obliged in 1524 to exhort the city fathers of every town in Germany to erect schools was the result of the propaganda issuing from the disciples of Karlstadt who were opposed to all forms of learning.

[1] *WA* 6, 450, 22–451, 19.
[2] *WA* 6, 381, 404–469, esp. 427 ff.
[3] A. Schultze, *Stadtgemeinde und Reformation*, 1918.
[4] H. Barge, 'Die älteste evangelische Armenordnung', *HV* 11 (1908), 193–225, 296; O. Winckelmann, 'Über die ältesten Armenordnungen der Reformationszeit (1522–1525)', *HV* 17 (1914–1915), 187–228, 361–400; F. Pischel, 'Die ersten Armenordnungen der Ref.-Zeit', *Deutsche Geschichtsblätter* 17 (1916), 317–330.
[5] See II. 8.
[6] F. Lau, 'Der Bauernkrieg und das Ende der lutherischen Reformation als spontaner Volksbewegung', *LuJ* 26 (1959), 109–134; *WA* 12, 16, 2 ff; *WA* 11, 401, 408–416.
[7] *WA* 12, 160, 169–196.

Another factor in the situation was that there was less incentive to take up clerical careers, and less need for clerical education.[1]

16. THE BEGINNINGS OF AN EVANGELICAL THEOLOGY

The Reformation originated in a German university. It can hardly be surprising that the Reformation brought into being a new Evangelical theology, before anything else. This theology is so markedly a scriptural theology that we must look for the signs of its development, to the exegetical lectures given by Luther and by other theologians who sympathised with him and which were subsequently printed.[2] This does not mean, of course, that Luther did not tackle theological questions in his other writings.[3] His translation of the New Testament with its prefaces (*Septembertestament*, 1522) and its exposition of principles of interpretation[4] was a theological event in its own right. Luther never attempted a systematic summary of Evangelical doctrine.[5] This service to the Reformation was performed by Philip Melanchthon (1497–1560),[6] who was a classical scholar, not a theologian. He was born in Bretten, a great-nephew of Reuchlin, received a humanist education at Tübingen and Heidelberg, became professor of Greek at Wittenberg in 1518, and in 1521 wrote his *Loci theologici rerum theologicarum seu hypotyposes theologicae*. This work, in its first edition, did hardly more than bring together various doctrinal topics, but it is a clear example of the new scriptural theology, with its renunciation of speculation, its Evangelical doctrine of justification, faith and gospel, and also a clear denial of free will (a position which

[1] *WA* 15, 9, 27–35; F. H. Löscher, *Kirche, Schule und Obrigkeit im Reformations-Jahrhundert*, 1925; G. Thiele, 'Das Schulwesen im Jahrhundert der Reformation', *Deutscher Kulturatlas* 3 (1936), 224–227a. J. Hahn, *Die evangelische Unterweisung in den Schulen des 16. Jahrh.s*, 1957.

[2] The first of Luther's commentaries to be printed was the *Operationes in Psalmos*, 1519; see *WA* 5. On this, see H. Beintker, 'Zur Datierung und Einordnung eines neuren Lutherfragments', *Wissenschaftliche Zeitschrift Greifswald* I (1951–1952), 70–78.

[3] *Von den guten Werken* (1520); *Von dem Papsttum zu Rom usw.* (1520); *De captivitate Babylonica* and esp. *De servo arbitrio* (1525).

[4] *WADB* 6 and 7.

[5] The Schmalkaldic Articles of 1536–1537 (*WA* 50), the Catechisms of 1529 (*WA* 30/I) and the last section of the Great Confession on the Lord's Supper of 1528 (*WA* 26, 499–509) are a kind of substitute for a systematic exposition of Luther's theology.

[6] C. Schmidt, *Philipp Melanchthon, Leben und ausgewählte Schriften*, 1861; W. Maurer, 'Zur Komposition der Loci Melanchthons von 1521', *LuJ* 25 (1958); and 'Melanchthons Loci communes als wissenschaftliche Programmschrift', *LuJ* 27 (1960), 1–50; W. Neuser, *Der Ansatz der Theologie Melanchthons*, 1957; A. Sperl, *Melanchthon zwischen Humanismus und Reformation*, 1959; R. Stupperich, *Melanchthon*, 1960; P. Meinhold, *Philipp Melanchthon, der Lehrer der Kirche*, 1960; W. Elliger (ed.), *P. Melanchthon, Forschungsbeiträge*, 1960; R. Stupperich, *Der unbekannte Melanchthon*, 1961; Melanchthon's works were published in *CR* 1–28, 1834–1860 and in a new edition by R. Stupperich, 1951 ff.

Melanchthon had not yet modified) and a strict doctrine of predestination.[1] The *Loci*, in their several editions (1521, 1522, 1535), provide a commentary on the whole history of the Reformation and also reflect the changes in Melanchthon's own thinking. The later developments in Luther's theology were determined by his struggle against the fanatics and particularly by the controversy over the Lord's Supper.[2] Zwingli, too, found an opportunity to develop his theology, for his closing addresses ('theses') at the First Zürich Disputation (1523)[3] allowed him to give a reasoned exposition of his views. His *Commentarius de vera ac falsa religione* (1520)[4] and other writings attempted to do the same. The Lord's Supper controversy brought other theologians into the fray: Oecolamped[5] (*De genuina verborum Domine expositione*, August 1525), Johann Brenz[6] (*Syngramma Suevicum*, October 1520), Johann Bugenhagen.[7] Lutheran and Swiss reformed theology parted company, not only in the controversy over the Lord's Supper, but also over Christology. Martin Bucer[8] began to publish in about 1523. He occupied a middle position, but his theology, like explicitly Lutheran and explicitly Swiss theology, did not fully establish itself before 1525.

17. HUMANISM AND THE REFORMATION

It might appear—and certainly many have assumed—that the humanists as a whole, or with perhaps a few exceptions, went over into the reformers' camp.[9] Luther's friends and colleagues, for the most part, came from the humanist movement—Melanchthon, J. Jonas,[10] G. Spalatin[11] and many others. One of them, N. von Amsdorf, can hardly be said to have been influenced by humanism.[12] It is impossible to deny that Luther himself was influenced by humanism, as is evidenced by his love of languages, his rejection of Karlstadt's tendency to suspect learning, his interest in teach-

[1] C. Trinkaus, 'The Problem of Free Will in the Renaissance and the Reformation', *Journal of the History of Ideas* X (1949), 51–62.

[2] See III. 10.

[3] *CR* 89 (1908), 1–457.

[4] *CR* 90 (1914), 590–912.

[5] E. Staehelin, *Das theologische Lebenswerk Oecolampads*, 1939.

[6] H. Hermelink, *Joh. Brenz als lutherischer und schwäbischer Theologe*, 1949.

[7] K. Harms, *Doktor Joh. Bugenhagen (1485–1558)*, 1958; W. Rautenberg (ed.), *J. Bugenhagen*, 1958.

[8] See p. 22 n. 9 and p. 40 n. 1.

[9] P. Kalkoff, 'Die Stellung der deutschen Humanisten zur Reformation', *ZKG* 46 (1927), 161–231; B. Moeller, 'Die deutschen Humanisten und die Anfange der Reformation', *ZKG* 70 (1959), 46–61.

[10] W. Delius, *J. Jonas*, 1952.

[11] I. Höss, *G. Spalatin*, 1956.

[12] H. Stille, *N. von Amsdorfs Leben bis 1542*, 1937; O. H. Nebe, *Reine Lehre, Zur Theologie des N. von Amsdorf*, 1935.

ing, his understanding of history and of the individual within history (cf.
To the city councillors of Germany, 1524,[1] etc.). The leading figures in the
Swiss Reformation were Zwingli, a humanist and student of Erasmus, and
men like Pellikan, Oecolampad, Bullinger and others, all of whom owed
much to humanism. Even the Anabaptist movement had certain roots in
Erasmian humanism.[2] The later history of Protestantism shows how great
was the humanist inheritance which the Reformation received. There were
few humanists, like Reuchlin or Mutian, who set their faces against the
Reformation. But it is just as important to notice that other humanists
like Pirckheimer, Crotus Rubeanus and others were for a time attracted
to the Reformation and gave it their sympathy, only to turn away from it
later on. Though they wanted, and were prepared to work for, a 'reform
of the Church', the 'Reformation' as a totally new expression of the faith
in Luther's or Zwingli's sense was foreign to them. Their faith in the
dignity and greatness of man was affronted by the reformers' insistence
on the total incapacity of sinful men to do any good. The hatred of Rome,
as expressed in von Hutten's *Vadiscus sive trias Romana* (1520), was by no
means all that was needed to bring the humanists to the reformers' side.
In England it was precisely the leading humanists like Colet,[3] More,[4]
and Fisher who conducted the intellectual campaign against the Reformation and Henry VIII's church policies, while in France it was difficult to
make out whether those who were suspected of heresy were humanists
or Evangelicals. Spain, despite its humanism,[5] remained Catholic. In
Poland the Renaissance was a hindrance to the Reformation rather than a
help. The history of the Reformation in Switzerland (cf. the Lord's Supper controversy) and in Hungary shows how strongly-held humanist
attitudes could affect very considerably the manner in which the Reformation proceeded.

18. OPPOSITION TO LUTHER AND TO THE REFORMATION

Even the first chapter of Reformation history cannot be written without taking into consideration the forces which operated against it. Although the first and surprising impression might be that things went on as
though the Edict of Worms had never existed, the Reformation movement did not advance altogether unopposed. Brutal force was exercised
against it; attempts were made to set in motion long overdue reforms, so
as to deprive the reformers of a cause, but naturally it was too late;
and a very considerable literary war was conducted against it. The Popes,
who were deeply involved in Italy's political problems and in the tension

[1] F. Lau, *Luther*, 1959, 80 ff.   [2] See p. 36 n. 2.   [3] See p. 9 n. 10.
[4] See p. 9 n. 11.   [5] See p. 9 n. 12.

between France and the Habsburgs, were unable to counter the Reformation with very much zeal. Clement VII (1523–1534)[1] was as impotent in this respect as Leo X (1513–1521) had been. Only Adrian VI (1522–1523),[2] who as Adrian of Utrecht had been Charles V's tutor and for a time Regent of Spain, had a clear understanding of the problem of Catholic reform, and at the second Diet of Nuremberg (1522–1523) announced, through Chieregati, a programme of reform which, however, he was unable to implement.[3] Charles V, as ruler of Burgundy (martyrdoms in 1523)[4] and also the rulers of Austria, Salzburg, Bavaria, Albertine Saxony and central Switzerland, took steps against Luther's supporters according to the terms of the Edict of Worms. The universities of Louvain and Cologne had pronounced judgement against Luther and had thus prepared the way for Luther's ban. Jakob Hochstraten, the inquisitor in Cologne, and Aleander both had some part in this. Johann Eck,[5] until his death, was continually appearing in public against Luther, and also wrote against him and against the Reformation. His *Enchiridion locorum communium adversus Lutherum et alios hostes ecclesiae* ran into 46 editions between 1525 and 1576. He was supported by other theologians, Johann Faber of Leutkirch[6] (*Malleus in haeresim Lutheranam*, 1522), the man who appeared against Zwingli at the First Zürich Disputation and with Eck at the Disputation at Baden in Switzerland. Among other supporters of Eck were Thomas Murner, who in 1522 published his attack *On the great fool, Luther*,[7] and also Caspar Schatzgeyer.[8] Those opponents of Luther who set themselves to conduct a literary campaign against him tended to gather in groups around theologically informed princes like Henry VIII of England, (cf. John Fisher),[9] for Henry had himself written against Luther's *De*

---

[1] L. v. Pastor, *Geschichte der Päpste* IV/2, 1956[13], 161 ff.; on Leo X cf. *ibid.* IV/1, 1956[13]. On the Counter-reformation understood as a renewal of the 'old Church' see *Reformationsgeschichtliche Studien und Texte*, 1906–1929; *Corpus Catholicorum* 1919 ff.; *Acta Reformationis catholicae ecclesiam Germaniae concernentia* I (=1520–1532), ed. G. Pfeilschifter, 1959.; K. Kupisch, *Feinde Luthers*, 1951; K. D. Schmidt, 'Katholische Reform und Gegenreformation', *Aus der Arb. des Evangelischen Bundes* 6, 1957.

[2] L. v. Pastor IV/2, 1 ff; E. Hocks, *Der letzte deutsche Papst Adrian VI.*, 1939; J. Posner, *Der deutsche Papst Adrian VI*, 1962. Bennos of Meissen was canonised under Adrian VI. Cf. Luther, *Wider den neuen Abgott und alten Teufel zu Meissen*, 1524 (*WA* 15, 170–198).

[3] *Mirbt*, no. 420 (Instruction).

[4] See K. Brandi, *Deutsche Geschichte*, 124.

[5] See *CCath*. 2, 6, 13, 14, 16 (bibliography); *Schl* I, 5184–5244; E. Iserloh, *Die Eucharistie in der Darstellung des Johann Eck*, 1950. J. Lortz, *Die Reformation in Deutschland*, 2 vols., 1949[3], II 9, passim.

[6] L. Helbling, *Dr. Johann Faber*, 1941; cf. *CCath*. 25–26; O. Vasella, *Abt Theodul Schlegel von Chur*, 1954.

[7] *Schl* II, 16024–16133; R. Newald, *Wandlungen des Murnerbildes*, 1938.

[8] *Schl* II, 18991–19001; K. Klomps, *Kirche, Freiheit und Gesetz bei Kaspar Schatzgeyer*, 1957.

[9] *RGG*[3] II, 970 ff.

captivitate Babylonica ecclesiae.[1] George of Saxony,[2] too, was among the most sober but inflexible of Luther's adversaries. Augustin Alvelt[3] in Leipzig, Hieronymus Emser[4] and Johann Cochläus[5] wrote against Luther unflinchingly. Among the Italian theologians who joined in were Cajetan,[6] Prierias[7] and Ambrosius Catharinus de Politi.[8] All these make a formidable array. In fact the theologians of the Reformation carried far more weight than those of the 'old faith', and Luther's conviction that papacy was nearing its end was understandable at that time.

19. THE FIRST ITALIAN WAR

How are we to account for the fact that the Reformation movement achieved such a powerful success, even after the excommunicate Luther had been formally outlawed at Worms, Charles V had made a solemn personal delcaration of his opposition to Luther, and the Edict of Worms, claiming to represent the will of all estates of the Empire, had passed judgement against Luther and his followers and had laid down the direct penalties on any who sought to emulate him? What actually happened must have detracted from Charles V's reputation and standing, for the only reason why he allowed developments to run their course unchecked was that he was in trouble with France. Francis I, sandwiched between Burgundy, Anterior Austria, Habsburg Württemberg and Spain, found his position intolerable, and he felt that he had to make good his defeat at the imperial election. His main anxiety was that Charles V might advance on Upper Italy (Milan had been in French hands since the battle of Marignano in 1515).[9] Francis judged it expedient to take action against Charles with all speed, because there were regular rebellions in Spain against the 'Burgundian'. Francis made speedy contact with the *Comuneros*

[1] C. S. Meyer, 'Henry VIII burns Luther's Books, 12 May 1521', *Journal of Ecclesiastical History* 9 (1958), 173–182.
[2] H. Becker, 'Herzog Georg v. Sachsen als kirchlicher und theologischer Schriftsteller', *ARG* 14 (1927), 161–269; O. Vossler, 'Herzog Georg und seine Ablehnung Luthers', *HZ* 184 (1957), 272–291; E. Werl, 'Herzogin Sidonia v. Sachsen und ihr ältester Sohn Herzog Georg', *Herbergen der Christenheit* 2 (1959), 8–19.
[3] *CCath.* XI, 1926; *Schl* I, 313–321; G. Hesse, 'A. von Alvelt', *Franziskanische Studien* 17 (1930) 160–178.
[4] *CCath* 4, 28; *Schl* I, 5400–5429; *RGG*[3] II, 462
[5] *Schl* I, 2986–3033; *RGG*[3] I, 1842. Cochläus wrote *De gratia sacramentorum* in 1522, and Luther's reply, *Adversus armatum virum Cochläum*, appeared in 1523 (see *WA* 11, 292–306).
[6] *EC* IV, 1506 ff. (bibliography); R. Bauer, *Gottesbeweis und Gotteserkenntnis bei Kardinal Cajetan*, 1955.
[7] E. Lauchert, *Die italienischen literarischen Gegner Luthers*, 1912; *RGG*[3] V, 568.
[8] *CCath* 27 ('Apologia pro veritate catholicae fidei' 1521), 1956.
[9] The Swiss had been in possession of Milan since the battle of Novara 1513, but at the battle of Marignano they were driven out.

in revolt. The war between Charles V and France was fought in the Pyrenees (the kingdom of Navarre; Ignatius of Loyola was wounded in the battle of Pamplona in 1521), along the Meuse and in Picardy, where Henry VIII joined Charles as an ally. But the main fighting was in Italy, for which reason the war is referred to as the First Italian War (1521–25/26).[1] Fortunes in the war were varied. On 27 April 1522 at Bicocca George of Frundsberg repelled a French counter-attack on Milan, which in November 1521 had revolted against France. On 26 October 1524 Francis I regained Milan, though in 1523 one of his major vassals, Charles of Bourgogne, had rebelled against him. The situation seemed to augur well for France, because on 12 December 1524 Clement VII, having transferred his attentions from the Emperor, concluded a separate peace with Francis I. But on 24 February 1525, on Charles V's 25th birthday—Charles was in Madrid at the time—his troops routed the French completely at the celebrated battle of Pavia.[2] It was not until January 1526 that Charles concluded with Francis the Peace of Madrid,[3] when Francis I was forced to renounce all claims to Milan, Naples, and even Bourgogne. The Peace contained the seeds of new and more serious conflict. It was because Charles was tied militarily and financially by these struggles that he was unable to act upon the decisions of Worms and therefore had to allow the Reformation movement to take its course.

20. THE DIETS OF NUREMBERG AND THE SECOND IMPERIAL GOVERNING COUNCIL

The tussle between the Habsburgs and France over, and for the most part in, Upper Italy explains why Charles V found it impossible to implement his statements at Worms. But it still does not explain why the German estates did not implement the Edict of Worms. Between 1522 and 1524 three Diets were held in Nüremberg. None arrived at decisions resulting in a check to the Reformation movement. The first, in March 1522,[4] was concerned with the Turkish question and did not discuss the religious question at all. The second (1522–23) contained an element of drama, because the Nuncio Chieregati arrived to deliver a confession of sins and a programme of reform on behalf of Adrian VI.[5] The Imperial Diet's decision (on 'the preaching of the pure Gospel according to true Christian understanding') had the effect of encouraging Evangelical

[1] W. P. Fuchs, 'Das Zeitalter der Reformation', Gebhardt-Grundmann 2, 1955[8], 8–11.
[2] Schl IV, 40703–725.
[3] Schl I, 37818–37819. See lit. on Charles V, p. 4 n. 3.
[4] Deutsche Reichstagsakten Jüngere Reihe 3 and 4 (1901 and 1905).
[5] Schl III, 27951–27956a.

preaching, though it was clearly intended (as is evidenced by the appeal to four Latin fathers) in the spirit of Catholic reform. The third Imperial Diet, held in January 1524, made a definite decision about something which the second had had in mind, namely the summoning of a German national assembly in Speyer in November 1524, in place of a Council which could not be held on account of the war.[1] But since Charles V, on 15 July 1524, forbade the holding of such an assembly, the estates could do nothing more than declare their general willingness, so far as was possible, to implement the Edict of Worms.

The Second Imperial Governing Council[2] (1521–1531) acted merely as a kind of holding body in the absence of the Emperor. This was in distinct contrast to the first (1500–1502), which had been constituted a body of the estates. At the second Council were men who wished to suppress the Reformation energetically. One was the archduke Ferdinand who took the chair (on a rota system) at the beginning. Another was George of (Albertine) Saxony, who employed all the means at his disposal, including a warning to Frederick the Wise that by shielding Luther he might be putting his position as elector in jeopardy. However, one of Frederick's diplomats, Hans von der Planitz,[3] was extremely skilful in warding off all attacks. Moreover, some of the princes' councillors, particularly the *Hofmeister* from Bamberg, Johann von Schwarzenberg,[4] were supporters of the Reformation. The reason why neither the Imperial Diet nor the Imperial Governing Council took any positive action against the Reformation (by implementing the Edict of Worms) was partly that there were tensions between Emperor, Imperial Governing Council and the estates of the Empire, but chiefly that everyone feared a popular rising and open revolution. It was certainly not that a sufficient number of the princes had reformist leanings, for even in the case of Frederick the Wise[5] this is by no means certain.

21. THE REFORMATION IN THE GERMAN TERRITORIAL STATES

Before the time of the Peasants' War none of the German territorial states had officially adopted the Reformation, nor was the situation essen-

[1] *Schl* III, 27957–27960.
[2] *Schl* III, 27886–27891; W. P. Fuchs, *op. cit.* (see p. 49 n. 1).
[3] E. Wülcker and E. Virck, *Des kursächsischen Rathes Hans v. d. Planitz Berichte an den Reichsregiment in Nürnberg 1521–1523*, 1899; J. Reimers, 'Dr. Hans Edler von der Planitz', *Herbergen der Christenheit*, 1957.
[4] *Schl* II, 19531–546a; V, 49221–49223; E. Wolf, *Grosse Rechtsdenker*, 1944², 97–133; H. Rössler, 'Johann von Schwarzenberg', *Fränkischer Geist – deutsches Schicksal*, 1953.
[5] P. Kirn, *Friedrich der Weise und die Kirche*, 1926; A. Koch, 'Die Kontroverse über die Stellung Friedrichs des Weisen zur Reformation', *ARG* 23 (1926), 213–260.

tially different in the towns. The Reformation movement was fully alive in almost all territories, even those in which the cause was a hopeless one (such as Albertine Saxony, the archbishopric of Magdeburg). It was still stronger in the towns. Frederick the Wise,[1] to whom the reformists owed very great gratitude for his intervention on Luther's behalf— whether out of a sense of justice, or out of pride in the celebrated professor from the university in his own territory—kept up his 'priceless' collection of relics till 1522, and received communion in Evangelical style only on his deathbed. Frederick's co-regent and brother, John, who succeeded Frederick as John 'the constant' (1525–1532),[2] was regarded hopefully by the advocates of the Reformation. Similarly regarded was a prince who occupied a clerical territory at the extreme edge of the Empire, Albert of South Brandenburg,[3] who since 1511 had been Grand Master of the Order of Teutonic Knights. He had been trying without success to get rid of Polish domination over the Order's territory, and in 1523 he came into contact with Luther, at whose suggestion he renounced his clerical calling and as a secular duke took Prussia in fee from Poland in April 1525. At this outer edge of the Empire, which owed its very existence to the Reformation, were the ideal conditions for the establishment of an Evangelical territory and an Evangelical territorial church.

A number of other princes, too, showed themselves favourably inclined towards the Reformation, among whom were the young and gifted Landgrave Philip of Hesse[4] (1518–1567—born in 1504; he was George of Saxony's son in law), George[5] and Kasimir[6] of South Brandenburg, Ernest of Lüneburg,[7] Wolfgang of Anhalt-Zerbst,[8] and the Danish king and duke of Holstein, Frederick I.[9] Before the Peasants' War there was no alliance by such men, say, for the purpose of protecting Evangelical preachers and preaching. This makes it the more noteworthy that the German territorial princes who were not content to remain at a cautious distance from the Lutheran upheaval but actively stressed their allegiance to the old faith actually formed an alliance, at least in South Germany,

---

[1] *Schl* III, 32975–33004; V, 51421 f; A. Koch, *op. cit.* (p. 50 n. 5); I. Höss, *Spalatin*, 1956.

[2] *Schl* III, 33097a–33125.

[3] *Schl* III, 32529a–32662; W. Hubatsch, *Europäische Briefe im Reformations-Zeit-altar*, 1949; P. Thielen, *Die Kultur am Hofe Herzog Albrechts von Preussen*, 1953; W. Hubatsch, *Albrecht von Brandenburg-Ansbach*, 1960; P. Tschackert, *Urkundenbuch zur Reformationsgeschichte des Herzogtums Preussen*, 3 vols., 1890.

[4] *Politisches Archiv des Landgrafen Philipp von Hessen* I/II (1904–1910, ed. Küch), III/IV (1954–1959, ed. Heinemeyer); *Urkundliche Quellen zur hessischen Ref. geschichte* I (1915, 1957[2], ed. Sohm), II–IV (1951–1955 ed. Franz); *Schl* III, 30293–30483; V, 51266–51270.

[5] *Schl* III, 29097a–29128; V, 51146a–51148.

[6] *Schl* III, 29147a–29156.   [7] *Schl* III, 29750–29759.

[8] *Schl* III 29020–29035.   [9] *Schl* III, 30648a–30650a.

to offer political opposition to the Reformation movement. Under the influence of the nuncio Lorenzo Campeggio,[1] Bavaria, Salzburg and a number of other bishoprics formed the Regensburg Convention[2] in June 1524, whereas the North German counterpart (the Dessau Convention), despite the activities of George of Saxony, was not formed until July 1525.[3] Outside Germany, with the exception of Switzerland, conditions were not favourable to the setting up of Evangelical territories, so that even after the Peasants' War the Reformation *movement* remained simply a movement.

22. THE PEASANTS' WAR AND THE REFORMATION

There is no direct connection between the Peasants' War[4] and the history of the Church. For its origins it is necessary to look a long way back.[5] The most famous peasant revolts outside Germany were the revolt in Flanders, 1323, the *Jacquerie* in Northern France, 1356, and the English Peasant Revolt of 1381. In Germany, serious unrest among the peasants came to the surface in 1476, when Hans Böhm, the piper of Niklashausen in the Tauber valley, appeared on the scene. At the end of the 15th and beginning of the 16th centuries important peasant confederations were formed, the *Arme Konrad* in *Württemberg*,[6] 1514, and the *Bundschuh*,[7] whose emblem (the low shoe of the peasant bound above the ankle with string, in contrast to the boot of the nobleman) became the banner of the peasant revolution. But these alliances were made only over relatively small areas (cf. the revolts in the bishopric of Speyer, 1502, Breisgau, 1503, and the Upper Rhine, 1517), and this was a limitation and a weakness in the peasant movement which had not been overcome by the time of the Peasants' War. There has been much discussion of the causes of discontent and unrest in the peasantry. Of much greater consequence than material poverty (which certainly existed in South-west Germany, where plots had been subdivided almost to vanishing point) was the fact that the peasants were without rights. They had no freedom, for they were subject to lords who had control over land, over justice, and over the pea-

---

[1] RGG[3] I, 1606; E. Cardinal, *Cardinal Lorenzo Campeggio, Legate to the Courts of Henry VIII and Charles V*, Boston 1935.
[2] *Schl* IV, 41253–41257;
[3] *Schl* IV, 36489 f.
[4] *Schl* IV, 34765–35241; V, 51510–51531; G. Franz, *Der Deutsche Bauernkrieg*, 1933, 1957[4]; A. Meusel, *Th. Müntzer und seine Zeit*, 1953 (marx).
[5] *Schl* IV, 35191–35209.
[6] Franz, *op. cit.* (n. 4 above); H. Oehler, 'Der Aufstand des Armen Konrads 1514', *Württembergische Vierteljahrhefte* 38 (1932), 401–486.
[7] *Schl* IV, 34885–34895a; V, 51516–51518; A. Rosenkranz, *Der Bundschuh*, 2 vols, 1927; W. Andreas, *Der Bundschuh*, 1953[2].

sant's own person, and hardly anywhere did they have official representation (though the *Landstube* of Tirol was an exception). Their rights were
even further diminished by unlimited compulsory service which heightened the tension. Although it is true that the peasant movement was a
political and social movement rather than a religious one, it is plain that
from its beginnings it allied itself to religious movements.[1] The use of
slogans like 'divine law' and 'divine justice' suggests that Wyclif, Huss
and the Waldensians had had some influence. It cannot be surprising
that the new righteousness of which the reformers spoke had a powerful
attraction for the restless peasants, despite the fact that not all the peasants
or peasant leaders who fought in the war were adherents of the new faith.
In many respects and for many people Reformation thinking and the
thinking of militant peasants tended to mingle with each other. During
the period in which the Reformation was spreading rapidly, everything
'revolutionary' was dubbed 'Lutheran', in the minds of the revolution-
aries as well as in the polemics of their adversaries; though this is not to
say that the influence of the Reformation upon the Peasants' War goes
back to Luther himself.[2] It is obvious that the peasant movement, which
since June 1524 (the revolt in Stühlingen) had become a peasants' war in
the Black Forest, Southern Swabia, Alsace, Tirol, with offshoots in Fulda
and Thuringia, had already been crushed in May and June of 1525 by the
superior force of the Swabian League (George Truchsess of Waldburg)
and of territorial princes like Philip of Hesse and George of Saxony (there
were battles at Leipheim on 4 April, Böblingen on 12 May, Frankenhausen on 15 May, Zabern on 17 May, Königshofen on 2 June, and
sequels in 1526). The main reason for the peasants' defeat was that they
fought in 'groups' (*Haufen*) and had leaders (Wendel Hipler, Friedrich
Weigandt, Michel Gaissmeier) but no coherent direction,[3] many 'programmes'—both utopian and realistic—but no actual policy. Division
amongst the peasants themselves—some advocating a return to the 'old
justice' by restoring lost liberties, and others seeking a 'divine justice' in
the shape of a new ordering of society[4]—positively encouraged their
opponents to play off one against the other. The *Twelve Articles of the
Swabian Peasants*[5] of February 1525, which demanded freedom to elect

[1] E. Bloch, 'Blick in den Chiliasmus des Bauernkriegs und Wiedertäufertums',
Genius 2 (1920), 310–313. See p. 2 n. 2.
[2] Christoph Schappeler, the reformer from Memmingen, who is supposed to have
composed the preamble to the Twelve Articles, was much more strongly influenced
by Zwingli than by Luther. Cf. also Goeters, *Hätzer*, 55 f.
[3] See *Schl* for literature on the various peasant leaders, and also Franz, *op. cit.* (p. 52
n. 4).
[4] I. Schmidt, *Das göttliche Recht und seine Bedeutung im Bauernkrieg*, 1939.
[5] *Schl* IV, 34830–34851; G. Franz, 'Die Entstehung der zwölf Artikel der deutschen Bauernschaft', *ARG* 36 (1940), 193–213.

E

the parson and freedom from compulsory feudal servitude, tithes, etc., in no way represent the considered policy of the peasants as a whole, for there was no such policy. But they gave Luther an opportunity of dissociating himself from the peasants' cause.[1] Other reformers like Melanchthon and Bucer differ from Luther only in the degree of severity with which they reacted to the peasants.[2] The significance of the Peasants' War, as also of the reformers' disowning the peasant movement, is not that it revealed who were the radicals—Müntzer was beheaded and Karlstadt was hard put to it to defecnd himself against the charge of complicity. The Anabaptist movement, in any case, did not really develop until after the Peasants' War. The decisive significance of the war is that it represents a half-way point in the history of the Reformation, a point at which it became abundantly clear that the Reformation could not be allowed to go on running wild. The period of uncontrolled growth had finally come to an end. There now remained only two possibilities: either to suppress the Reformation, or to give it public and official recognition by setting up an Evangelical church order in Evangelical territories. This does not mean that the Reformation, as a spontaneous popular movement, was immediately and forcibly arrested. Within Germany, and even to a greater extent outside Germany, the Reformation continued as a reform movement. The notion that the Peasants' War marks the end of the Reformation as a spontaneous popular movement is a notion that has only limited validity.[3] But it had now become essential to set up a new and reformed church order.

[1] *WA* 18, 279–334; P. Althaus, *Luthers Haltung im Bauernkrieg*, 1953; W. Elliger, *Luthers politische Denken und Handeln*, 1952; F. Lau, 'Luther—Revolutionär oder Reaktionär?' *Luther* 28 (1957), 109–133.
[2] W. Stolze, *Bauernkrieg und Reformation*, 1926.
[3] See III. 3.

CHAPTER III

THE DEVELOPMENT OF REFORMED CHURCH ORDER

I. THE ADOPTION OF THE REFORMATION BY GERMAN TERRITORIAL
PRINCES AND CITY AUTHORITIES, AND THE BEGINNINGS OF
PROTESTANT ALLIANCE POLITICS

In putting down the Peasants' Revolt George of Saxony and Philip of Hesse, father in law and son in law, joined forces. But they held quite contrary opinions about what was to be done afterwards, having won the victory. George of Saxony in July 1525 gathered together princes from Central and North Germany and formed the Dessau Alliance,[1] which included Albert, elector, cardinal and archbishop of Magdeburg-Mainz,[2] Joachim, elector of Brandenburg,[3] Henry of Wolfenbüttel[4] and Erich of Brunswick-Calenberg.[5] The aim of the alliance was to reinforce the princes' territorial government and also to blot out the Lutheran heresy. Philip of Hesse,[6] on the other hand, not only recognised the strength of the Lutheran movement even in his own territory, but had also been won over to the Reformation by Melanchton in 1524. He dissociated himself from his father-in-law's anti-Reformation measures and instead formed an alliance with John ('the constant') of Saxony,[7] who personally favoured the Reformation and Luther in a way that his predecessor and brother, Frederick the Wise (who died on 5 May 1525), had not. Thus on 4 May 1526 the Gotha (or Torgau) Alliance came into being,[8] which at Magdeburg on 12 June 1526 was joined by Ernest and Francis of Brunswick-

---

[1] See p. 52 n. 3.
[2] *Schl* III, 31208–31267; V, 51321; W. Delius, *Die Reformationsgeschichte der Stadt Halle*, 1953.
[3] *Schl* III, 29540a–29559.   [4] *Schl* III, 29766–29836a; V, 21206a-f.
[5] *Schl* III, 29732–29738.   [6] See p. 51 n. 4.   [7] See p. 51 n. 2.
[8] W. Friedensburg, *Zur Vorgeschichte des Gotha-Torgauschen Bündnisses 1525–26*, 1884.

Lüneburg, Philip of Brunswick-Grubenhagen, Henry of Mecklenburg, Wolfgang of Anhalt and others. An attempt to persuade Nuremberg to join failed at first. The members of this alliance decided to take steps to protect themselves from attacks made on them in the cause of religion. The experience of the Peasants' War, however, meant that they could not allow the reform movement simply to go on growing unchecked. It had become necessary to take precautions against anti-authoritarian outbursts and to make quite clear that the principle of obedience to authority, which Luther had enunciated during the Peasants' War, held good. This meant that it was now essential to introduce a clear and definite church order and a clarification of the doctrine on which clerics were to base their preaching. This drive towards an Evangelical ordering of the church gained a momentum which was felt even in territories which did not belong to the political alliance. Prussia[1] was the first territory to establish such a church order. The South Brandenburg regions followed suit.[2] The cities were even more strongly inclined to set up a 'civic church order',[3] and certainly where the chief cities of the territories were concerned it sometimes took centuries to persuade them to align themselves with the other churches of the territories. Even in territories which continued to remain loyal to the old church the attempt was made—in so far as was possible within the framework of the papal church—to organise church order on territorial principles.[4]

2. THE CREATION OF EVANGELICAL TERRITORIAL CHURCHES

The most difficult, in fact the most questionable, task was that of laying the theoretical foundations on which the new church order was to be built. The sharp distinction proposed by Luther between the 'two kingdoms' or 'governments'[5] and the powers which he allotted to the congregations[6] made it quite difficult to appeal to the 'authorities' to take the initiative. Luther made his appeal to the nobility as to those who were

[1] See p. 51 n. 3.
[2] The Reformation was already being formally introduced in Nuremberg in 1524—see p. 22 n. 5. The visitation of Ansbach-Bayreuth did not being until 1528. See *Schl* III, 29105–29128, 29147c–29156, 29176d–29188; V, 51146a–51148.
[3] H. Baron, *Religion and politics in the German imperial cities during the Reformation*, 1937.
[4] H. Lehnert, *Kirchengut und Reformation*, 1931; G. Bossert, 'Beitrag zur Geschichte der bayrischen Religionspolitik in der Reformationszeit', *Beiträge zur bayrischen Kirchengeschichte* 15 (1909), 1–16.
[5] *WA* 11, 229–281; H. Diem, *Luthers Lehre von den zwei Reichen*, 1938; G. Törnvall, *Geistliches und weltliches Regiment bei Luther*, 1947; F. Lau, *Luthers Lehre von den beiden Reichen*, 1952; J. Heckel, *Lex charitatis. Eine juristische Untersuchung über das Recht in der Theologie M. Luthers*, 1953; and on this P. Althaus, *ThLZ* 81 (1956), 129 f.
[6] *WA* 11, 406–416; K. Müller, *Kirche, Gemeinde und Obrigkeit nach Luther*, 1910.

bound to the Gospel for Christian love's sake,[1] and this provided the motive for an urgent solution which in the historical circumstances was the only one possible. Another quite different approach, based on natural law, was Melanchthon's thesis that the 'authorities' were the guardians even of church services (*custodia utriusque tabulae*).[2] Philip of Hesse had the powers of jurisdiction belonging to the archbishop of Mainz temporarily transferred to himself,[3] and thereby foreshadowed developments in the establishment of a reformed Church order which by the middle of the century were to become of crucial importance.[4] There can be little doubt that the ostensible reasons for the establishment of Church government by the territorial princes were relatively insignificant. The real reasons were provided by the immediate historical circumstances, and also by the fact that the local authorities had exercised a controlling influence over church life for a very long time and in Western Europe this had proved a very practical solution.[5] It was by means of visitations that this kind of church order was established, both in Saxony and Prussia and in South Brandenburg, and subsequently in many other areas. These visitations naturally grew out of the earlier episcopal duty to make visitations. But now the territorial governor or city council appointed visitation commissions containing theologians and lawyers. Visitations of this sort were begun in Prussia as early as 1525. There the Reformation[6] was greeted by a good omen, in so far as the bishops of Samland (George of Polenz)[7] and Pomesania (Eberhard of Queiss;[8] and after 1529 Paul Speratus[9]) surrendered their secular territorial rights to the duke but kept their clerical functions. The 'Visitation of schools and churches in electoral Saxony' lasted from 1526 until 1530. A visitation entailed not a visit to every single village, but a summons to village parsons and church office-holders to attend at the nearest administrative centre. The purpose was to examine on the one hand the spiritual and moral qualifications of the clergy (together with their 'housekeepers' and children), and on the other hand to discover what the clergy's possessions were. The result of examinations in the first sense was that countless numbers of clergy were dismissed

---

[1] *WA* 26, 197, 12 ff.
[2] F. Lau, 'Melanchthon und die Ordnung der Kirche', *Philipp Melanchthon. Forschungsbeiträge*, 1961, 98–115.
[3] K. Dülfer, *Die Packschen Händel im Lichte der hessischen Politik*, 1956.
[4] K. Müller, 'Zur Geschichte und zum Verständnis des Episkopalsystems', *ZSavRG* (Kan. Abteilung) 8 (1918), 1–26; M. Heckel, 'Staat und Kirche in der ersten Hälfte des 17. Jahrhunderts', *ibid.*, 42 (1956), 117–247; 43 (1957), 202–308.
[5] See I. 7.
[6] See p. 51 n. 3.
[7] *Schl* III, 33476–33486; H. Laag, 'Die Einführung der Reformation im Ordensland Preussen', *NKZ* 36 (1925), 857–873.
[8] Ibid.
[9] *Schl* II, 20373–20396; P. Gennrich, *Die ostpreussischen Kirchenliederdichter*, 1938.

from their posts on the grounds that they did not meet even the most minimal requirements, such as the ability to say the creed or the Lord's Prayer or to 'read off' a sermon, or because they were immoderate frequenters of hostelries, etc., or because they were unwilling to accept the reformed faith. This meant that other parsons had to be found, whose qualifications were frequently only fractionally better. The reason for examining the parishes' economic circumstances was simply to safeguard their rights and their property against secularisation, by gaining protection from the local nobility, and to ensure adequate remuneration for married clergy.[1] In the cities there were monasteries to be disposed of, and these were normally used for educational purposes (usually for schools; but in Marburg for the foundation of the first explicitly Evangelical university[2]), though sometimes they became the property of the city itself or were added to the resources of the local prince. The proceeds from legacies left for the saying of masses etc. were paid into a 'common chest' and were used for poor relief and to meet other ecclesiastical expenditure. It seemed important to establish certain principles and aids which would assist in developing the spiritual life of the congregations. Melanchthon, for example, was largely responsible for the *Visitors' instructions to the clergy of electoral Saxony* (1528),[3] which goes into great detail, even giving recommendations about which books of the Bible may suitably be discussed with the young. As visitations developed, an increasing preoccupation was with the establishment of firm and acceptable teaching, and evidence of this concern is to be found in the Catechisms[4] which Luther produced during the period of the visitations (in 1529 the *Short Catechism* was produced on loose boards, followed by the *Great Catechism*, after which the Short Catechism was issued in book form). The influence of Luther's catechisms was very great indeed, but other catechisms, such as Brenz's catechism, did not simply go under.[5] The visitations did not in themselves represent a new means of ordering church life, for the commissions were not permanent institutions but were appointed *ad hoc*. They could of course be repeated, and sometimes went on, at intervals, for decades.[6] A

[1] *Schl* I, 39078–39096; also *WA* 26, 175 ff.
[2] H. Hermelink, 'Die Universität Marburg in den Jahren 1527–1645', *Die Philipp-Universität Marburg*, 1927, 1–224.
[3] *CR* 26, 51–96; *WA* 26, 195–240.
[4] *Schl* I, 12790–12876; V, 47825–47841; *RGG*[3] III, 1179–1186.
[5] *Schl* IV, 38501–38607; V, 51811–51816; E. V. Wills, 'Joh. Brenz's Catechisms of 1528 and 1535', *Lutheran Church Quarterly* 19 (1946), 271–280.
[6] C. A. H. Burckhardt, *Geschichte der sächsischen Kirchen-und Schulvisitationen*, 1879. Visitations were made for the first time in Prussia 1525, in Electoral Saxony 1526–1530, in Hesse 1527, in South Brandenburg 1528, and in Schleswig-Holstein 1528. In Hesse there was an attempt to found a church of the converted (Synod of Homberg an der Efze, 6 October 1528—Reformatio ecclesiarum Hassiae, François Lambert of Avignon), but Luther strenuously warned the Landgrave against attempt-

first step towards a new constitution of the church was the appointment of *Superattendenten*, such as Melanchthon had envisaged earlier, and who were subsequently called Superintendents. The fact that it was necessary for these men to work in close collaboration with the local authorities offered new possibilities for development which were admittedly not always taken (cf. the inspection of the churches in Saxony). It was not until 1532 that specifically church authorities, under the territorial prince, came to be set up.

3. REFORMATION IN THE NORTH GERMAN CITIES AND SPONTANEOUS REFORMATION ELSEWHERE

There is no mistaking the fact that the establishment of Evangelical territorial churches after the Peasants' War brought about a marked change in the character of the Reformation. Until 1525 the Reformation had been a spontaneous popular movement which no one had created— it was simply there and it triumphed. According to Luther (WA 15.32) the Word of God 'came like a cloudburst' and saturated the land. It called for recognition as a valid cause. Its advocates expected to find faith, or, since faith is a gift of God, at least an attitude which could be taken for tolerance. But the events of 1525 and the years following saw the Word of God being introduced at the command of authority, and all clergy were required to preach it. The people of the parishes were not only expected to come to church services and receive communion in both kinds—it was demanded of them. The visitations were increasingly concerned to see that a new church order was constructed on the basis of the reformers' gospel and that everyone should conform to it. The Reformation spring-time was followed by an intolerant church order based on compulsion. And yet although it is undeniable that with the visitations the first step had been taken towards a church order dependent on authoritarian sanctions, it would be wrong to suppose that after the Peasants' War the Reformation as a spontaneous popular movement ceased to exist altogether. In the cities of South and South-West Germany[1] the Reformation was 'introduced' in the same way as it was in the territories: authority checked the undisciplined growth of the Reformation, the city authorities appointed Evangelical preachers, introduced communion in Evangelical form, sequestrated the monasteries (except in cases

ing to implement it. Cf. G. Müller, 'Franz Lambert von Avignon und die Reformation in Hessen', *Theol. Diss. Marburg* 1955.

[1] B. Moeller, *Stadtgemeinde und Reformation*, 1962. The first church to be ordered along evangelical lines was undoubtedly Zürich (cf. p. 35 n. 1). In South Germany Nuremberg, Strasbourg, Memmingen and Constance followed. See B. Moeller, *Joh. Zwick und die Reformation in Konstanz*, 1961.

where the monasteries were able to assert themselves and their rights)
and so on. In contrast to these cities, the cities of North Germany[1] were
for the most part not imperial cities but territorial cities, though the
majority were bound only very loosely to the territorial prince. These
cities had literally bought themselves a position which came quite close
to the freedom of the imperial cities, and a whole series of them, namely
those which belonged to the Hanseatic League, now introduced the
Reformation. They were: the old city of Magdeburg (1524),[2] Stralsund
(1525),[3] Celle (1526), Goslar (1528),[4] Brunswick (1529),[5] Göttingen
(1529)[6], Hamburg (1529),[7] Lübeck (1530).[8] Rostock (1531),[9] Greifswald
(1531/32),[10] Hannover (1533)[11] and others. They did it independently of
their territorial overlords, many of whom continued to be adherents of
the old faith for a very long time. In not a single case did the initiative
come from the patriciate (or from the territorial prince). It was always
from below that the impetus towards reform came, from the craft guilds
and commoners, and in every case the campaign for the 'Word of God'
was inextricably linked with a campaign for the rights of the townspeople.[12]
New forms of representation for the burghers (councils of 24, 48, 60,
etc.) brought pressure to bear on the city authorities to establish a reformed church order. In many of the most important instances in which

[1] F. Lau, 'Die Reformation in den norddeutschen lutherischen Städten', *Infor-mationsblätter für die norddt. luth. Landeskirchen* 5 (1956), 113–118; also F. Lau's article in *LuJ* 26 (1959), 109–134.
[2] M. Ullrich, *Wie Magdeburg evangelisch wurde*, 1917; I. Höss, *Spalatin*, 1956, 256 ff.
[3] H. Heyden, *Die Kirche Stralsunds und ihre Geschichte*, 1962.
[4] U. Hölscher, *Die Geschichte der Reformation in Goslar*, 1902; G. Cordes, *Die Goslarer Chronik des Hans Geismer*, 1954.
[5] W. Meyer, 'Die Einführung der Reformation in der Stadt Braunschweig', *Die Wartburg* 7 (1908), 377–399; G. Kalberlah, 'Der soziale Gedanke in Bugenhagens Braunschweiger Kirchenordnung', *Jahrbuch für niedersächsische Kirchengeschichte* 51 (1953), 113–117. For the Brunswick Church Ordinance, see *KlT* 88, ed. Lietzmann, 1912.
[6] G. Erdmann, *Geschichte der Kirchenreformation in der Stadt Göttingen*, 1888; R. Leewe-Scharrenberg, 'Die Ordnung der Kirchengemeinde in der Stadt Göttingen U.S.W.', *Jahrbuch für niedersächs. Kirchengeschichte* 50 (1952), 1–50, 52 (1954), 34–97.
[7] C. H. W. Sillem, *Die Einführung der Reformation in Hamburg*, 1886; H. von Schubert, *Kirchengeschichte Schleswig-Holsteins*, 1907; K. Beckey, *Die Reformation in Hamburg*, 1929; W. Jensen, *Das Hamburger Domkapitel und die Reformation*, 1961.
[8] W. Jannasch, *Reformationsgeschichte Lübecks*, 1958; W. Ebel, *Lübecker Ratsurteile 1526-1550*, 1958.
[9] A. Vorberg, *Die Einführung der Reformation in Rostock*, 1897; K. Schmaltz, *Kirchengeschichte Mecklenburgs II*, 1936.
[10] K. Uckeley, 'Reformationsgeschichte der Stadt Greifswald', *Pommersche Jahrbücher* 4 (1903), 1–88; O. Plantiko, *Pommersche Reformationsgeschichte*, 1922.
[11] W. Bahrdt, *Geschichte der Reformation der Stadt Hannover*, 1889.
[12] A. Schultze, *Stadtgemeinde und Reformation*, 1918; E. Naujoks, *Obrigkeitsgedanke, Zunftverfassung und Reformation*, 1958; E. Maschke, 'Verfassung und soziale Kräfte in der deutschen Stadt des späten Mittelalters', *Vierteljahrsschrift für Sozial- und Wirtschaftsgeschichte*, 46 (1959), 289–349, 433–476.

this was done, Johann Bugenhagen[1] was brought in to assist in the process. In the North German cities the Reformation took Wittenberg as its model, whereas in South Germany the impetus was provided by the example of Bucer in Strasbourg or even of Zwingli in Zürich.

4. EVANGELICALS IN CATHOLIC TERRITORIES

The German territorial princes and city fathers who gave their allegiance to the Reformation were at first, and for a long time remained, a minority. Side by side with Evangelical territories there were many whose rulers held fast to the old faith. Among the latter were all the Habsburg areas, the Netherlands as well as the Austrian territories and so-called Anterior Austria, Württemberg (which Ferdinand administered), Albertine Saxony (under George of Saxony), Brandenburg (Joachim I), Bavaria and many more. In large European countries, too, like France, Spain, Portugal, the Reformation stood little chance of success—not even in England.[2] Some of the Catholic rulers were staunchly anti-Luther, while others, being dependent on neighbouring territories, felt that they could not yet risk adopting the Reformation. There were even some imperial cities which had to take account of the mood in the surrounding territories.[3] Persecutions were frequent and there were some martyrdoms,[4] for example, in Bavaria.[5] There, under the influence of Eck and the university of Ingolstadt, something amounting almost to a Counter-reformation 'front' was established.[6] Nevertheless, despite a stiffening of opposition here and there, Evangelical influence continued apace in Catholic regions. It found least resistance where Evangelical imperial cities were totally enclosed within Catholic territories (cf. Württemberg) or where territorial cities had won a large measure of independence. It was also irresistible in those areas where the territorial rulers had not yet developed centralised authority and where the estates claimed for themselves the *ius reformandi* (as in parts of Austria and the whole of Bohemia).[7] In the clerical dominions the situation had not reached the point at which a 'heretical' cathedral chapter could elect a 'heretical bishop'.[8] But it was certainly possible for

[1] W. Jensen, 'Joh. Bugenhagen und die lutherischen Kirchenordnungen von Braunschweig bis Norwegen', *Luther* 29 (1958), 60–72; K. D. Schmidt, 'Bugenhagens geschichtliche Bedeutung', *Informationsbl. für die norddt. luth. Landeskirchen* 7 (1958), 128–130; *Sehling* 6, Niedersachsen 1/1, 1955.
[2] On the so-called 'English Reformation' see p. 62 nn. 5, 6.
[3] R. Dollinger, *Das Evangelium in Regensburg*, 1959.
[4] H. Bornkamm, *Das Jahrhundert der Reformation*, 1961, 153.
[5] Köstlin-Kawerau, *Martin Luther II*, 1903⁵, 104 ff.
[6] R. Stadelmann, *Vom Geist des ausgehenden Mittelalters*, 1929, 102.
[7] G. Mecenseffy, *Geschichte des Prostestantismus in Österreich*, 1956.
[8] Lortz, *op. cit.* II, 117.

noblemen in such territories, many of whom were only too ready to rise in opposition to their overlord, to encourage the reformers' gospel within their own possessions. When Eck demanded that the bishops should banish all Lutherans from their entourage (e.g. councillors, secretaries, chaplains) he was giving an indication of the actual state of affairs at many of the courts of ecclesiastical princes. The reformers' message gained entry at many places in Catholic areas, whereas the old faith, in territories which had become Evangelical, hardly had a chance.[1]

5. EVANGELICAL CHURCH ORDER AND THE REFORMATION MOVEMENT IN EUROPE

Between 1525 and 1532 a regular Evangelical church order was established in only a few areas outside Germany, as for instance in Sweden and Denmark, and in somewhat different style among the Waldensians in Southern France and Piedmont. In any case, this period sees only the beginnings of a reordering of the church. In Denmark[2] the Rulers' Diet of Odense in 1529 officially tolerated the Evangelicals. The New Testament was translated into Danish by Christian Peterson in 1529. The *Confessio Hafnica* of 1530 represents the confession of the Protestant party. The popular Lutheran movement was stimulated by the Reformation-minded population of Lübeck. Gustav Wasa of Sweden[3] proceeded more purposefully. He deprived the bishops of their powers and in 1527/28 created a new arrangement of dioceses with 12 bishoprics. The bishops remained in the apostolic succession, and Lorenz Petersen, brother of Olaf Petersen, became the first Evangelical archbishop of Uppsala in 1531. To a greater extent than in Denmark and Germany church order was in the hands of the hierarchy and only became a popular matter at the end of the century.[4] In England too, there was an ecclesiastical revolution, but no actual Reformation was ever intended, even though it was the Evangelically-minded Thomas Cranmer[5] who arranged Henry VIII's divorce from Catherine of Aragon,[6] after cardinal Thomas Wolsey had failed to secure it and was therefore removed in 1529. But this merely

[1] Lortz, *op. cit.* II 97.
[2] See p. 28 nn. 3, 4.; N. H. Andersen, *Confessio Hafniensis*, Copenhagen 1954.
[3] See p. 28 nn. 5–7; E. E. Yelverton, *The Manual of Olavus Petri 1529*, 1953.
[4] J. Paul, *Gustav Adolf I*, 1927, 67 f; G. Schwaiger, *Die Reformation in den nordischen Ländern*, 1962.
[5] See p. 27 nn. 5–7; C. Jenkins, *The Life and Times of Cranmer*, 1936; G. W. Bromiley, *Thomas Cranmer*, 1956; J. Ridley, *Thomas Cranmer*, New York, 1962.
[6] J. Scarisbrick, 'The Pardon of Clergy 1531', *Cambridge Hist. Journal* 12 (1956), 22–39; R. C. White, *The Tudor Books of Private Devotion*, 1951; G. Mattingly, *Catherine of Aragon*, 1941; H. Kressner, *Schweizer Ursprünge des anglik. Staatskirchentums*, 1953.

brought about the separation of the English church from Rome. The Act of Supremacy was passed in 1534, but in 1533 the English church had already allowed Henry's divorce from Catherine of Aragon in order to make possible his marriage to Anne Boleyn. The heads of the Roman party fell (More and Fisher were executed in 1535). Thomas Cromwell[1] had replaced More as Chancellor in 1532, and Cranmer, a secret Protestant, became Archbishop of Canterbury in 1533.

In France,[2] the humanist friends of Luther lived as crypto-Protestants, among them John Calvin (from 1529?). The Waldensians[3] established a genuinely Evangelical church order in Piedmont, influenced by Farel and by the debate on Luther's De servo arbitrio at the Synod of Chianforan/Angronia on 12 September 1532. In the case of the small persecuted groups in Spain[4] it is difficult to distinguish with any certainty Erasmian from Lutheran influences. In Bohemia[5] the advocates of communion in both kinds (e.g. Gallus Cahera) as well as the Bohemian Brethren had contacts with Luther, the latter regarding him with some suspicion. A change of attitude among the Brethren did not come about until 1532, when John Augusta became leader. Their hymn-book of 1531 is of importance. The history of the Anabaptist movement after 1525[6] shows how open many of the nobility could be to Protestant influence. Reformist influence in Hungary, especially in so-called Turkish Hungary, was strong and went unimpeded. Matthias Dévay, who was to become a figure of some importance later on, was active in 1531 as an Evangelical preacher in Buda and Kaschau. In Hungary there was rivalry between christian humanists and Evangelical preachers.[7]

6. THE CONTROVERSY BETWEEN THE WITTENBERG REFORMERS AND THE 'FANATICS'

The consolidation of reformed church order in Central Germany was facilitated by the fact that Luther—for reasons which stem largely from his personal history—had definitely broken with the so-called 'fanatics'

[1] T. Maynard, The Crown and the Cross, A Biography of Thomas Cromwell, 1950.
[2] See p. 27 nn. 1, 3.
[3] J. Jalla, 'Farel et les Vaudois du Piemont', G. Farel, Biographie nouvelle (1930), 285–297; G. Gonnet, 'Beziehungen der Waldenser zu den oberdeutschen Reformatoren vor Calvin', ZKG 64 (1953), 208–211; and 'Le premier Synode de Chianforan de 1532', Bulletin de la société de l'histoire du Protestantisme français 99 (1953), 201–220.
[4] See p. 28 n. 3; J. E. Longhurst, Luther and the Spanish Inquisition. The Case of Diego de Uceda, 1528–1529, 1953; Domingo de Sta. Teresa, Juan de Valdes, 1957.
[5] EKL III (1959), 520–523; R. Ričan, Das Reich Gottes in den böhmischen Ländern, 1957; M. Weisse, Gesangbuch der Böhmischen Brüder 1531, 1957.
[6] See p. 65 n. 12 and p. 66 n. 1.
[7] See p. 28 n. 10 (Bucsay); F. Valjavec, 'Geschichte der deutschen Kulturbehziehungen zu Südosteuropa' 2, Reformation und Gegenreformation, 1955.

(*Schwärmer*) even before the end of the Peasants' War.[1] He began to write against Müntzer in 1524, and Müntzer replied to Luther's attacks with passionate intensity.[2] Because Müntzer, who was not in fact the man who had inspired the entire peasant revolution—as Luther thought he was[3]—had identified himself so completely with the peasants' cause in the war, it was impossible for his supporters ever to become a permanent alternative party to the Evangelicals in Central and North Germany. The same appears to be true of Karlstadt, who in 1524 had to leave Orlamünde, where he had been occupying an incumbency pertaining to his archdeaconry at Wittenberg. In 1525 he returned to Wittenberg for a while, but in 1529 left Saxony for ever and spent the rest of his life (i.e. until 1541) as a professor in Basle. Thus the 'Karlstadtians' no longer counted for anything, either in Saxony or elsewhere. But in two respects the apparently rigid separation of Evangelicals from the radicals in Central Germany was not so drastic as to deprive the radicals of influence in the period which followed. For on the one hand the Anabaptists and the later 'Spiritualists',[4] though not stemming directly from Müntzer or Karlstadt, were none the less linked to them in hidden ways and thus carried their ideas further.[5] On the other hand the controversy between Luther and Karlstadt over the eucharist passed imperceptibly into the controversy between Luther and Zwingli which dragged on during the years between the Peasants' War and the battle of Kappel, and which became the occasion of the split within the Evangelical camp.[6] So it certainly cannot be said that the 'fanaticism' of Müntzer and Karlstadt was entirely without abiding influence. From 1525 onwards the campaign against the 'heavenly prophets', the destroyers of images and the 'disparagers of sacraments' increased in intensity, particularly in the direction of Switzerland.

7. ANABAPTISTS AND 'SPIRITUALISTS' AFTER THE PEASANTS' WAR

It was not only Luther's Reformation and Zwingli's Reformation which from 1525 were seeking to form churches of the Gospel. The Anabaptists, too, who began as a Swiss phenomenon, were spreading powerfully through the whole of Germany.[7] For them it was admittedly not a matter of forming churches in the strict sense, for they regarded the Church as a community aligned on the Bible and led by the Spirit

[1] See E. Wolf, *Luther* (3 I in this series).
[2] C. Hinrichs, (ed.), *Th. Müntzer, Politische Schriften*, 1951; *WA* 15 (199), 210–221; cf. II. 7 above.
[3] Smirin, *op. cit.* (p. 29 n. 6.).   [4] See II. 11.
[5] See III. 7.   [6] See III. 10.
[7] B. R. Smithson, *The Anabaptists*, 1935; J. Horsch, *Mennonites in Europe*, 1950[2]; J. H. Smith, *The Story of the Mennonites*, 1950[3].

which refused to recognize any church which claimed a doctrinal authority higher than these. Anabaptist propaganda exerted an enormous influence throughout Switzerland, including Central Switzerland.[1] Several religious conferences with the Anabaptists were held, e.g. at Teufen and Zofingen.[2] The Anabaptist mission extended beyond the frontiers of Switzerland as far as Venice[3] and Tirol,[4] where for a time their movement was stronger than all other Evangelical bodies. Their influence spread, too, into other regions of Austria.[5] Pilgram Marbeck was active in Tirol between 1525 and 1528. Augsburg[6] and Strasbourg[7] became centres of the movement. Denck,[8] who was Rector in Nuremberg and Hut[9] were instrumental in introducing new features, namely a pronounced 'spiritualism' and apocalypticism which they inherited from Müntzer. The heterogeneous elements within the Anabaptist movement develop along widely divergent lines, so that there exist side by side both peaceable Anabaptists, devoted to pious study of the Scriptures and willing to accept suffering, and revolutionary Anabaptists advocating force and violence. There is a tendency among some scholars to express this schematically, by drawing a distinction between 'biblicist' and 'spiritualist' Anabaptists,[10] but this hardly does justice to the very subtle differences of temperament within the Anabaptist movement. The incumbent of Waldshut, Balthazar Hubmair, was and remained a disciple of Zwingli in his theology,[11] but he campaigned and died (he was burned to death in Vienna 1527) simply for the right to baptise adults after the biblical model. In Mähren,[12] where certain noblemen allowed the Anabaptists to live at peace on their property and where a kind of 'communist' order was developed, the pacifist Anabaptists separated (there were groups in Nikolsburg, Auster-

[1] J. Horsch, 'The Rise and Early History of the Swiss Brethren Church', *MQR* VI (1932), 169–191, 227–249; P. Peachey, 'Social Backgrounds and Social Philosophy of the Swiss Anabaptists 1525–1540'; *MQR* 28 (1954), 102–127.
[2] O. Farner, *H. Zwingli IV*, 1960, 144–158, 532–544.
[3] D. Cantimori, *Italienische Häretiker der Spätrenaissance*, 1949; H. A. Dewind, 'Anabaptism and Italy', *ChR* 21 (1952), 20–38.
[4] G. Mecenseffy, *Geschichte des Prot. in Österreich*, 1956, 35 ff. (bibliography); E. Widmoser, 'Das Tiroler Täufertum I and II', *Tiroler Heimat* XV (1951 f.), 45–90 and XVI (1952 f.), 103–128.
[5] G. Mecenseffy, *op. cit.*; H. G. Klassen, 'Ambr. Spittelmayr', *MQR* 32 (1958), 251–272.
[6] J. Hans, *Aus Augsburgs kirchlicher Vergangenheit*, 1930; J. F. G. Goeters, *L. Hätzer*, 1957, 42 ff., 54 ff.
[7] J. Adam, *Evangelische Kirchengeschichte der Stadt Strassburg*, 1922; J. F. G. Goeters, *op. cit.*, 87 ff.
[8] See p. 37 n. 7.
[9] See p. 37 n. 5.
[10] N. van der Zijps, *Geschiedenis der Doopsgezinden in Nederland*, 1952, 24 f.
[11] *Schl* I, 9057–9075; T. Bergsten, *Balth. Hubmair*, 1962.
[12] J. Loserth, *B. Hubmair und die Anfänge der Wiedertäufer in Mähren*, 1923; G. J. Neumann, 'Nach und von Mähren', *ARG* 48 (1957), 75–90.

litz, Rossitz, Auspiz) until Jakob Huter[1] brought all the 'brothers in Mähren' together at Austerlitz in 1529. Melchior Hoffmann,[2] a furrier from Schwäbisch-Hall who while in Livonia in 1523 had been won over to Luther's cause, travelled north by way of Strasbourg, and the Anabaptist movement came to Westphalia (Münster ca. 1530),[3] East Friesland[4] and the Netherlands.[5] Research has brought to light that there were hundreds of Anabaptist congregations in a very considerable number of territories, including Hesse (Melchior Rinck)[6] and Thuringia (between Eisenach and Bebra),[7] in Franconia[8] and in the Palatinate.[9] The records listing the number of executions[10] are no doubt exaggerated, but the Anabaptist movement certainly aroused strong opposition. The documents which enshrine the Anabaptists' confessions of faith[11] (the *Schleitheim Confession* of 1527, the *Schlatt am Randen Articles* and the *Nikolsburg Articles*, etc.) are for the most part the statements of particular groups. Much the same is true of individual leaders of the movement like Marbeck,[12] Michel Sattler[13] and others. Synods and councils (such as the Synod at Augsburg on 20 August 1527) failed to unite the Anabaptists and served merely to encourage their opponents to regard them as a more united force than they were in reality. Luther[14] and Melanchthon[15] wrote vigor-

---

[1] *Schl* I, 9143–9145; H. Fischer, *Jakob Huter*, 1956; R. Friedmann, *The Epistles of the Hutterian Brethren*, 1946; and 'The economic aspects of early Hutterite life', *MQR* 30 (1956), 259–266.

[2] *Schl* I, 8517–30; P. Kawerau, *Melchior Hoffmann*, 1954.

[3] R. Stupperich, *Das münster. Täufertum*, 1958.

[4] C. Krahn, 'Anabaptism in East Friesland', *MQR* 30 (1956), 247–255.

[5] A. L. E. Verheyden, 'An Introduction to the history of the Mennonites in Flanders, 1530–1650', *MQR* 21 (1947), 51–63; H. W. Meihuizen, 'Spiritualist tendencies and movements among the Dutch Mennonites of the 16th and 17th centuries', *MQR* 27 (1953), 259–304.

[6] *Schl* II, 18153–18156; J. S. Dyer, 'Anabaptism in Central Germany', *MQR* 34 (1960), 219–248; 35 (1961), 5–57; G. Franz (ed.), *Wiedertäuferakten für Hessen 1527–1626*, 1951.

[7] P. Wappler, *Die Täuferbewegung in Thüringen 1526–1584*, 1913; and *Die Stellung Kursachsens und des Landgrafen Philipp v. Hessen zur Täuferbewegung*, 1910; G. Zschäbitz, *Zur mitteldeutschen Täuferbewegung nach dem grossen Bauernkrieg*, 1958 (marx).

[8] See p. 37 nn. 5, 7.

[9] M. Krebs (ed.), *Täuferakten für Baden und Pfalz*, 1951.

[10] Neumann, 'Nach und von Mähren', *ARG* 48 (1957), 80 f.

[11] R. Friedmann, 'The Schleitheim Confession (1527) and Doctrinal Writings of the Swiss Brethren in a hitherto unknown Edition', *MQR* 16 (1942), 82–98; B. Jenny, *Das Schleitheimer Täuferbekenntnis 1527*, 1951; J. F. G. Goeters, *op. cit.*, 94 (see p. 65 n. 6).

[12] J. J. Kiewit, *Pilgram Marbeck*, 1954; W. Klassen, 'The Hermeneutics of Pilgram Marbeck', *Theol. Diss. Princeton*, 1959; and 'Pilgram Marbeck in Recent Research', *MQR* 32 (1958), 211–231, 248.

[13] *Mennonite Lexicon* IV (1959), 29 ff. See n. 11 above.

[14] *WA* 26, 137–174; *WA* 50, 6–15; M. Burgdorf, *Luther und die Wiedertäufer*, 1928.

[15] J. S. Oyer, 'The Writings of Melanchthon against the Anabaptists', *MQR* 26 (1952), 259–279.

ously against the Anabaptists, as Catholic theologians did also. Bucer[1] and Capito,[2] who sympathised with the Anabaptists' desire to let faith be expressed in good works, came to their defence. By an imperial mandate of 4 January 1528 and by decisions of the Imperial Diets of Speyer (1529) and Augsburg (1530) the Anabaptists were adjudged heretics. As early as 1527 Zürich had had Felix Manz[3] drowned. Philip of Hesse[4] and Vadian[5] took a more lenient view. But by 1530 a number of influences were beginning to make themselves felt which eventually issued in the great Anabaptist catastrophe at Münster in 1534/35.[6] Rebaptism was held to be an offence worthy of the death-sentence. The 'spiritualists', who were not directly involved in baptismal controversies but who were nevertheless closely akin to the Anabaptists and had assisted in bringing the movement into being, were generally not affected. Karlstadt, who had finally been driven from Saxony in 1529, was allowed to remain as a professor in Basle from 1534 to his death in 1541. The Silesian nobleman Caspar Schwenckfeld,[7] through whose efforts the Reformation took deep root in Silesia, lived and worked in Swabia and died in 1561 at Ulm. Sebastian Franck's influence[8] dates from 1530. The Anabaptist spirit did not die, but survived to be of great significance for the churches of the English revolution and for the pietist movement in and beyond Germany.

8. THE CONTROVERSY BETWEEN LUTHER AND ERASMUS

Until Luther had become famous as a result of his *Theses* in 1517, it was Erasmus[9] who had been the dominant figure in the intellectual life of Germany. After 1517 Germany, indeed the world, looked not only to Erasmus but also to Luther. It could never have been seriously supposed that these two totally contrasted personalities would 'hit it off'.[10] Erasmus found highly distasteful Luther's desire and capacity to influence the

[1] *Menn. Lex.* I, 307–313.   [2] *Menn. Lex.* I, 326–333.
[3] E. Krajewski, *Leben und Sterben des Zürcher Täuferführers Felix Manz*, 1957; J. F. G. Goeters, 'Ein Auszug aus Zwinglis "In katabaptistarum strophes elenchus" als antitäuf. Flugblatt', *ThZ* 9 (1953), 395–397; H. Fast, *H. Bullinger und die Täufer*, 1959.
[4] P. Wappler, *op. cit.* (see p. 66 n. 7).
[5] See p. 72 n. 2 and p. 34 n. 6.
[6] F. J. Wray, 'The "Vermanung" of 1542 and Rothmann's "Bekenntnisse" ', *ARG* 47 (1950), 243–251.
[7] See p. 41 n. 1.
[8] *RGG*[3] II, 1012 f.; W. E. Peuckert, *Sebastian Franck, ein Sucher*, 1943.
[9] Edition of Erasmus's works (ed. W. Allen), 9 vols., Oxford 1906–1928; a selection, ed. H. Holborn, 1933; J. Huizinga, *Erasmus*, 1924; A. Renaudet, *Études Erasmiennes*, 1939; W. Kaegi, *Erasmus and the age of Reformation*, 1957.
[10] See *WA* 18, 551–596.

popular masses, while Luther, for his part, was deeply hurt by the note of detachment in the scholar's utterances, and by the fact that Erasmus recoiled from committing himself when commitment was required. It was in any case inconceivable that Erasmus, who was flattered by a considerable reputation and the desire of so many to pay court to him, should openly declare himself to be on the side of a man who was under the ban. Even so, until 1524 Erasmus maintained a benevolent neutrality towards Luther which was much to Luther's advantage; and Erasmus' criticism of Luther's personal style and manner led many other men of reformist inclination to suppose that Erasmus was an ally. In his *Diatribe de libero arbitrio* of 1524[1] Erasmus went as far in attempting to come to terms with Luther as he could possibly have done, saying that it is by grace, *almost* alone, that men are saved, but none the less men have to do something, namely accept grace and appropriate it. That Luther's sharp attack on Erasmus in *De servo arbitrio* (1525)[2] finally forced the two men apart was not the only consequence of the controversy. Even more important was the fact that those who sought church reform in terms other than Luther's now had an acknowledged intellectual leader.[3] Erasmians became the active exponents of Catholic reform which even at that early date began to assume the character of a Counter-reformation. It is necessary to notice that Erasmus' teaching on justification, as expressed in his writings on free will, made a lasting impression on Evangelical humanists who, unlike others who followed Erasmus on this issue, did not dissociate themselves from the Reformation, even though they could not themselves adopt the particularist view of grace attendant on Luther's doctrine of predestination. Melanchthon, for example, perhaps as early as 1523 but certainly by 1525 had become a 'synergist';[4] and not only the 'synergism' of the years which followed the Interim but also the doctrine of predestination given in the *Formula Concordiae*[5] were derived in the last resort from the controversy between Luther and Erasmus.

---

[1] J. v. Walter (ed.), *De libero arbitrio*, 1935[2]; O. Schumacher, *Vom freien Willen*, 1956[2].

[2] *WA* 18, (551), 600–787; F. Gogarten, 'Sittlichkeit und Glaube in Luthers Schrift "De servo arbitrio" ', *ZThK* 47 (1950), 227–275; E. Schweingruber, *Luthers Erlebnis des unfreien Willens*, 1947; H. Bornkamm, 'Erasmus und Luther', *LuJ* 25 (1958), 3–22; O. J. Mehl, 'Erasmus contra Luther', *LuJ* 29 (1962), 52–64.

[3] A. Flitner, *Erasmus im Urteil seiner Nachwelt*, 1952; H. Schätti, *Erasmus v. Rotterdam und die römische Kurie*, 1954; F. W. Kantzenbach, *Das Ringen um die Einheit der Kirche im Jahrhundert der Reformation*, 1957; J. P. Dolan, *The influence of Erasmus, Witzel, Casander etc.*, 1957; F. Heer, *Die dritte Kraft*, 1959.

[4] G. Ellinger, *P. Melanchthon*, 1902, 175, 199 ff.; W. Maurer, 'Melanchthons Anteil am Streit zwischen Luther und Erasmus', *ARG* 49 (1958), 89–115.

[5] *BSLK* 816–822, 1063–1091; H. R. Franck, *Theologie der Concordienformel IV*, 1865, 120–344.

9. CONTROVERSIES AMONG THE LUTHERANS

Another controversy worthy of note took place within the Lutheran camp among the Wittenberg theologians between 1524 and 1530. During that period it did not have anything like the public notoriety of the controversy between Luther and Zwingli on the Lord's Supper, but it represents the beginning of the controversies which later on were to divide Lutherans into two irreconcilable factions—the 'Gnesio-Lutherans' and the 'Philippists'. In 1524 at Tetschen in the Saalhausen region Dominikus Beyer[1] became involved in an argument with a certain Master Martin Becker about the significance of the law for the Christian Church.[2] In 1527 the rector of Eisleben, Johann Agricola,[3] came into head-on collision with Melanchthon over 20 Articles[4] which the latter had drawn up in connection with the visitation of churches and schools in Electoral Saxony. In these articles Melanchthon presented a doctrine of penance in which atonement was said to be effected by the law, and Melanchthon demanded that emphasis be given in the churches to the preaching of the law. Agricola, not entirely unreasonably invoking certain of Luther's propositions in support of his case,[5] would accept no other atonement but what is effected by the Gospel, and he challenged the idea that the preaching of law could rightly be called christian, for the law's proper place is at the town hall. Agricola was not alone; Kaspar Aquila,[6] superintendent at Saalfeld, supported him, as did Amsdorf[7] also. Without actually branding Agricola as a 'heretic' (he did not do that until 1537), Luther sided with Melanchthon, saying that the whole controversy was purely an argument about words, and formally giving his approval to a 'christian preaching of the law'. Although temporarily subdued, the controversy flared up again in 1537.[8] But even in the second antinomian conflict there was no greater clarification of the question of the status of law than there had been in 1527.[9] The position adopted by Luther in this controversy in 1527 is really responsible for the enormous influence which Melanchthon exerted over orthodox Lutheranism in the post-Reformation period.

[1] O. Clemen, 'Dominikus Beyer', BSKG 14 (1889), 224–229.
[2] G. Hammann, 'Nomismus und Antinomismus innerhalb der Wittenberger Theologie 1524–1530', Bonner theol. Diss., 1952, 1–8; W. Joest, Gesetz und Freiheit, 1951.
[3] G. Kawerau, J. Agricola v. Eisleben, 1881. See n. 5 below.
[4] Cf. Hammann, op. cit., 57–60.
[5] J. Rogge, J. Agricolas Lutherverständnis, 1961.
[6] M. Saupe, 'Vita Aquilae', Thüringer Kirchliches Jahrbuch 177 (1912), 16–48; G. Biundo, Caspar Aquila, 1963.
[7] H. Stille, 'N. von Amsdorf', Phil. Diss. Leipzig, 1937, 95 f.
[8] See below, Bizer I.
[9] L. Haikola, Usus legis, 1958 (bibliography).

F

10. THE CONTROVERSY BETWEEN THE GERMAN AND SWISS REFORMERS ON THE LORD'S SUPPER

Even more important and far-reaching than the antinomian controversy within Lutheranism is the great controversy between Luther and Zwingli over the Lord's Supper, which raged from 1524 onwards.[1] This controversy has never been closed, for today the split between Lutheran and Reformed churches has yet to be ovecome. The controversy is rooted in the personal histories of Luther and Zwingli,[2] and it also represents a chapter in the debate between humanism and the Reformation. The doctrine of the Lord's Supper which Zwingli adopted for himself—not without adding distinctive notes of his own—originated not in Switzerland but in the Netherlands, where humanism had taken deep root[3] and where the *Devotio moderna*[4] and other features derived from late mediaeval mysticism and theology lived on. In a letter written by Cornelisz Hendrixz Hoen of the Hague[5] the writer had suggested that the verb *est* in the words of institution means *significat*,[6] and Hinne Rode[7] of Utrecht, who was rector of a community house there, had travelled around seeking to propagate this view of the Lord's Supper; and though he met Luther he did not find in him a sympathetic listener. As humanists, Zwingli and Oecolampad alike adopted this view as their own. They regarded the Lord's Supper simply as an act of remembrance and a thanksgiving for the death on the Cross on Good Friday. They rejected the view that a particular saving event took place on Maundy Thursday which is repeated at every celebration of communion. With church people in Zürich and elsewhere their view was so popularly held that when Zwingli and his colleagues went to the discussions at Marburg (1–3 October 1529)[8] they were unable to make any real concessions, for fear of causing offence

[1] *Schl* IV, 34285a–34292b; V, 51465–51466; W. Köhler, *Zwingli und Luther. Ihr Streit um das Abendmahl* I 1924, II 1953; E. Bizer, *Studien zur Geschichte des Abendmahlsstreits im 16. Jahrh.*, 1940; W. Maurer, 'Zum geschichtlichen Verständnis des Abendmahlsartikels der Confessio Augustana', *Festschrift für G. Ritter*, 1950, 161–209.

[2] Wolf; *Luther.* Bugenhagen (*Contra novum errorem de sacramento*), Urb. Rhegius (*Wider den newen irrsal Doctor Andres v. Carlstadt*) and Brenz (*Syngramma Suevicum*, Oct. 1525) supported Luther, while Oecolampad (*De genuina verborum domi*) supported Zwingli. In Augsburg Lutheran and Zwinglian parties opposed one another.

[3] See I. 6 and Moeller/Liebing, *Spätmittelalter/Humanismus*; G. Krodel, 'Die Abendmahlslehre des Erasmus', *Diss. Erlangen* 1955.

[4] Moeller/Liebing, Spätmittelalter/Humanismus.

[5] *Schl* I, 8892–8898; *RGG*³ III, 411.

[6] A. Eckhof, *De Avondmaalsbrief van Cornelis Hoen*, Hague 1917.

[7] *Schl* II, 18183–18187; *RGG*³ V, 1135.

[8] See n. 1 above; also *Schl* IV, 41337–413362; J. G. Beto, 'The Marburg Colloquy of 1529', *CThM* 16 (1945), 73–94; R. H. Bainton, 'Luther and the Via Media at the Marburg Colloquy', *LQ* 1 (1949), 394–398.

at home. This shows how deeply humanist thinking had embedded itself in Swiss cantons and also in the cities of South Germany. However, neither Luther nor Melanchthon (who at Marburg was, if anything, even more rigid than Luther) made an issue of the Lord's Supper or of the meaning of *est* in their controversy with the humanists. At an earlier stage Karlstadt, while at Orlamünde, had issued five pamphlets[1] against Luther in which he proposed a similar view of the Lord's Supper, based on somewhat primitive biblical exegesis. He subsequently sought to propagate his view at Strasbourg.[2] *Against the 'heavenly prophets'* (1525)[3] was Luther's answer to Karlstadt. The campaign which he conducted against Zwingli was in effect an extension of the campaign he waged against 'fanatics' and those who despise the sacraments, so that the controversy took the form of a battle on the part of 'the Word' against those who treated 'the Word' with contempt. In reality, Zwingli's doctrine of the Lord's Supper[4] had a very strong biblical basis, and Zwingli, no less than Luther, had campaigned against the radicals and had dissociated himself from them.[5] Luther's estimate of Zwingli as a 'fanatic' and disparager of the sacraments was not wholly without foundation, but as a total picture was false; and it created a chasm from the outset between the German Reformation and the Swiss Reformation. Although the gap has narrowed appreciably in course of time, it has not been entirely bridged even today.

II. THE PROGRESS OF THE REFORMATION IN SWITZERLAND

In Germany it was the Peasants' War which made it necessary to regulate the indisciplined growth of the Reformation. In Switzerland such regulation was made necessary, not by troubles with the peasantry (for their difficulties were solved more peaceably than in Germany) but by the radical tendencies which manifested themselves in the Anabaptist movement. By 1527 the controversy with the Anabaptists had reached the point at which they were clearly marked off and branded as heretics, by Catholic and Reformed alike.[6] It is significant for the future course of the Reformation in Switzerland that the reformed christians who accepted the authority of the state and its rulers failed in their attempt to persuade the whole Confederacy to adopt the Reformation. The Disputation at Baden in Aargau (May 1526)[7] made it impossible for the Reformation to spread throughout Switzerland, just as the Imperial Diet of Speyer held

[1] See *WA* 18, 37 ff.   [2] See *WA* 18, 41 ff.
[3] *WA* 18, (37) 62–214.   [4] *CR* 90, esp. 773 ff. (De eucharistia).
[5] See II. 11 and III. 7.   [6] See p. 65 n. 1.
[7] *Schl* IV, 41283b–297; L. v. Muralt, *Die Badener Disputation*, 1926 (= *Schl* IV, 41296a).

at roughly the same time in Germany made it improbable that the Reformation would have free course throughout Germany (no matter how favourable its decisions were to the reformers' cause). But the Disputation at Bern(January 1528)[1] did lead to the formal adoption of the Reformation there, though the council was inclined to tolerate the 'old faith' in the Bernese Oberland for quite a long time. Capito played a leading part at the Synod of Bern, which in 1532 established a reformed church order in Bern. Vadian, who had been active in promoting the Reformation in St. Gallen since 1520, was able to secure its triumph there in 1525/26.[2] Schaffhausen,[3] Biel[4] and Mühlhausen[5] also went over. In Basle[6] Johann Oecolampad[7] had been active since 1522, and at the beginning Konrad Pellikan,[8] too. However, a reformed church was not set up in Basle until 1529. After 1531 Myconius[9] worked there. In 1530 the Reformation was adopted in Neuchâtel and the valleys of the Jura. Certain developments in the reformed camp evoked counter-measures from Catholic areas: the Reformation was making progress in some of the smaller dependencies; Zürich began to take extreme measures against the Catholic opposition; martydoms aroused strong public reaction(Jakob Kaiser,[10] a preacher in Zürich, was executed by the people of Schwyz on 29 May 1529); Zwingli entered into a conspiracy with Philip of Hesse with the aim of establishing a large political alliance of all Protestants with France against the Habsburgs.[11] The result was that in Waldshut in 1529 Schwyz, Uri, Unterwalden, Lucerne, Zug, Wallis, Fribourg all concluded a 'Christian Alliance'[12] with Austria. The war (the so-called 'First Kappel War'[13])

[1] *Schl* IV, 41299–41311; K. Lindt, 'Der theologische Gehalt der Berner Disputation', *Gedenkschrift zum Vierhundertjahrfest der Bernischen Kirchenref.* I, 1928, 301–344.
[2] *Schl* II, 21628–21656, 26623–26647a; V, 48619–48621, 50807a–8; J. Ninck, *Arzt und Reformator Vadian*, 1936; Näf (see p. 34 n. 6).
[3] J. Wipf, *Reformationsgeschichte der Stadt und Landschaft Schaffhausen*, 1929.
[4] W. Bourquin, 'Die Reformation in Biel', *Gedenkschr. zur Vierhundertjahr feier der Bernischen Kirchenref.* I, 1928, 345–388.
[5] H. Strohl, 'Quatrième centenaire de l'introduction de la réforme à Mulhouse 1523', *Société de l'histoire du Protestantisme français*, Bulletin 72 (1923), 280–282.
[6] *Schl* II, 27706–27758; V, 49908–49914. See also p. 34 n. 6; P. Roth, *Durchbruch und Festsetzung der Reformation in Basel*, 1942.
[7] *Schl* II, 16520–16567; V, 48493a–48500. See also p. 34 n. 6.
[8] *Schl* II, 17054–17066; V, 48635–48636; E. Bonjour, *Die Universität Basel*, 1960.
[9] See p. 34 n. 6; *Schl* II, 16212–16216b; V, 48429–48429a; F. Rudolf, 'Oswald Myconius', *Basler Jahrbücher* 1945, 14–30; W. Brändly, *Geschichte des Prot. in Stadt und Land Luzern*, 1945.
[10] *Zürcher Pfarrbuch*, 1953, 70; O. Farner, *H. Zwingli* 4, 1960, 307 ff.
[11] F. Rohrer, *Das 'christliche Burgrecht' und die 'christliche Vereinigung'*, 1876; M. Lenz' 'Zwingli und Philipp', *ZKG* 3 (1879), 38–62, 220–274, 429–463. H. Escher believed that the idea of an alliance came from Philip rather than from Zwingli.
[12] T. Scherer-Boccard, 'Akten zum Christlichen Bündniss ... Anno 1528 u. 1529', *Archiv für schweizerische Reformationsgeschichte* 3 (1875), 555–598.
[13] J. Häsne, 'Der zürcherische Kriegsrodel des ersten Kappeler Krieges', *Nova*

which threatened to break out in 1529 never took place, thanks to the efforts of the magistrate Aebli (the first Peace of Kappel was concluded in 1529).[1] But the Second Kappel War ended with the battle of Kappel on 11 October 1531, at which Zwingli died, and the Second Peace (1531),[2] which although it did not undo the Reformation in Switzerland made its further spread impossible. The result was that by and large only Zürich, Basle, Bern and St. Gallen remained officially Evangelical.

12. CATHOLIC RESISTANCE TO THE REFORMED CHURCHES

Pope Adrian VI's so-called 'Confession of sins' which was delivered by Chieregati to the Second Diet of Nuremberg in 1522/23[3] has been described as the beginning of the Counter-reformation or of Catholic reform in Germany.[4] If this is correct, then we may suppose that during the years between the Peasants' War and the Nuremberg Standstill Counter-reformation forces were at work. It is well known that as soon as Luther became notorious as a result of his *Theses* and subsequent writings a whole succession of Catholic writers mounted opposition. In the period before 1525 names like Eck, Emser, Cochläus, Murner, Schatzgeyr, Alvelt, Catharinus de Politi are well known.[5] Catholic theological polemics persisted during the period in which Evangelical territorial churches were being established. New writings against Luther and against reformed doctrine were being published. What is astonishing, however, is that the number of Catholic theologians engaged in the controversy did not increase. No new personalities—and certainly no great dominant figures—appear on the scene.

But Counter-reformation[6] was not just a campaign against the Reformation movement, whether conducted with a pen or with a sword; it was also the expression of a new mood, a spirit of renewal within the Catholic camp. It is only recently that research has brought to light some of the developments that were taking place in the early period of the Reformation.[7] Attention has been drawn to Eck's attempts to bring about a Catholic renewal, and to the Carthusians at Cologne, whose work was

---

Turicensia, 1911, 165 ff.; W. Oechsli, 'Zwingli als Staatsmann', *Ulrich-Zwingli-Gedenkwerk*, 1919, 75–200; O. Farner, *op. cit.* (see p. 72 n. 10), 310–322. See also n. 2 below.

[1] E. Walder, *Religionsvergleiche des 16. Jahrhunderts* I, 1945, 5–14; O. Farner, *op. cit.* 322–330.

[2] O. Farner, *op. cit.*, 482 ff., 560 (see esp. footnote on p. 483).

[3] *Mirbt* 421; cf. also II. 20.

[4] Lortz, *Die Reformation in Deutschland*, 1949³, vol. II pp. 108.

[5] See II. 18.

[6] K. D. Schmidt, *Katholische Reformation u. Gegen-reformation*.

[7] Lortz, *op. cit.* II, 82 ff.

later taken up by the Jesuits in Germany,[1] and also to the efforts of Catholic
bishops in Germany to bring about reform.[2] Yet the results of all this
research have remained astonishingly meagre, and Catholic scholars have
openly stated that Catholic polemics, like Protestant polemics, did not
escape the distortions of prejudice. Certainly during the period in which
the Emperor was unable to take any positive action there was no attempt
on the part of Catholic princes to take military measures.[3] Apparently
there was an attempt to form an alliance of Catholic rulers against the
territorial princes who had consented to the Reformation, with the aim
of stripping them of their power and putting an end to the Reformation
by force. But the so-called 'Pack affairs'[4] did not in fact amount to anything
like a Counter-reformation, for they were merely an indication of the
kind of steps which would be taken later on in opposing the Reformation.
Their principal effect (especially after the sad discovery of the swindle)
was to encourage the Protestant princes to band together against any
possible military activity on the part of the Catholics.[5]

13. THE SECOND ITALIAN WAR[6]

The fact that the Evangelical movement was able to make such powerful
progress after the Diet of Worms is in itself surprising. It can only be
explained by Charles V's preoccupation with the so-called First Italian
War.[7] In the same way, it is entirely due to the state of European politics
that it was possible to establish reformed churches at all, for the territorial
princes and the Swabian League had only brought the Peasants' War to a
successful conclusion because after the battle of Pavia large numbers of
Landsknechte were available for military service. The dictated Peace of
Madrid (14 January 1526) was not only intolerable for Francis I, who
immediately upon his release declared himself in the presence of his
nobles not bound by the concessions which had been forced from him;[8]
it was also intolerable for all the European powers. Pope Clement VII
made an alliance with countless Italian states like Venice and Milan and
with France, in order to protect Italy against the grasping Habsburgs,
who threatened to become the leading European power. On 30 April

[1] Lortz, *op. cit.* II, 134 ff.
[2] G. Pfeilschifter, *Acta reformationis catholicae ecclesiam Germaniae concernentia I*
(*1520–1532*), 1959.
[3] II. 19; III. 13; III. 14.
[4] P. 77 n. 4.
[5] III. 16.
[6] K. Brandi, *Kaiser Karl V*, I (1961[6]), 205 ff., II (1941), 173–177; W. P. Fuchs, *Das
Zeitalter der Reformation*, 64 f.
[7] See II. 19.
[8] *Schl* III, 28535b, 28538; IV, 39818b–9b.

1527 England joined the Holy League of Cognac[1] which had been formed on 22 May 1526, and because it was concerned to maintain the best possible relations with the Curia (Henry VIII was hoping to be granted a divorce) it renounced its oft repeated claims to the French crown.[2] Charles V recognised very clearly that the new anti-Habsburg coalition afforded a wonderful opportunity to the 'German heresy'. He expressed this in a manifesto drawn up by the imperial secretary, Alfonso de Valdez,[3] in which Charles branded Clement VII as an unfaithful chief shepherd of Christendom. The fearful massacre inflicted by the imperial troops at the *Sacco di Roma*[4] in May 1527 (from which the Pope himself only just managed to escape by betaking himself to the castle of St. Angelo) was not deliberately planned. It came about because the *Landsknechte* were owed arrears of pay, and on the march towards Rome, or perhaps as the attack on the city was being mounted, the main leaders of the army (Frundsberg, Pescara) dropped out. Military conflicts continued until 1529. The fortunes of war alternated: for a time the imperial troops in Naples and in the North were actually cut off and surrounded. The end of hostilities came with the conclusion of the Peace of Barcelona by Charles V and Clement VII on 28 June 1529,[5] and the Peace of Cambrai on 3 August 1529.[6] (This was called the 'Ladies Peace', because an understanding was reached between Louise of Savoy, Francis I's mother, and Margaret, Charles V's aunt. Both Charles and Francis made mutual concessions.) This second conflict with France prevented Charles V from putting the Edict of Worms into effect, and thus made possible the establishment of reformed churches in Germany.

14. THE TURKISH INVASION

Beside the Second Italian War another series of events must rank as of equal significance for the progress of the Reformation in the period between the Peasants' War and the Imperial Diet of Augsburg of 1530, namely the conflicts with the Turks in the Eastern part of Europe which caused so much excitement. It is quite apparent that what happened there had a much greater emotional effect than the events of the Italian Wars. The recognition that the Turkish army might well overrun Germany, coupled with the fact that the Turks were traditionally regarded as the arch-

[1] Brandi, *op. cit.* I, 207 ff.
[2] Brandi, *op. cit.* I, 228.
[3] *Schl* I, 21695a–e; J. E. Longhurst, *Alfonso de Valdés and the Sack of Rome*, New Mexico 1954.
[4] *Schl* I, 41550–41577; Longhurst (see n. 3).
[5] L. v. Ranke, *Deutsche Geschichte im Zeitalter der Reformation*, ed. Duncker and Humblot, 1924, bk. 5, ch. 4.
[6] As n. 5.

enemy of Christendom—the forces of anti-Christ—gave an almost apocalyptic urgency to the situation. Since the period of the Crusades the Turks had pushed farther and farther towards the West.[1] Serbia, Bulgaria and Wallachia had been tributary to the Turks in the 14th century and had been made totally subject during the 15th century. The conquest of Constantinople (1453)[2] had set the whole of Christendom on the alert. Hungary had been seriously threatened for more than a century. Although Selim I (1512–1520)[3] was mainly interested in the Middle East and had overthrown Syria and Palestine, Suleiman I (1520–1566)[4] resumed the drive to the West and advanced steadily towards the Hungarian Plain. But the field of conflict with the Turks was not only Hungary but the entire Mediterranean. The sharp struggle for Hungary and even Austria coincided with the Second Italian War.[5] On 29 August 1526 Suleiman decisively defeated the army of king Ludwig of Hungary at Mohač.[6] He laid siege to Vienna from 26 September 1529,[7] but was unable to conquer it. Disturbances in the East compelled him to withdraw during the night of 14/15 October. The house of Habsburg gained from the fact that Ferdinand I, Charles's brother, became king of Bohemia and Hungary. But only a part of the Hungarian nobility voted. Another party supported Jan Zapolya[8] of Transylvania. From that time onwards there were three Hungaries, Habsburgian Western Hungary, Transylvania and the part of Hungary which was directly under the Turks. In the last of these, not unnaturally, the Reformation movement met with no resistance.[9] Zapolya came to be regarded as nothing less than the predestined ally of all who were the enemies of the house of Habsburg, which was tolerated in so far as it fought for the Empire against the Turks, but received little sympathy for defending the Empire's interests in Italy. Even the estates which were sympathetic to the Reformation were prepared to assist the Habsburgs against the Turks.[10] Giving such assistance

---

[1] A. Fevret, *Essai de bibliographie pour servir à l'histoire de L'Empire ottoman I*, 1911; P. Wittek, *The Rise of the Ottoman Empire*, 1938; A. Bombaci, 'Das Osmanische Reich', *Historia Mundi VII* (1957), 439–485.

[2] Moeller/Liebing, *Spätmittelalter/Humanismus*.

[3] A. Bombaci, *op. cit.*, 461 ff.

[4] F. Downey, *Soliman the Magnifique*, 1930; A. H. Lybyer, *The government of the Ottoman Empire in the time of Suleiman the Magnificent*, 1913; A. Bombaci, *op. cit.*, 463 ff.

[5] *Schl* IV, 43461b–43464d, 43500–43501; Ranke, *op. cit.* IV, ch. 5.

[6] *Schl* IV, 40168–40174; V, 51102a; Ranke, *op. cit.*, vol. 11, 292 ff.

[7] *Schl* IV, 42518–42520.

[8] *Schl* III, 33652c–33656a; IV, 43538–43539a.

[9] *Schl* IV, 43528a–43559; M. Bucsay, *Geschichte des Prot. in Ungarn* (1959), 40 f.

[10] On the various Imperial Diets see *Schl* III; on the question of assistance against the Turks see *Schl* IV, 43455–43520; S. A. Fischer-Galati, *Ottoman Imperialism and German Protestantism 1521–55*, 1959.

only after concessions had been granted in religious matters) became one of the most effective weapons in the hands of those who had to defend an Evangelical territorial church.

15. THE IMPERIAL DIETS OF SPEYER, 1526 AND 1529

In the year of the Peasants' War, 1525, no meeting of the Imperial Diet took place, even though one was called for November 1525.[1] Naturally, after the dictated Peace of Madrid (January 1526) and immediately after the formation of the Cognac League, which had demonstrated to Charles V that he was not the master of Europe, the estates at the Diet of Speyer (25 June–27 August)[2] which were favourable to the Reformation had a good basis for negotiation. The representatives from Saxony and Hesse wore on their lapels the slogan: *Verbum Dei manet in aeternum*. That once again the Emperor was not present to take part himself was a blow to the prestige of the Catholic group. The Emperor had forbidden reform of any kind, including the kind of 'Catholic' reform which the princes would have favoured and which might have served to dampen the passions of those who were set on reform, since it was plain to all that it would be quite impracticable to carry out the provisions of the Edict of Worms. The effect of all this was to unite all the estates in resolving that each should conduct himself 'as answerable to God and to his imperial Majesty' until a Council could be held. Obviously this did not mean that the estates were formally granted the *ius reformandi*, but the First Imperial Diet of Speyer marks the point at which the Reformation was set in motion within the German territories.

At the Second Imperial Diet of Speyer (15 March–22 April 1529)[3] the adherents of the new faith were less favourably placed than at the Diet of 1526, as a result of a shady affair which Philip of Hesse had allowed himself to get involved in, which has come to be known as the 'Pack Affair'.[4] Otto von Pack, who was George of Saxony's vice-chancellor, had informed Philip (presumably to get financial reward) that in May 1527 at Breslau an alliance had been formed between Ferdinand of Austria, Joachim I of Brandenburg, Cardinal Albert, the dukes of Bavaria and several South German bishops, the aim of which was to stamp out

---

[1] *Schl* III, 27910a–27912.
[2] *Schl* III, 27960b–27974. We do not have all the documents of these imperial diets.
[3] *Deutsche Reichstagsakten*, Jüngere Reihe 7 (ed. J. Kühn), 1935; also *Schl* III, 27975–28010; E. Mayer, *Der Speyrer Reichstag 1529*, 1929; J. Kühn, *Geschichte des Speyrer Reichstags von 1529*, 1929; E. Lund, *Speyer und der Protestantismus II*, 1930; J. Boehmer, *Protestari 1529*, 1929; H. Bornkamm, *Das Jahrhundert der Reformation*, 1961, 112–125.
[4] *Schl* II, 13674a; III, 29120; IV, 40566a–40591; V, 52009a; H. Dülfer, *Die Packschen Händel*, 2 vols., 1958.

'heresy'. Philip of Hesse and John of Saxony formed a counter-alliance in May 1528 and conducted far-reaching negotiations with the European powers. Only when Philip had already begun military operations against Würzburg and Mainz did it emerge that the 'Breslau Alliance' was an invention of Packs. Indeed Philip himself was suspected of having initiated this fake as an excuse for military action.[1] At the Second Diet of Speyer the Catholics, even though the struggles against the French and against the Turks were still continuing, took a rigorous line. Ferdinand made a proposal which was even fiercer than the Emperor's, which anyhow arrived late. The decision of the 1526 Diet was annulled, and the reformist measures which the earlier Diet had introduced were allowed to continue in force for a time, though no new measures were to be taken. Catholic services were to be allowed everywhere, and those who debased the sacraments (i.e. Zwinglians and Anabaptists) were to be stamped out. The 'Protestants' held firmly to the decisions of 1526 and on 19 April 1529 lodged their celebrated *Protestation*: 'In matters pertaining to God's honour and the soul's felicity each (i.e. each estate of the Empire) must stand before God and answer for itself'. The 'Protestants' were Electoral Saxony, Hesse, Brandenburg-Ansbach, Lüneburg, Anhalt-Köthen, and also 14 cities. Electoral Saxony, Hesse, Nuremberg, Strasbourg and Ulm formed a secret alliance.

16. PROTESTANT ALLIANCE POLITICS

The attempt to form an alliance of Evangelically-minded estates of the Empire against a non-existent Catholic military alliance which was the pure invention of a speculator was seriously damaging to Philip's prestige and the prestige of his colleagues. But the situation in 1529, which resulted from the Diet of Speyer and also from the tense situation in Switzerland,[2] made it necessary to think seriously about forming an Evangelical union. But the Evangelical camp was divided into two major factions, each based on conflicting conceptions, so that it proved to be impossible to unite all Evangelicals. Philip of Hesse was anxious to establish as comprehensive an alliance as possible against the Habsburgs. While the Pack Affair was on, contact had already been made with France and with Transylvanian Hungary. Electoral Saxony, on the other hand, would not contemplate resistance to the Emperor except in self-defence; and even this position was not arrived at until the lawyers had fought for it against the theologians. Nuremberg and South Brandenburg held that under

[1] S. Ehses, *Geschichte des Packschen Händels*, 1881; another view in H. Schwarz, *Landgraf Philipp und die Packschen Händel*, 1884.
[2] P. 72 nn. 10–13.

no circumstances would they have the right to resist the Emperor.[1] While Saxony, Hesse, Strasbourg and Ulm had concluded a secret treaty of mutual defence in Speyer on 22 April 1529, an alliance between Saxony and Franconia came into being on 3 October 1529 at Schleiz.[2] The Religious Conversations at Marburg[3] which had only just taken place (1–3 October) resulted in an attempt being made, at the political level, to draw the Central Germans into a great anti-Habsburg coalition which would be founded on the idea of autonomy in religious affairs (*Christliches Burgrecht*). The attempt failed, though contacts were not completely broken. In December 1529 negotiations were already going on in Schmalkalden.[4] At the Diet of Augsburg early in 1530 the Protestants did not even manage to represent themselves in two groups but appeared as individual factions. This was due not merely to differences in political outlook but also to growing confessional preoccupations.

17. THE CONFESSIONAL STRUGGLE

In the years 1526–30 we find what looks like a new phenomenon in the history of the Reformation, namely the drawing up of so-called 'Confessions'.[5] Actually this process began before 1525 in Nuremberg and the surrounding area (i.e. South Brandenburg). As a result of the discussions at the Imperial Governing Council during the period of the three Diets of Nuremberg[6] and also as a result of the Nuremberg city council's attempt to unify preaching in order to establish the Reformation formally, it had become a matter of urgency to define doctrinally what the content of preaching was to be. Kasimir of Brandenburg-Ansbach (d. 1527),[7] a Hohenzollern who at the end of his days remained loyal to the old faith, has the distinction of being the first to have drawn up an Evangelical confession. The *Ansbach Recommendations* of 1524[8] had a

---

[1] L. Cardauns, *Die Lehre vom Widerstandsrecht des Volks gegen die rechtmäsige Obrigkeit im Luthertum und Calvinismus des 16. Jahrhunderts*, Diss. Bonn, 1903; K. Müller, *Luthers Äusserungen über das Recht des bewaffneten Widerstands gegen den Kaiser*, 1915; H. Lüttge, 'Melanchthons Anschauung vom Recht des Widerstandes gegen die Staatsgewalt', ZKG 47 (1928), 512–542; J. Heckel, *Lex charitatis*, 1953, 148–154, 184–191; E. Wolf, 'Widerstandsrecht', RGG³ VI, 1681–1692.
[2] T. Kolde, 'Der Tag von Schleiz und die Entstehung der Schwabacher Artikel', *Festschrift Köstlin* 1896, 94–115.
[3] See p. 70 n. 8; p. 80 n. 3.
[4] E. Fabian, *Die Entstehung des Schmalkaldischen Bundes und seine Verfassung 1529–1531/33*, 1956, 63 ff.
[5] H. Bornkamm, 'Die Bedeutung der Bekenntnisschriften im Luthertum', *Das Jahrhundert der Reformation*, 1961, 219–225; W. D. Allbeck, *Studies in the Lutheran Confessions*, Philadelphia 1952.
[6] See p. 50 nn. 2, 3.
[7] Schl III, 29147c–29156.
[8] W. F. Schmidt and K. Schornbaum, *Die fränkischen Bekenntnisse*, 1930, esp. 183 ff.

number of successors. On the one hand certain doctrinal summaries were formulated for visitation purposes,[1] and the most celebrated of these were the *Great Catechism* and the *Short Catechism*, both from Luther's hand.[2] On the other hand a certain amount of doctrinal definition was felt to be necessary for political reasons. No estate of the Empire could risk making a treaty with another for the purposes of defending the faith unless it could be assured of the other's 'orthodoxy', or—to put it another way—unless it could be assured that what was preached in the other's territory was warrantable from Scripture and did not run counter to the true *consensus ecclesiae*. Even before Marburg, in the summer of 1529, there had been drawn up in connection with the discussions between Nuremberg and Saxony the *Schwabach Articles*,[3] which were not published until 16 October. But on 1 October Luther, Melanchthon, Jonas, Brenz and Osiander took them with them to Marburg.[4] They managed to win assent from Zwingli, Oecolampad, Bucer and Hedio, and to produce 14 *Marburg Articles* on which all were agreed. But the 15th article, on the Lord's Supper, was disputed and no agreement was reached. If agreement had been reached, it might have been possible for the Swiss and the South Germans to combine politically against the Habsburgs and the Emperor; but this would in all probability have been very risky, and for this reason Saxony, Nuremberg and South Brandenburg fought shy of it. Moreover, if Luther and his followers had made concessions to the Swiss over the Lord's Supper question it would have put the Protestants of Central Germany in a very awkward position in discussions at the Imperial Diet (note Augsburg 1530). At Marburg Luther certainly did not see this, for he was solely concerned with the verb *est* and nothing else; but it is plain that Melanchthon had seen the problem. Alliance politics in the years 1528–30 came to grief for both political and religious reasons. It would be pointless to debate whether it was political reasons rather than religious reasons, or vice versa, which caused the collapse, for they were intertwined. On the question of the right to resist the Emperor, for instance, the positions adopted were based on theological arguments and conditioned by religious convictions.[5]

18. THE IMPERIAL DIET OF AUGSBURG AND THE AUGSBURG CONFESSION

For the Reformation movement in Germany 1530 was the most dangerous year between the Diet of Worms in 1521 and the Schmalkaldian

[1] III. 2. [2] p. 58 n. 4.
[3] *Schl* I, 42437–42444; V, 52116; *BSLK* XVI f.
[4] p. 70 n. 8; p. 79 n. 3. [5] p. 79 n. 1.

War. The Emperor, who at Worms had committed himself unequivocally to stamping out heresy,[1] was obliged during the nine years from 1521 to 1530 to let things slide and to allow the Reformation movement to gain in strength, because he was fully occupied by conflicts with the French,[2] the Turks[3] and the Pope.[4] After the peace treaties of Barcelona and Cambrai[5] and the departure of the Turks from Vienna[6] he was free. Although (to use Ranke's words) 'nothing could have been more redolent of peace than the Emperor's written charge to the Imperial Diet', it was nevertheless necessary to expect the worst, namely a brutal implementation of the Edict of Worms.[7] The Evangelicals, disunited among themselves, could not have begun discussions at greater disadvantage. Their spokesman, Melanchthon, was fully aware of the danger they were in. In fact, he could hardly think of anything else. Luther, still under the ban, could not be brought to Augsburg, but only as far as Coburg. From there he wrote his famous letters of admonition and encouragement.[8] The preparations for the discussions were entirely inadequate. John of Saxony had the Schwabach Articles with him[9] when he went to meet the Emperor (who arrived in Augsburg on 15 June). Melanchthon, who had already made up his mind to concentrate only on criticising abuses and requesting reforms, though without getting involved in argument over fundamentals, had brought with him a very thorough list of statements which, because they had been drawn up at Torgau on 20 May, were known as the *Torgau Articles*. On 9 July the South German cities of Strasbourg, Constance, Lindau, and Memmingen presented an independent confession called *Tetrapolitana*.[10] Zwingli did not come to Augsburg, but merely sent a document entitled *Fidei ratio ad Carolum imperatorem.* Philip of Hesse assumed virtually the role of an observer at the Imperial Diet.[11] The Catholics were brilliantly prepared. Eck brought with him a catalogue of 404 heretical propositions.[12] The Emperor had about 20 theologians at hand who were made to assist the legate Campeggio in

[1] p. 21 n. 3.   [2] II. 19 and III. 13.   [3] III. 14.
[4] L. v. Pastor IV, 2, 161 ff.; E. Rodocanachi, *Les pontificats d'Adrian VI et de Clemens VII*, Paris 1933.
[5] p. 75 n. 6.   [6] p. 76 n. 7.   [7] p. 21 n. 4.
[8] *Schl* I, 12109–12121; H. v. Schubert, 'Luther auf der Koburg', *LuJ* 12 (1930), 109–161; *WAB* 5, 275–650; P. Rassow, 'Die Reichstage zu Augsburg in der Ref.-Zeit', *Forschungen und Studien zur Kultur- und Wirtschaftsgeschichte Augsburgs*, 1955, 273–282; J. v. Walter, 'Der Reichstag zu Augsburg', *LuJ* 12 (1930), 1–90.
[9] p. 79 n. 8.
[10] *Schl* IV, 43093–43095; see also n. 12.
[11] W. Köhler, 'Der Augsburger Reichstag von 1530 und die Schweiz', *Schweizerische Zeitschrift für Geschichte* 3 (1953), 169–190; H. Grundmann, *Landgraf Philipp v. Hessen und der Augsburger Reichstag 1530*, 1959.
[12] W. Gussmann, *Quellen und Forschungen zur Geschichte des Augsburger Glaubensbekenntnisses* I, 1912, II, 1930.

drawing up a reply to the *Confessio Augustana*.[1] The final result was the *Confutatio*,[2] the reading of which was adopted, which meant that the Confessio Augustana was regarded as refuted. The *Augsburg Confession* was drawn up in Augsburg itself by Melanchthon, who conflated the two earlier sets of articles. Articles 1–21 of the Augsburg Confession correspond to the Schwabach Articles, and 22–28 to the Torgau Articles. He got Brück to write a preface.[3] The aim was to provide a set of articles which, after due discussion, would be handed to the Emperor as a Confession (in German and Latin) representing the views not only of Electoral Saxony but also of a considerable number of Evangelical estates (Hesse, Brandenburg-Ansbach, Nuremberg, Reutlingen, Anhalt-Zerbst and Lüneburg).[4] The Augsburg Confession did not claim to set out a new doctrine but to give an account of what was taught publicly in the *ecclesiae apud nos*, and the purpose was to show that there was no disparity between this teaching and Holy Scripture or the teaching of the whole Church or even the teaching of the Church of Rome.[5] Only abuses were abolished. This meant that many matters, such as the denial of purgatory and the sacrificial character of the mass and the papal primacy, were not mentioned. Only in Melanchthon's *Apology*[6] of 1531 (which he wrote in reply to the Catholic *Confutatio*) is there any open recognition that the doctrine of the churches of the Reformation is a denial of many of the doctrinal propositions of the Schoolmen. In the private negotiations which Melanchthon conducted repeatedly (to the great annoyance of the politicians) with men like de Valdés (Charles V's secretary) and Campeggio, he confined himself to seeking concessions only on the administration of the chalice to the laity and the right of the clergy to marry. Consonant with this is the fundamentally 'catholic' tone of the Augsburg Confession, though the *Confutatio* of course denied its 'catholicity'

[1] Crit. ed. *BSLK* 31–137 (see XV–XXI, ed. Bornkamm); *Schl* IV, 34504–34679; V, 51502; J. Ficker, 'Die Originale des Vierstädtebekenntnisses und die originalen Texte der Augsburger Konfession', *Geschichtliche Studien für A. Hauck*, 1916 240–251; R. Hermann, 'Zur theologischen Würdigung der Augustana', *LuJ* 12 (1930), 162–204; W. E. Nagel, *Luthers Anteil an der Confessio Augustana*, 1930; W. Maurer, 'Zum geschichtlichen Verständnis der Abendmahlsartikel der CA', *Festschrift für G. Ritter*, 1950, 161–209.

[2] *Schl* IV, 34680–34687a; J. Ficker, *Die Konfutation des Augsburger Bekenntnisses*, 1891.

[3] Bornkamm, *op. cit.* (see n. 1), 35–43, 44–49.

[4] The two texts (Latin and German) are supposed to be of equal value, though they do not correspond exactly. The Latin copy was destroyed in Spain and the German lost without trace. See H. Bornkamm, 'Der authentische Text der CA (1530)', *SAH* 1956, section 2.

[5] W. Elert, *Die Augustana und der Gedanke der christlichen Solidarität*, 1931; A. Lackmann, *Katholische Einheit und Augsburger Konfession*, 1959.

[6] In its first form, *CR* 27, 244–378, and its final form, *BSLK* 139–404 (XXII f.); K. Thieme, *Der Geist der lutherischen Ethik in Melanchthons Apologie*, 1931.

completely. The reason for Melanchthon's caution was his acute awareness that the time was unfavourable.[1] John and the other princes—and
their lawyers, too—could see that certain opportunities were still open
to them, for the Turkish menace was by no means overcome, and the
power of Reformation preaching continued unabated. The fact that the
Confessio Augustana was actually given a public reading endowed it with
a certain prestige which was not to be underestimated. Admittedly the
final verdict of the Imperial Diet, as given on 19 November 1530, was a
harsh one, for the Edict of Worms continued in force. But on 23 September there had been a proposal that a moratorium be granted until
15 April 1531. Even though the moratorium was not extended, it nevertheless indicated that the Edict of Worms, though formally in force,
was no more practicable after 19 November than it was before.

19. ZWINGLI'S END

Less than a year after the Diet of Augsburg Zwingli died in the battle
of Kappel on 11 October 1531.[2] In the summer of 1530 Philip of Hesse
had made an alliance with Zürich and Basle. It did not go further than
that, for Bern would not allow Philip to be admitted to the *Christliches
Burgrecht*. Despite this, Zwingli challenged the Catholic Cantons of
Central Switzerland to military combat, and Zürich, inadequately armed,
was speedily defeated. But the Catholic victory at Kappel did not spell
the end of the Reformation, for in the four Evangelical Cantons[3] the
Reformed faith had taken such deep root that there could be no prospect
of stamping it out. In Zürich Heinrich Bullinger[4] succeeded Zwingli,
and at Basle Oswald Myconius[5] took the place of Oecolampad who had
gone home in 1531. Even the Counter-reformation was not able to
suppress or diminish Evangelical faith and order in those four Cantons.[6]
But the Catholic victory at Kappel meant that there was now no likelihood

[1] H. Virck, 'Melanchthons politische Stellung an dem Reichstag zu Augsburg',
ZKG 9 (1888), 77–104, 293–340; G. Kawerau, *Die Versuche, Melanchthon zur
katholischen Kirche zurückzuführen*, 1902; J. v. Walter, *Luther und Melanchthon während
des Augsburger Reichstags*, 1931.
[2] O. Farner, *H. Zwingli IV* (1960), 482–509.
[3] III. 11.
[4] *Schl* I, 2025–2122; V, 45237–45250; E. Dollfuss-Zodel, *Bullingers Einfluss auf
das zürchersche Staatswesen von 1531 bis 1575*, 1931; A. Bouvier, *H. Bullinger d'après sa
correspondance avec les réformés et les humanistes de langue française*, 1940; F. Blanke, *Der
junge Bullinger*, 1942; W. Hollweg, *Bullingers Hausbuch*, 1950; P. Walser, *Bullingers
Lehre von der Prädestination*, 1956.
[5] *Schl* II, 16212–16218; V, 48429–48429a; F. Rudolf, 'O. Myconius', *Basler
Jahrbücher* 1945, 14–30; W. Brändly, *Geschichte der Protestanten in Stadt und Land
Luzern*, 1955.
[6] K. Egli, *Schweiz. Ref.-Geschichte*, 1910.

of the Reformation gospel making inroads into other parts of Switzerland, though it won new adherents in the Italian speaking districts. But anyone who adopted the Evangelical faith was obliged to move into an Evangelical Canton or to emigrate to Evangelical territory outside Switzerland.[1] Only in Geneva[2] did new opportunities present themselves to Protestantism, which was just beginning to take effect there during this period.[3]

20. THE LEAGUE OF SCHMALKALDEN AND THE NUREMBERG STANDSTILL

The final recess of the Imperial Diet of Augsburg compelled the Protestants, who at the beginning of 1530 had somewhat fallen apart, to make a formal compact, at least within Germany itself. For even though it was unlikely that the Emperor and the Catholic estates would take military measures against them, they had to anticipate adverse judgements at the Imperial Cameral Tribunal which made it uncertain whether they would be allowed continued possession of ecclesiastical properties already secularised. Since speedy action was called for, the signatories of the Augsburg Confession (John of Saxony, Philip of Hesse, Wolfgang of Anhalt, Albert and Gebhard of Mansfeld, George of Brandenburg, and ten German cities) met at Schmalkalden on 29 December 1530 and pledged themselves to joint resistance. On 27 February 1531 the League of Schmalkalden[4] was formally established, in the first instance for a period of one and a half years. South Brandenburg was not included, and two North German cities, Magdeburg and Bremen, joined in. They were followed by a further seven South German cities and seven North German cities. The defeat of the Protestants at Kappel had forced cities which previously had looked to Switzerland to orientate themselves afresh towards the Schmalkaldic League. At Frankfurt in December 1531 a formal constitution was drawn up.[5] The effect of this Protestant compact was astonishing, for although not all the Evangelical territories were able to risk joining the League, other estates of the Empire were em-

---

[1] R. Pfister, *Um des Glaubens willen. Die evangelischen Flüchtlinge von Locarno und ihre Aufnahme in Zürich im Jahre 1555*, 1955.
[2] See vol. 3 I in this series (Locher, *Zwingli u. die schweiz. Reformation*).
[3] H. Ammann, 'Oberdeutsche Kaufleute u. die Anfänge der Ref. in Genf', *Zeitschrift für württembergische Landesgeschichte* 13 (1954), 150–193.
[4] *Schl* IV, 41646–41671; V, 52101–52102; O. Winckelmann, *Der Schmalkalische Bund und der Nürnberger Religionsfriede*, 1892; E. Fabian, *Die Entstehung des Schmalkaldischen Bundes und seiner Verfassung 1529–1531/33*, 1956; C. Glitsch, *Die Bündnispolitik der oberdeutschen Städte des Schmalk. Bundes unter dem Einfluss von Strassburg und Ulm 1529/31–32*, Diss. Tübingen 1960.
[5] E. Fabian, *op. cit.* (see n. 4); and *Die Schmalkaldischen Bundesabschiede 1530–1532*, 1958.

boldened to embrace Evangelical church order.[1] Electoral Saxony had been alone in refusing to ratify the election of Ferdinand as Roman king[2] on 5 January 1531; but from October 1531 onwards the entire Schmalkaldic League refused to recognise the choice. There was an element of danger in the fact that enemies of the Habsburgs who had nothing in common with Protestantism were drawn towards an alliance which was founded for the purpose of defending Evangelical faith (note the attitude of Bavaria on the question of Ferdinand's election). France, and for a time England also, regarded themselves as natural allies of the Schmalkaldians. Since Charles V needed the support of all estates of the Empire once more against the Turks, he had no option but to introduce in 1532 the *Nuremberg Standstill* (also known as the 'Religious Peace of Nuremberg')[3], by which Protestants were assured that any proceedings taken against them at the Imperial Cameral Tribunal would be suspended, and that no estate of the Empire would be permitted to go to war against another over matters of faith and religion. Thus the formation of the League of Schmalkalden marks at once a beginning and an end: the end of the struggle to implement the Edict of Worms, and the beginning of the establishment of a reformed church order—the beginning of a period in which a politically established Protestantism would play its part in shaping German history.

[1] See the Reformation history of Württemberg, Anhalt, Pomerania, Mecklenburg, etc., in the second part of this volume (E. Bizer).

[2] *Schl* III, 28433, 28760, 28761.

[3] *Schl* IV, 40502a–40504; O. Winckelmann, *op. cit.* (see n. 1); S. Fischer-Galati, 'Ottoman Imperialism and the Religious Peace of Nuremberg', *ARG* 47 (1956), 160–179.

G

PART II

THE HISTORY OF
THE REFORMATION FROM 1532 TO 1555

Ernst Bizer

THE Nuremberg Standstill was regarded by Luther as a heaven-sent gift. Its effect was to put in abeyance the decisions of the final recess of the Diet of Augsburg which constituted a direct threat to the Reformation; and it allowed the Reformation an unspecified period (i.e. 'until the Council') in which to establish and extend its influence. It also secured unity within the Empire, at least to the extent that the Evangelical estates would now take part in the war against the Turks—though it was not, in fact, their participation which directly accounted for the successful outcome of the campaign of 1532. Nevertheless, the situation remained unstable. The attitudes of those who opposed the Reformation had not basically changed. The Standstill rested only on a decree by the Emperor himself, and not on a decision of the Imperial Diet. The competence of the Imperial Cameral Tribunal to decide in matters of religion had not been set aside; and the sheer difficulty of drawing a line between religious and political issues was such that every new dispute brought new difficulties to light. Moreover the very existence of a time-limit 'until the Council' was a threat to peace efforts, particularly because it quickly became apparent that the two parties regarded this Council very differently. Whether the Reformation would succeed in the future depended on the capacity of its theology to carry conviction. Politically, its fate would be determined by the outcome of the Council question.[1]

[1] Recent presentations of the second part of the history of the Reformation may be found in the general works noted in the bibliography, though most treat the years 1532 to 1555 in all too summary a fashion, with the notable exception of *Lortz* (see list of abbreviations). The bibliographies of Schottenloher (*Schl*) and Franz (*BWDG*, *SWDG*) have already been mentioned (see abbrev.). For sources, the great works of the 16th and 17th centuries are still indispensable: *Sleidan, Ursachen, Rechtmässigkeit* (see abbrev.) and Seckendorff's *Commentarius historicus et apologeticus de Lutheranismo*, 1692. Among more recent works, *Pol. Corr.* (see abbrev.) is worthy of special mention. Research into the Anabaptist movement has made considerable progress, and particularly important are *Franz, Wiedertäufer* (see abbrev.), *Mennonitisches Lexikon* (ed. C. Hege, C. Neff and others), 1913 ff., and *The Mennonite Encyclopaedia* (ed. H. S. Bender, H. Smith), 1955–1959. A review of research in this field is contained in G. F. Herschberger, *Das Täufertum. Erbe und Verpflichtung*, 1963. In other fields most research has been conducted by secular and Roman Catholic

CHAPTER I

DEVELOPMENTS WITHIN PROTESTANTISM DURING THE THIRTIES

LUTHER remained the leading theologian of the Reformation, despite the fact that his activities as lecturer and writer were impeded by illness and a variety of other hindrances, which meant that some territories in many respects simply went their own way. The enormous number of his letters, considered judgements and 'table conversations' show how much he was occupied with all the problems of the period, and they also show what authority was attached to his utterances.

With his translation of the Bible he made a lasting impression on the consciousness of German Protestantism. Early in 1532 he produced *The Prophets, in German*, and in 1534 the first provisional translation of the whole Bible was completed. For this edition, as with his *Psalter* in 1531,[1] those parts which had already been printed earlier were meticulously revised, with the aid of a working committee in which Melanchthon, Cruciger, Bugenhagen, Jonas, Aurogallus (a Hebraist) and Rörer[2] (secretary) took part. During the years 1539–1541 a similar revision was made of the whole Old Testament and in 1541 a revision of the New Testament. Finally in the autumn of 1544 the Pauline letters as far as II Cor. 3 were closely revised in preparation for the publication of the entire New Testament in its final form in 1546. The minutes of this working committee[3] are an impressive testimony to the care with which Luther sought to make an exact rendering of the biblical text into German. In consequence he profoundly influenced not only the work

---

historians. The most important works are *Brandi* (and *Brandi Quellen*), *CT*, *Jedin*, *ARC*, *DThC* (see abbrev.) and G. Dommasch, *Die Religionsprozesse der rekusierenden Fürsten und Städte und die Erneuerung des Schmalkaldischen Bundes 1534–1536*, 1961. For older specialist literature see list by H. Hermelink in *HKG* pt. 3, 1911, 2nd ed. 1931.

[1] *WADB* III, 1–166.
[2] B. Klaus, 'G. Röhrer, ein bayrischer Mitarbeiter Luthers', *ZBKG* 26, 1957, 113 ff.
[3] *WADB* IV.

done on the Bible during his own period but also the development of German language and culture.[1]

Here we shall list only those of Luther's works which are important but which we shall not have further occasion to mention. Rörer collected together the notes of lectures which Luther delivered during the session from July to December 1531, from which resulted the 'Great Commentary' on Galatians, published in 1535, which is the most important source for the theology of the older Luther, particularly for his view of the doctrine of justification. In the preface he states that this doctrine occupies him day and night, and in the first lecture he says that it is impossible for anyone to study it sufficiently, for *et si perit haec doctrina, universa perierunt* (WAR 40/I,39,10f).[2] In June 1535 he made a start with his lectures on Genesis, the last and longest lecture course of his life, which occupied him—with frequent interruptions —until November 1545.[3] Luther's very considerable activity as a preacher led Cruciger in 1538 to make a collection of expository sermons entitled *An Exposition of the 14th and 15th chapters of St. John's Gospel*. Mathesius tells us that Luther 'took this book with him often to church' and that he 'delighted to read it' and that he had called it 'his best book'.[4] In his admonition *To the Clergy, that they should preach against usury*[5] he returned to a theme in the field of social ethics which he had taken up twice in his early writings. His exposition of *The Last Words of David*[6] is a sequel to earlier writings against the Jews (including *On the Jews and their lies*, WAR 53, 412 ff., and *Schem Hamphoras*, WAR 53, 573 ff.). It is a piece of exegetical writing which aims not only at improving translation but also at showing Christ in the Old Testament, and it is therefore an important source for Luther's christological views. The preface to the first volume of his collected Latin writings is an important but much disputed account of his early life, in which he gives an account of the experience which made him the protagonist of reform.[7] The majority of scholars feel that it is an account which at several significant points needs to be corrected. Finally, the collection of Luther's 'table conversations', made by zealous disciples, together with the collected edition of his Wittenberg writings which was requested by Strasbourg Protestants[8] are an indication of the grateful reverence in which he was held, and of the authority which his colleagues ascribed to him.

But besides Luther's activity, that of Melanchthon assumed increasing importance.[9] He lectured regularly, wrote methodical text books for

[1] *WADB* IC, LIV; VI, L ff. and VII, XX ff.; W. Walther, *Luthers deutsche Bibel*, 1917.
[2] 2nd ed. 1538, German 1539 in the complete edition.
[3] Pt. I ed. Veit Dietrich 1544, pt. II 1550, pt. III by H. Besold 1552, pt. IV 1554. Text in *WAR* 42–44.
[4] *WAR* 45, XXXIX ff. and 465.   [5] *WAR* 51, 325 ff.
[6] *WAR* 54, 16 ff.   [7] *WAR* 54, 176 ff.   [8] *WAR* 50, 654 ff.
[9] Melanchthon studies have revived after a period of neglect. R. Stupperich, *Melanchthon*, 1960, and *Der unbekannte Melanchthon*, 1961; R. Schäfer, *Christologie und Sittlichkeit in Melanchthons frühen Loci*, 1961; P. Fraenkel, *Testimonia Patrum. The function of the patristic argument in the theology of Philip Melanchthon, 1961*.

students, conducted an extensive correspondence, and took part in all the decisive conferences and discussions of the period. All this, coupled with his great concern to assist in the work of education by striving for clarity of method (which Luther always gratefully acknowledged), meant that in the thirties Melanchthon's influence was more penetrating, more widespread, and more sustained than that of Luther himself. Disciples of Melanchthon exercised a determinative influence upon the second generation of Lutherans, and they betrayed their indebtedness to their master even when they took sides against him. Although it was Melanchthon's desire, even in his later years, to be nothing more than a faithful interpreter of Luther, he nevertheless became a theologian in his own right, whose thinking diverged from Luther's at certain key points.

> From 1527 onwards, the testimony of the ancient church with regard to the doctrine of the Lord's Supper became increasingly important to Melanchthon, and he began to move away from Luther's doctrine of 'ubiquity'. Of decisive significance for his theological development was his attempt to formulate a forensic, imputative doctrine of justification based on Anselm's doctrine of 'satisfaction', which he adopted in the article on justification in the *Confessio Augustana* and which he argued more fully in his *Apology*.[1] For Melanchthon, the saving death of Christ guarantees the objectivity of justification, but at the same time the necessary subjective acceptance of justification is something that cannot be ignored. Thus Melanchthon's interest in human responsibility leads him to qualify the earlier determinism. In his commentary on Romans of 1532 (not included in CR) he states that it is man's natural awareness of God which makes possible the appropriation by man of God's saving grace. This natural awareness of God Melanchthon finds presupposed in the first two chapters of Romans, and it is to be sharpened and intensified by the preaching of the law. Thus conscience, understood as a capacity of man's psyche, is made to occupy a central place in theology. He persistently warns against what he calls 'dangerous illusions' about predestination, for predestination is something discernible only to the eye of faith, *a posteriori*. In his lectures on the *Loci Communes* of 1533[2] Melanchthon felt driven to take issue with Servet over his teaching on the Trinity, and from that point onwards he makes frequent appeal not only to Scripture but also to the creeds of the ancient church as sources of faith.[3] It was Melanchthon who devised, with regard to the doctrine of election, the formula which has remained standard within Lutheranism: *Neque ex ratione neque ex lege, sed ex evangelio iudicandum est . . . Sicut cum de iustificatione quaerimus ordimur a verbo, ita cum de praedestinatione quaerimus, ordiendum est a verbo seu evangelio.*[4] He acknowledges a *causa electionis in accipiente*, in so far as a person who accepts the promise offered to

[1] Cf. H. E. Weber, *Reformation, Orthodoxie, Rationalismus* I, 106 ff.
[2] CR 21, 253 ff.
[3] O. Ritschl, *Dogmengeschichte des Protestantismus I*, 1908, 301 ff.
[4] CR 21, 330 cf. 450.

him has not rejected it. This non-rejection is indeed effected by the Spirit, but it could not happen without the participation of the human will. This means that the human will must play a vital part in justification. In the 1535 edition of the *Loci*[1] Melanchthon completed the task of reformulating his theology and of casting it in a form which would facilitate its use as a basis for instruction. In the first part he deals with what he calls the 'objective' dogmas, i.e., the doctrines of God, of the Trinity, of the two natures of Christ, and of creation. He did not attempt to deal with these in 1521. At the heart of the work (*De evangelio*) is the doctrine of the satisfaction offered by Christ, and of justification by a faith which accepts Christ's satisfaction. In his definition of the Gospel as *praedicatio poenitentiae et promissio* Melanchthon bases himself on Luke 24: 47. Accordingly he describes repentance as 'necessary' in the same way as good works also are 'necessary to eternal life, because they must necessarily follow from reconciliation' (p. 429). Faith, so Melanchthon claims, is the product of the joint operations of Word, Spirit and will; the will is not merely passive but struggles against its own weakness (p. 376). In the doctrine of justification, it is to be noted, *quod et gratis promittit iustitiam et quod promissio est universalis*—anyone who attempts to reduce this universal promise to a particular promise makes that promise uncertain and destroys faith (p. 451). Melanchthon supports his argument not only by examples from Scripture but also by examples from the ancient church. Troeltsch has already pointed out that Melanchthon has not simply made minor changes in matters of detail, but has established a new relationship between faith and reason.[2]

Luther never gave an explicit judgement on all this, but the more suspicious of his friends and the Wittenberg students could not fail to notice the difference between the two men. Amsdorf complained to Luther about Melanchthon's view that good works are necessary to salvation[3] and later gave it as his opinion[4] that in Melanchthon Luther was harbouring a snake in his bosom. Then Konrad Cordatus, who was a clergyman in Niemegk, informed first Luther, then Jonas (who was Rector of the university) and subsequently—when Jonas sent him away—informed Brück (the elector's chancellor) of his opposition to Melanchthon's theory, which Cruciger had apparently given in a lecture, that contrition is *causa sine qua non* of justification[5] and that good works are necessary to salvation,[6] and he based his objections on what he had learned earlier from Luther and Melanchthon themselves. Melanchthon justified his statement[7] by saying that it was *docendi causa* that he considered good

[1] CR 21, 333 ff.
[2] E. Troeltsch, *Vernunft und Offenbarung bei J. Gerhard und Melanchthon*, 1891, 144 ff., 206 ff.
[3] CR 3, 162 (note).
[4] CR 3, 503. [5] CR 3, 159 ff.
[6] CR 3, 185 passim. [7] CR 3, 179 ff., 1 Nov. 1536.

works to be necessary, but that he had no wish to deviate from the Wittenbergers' common teaching or to destroy their unity; and on 5 November he wrote to Cordatus, but without much effect.[1] Luther eventually managed to pacify him, though at a disputation on 1 June 1537 Luther specifically rejected the theory that works are necessary to salvation.[2] He did not wish to deny that the law is God's Word and commandment, but it is precisely as such that the law is a standing condemnation of man, who can have a good conscience only by having faith; works can never become a kind of 'sacrament of faith' with the aid of which faith could somehow stand up on its own.[3] Melanchthon, for his part, subsequently abandoned his thesis, and later on, when it was taken up again by Georg Major, dismissed it with Luther's argument that it encouraged a catholic view. At the same time he held fast to his opinion 'that faith must be supported by means of good works, for without them it would die'.[4] There was thus no overcoming the difference in substance between his view and Luther's.

Melanchthon had just got back from Tübingen, where he had been involved in efforts to reform the university, when he had to occupy himself with the accusations brought against him by Cordatus. In Nuremberg, on the same journey, he had been called in to mediate in a dispute which we must mention here, because it brings to light a far-reaching difference of opinion between Andreas Osiander and the theologians of Wittenberg. In Nuremberg it had become customary, in the service of the Lord's Supper, to follow the admonition with a formula of 'general confession' devised by W. Linck. A church ordinance of 1533 set this aside,[5] in order to introduce a form of private confession and absolution.[6] The city council asked for the general confession to be reintroduced, but Osiander withstood the request passionately, to the point of asserting that neither preaching nor general confession could effect genuine absolution. The Wittenberg theologians, who were twice asked to mediate, supported the council but failed to convince Osiander. On S. Bartholomew's Day 1536 Osiander once again preached against this 'utterly blasphemous deception' which mocked both God and the conscience. The council approached Melanchthon, who on 22 October gave his considered judgement,[7] which recognised the abuses of which Osiander complained and proposed for consideration an altered version of the formula which had been customary in Nuremberg. It failed to solve the

[1] CR 3, 181.   [2] WAR 39 I, 198 ff.
[3] Ibid., 214.
[4] O. Ritschl (see n. 16), II, 316 ff; cf. WAR 39 I, 198.
[5] Sehling XI, 498 n. 'k',
[6] W. Möller, Osiander, 1870, 187 f.; WATR 4, 5004 and 5047.
[7] CR 3, 173.

dispute. The council made an approach to Wittenberg,[1] but received only a tentative decision from there.[2] In 1539 the dispute broke out again in Nuremberg, and the Wittenberg theologians in February 1540 sent two new formulae of general confession, because the Nuremberg formula displeased them: 'If you are going to mention one commandment—the command to forgive one's neighbour—as the condition for receiving God's forgiveness, then why do you not go all the way and include the whole Decalogue?'[3] But even then the question was not brought to a satisfactory conclusion.

The Cordatus affair brought to light the contrasting views of Luther and Melanchthon, but in the controversy with Johann Agricola, who had been Luther's graduate assistant and was now a schoolmaster in Eisleben, the two Wittenbergers fought side by side against antinomianism, which seemed to both of them to be highly dangerous.[4] In December 1537 Luther published a series of eighteen theses which had been circulating in Wittenberg since the summer and which challenged his teaching on the law. Agricola claimed to have no part in them, but his statements are not above suspicion. Added to the series were a few propositions in which Luther was said still to represent 'the true doctrine' and others in which he is said to have denied it. Finally there came eight theses which Luther presumably formulated himself against Agricola.

Evidently this was an attempt to play off the teachings of the older Luther against his statements as a young man, though there can in fact be little doubt 'that anyone who looks at the matter closely must see that with Luther there is no going back on his reformist teaching'.[5] The first of the theses (*Poenitentia docenda est non ex decalogo aut ulla lege Mosi, sed ex violatione filii per Evangelium*) shows moreover that 'antinomianism' did not mean libertinism; it sought 'merely' to base obedience on the Gospel rather than on the law. But Luther regarded the attack as an extremely serious one, and as with Müntzer and with the Pope he saw the devil at work, and his reaction was to produce no less than six series of theses. Disputations on the first series were held in December 1537 and on the second series in January 1538. After that there was a reconciliation, and Luther gave Agricola a formal apology. But in August 1538 Agricola wrote a letter which 'set the Rhine on fire' once more and caused Luther to produce a fifth series of theses which were presumably debated on 6 September 1538. Records of the disputation have been preserved. They show that Luther regarded Agricola's recantation as insufficient, and

[1] *WAB* 7, 588 ff.   [2] *Ibid.*, 594 f.
[3] *CR* 3, 954; *Enders* 12, No. 2825; G. Rietschel, *Lehrbuch der Liturgik I*, 1900, 430 n. 15.
[4] *WAR* 39 I, 342 ff., 359 ff.; *WAB* 8, 279; *WAR* 50, 461 ff.
[5] Hermann, *op. cit.*, 12.

although Melanchthon made an attempt at mediation, Luther wrote, early in 1539, a polemic *Against the Antinomians*.[1] It was taken to be a condemnation of Agricola, and the prince elector had Agricola brought before a hastily convened consistory court. A disputation in February 1539 failed to satisfy Luther and his wrath flared up once more. Friends sought in vain to achieve a settlement, and Agricola lodged a formal complaint with the elector against Luther,[2] but while proceedings were on Agricola went to Berlin to become court chaplain to Joachim II. In connection with a doctoral dissertation in September 1540 Luther took up the theme once again in a sixth series of theses. In antinomianism Luther saw a threat to Protestant doctrine as a whole. To those who attempted to base the preaching of repentance solely on Christ and his Gospel Luther replied that though Christ did indeed summon men to repent, he did so by means of an exposition of the Law and not by means of the Gospel. To reject the preaching of the Law is no less a rejection of Christ than was the Pharisee's passion for legal rectitude. Secondly, he warns against making Christ, 'who came as mediator and redeemer, in order to fulfil the Law',[3] into a new lawgiver, by basing repentance on the Gospel. The antinomians were arguing that one should start with Christ's generous deeds and by means of these move people to repentance; Agricola was merely 'juggling' with the Law.[4] Luther agreed that he had indeed taught this himself,[5] but this also is a law, often (as he would show by means of an example) a most difficult and incriminating law, for it compels us to ask 'what I have done and what I have failed to do', and it forces us to recognise the extent of our own ingratitude, which has as its consequence both despair and death. 'This is the moment at which we must be directed by John the Baptist, whose finger points towards the Lamb who takes away the sin of the world'[6] and proclaims the Gospel to the poor. This is an extreme testing which must leave the antinomians dumbfounded, for the devil has transformed himself into Christ. So there is good reason for making a clear distinction between Christ the preacher of the Law and Christ the Redeemer, who has fulfilled the Law.[7]

Melanchthon allowed nothing to divert him from his purpose. The most important formulation of his views during this period is the 1540 edition of the *Confessio Augustana*, the so-called *Variata* in which, without letting the reader realise it and without any change in the preface, he has in fact done a new version of the text in such a way that it incorporates all the characteristic features of his most recent thinking.[8] This caused no

[1] *WAR* 50, 461 ff.   [2] *WAR* 51, 425 ff. (Luther's reply).
[3] *WAR* 39 I, 535, 10.   [4] *WAR* 51, 438, 26.
[5] *WAR* 50, 471, I.   [6] *WAR* 39 I, 537, 11.   [7] *Ibid.*, 538, 13.
[8] T. Kolde, *Die Augsburger Konfession, lat. u. deutsch kurz erläutert*, 1896 (*BSLK* gives only a few excerpts which give no idea of the scope of the changes).

stir among his Evangelical contemporaries, though Eck drew their attention to it at the religious conversations at Worms in 1541. The alterations
were more than mere additions and rearrangements, and they were not
confined simply to the article on the Lord's Supper, which now taught
*quod cum pane et vino vere exhibeantur corpus et sanguis Christi vescentibus in
coena domini.* This is so obviously reminiscent of the Wittenberg Concord
(see below) that it would be reasonable to suppose that Melanchthon is
here simply placing on record the result of the efforts to achieve Protestant
unity. Considerable emphasis is placed on repentance and good works,
on the necessity of good works and the incompatibility of faith with
'deadly sins'. Ecclesiastical customs are described as matters of indifference
(*Adiaphora*), and the polemic against Catholics and Anabaptists is intensi-
fied. Of special interest is the Postscript to Article 21, in which an appeal
is made to the Emperor to call—as is his right and his duty—a Council
of pious and learned men. In the section dealing with the marriage of
priests Isaiah 49: 23 and the 'men of valour' from Gideon to Constantine
are quoted as illustrations of the duty which is placed upon devout
princes, and particularly upon the Emperor, to care for the Church. Thus,
by introducing it in this way, Melanchthon has managed to smuggle into
the Confession 'what amounts to an article of faith dealing with the
ecclesiastical rights of the princes'.[1]

Here we must at least mention, side by side with Luther and Melanchthon, some of the lesser reformers. In 1538 Philip of Hesse summoned
the Strasbourg reformer Martin Bucer[2] to assist in the reordering of the
church in his territory. From 30 October to 1 November he held a public
discussion with the leaders of the Anabaptists in Hesse, and although he did
not manage to persuade them to retract their teachings, he did get from
them an admission that their separatism 'could do nothing but harm' and he
led nine of them back into the fellowship of the territorial church. He
wrote to Philip: 'The most obvious objection of these people is that we
are so bad at keeping our house in order, and with this argument they
are leading many people astray.'[3] So the ordering of the church was an
urgent requirement which he sought to do something about in his essay
'*On the true care of souls and the proper service of pastors* (1538).[4] He presented

---

[1] Kolde, *op. cit.*, 13.
[2] F. Wendel (ed.), *Opera auspiciis ordinis theologorum evangelicorum Argentinensis
edita, XV, De regno Christi,* 1955; *XVbis Du royaume de Jésus Christ* (éd. critique de la
traduction française), 1954; J. V. Pollet, *M. Bucer, Etudes sur la correspondance I,* 1958;
R. Stupperich (ed.), *Butzers Deutsche Schriften I,* 1960; C. Hope, *Martin Bucer and
the English Reformation,* 1946; J. Courvoisier, *La notion d'Eglise chez Bucer,* 1933;
H. Bornkamm, 'M. Bucers Bedeutung für die europäische Reformationsgeschichte'
SVRG 169, 1952 (*Bibliographia Buceriana*); accounts of recent research by B. Thompson, *ChH* 25, 1956, 63 ff.
[3] *Franz, Wiedertäufer,* 213 ff. and 238.   [4] *SVRG* 169, 1952 (Bibl. Buceriana, No. 59).

it at the Synod of Hesse[1] which met at the end of the year in Ziegenhain. Here he managed to achieve what he had sought in vain to achieve in Strasbourg, namely congregational participation in the running of the church's affairs through the agency of elected elders, who together with the minister would be responsible for discipline, including excommunication. Also instituted were confirmation and, in connection with confirmation, a programme of school instruction.[2] This *Ziegenhain Ordinance*[3] was later recommended by Luther for the duchy of Saxony.[4] Bucer's subsequent attempt in Strasbourg to gather together small groups within the church met with opposition from the council and failed.[5] But his ideas became normative for Calvin and the 'four offices' of the Geneva church order, and they thus attained world-wide significance.[6] In spite of the Concord over the Lord's Supper, Bucer never became a 'Lutheran', because he could not depart from the earlier 'spiritualist' bias in his theology.[7] He continued to think of the divine Spirit as 'a universal power whose operations extend far beyond the historical limits of Christianity'. 'Above all, he did not make the sharp contrast between Law and Gospel which for Luther was the key to understanding the Bible in its entirety.'[8] This accounts for the attitude which Bucer adopted in the efforts towards unity, and it made him the champion of Erasmus' idea of a twofold justification. It is in this latter capacity that we shall come across him again.

In one of his table conversations (WATR 3, 3426) Luther said that after his death there would be three theologians left, namely Bugenhagen, Brenz and Cordatus. We have already mentioned the last, and it is quite true that Bugenhagen and Brenz were the most loyal champions of Luther's cause.

Johannes Bugenhagen (1485–1558),[9] who had been won over to Luther's theology by Luther's *Babylonian Captivity of the Church*, came to Wittenberg in 1521, was appointed as a clergyman there in 1523 and in 1532 became '*Ober-Superattendent*'. He became a doctor of theology in

[1] The participants are listed at the end of the Order.
[2] W. Diehl, 'M. Butzers Bedeutung für das kirchliche Leben in Hessen', SVRG 83, 1904, 39 ff.
[3] A. Uckeley, *Die Kirchenordnungen von Ziegenhain und Kassel 1539*, 1939; SVRG 169, 1952 (Bibl. Buceriana, No. 60).
[4] WAB 10, 284.
[5] G. Anrich, 'Ein Bedacht Butzers', ARG suppl. vol. V, 1929, 46 ff.; W. Bellardi, 'Die Geschichte der "Christlichen Gemeinschaft" in Strassburg 1546–50' QFRG 18, 1934.
[6] G. Anrich, 'Strassburg und die calvinistische Kirchenverfassung', *Tübinger Rektoratsrede* 1928.
[7] H. Strohl, 'Bucer interprète de Luther', RHPhR 19, 1939, 223 ff.
[8] H. Bornkamm, *op. cit.*, 28.
[9] Bibliography by G. Geisenhof, 1908; correspondence ed. O. Vogt, 1888; see Schl 1948–2048, 45201–45236; also E. Wolf, *Peregrinatio* 1954, 257 ff.

1533 and a member of the faculty in 1535. His work in Wittenberg suffered constant interruptions, for he was regularly asked to assist in the establishment of the Reformation in other places (from November 1534 until the summer of 1535 he was in Pomerania, and from July 1537 until April 1539 in Denmark). Luther took over his preaching duties while he was away. The two men were close friends and colleagues. It was Bugenhagen who officiated at Luther's marriage; he was also Luther's confessor, he assisted him in the preparation of the Catechisms, the revision of Bible translations, and he translated Luther's Bible into Low German. At the end, he gave Luther's funeral oration. After Luther's death, Bugenhagen lost favour with strict Lutherans on account of his attitude towards the Interim.[1] His academic activity showed him as a grateful pupil of Luther's, and his writings reveal a 'teaching bishop' who could present things in a simple and popular manner. But his particular gift lay in church organisation and leadership. Luther often sought his advice on practical matters, and many of Luther's judgements carry Bugenhagen's signature, too. His particular field was that of church order—school ordinances, and ordinances concerned with worship and finance. For all his efforts to achieve an ordered ceremonial and methods of procedure, he nevertheless succeeded in preserving Lutheran freedom, and allowed himself to be guided entirely by the needs of the particular congregation. His concern was to make it possible, within a Lutheran framework, for the congregation to play its part responsibly, and it is no doubt this feature which prompted E. Wolf[2] to see in his work the basic features of a presbyterian church order.

Johannes Brenz from Weilderstadt (1499–1570),[3] who carried through the Reformation at Schwäbisch-Hall, was very like Bugenhagen in both manner and achievement. He might almost be called the Lutheran counterpart of Bucer in South Germany. 'We owe it to Brenz that a Lutheran church exists in South Germany, for it was he who helped the Lutheran pattern to achieve its successes throughout South Germany'.[4] He had witnessed Luther's Heidelberg Disputation in 1518, and in 1522 went as parish minister to Schwäbisch-Hall, where he proceeded resolutely to lead both the town and the surrounding area towards Lutheranism (cf. the first Church Ordinance of 1526).[5] As leader of the 'literalists'

---

[1] O. Vogt, 'Melanchthons und Bugenhagens Stellung zum Interim und die Rechtfertigung des letzteren in seinem Jonaskommentar, *JpTh* 13, 1887, 1 ff.

[2] E. Wolf, *op. cit.*, 276.

[3] *Opera* in 8 folio-vols., Tübingen 1576–1590. The bibliography by W. Köhler, 1904, includes some of these as Nos. 541–544, 546, 551, 554, 558, 568, 571. See E. Bizer, 'Analecta Brentiana', *BWKG* 1957–1958 (Sonderdruck); see also n. 14 above.

[4] G. Bossert, *AELKZ* 1899, 781.

[5] Richter, *Kirchenordnungen* I, 40 ff.

(*Syngrammatisten*) in the controversy over the Lord's Supper he took sides with Luther against his former teacher, Oecolampad. It is to him that credit is due for the Nuremberg and Brandenburg-Ansbach Church Ordinance of 1533. At first he took no part in the Reformation of the duchy of Württemberg, but his little Catechism of 1535 was included in duke Ulrich's Church Ordinance and was subsequently widely used. In the autumn of 1536, on Melanchthon's recommendation, he was asked to go to Tübingen to assist in the reform of the univeristy, and from April 1537 he worked there with great success for a year. When he got back to Schwäbish-Hall he withdrew his opposition to the town's entry into the League of Schmalkalden, so that the town was able to join the League in 1538, and in 1543 it received a new Church Ordinance.[1] From 1535 onwards he published a whole series of books containing commentaries on the Old and New Testaments in the form of homilies, which Luther reproached for being too wordy.[2] The most valuable, theologically, is the commentary on Exodus, which is the result of his lectures at Tübingen in 1538.[3] Brenz attained his greatest stature in the period following the Interim, when he led the opposition in South Germany. In exile in Basle he produced his commentary on Isaiah.[4] After that, he became the confidant of duke Christoph and provost of Stuttgart (on January 1553) and a leading figure in the Württemberg church. His *Confessio Virtembergica* and the 'Great' Church Ordinance of 1559 made a mark upon that Church which was to prove enduring. He made his voice heard in the controversy with Osiander, combated the reformed doctrine of the Lord's Supper, but wrote the doctrine of 'ubiquity' into the confession of the Württemberg church and thus stands on the boundary between the Reformation and orthodoxy.

[1] *Ibid.*, II, 14 ff.; Köhler, *Bibl.* No. 102 f. Note the link between the Lord's Supper and preaching, a link which was not preserved in Württemberg.
[2] *WATR* 4, 4025.
[3] Köhler, *Bibl.* No. 102 f.
[4] *Ibid.*, No. 175.

CHAPTER II

CLARIFICATION AND DEMARCATION

I. THE CONTROVERSY WITH THE ANABAPTISTS IN STRASBOURG

THE Anabaptists,[1] as a result of an order of the Emperor on 4 January 1528 and of the Imperial Diets of 1529 and 1530, were banned everywhere and were consequently persecuted and threatened with the death sentence. But in spite of countless executions it was not possible to suppress them completely. In South Germany Strasbourg, despite an order of the council on 27 July 1527, remained a place of refuge for some time. Capito, Matthew Zell and his wife Catherine had certain theological sympathies with Anabaptist 'spititualism'; Bucer respected their piety and condemned only their sectarian particularism.[2] Pilgram Marbeck,[3] who in May 1525 had fled from Tirol and had come by way of Augsburg to Strasbourg, held meetings in his house in the Steintal and according to Bucer was revered by his followers 'like a god'. But when he started to perform baptisms he was imprisoned in 1531, brought before the council several times, and in 1532 was banished on account of his activities and his teaching.[4] His mantle was assumed by Leopold Scharnschlager, who did not baptise but in 1534 also had to leave the city.[5] In Tirol the year 1533 marked the climax of the persecution; but in Mähren, thanks to a large-scale secession from the Austerlitz church and to the organisational talents of Jakob Huter of Tirol (who was burnt at the stake in Innsbrück on 25 February 1536), a 'communist' fellowship was set up, known as the

[1] J. Loserth, *AÖG* 78, 1892, 427 ff., and 79, 1893, 127 ff., and 81, 1895, 135 ff.; W. Köhler, *ARG* 37, 1940, 93 ff.; 38, 1941, 349 ff.; 40, 1943, 246 ff.; 41, 1948, 164 ff.; also E. Teufel, *ThR* (new series) 13, 1941, 21 ff., 103 ff., 183 ff.; 14, 1942, 27 ff., 124 ff.; 15, 1943, 56 ff.; 17, 1948–1949, 161 ff.; 20, 1952, 361 ff. On Strasbourg see M. Krebs and H. G. Rott, *QFRG* 7/8, Elsass I/II, 1950–1960.
[2] *Krebs-Rott I*, No. 266.
[3] J. J. Kiwiet, *Pilgram Marbeck (1495–1556), sein Kreis und seine Theologie*, 1957.
[4] *Krebs-Rott I*, No. 277 ff. and 302.
[5] *Krebs-Rott II*, No. 576.

Huterite Brotherhood, which became a regular place of refuge for those who had suffered persecution in Germany.[1] In almost every Evangelical region Anabaptists were to be found, either individually or in groups.

On the face of it one cannot properly speak of an Anabaptist theology. The many controversies which raged among them rarely had to do with actual theological issues, but rather with practical problems of Church order or of the relationship of the Church to the world. What they had in common was a spiritualism which rejected all appeals to the external word or sacrament and therefore also rejected a national church which made its appeal to such things. Their concern was to seek personal gifts of the Spirit, sanctification and separation from the world. They recognised baptism and the Lord's Supper as necessary signs, but their necessity is something which only the man of faith understands. They rejected the idea that the civil authority has any part to play in the external organisation of the Church, and they refused to take any oath. But the fact that the Anabaptists acknowledged the fellowship of the Church and also acknowledged 'signs' (i.e. baptism and Lord's Supper) served to distinguish them from more radical spiritualists like Denck, Bünderlin (a pupil of Denck from Linz who also appeared on the scene in Strasbourg), Franck or Schwenkfeld. These latter, after attempting some kind of harmony with the Anabaptists—with varying degrees of enthusiasm—eventually parted company with them.[2]

Melchior Hoffmann is a figure of decisive significance in Anabaptist history, and he, too, had links with Strasbourg.[3] Born in Schwäbisch-Hall at an unknown date, this self-educated furrier appeared in Livonia in 1523 as a lay preacher. In June of the same year, at the request of the town council of Dorpat, he was sent to Luther in Wittenberg in order to get a report on his ability as a preacher. As it happened he got a favourable one, but nevertheless by the autumn he had been told to leave Dorpat. He then turned up in Reval, in Stockholm (only to be sent away again in 1527) and in Lübeck. From Holstein he made a second journey into Saxony, but this time he was turned away from Magdeburg by Amsdorf and from Wittenberg by Luther. But Frederick I of Denmark gave him a preaching post in Kiel, where he got involved in a literary feud with Amsdorf and one of his Kiel students. This was due to be settled at a disputation in Flensburg on 8 April 1529. Bugenhagen was called in and got him convicted of being a disparager of the sacraments and had him dismissed on that account. Hoffmann and Karlstadt then went together

[1] L. Müller, 'Der Komminismus der mährischen Wiedertäufer', *SVRG* 142, 1927; H. Fischer, *Jakob Huter*, 1957; R. Wolkan, *Geschichtsbuch der Hutterischen* Brüder, 1923.

[2] *CS* 8, 168 ff.

[3] *Krebs-Rott II* passim; P. Kawerau, *Melchior Hoffmann als religiöser Denker*, 1954.

to East Friesland. From there he paid several visits to Strasbourg, in the intervals pursuing his activities in East Friesland and in Holland. From 1530 onwards he administered believers' baptism. He had learned from a prophecy that he would be imprisoned in Strasbourg for six months and thereafter, at the head of his faithful followers, he would lead them to witness the triumph of (believers') baptism. So in 1533 he went up the Rhine once more, got himself imprisoned in Strasbourg, and remained in prison until his death (1543 or even later). At first he was allowed to issue directives to his followers from the tower, and he was able to continue writing.[1]

Fundamental to Hoffmann's theological thinking[2] is his 'figurative' understanding of Scripture. He speaks of Scripture just like any of the reformers, but for him the 'word' is merely a sign or 'figure' of the inner meaning which step by step leads men into the Spirit. God's converse with men is always by means of 'figures', and it is by means of 'figures' that God wills to be recognised, but he can be recognised only by those who already have the Spirit. All Hoffmann's peculiarities are directly related to his 'Spirit' theology. What is most striking, in a man of his period, is his christology: the eternal Word of God remains utterly and completely heavenly, even after the Incarnation, 'without any admixture of earthly, created stuff'. This incarnate Word is not 'half earthly and half heavenly', but is Spirit which has become, or changed into, flesh, and has taken nothing from Mary. This notion has close affinities to his notion of redemption, which Hoffmann imagines as a ransom paid to the devil for fallen flesh. This ransom cannot be paid with human flesh, for human flesh belongs to the devil anyhow. As Adam was called to obedience, so humanity is called to obedience by the Spirit who leads men through the stages of 'un-becoming' to the 'second bliss'. That is why the man who has the Spirit is under obligation to chastise the rebellious and to suppress them. The highest stage of perfection is represented by a figure called the 'Apostolic Teacher', who is at once a religious and political leader 'who rules over the faithful and destroys the unbelievers'. Christ himself is present in him, he administers baptism and through him God creates for himself the universal church of the Spirit. Among his special gifts are the interpretation of the signs of the times and the gift of prophecy (which Hoffmann also recognised in others). Prophecy is essential, because it serves to warn and to prepare the faithful. Hoffmann was certain that he was living in the last days, and he listed the signs which assured him of this. He claimed that the 'two witnesses' mentioned in Rev. 11.3 were active in his day, for he considered himself to be Elijah and another prophet (presumably in Strasbourg) to be Enoch. He did not claim to have knowledge of every detail in the programme of the last things, but he was quite clear that the revelation at the last day would be

[1] *Krebs-Rott* II No. 390 and 395; P. Kawerau, 'Zwei unbekannte Wiedertäuferdrucke', *ZKG* 69, 1958, 121 ff.; E. W. Kohls, *ThZ* 17, 1961, 356 ff.
[2] This paragraph follows P. Kawerau.

H

given at a particular place, and that place, for Hoffmann, was Strasbourg. He was also convinced that the Spirit would employ human hands to wreak bloody revenge upon his adversaries and to plunge the entire clergy, the Pope, and all Lutherans and Zwinglians into ruin. Nevertheless Hoffmann gave an assurance in Strasbourg that he himself had no intention of taking up the sword; and although he was by no means averse to apocalyptic number-games, it seems that he never actually fixed a date for the End. The link between Hoffmann and the Anabaptists appears to be an indirect one, and the 'spiritualism' of his doctrine of the Lord's Supper is the result of his figurative interpretation of Scripture.

From 1530 onwards the clergy of Strasbourg sought to tackle the confusion which reigned in the city by demanding a public discussion with the Anabaptists and the dissidents,[1] for quite apart from those whom we have already mentioned, the town was sheltering Karlstadt, Servet, Schwenkfeld, Sebastian Franck, and in Ruprechtsau Clemens Ziegler was writing about 'The salvation of all men's souls'. In November 1532 the town clergy proposed to the council that a 'synod' be held, at which everyone could state his objections to their teaching, for they were quite certain that the Word of God would triumph. They suggested as themes for discussion the teaching, the ecclesiastical practices and the life of the clergy; and as a basis for discussion a committee drew up sixteen articles of faith, the last three of which dealt with the right and duty of the civil authority to take part in church affairs. The preliminary synod for the town clergy lasted from 3–6 June 1533, and the main synod was held on 10–14 June. Some of the clergy had difficulties over the doctrine of the sacraments, but the question which caused most difficulty was the question of the civil authority's rights over the church. This was contested particularly by Engelbrecht, who regarded it as papacy in a new guise. Bucer, however, laid great stress on the duty of the civil authority to further the kingdom of God and therefore also to promote right preaching. At the main synod Ziegler, Hoffmann, Schwenckfeld and two others were 'given a hearing'. Schwenckfeld was treated with great courtesy, but nothing could conceal the contrast between his views and those of the town clergy—a contrast which subsequent literary exchanges made manifest. Discussions were not resumed until 23 and 29 October, when a draft of a Church ordinance was discussed, and when the same two points occasioned difficulties for some of the clergy. In the end, on 28 January 1534, the clergy asked the council to bring the whole matter to a conclusion. On 4 March it was decided that they should rest content with the *Tetrapolitana* and the sixteen articles drawn up for the synod. A standing

[1] *Krebs-Rott II* (Strasbourg Synod); F. Wendel, *L'Eglise de Strasbourg, sa constitution et son organisation 1532–1535*, 1942.

committee of the council was appointed to deal with Anabaptist affairs. It was not until June that the decision was reached to adopt the town clergy's viewpoint and not to tolerate any longer those sects which refused to adopt the recognised Confession. Then followed a reordering of the whole church (including, for example, a provision that children be baptised within six weeks of their birth, and that a standing committee of the city council be appointed to hear complaints and grievances). But the new Church Ordinance[1] was not published until November 1534, and only on 7 February 1535 were the guilds informed of the council's 'report' on sects, compulsory baptism, attendance at sermons, etc. Engelbrecht,[2] formerly suffragan bishop of Speyer, was dismissed, and Schwenckfeld, when he appeared again in the city, was sent away.[3] Thus the idea of the confessional and national church won the day in the great controversy with the fanatics.

The opposition to Schwenckfeld,[4] who previously had been a guest in Capito's house, flared up because he refused to recognise the Strasbourg church as a church of Christ or its preaching as right preaching—even though he did not specify any points on which he differed from its doctrine.[5] The clergy were well aware that on the major points of doctrine they were one with him—and incidentally showed at the same time how far they were from Luther;[6] but Schwenckfeld's spiritualism prevented him from acknowledging God's Word or a genuine call in any place where he could find no evidence of its bearing fruit. The Strasbourg clergy realised that Schwenckfeld's position could only lead to separatism, the establishment of conventicles and to contempt of their office—all of which amounted to the destruction of their church—and so they told him that they could not blame the authorities if they would not allow his preaching or writing. From the time of the Tübingen discussions onwards[7] Schwenckfeld frequently aired his peculiar christology. First he disputed that the transfigured body of Christ belonged to the order of created things, and from 1538 onwards he asserted the divinity of the earthly body of Christ, thus calling forth opposition from the orthodox.[8] He found refuge first of all in Ulm, but was driven out by Frecht in 1539,[9] and subsequently lived in various castles in Swabia. He died in Ulm in 1561.

---

[1] Richter, *Kirchenordnungen I*, 231 ff.; *Krebs-Rott II*, No. 620.
[2] *Krebs-Rott I*, p. 51 n. 1.   [3] *Ibid.*, No. 584–588.
[4] *CS* (see p. 100 n. 2); S. G. Schultz, *Caspar Schwenckfeld von Ossig*, Norristown 1946.
[5] *Krebs-Rott II*, No. 418, 435a, 436, 444.
[6] P. G. Eberlain, 'Schwenckfelds Urteil über die Augsburger Konfession', *Jahrbuch für schlesische Kirche und Kirchengeschichte* (new series) 34, 1955, 58 ff.
[7] See p. 111 n. 1.
[8] *CS* 7, 454, 484–884; also *CS* 7, 281–361.   [9] *CS* 6, 398 ff.

2. 'THE COUNCIL QUESTION'

Emperor Charles left the Empire again in October 1532 in order to return to Spain by way of Italy. Preoccupation with his other territories were to keep him away from Germany again virtually for another decade. This was the period of overseas discovery (Pizarro conquered Peru between 1532 and 1535), of campaigns against the Turks in the Mediterranean area (e.g. Tunis, 1535) and against their French allies. In 1536 war with the French flared up again in Provence and on the northern frontier. In June 1538 the Emperor met the Pope and king Francis at Nice for a peace conference, but this resulted merely in an uncertain armistice for a period of about ten years. In the winter of 1539/40 Charles went through France to the Netherlands in order to put down a rebellion in Ghent, and this brought him within reach of German affairs. He did not appear again in the Empire until 1541, when religious conversations took place at Regensburg.[1]

When Charles left Germany in 1532, his major preoccupation was with the 'question of a Council, which he regarded as of critical importance to Germany, but which could only be achieved if there were peace in Italy, if the Pope would put the interests of the Church before his own dynastic interests, and if France would observe the treaties to which it had pledged itself. But all these things were extremely doubtful.'[2] At the end of that year he met the Pope at Bologna and seemed to have achieved his goal.[3] Letters from the Pope and the Emperor to the estates of the Empire gave the impression that a Council was imminent.[4] No one in Germany could have guessed that the Pope was playing politics, that he would immediately give up the idea of calling a Council, that the show at discussions was 'nothing more than a façade'.[5] After a secret agreement of 24 February 1533[6] the bishop of Reggio, Rangoni, came as papal nuncio to Germany, and he was accompanied by one of the Emperor's officials whose job it was to keep a watch on him.[7] Rangoni brought with him the Pope's conditions for a Council,[8] and the princes had to decide whether they were acceptable. The elector of Saxony received the legations in Weimar on 3 and 4 June, but was extremely hesitant about accepting the conditions, because Saxony ought not to make a decision without first consulting its allies.[9] From the doctrinal point of view the most suspicious parts of the Pope's

---

[1] Further details in *Brandi*.   [2] *Brandi*, 282.   [3] *Jedin I*, 225.
[4] *CT* IV, LXXXIV; J. le Plat, *Monumentorum ad Historiam Concilii Tridentini II*, 1782, 513 f.; Lünig, *Reichsarchiv* II, 606 f.; *Ursachen* I, 13 f.
[5] *Jedin I*, 226.
[6] Ed. S. Ehses, *RQ* 5, 1891, 299–307.
[7] K. Lanz, *Staatspapiere zur Geschichte des Kaisers Karl V*, etc., 1845, 101 f.
[8] *CT* IV, LXXXVII f.; cf. also *Ursachen* I, 15 (appendix).
[9] *CT* IV, XCII f.; *Ursachen* I, 15.

message were his declarations that the Council was to be held in 'free-dom' according to the established custom of the Church, that the partici-pants should submit to its decisions in advance, and that in the event of any disobedience the *senior pars* would be under obligation to assist the Pope.[1] Consultations were held in Wittenberg on the matter. The considered judgements of the Wittenbergers[2] reveal immediately that they had a totally different view of the Council, for 'freedom' can only mean being free to decide any issue in the light of God's Word. All the same, Luther recommended that the articles should be accepted, though the first—dealing with the Council's 'freedom'—should be accepted only under protest. He argued that by acting in this way the Evangelicals could not then be accused of sabotaging the Council if it failed to come to pass. The papal articles were also discussed in other places. The judge-ments of Osiander, Urban Rhegius[3] and Bucer[4] have been preserved. The Evangelicals gave their answer to the legation at a meeting of the Schmalkaldians on 30 June. In it they stated that the proposed Council was not what the Protestants had asked for, and they appealed to the Emperor to fulfil the obligations of his office by making every effort to get a genuine Council convened. However, the legation was not refused. The Evangelicals' answer was sent by special messenger to the imperial legate and reached him at Flonheim in Hesse on 22 July.[5] The minutes of the discussion were published with prefaces by Melanchthon and Luther.[6] On this occasion the Council came to grief, not because of opposition on the part of the Protestants, but because the Pope declared that he must have the agreement of the French king, and this was not forthcoming. Between 11 October and 12 November 1533 the Pope and Francis I met in Marseilles, and afterwards the Pope declared that the whole question of a Council 'has been finally abandoned for the rest of this pontificate'.[7] Pope Clement died on 25 September 1534,[8] having buried Hadrian VI's programme of reform. Like his uncle Leo X he was more a politician than a pope and invariably placed the interests of the house of Medici above the interests of the Church.[9]

Under Alessandro Farnese, who on 13 October 1534 became Pope

---

[1] *CT* IV for the 8 articles.
[2] *CR* 2, No. 654 ff.; *WAB* 6, 480 ff.
[3] Quoted *WAB* 6, 483 n. 8.
[4] Bibl. Buceriana, *SVRG* 169, 1952, No. 41.
[5] *CT* IV, XCVII; J. G. Walch, *Lutherausgabe*, 1740 ff., 16, 2281–2289; *Ursachen* I, 16.
[6] *CR* 2, No. 667–670; *WAB* 6, 489.
[7] *Jedin* I, 228.
[8] *V. Pastor* IV/2, 542.
[9] Ranke (I, 82) describes him as the most sinister of all Popes; cf. *v. Pastor* IV/2, 544; *Jedin* I, 228.

Paul III,[1] the policies of the Curia changed, for he genuinely had the Council and reform at heart. In February 1535 papal legates once more went into all the countries of Europe, this time with the task of informing them of the Pope's definite intention to call a Council, and offering as a possible venue either Mantua or Turin, or Piacenza or Bologna. It was Peter Paul Vergerio who was sent to Germany. He had been papal nuncio at the court of Ferdinand, and was himself convinced that a Council was necessary. He was received as the bearer of good tidings, and was profoundly aware of the extent to which the Church had fallen into decline.[2] Politically, his efforts were not as successful as he had hoped, for neither Charles nor Ferdinand would agree to Mantua as a venue.[3] On 6 November 1535 he arrived in Wittenberg and invited Luther to meet him at the castle.[4] At this celebrated discussion Luther did not conceal his opinion, but he promised that he personally would come to the Council 'even if I knew that you would burn me at the stake'. Vergerio met the elector of Saxony in Prague on the journey back from Vienna and eventually, after much resistance, managed to get an audience with him, at which he emphasised strongly that his mission was different from Rangoni's. He mentioned Mantua as a possible venue for the Council, but he did not get the agreement he had hoped for.[5] Once again the elector stated that he wished to consult his confederates. He reported to the Schmalkaldian Diet in December, but since the representatives there had no instructions, the answer drawn up by Melanchthon represented only the opinion of the princes who were present, namely Saxony, Lüneburg and Hesse.[6] Again the main question for the Evangelicals was the question about the 'freedom' which would be allowed at the Council, and they renewed their request for 'a general and devout and free Council'. Their document attempted to make clear the Protestant point of view, but it did not commit them to attend, even if their wishes were granted. After the answer had been drawn up and approved, an envoy from England made a long speech against the Pope and against the Council. In the articles drawn up in preparation for an alliance with England it is expressly stated that if the Pope were to summon a Council without the agreement of the Protestants, they would refuse to participate.[7] But since

[1] V. Pastor V and Jedin I, 545 n. 3; W. Friedensburg, Kaiser Karl V und Papst Paul III, 1932; F. X. Seppelt, Geschichte des Papsttums, V, 1959².
[2] NBD I, 1; Jedin I, 234 ff.; F. Roth, Augsburger Reformationsgeschichte II, 246.
[3] Jedin I, 238 f.
[4] WATR 5, 6384 and 6388; NBD I, 1, 539 ff.; CT IV, CXVIII n. 8; v. Pastor V, 50 (n.).
[5] CR 2, 991 ff.; Ursachen I, 19.
[6] CT IV, CXVI–CXIX; CR 2, 1018 ff.; Ursachen I, 20.
[7] F. Prüser, England und die Schmalkaldener 1535/40, 1929.

this alliance was never concluded,[1] these articles have no practical significance. Vergerio got the reply on 7 February while he was on his way to meet the Emperor in Naples, and immediately he began discussions with officials of the Emperor. It is not known whether anything came of these. Again the real difficulties were caused, not by the attitude of the Evangelicals, but by the tortuous paths of French and English diplomacy.[2] An episode which is characteristic of the policies of Francis I at the time is that he tried to get Bucer and Melanchthon to go to Paris, in order to achieve unity by discussions among theologians without the necessity of calling a Council.[3] Melanchthon did in fact draw up a statement on this,[4] but the elector refused him leave, and so the extraordinary plan was never carried out. At the beginning of 1536 Francis I brought war again by attacking Savoy. On 17 April, Easter Monday, the Emperor made a great speech in Rome, urging the Pope to remain neutral and to continue his efforts for a Council,[5] On 8 April the congregation of cardinals decided to convene a Council,[6] and on 2 June 1536 was published the papal bull *Ad domini gregis curam*.[7] This bull brought Protestants to the point of decision.

[1] The Protestants made a condition that agreement should be established in matters of doctrine. This gave rise to the discussions at Wittenberg, out of which came the Wittenberg Articles.

[2] *Jedin I*, 242 ff.

[3] Imbart de la Tour, *Les origines de la Réforme*, 3 vols., 1905–1914, III, 497 ff.

[4] *CR* 2, 741 ff.; cf. 1009 ff.

[5] Text in P. Rassow, *Die Kaiseridee Karls V.*, 1932, 421 ff. Lit. in Brandi, *Quellen* 258 ff.; *Ursachen* I, 21.

[6] *CT* IV, 1 f.

[7] *CT* IV, 2 ff.; *Ursachen* I, 22 (the original has been lost).

CHAPTER III

THE REFORMATION ACHIEVES STABILITY

I. THE CONTINUED EXTENSION OF THE REFORMATION
AND ITS CONQUEST OF WÜRTTEMBERG

THE Nuremberg Standstill, as its Catholic opponents had feared, at first brought the Evangelicals further gains. Augsburg, where the town clergy had been Zwinglian since the summer of 1531, decided in 1533 to adopt the Reformation and took the first steps towards implementing it.[1] In Ulm and in Strasbourg[2] the Church was reordered on permanent lines. After bitter struggles the town of Hannover decided in 1533 to adopt the Reformation.[3] In 1534 Anhalt-Dessau,[4] Pomerania,[5] and the Silesian territories of Liegnitz and Brieg[6] went Lutheran; and Bremen passed a Church ordinance which gave to the city council the ecclesiastical rights which had belonged to the archbishop.[7] The most important gain, however, was the duchy of Württemberg, where the Reformation was established in 1534.

[1] F. Roth, *Augsburger Reformationsgeschichte II*, 100 ff. The council made its decision on 22 July 1534. See Roth II, 175 ff.; and P. Fuchs, 'Bayern and Habsburg 1534–1536', *ARG* 41, 1948, 1 ff.

[2] See II. 1.

[3] G. Uhlhorn, *Hannoversche Kirchengeschichte*, 1902; J. Meyer, *Kirchengeschichte Niedersachsens*, 1939, 69 ff.

[4] *Schl* 28984–29004; *RE³* VI, 521.

[5] K. Graebert, 'Der Landtag zu Treptow 13 Dec. 1534', *Diss. Berlin* 1900; M. Wehrmann, 'Die Pommersche Kirchenordnung von 1535', *Baltische Studien* (old series) 43, 1893, 128 ff.; H. Heyden, 'Protokolle der Pommerschen Kirchenvisitation 1535–1539', *Veröffentlichung der Hist. Kommission für Pommern*, IV, 1, 1961.

[6] *Schl* 26705 ff.; P. Conrad, *Die Einführung der Reformation in Breslau und Schlesien*, 1917; K. Engelbert, 'Die Anfänge der luth. Bewegung in Breslau und Schlesien', *Archiv für schlesische Kirchengeschichte* 18, 1960, 121 ff.; 19, 1961, 165 ff.; 20, 1962, 291 ff. (being continued); G. Kretschmar, *Die Reformation in Breslau. I: Ausgewählte Texte*, 1961.

[7] J. F. Iken, 'Die Bremer Kirchenordnung von 1534', *Bremer Jahrbücher*, 2nd series, II, 1891.

Since duke Ulrich had been deposed, Württemberg[1] had been administered by Austria, and in 1530 the Imperial Diet of Augsburg had ceded it to the archduke Ferdinand. It had thus been added to the possessions of the house of Habsburg. Meanwhile duke Ulrich was living at Mömpelgard, one of his estates, and there he came into contact with the Swiss and was won over to the Reformation. He later went to the court of his 'cousin', Philip of Hesse. Even though Ulrich was himself capable of uncontrolled violence, the fact remained that his expulsion was an act of violence. He had been deprived of his duchy in breach of imperial law, and this was a violation of German liberty which had particularly embittered his Bavarian relatives.

Thus Bavaria and Hesse were both involved, and they were promised assistance from the king of France. The Swabian League, which was responsible for banishing Ulrich, had lost its effectiveness because it was torn by religious differences, and Philip made sure that it continued so. It soon transpired, however, that in this matter as in so many others Bavarian policy was unreliable, and so Hesse took the initiative alone. In January 1534 Philip met king Francis at Bar le Duc and obtained promises of the necessary financial assistance. It is not certain whether the Pope was informed of the project. Francis hoped that this affair would unleash a general war against the Habsburgs, but Philip left him in no doubt that he was solely interested in reinstating duke Ulrich. Warnings which reached the Habsburgs were treated by them with amazing indifference, so that the military aspect of the project was settled quickly and decisively.[2] Philip's troops gathered at Wimpfen, invaded Württemberg, and on 12 May 1534 defeated the Austrian army at Lauffen without difficulty. After this, the territory reverted to its prince almost of its own accord. But the political situation after this victory was even more complicated than before. John, elector of Saxony, had withheld his support, for he disapproved of the whole undertaking and regarded it as a breach of the peace, a contravention of the terms of the Schmalkaldic League which permitted only a defensive alliance, and also as rebellion against the Emperor. The Bavarians still offered no assistance. It had proved simpler to conquer the territory than to hold the field, should Austria decide to counter with all the forces at its disposal. All the same, it was John of Saxony who finally assumed the role of mediator, for he was already engaged in discussions with Ferdinand anyhow. Much against Ulrich's will, Philip accepted a peace proposal which reinstated duke

---

[1] J. Wille, *Philipp der Grossmütige und die Restitution Ulrichs von Wirtemberg 1526–1535*, 1882, and 'Die Übergabe des Herzogtums von Wirtemberg an Kar V.', *Forschungen zur deutschen Geschichte* 21, 1881, 430 ff.; Fuchs (see n. 1), 1 ff., 17 ff.

[2] *Ursachen* III, 9 f. and 10 f.

Ulrich but made the territory an under-fief of Austria. This made for no little confusion, because the legal significance of such tenure was by no means clear. But however that may be, the Peace of Kadan on 17 June 1534[1] conceded to duke Ulrich the right to reform the Church in his territory, provided that Zwinglianism was excluded. The two princes would be pardoned for lese-majesty on prostrating themselves.

The Reformation of the territory began forthwith.[2] The main problem was again the doctrine of the Lord's Supper.[3] We do not know what duke Ulrich's views on this were. He had to make sure that his territory did not get out of step with the South German cities which were Zwinglian, though at the same time Zwinglianism was forbidden in his own territory as a result of the Peace of Kadan and his commitment to Hesse and Saxony. Only five days after the victory at Lauffen the Strasbourg leaders proposed a religious conference and suggested as reformers Ambrosius Blaurer of Constance and Simon Grynäus of Basle who, it was suggested, would reform the university. But Philip of Hesse presented his chaplain, Erhard Schnepf,[4] a Lutheran. Ambrosius Blaurer was summoned, and it was Bucer who gave him his instructions. They collided at their first encounter, because Schnepf presented Lutheran doctrine at its most uncompromising. Blaurer, whose outlook was similar to Bucer's, referring to Luther in support of his case, proposed the formula which had been proposed by the Lutherans at Marburg as a means of securing unity, but which Zwingli had rejected. Both agreed to adopt this formula, though Blaurer did not wish this to be taken as a change of view on his own part. Melanchthon and Osiander were glad to agree to the formula; but in Switzerland the facts of the case came to be known, and Blaurer and Bucer were hard put to it to justify themselves. In the end, Jakob Sturm persuaded the duke that the clergy of Württemberg should be bound, not by this Confession—for the words used in the formula of concord were not Scriptural—but by the Augsburg Confession. Further, for the purposes of reformation, the territory was divided into two regions. But relations between the two reformers remained strained, because Blaurer was naturally enough on good terms with the Zwinglians. The duke took over a large amount of ecclesiastical possessions and treated them as public revenue. Grynäus was supposed to have reformed the university of Tübingen, but neither he nor his successor, Paul Phrygio,

[1] *Ursachen* III, 13.
[2] J. Rauscher, *Württembergische Reformationsgeschichte*, 1934; H. Hermelink, *Geschichte der Evangeslische Kirche in Württemberg von der Reformation bis zur Gegenwart*, 1949.
[3] W. Köhler, 'Zwingli und Luther, Ihr Streit über das Abendmahl nach seinen politischen und religösen Beziehungen', *QFRG* VII, II, 1953, 320 ff.
[4] Bibliography (typescript) by K. H. May in the university library at Marburg.

met with any success. Only after Melanchthon had spent four weeks in Tübingen and had subsequently put the work into the hands of Johannes Brenz (from 1537 to 1538) did the university become Evangelical. The Anabaptists were a menace from the start, and within three years a good half-dozen decrees were issued against them. Kaspar Schwenckfeld[1] came from Strasbourg and got support from powerful noblemen. A religious conference with him, held in Tübingen,[2] failed to prevent his influence from spreading through the territory. In terms of its inner substance duke Ulrich's Reformation remained an unsatisfactory and fragmentary enterprise.[3]

2. THE DISTURBANCES IN MÜNSTER[4]

At roughly the same time as all this was going on in Württemberg, other events were taking place which were hardly calculated to improve the Reformation's public image, namely the catastrophic attempt to set up an Anabaptist state at Münster.

Like other city bishoprics, Münster had conducted a long and successful resistance campaign against the clerical overlord of the territory, who was by no means at one with his own cathedral chapter. At the same time the burghers of Münster were revolting against the traditional privileges of the city's aristocracy. In these explosive conditions Bernhard Rothmann came to St. Mauritz as preacher in 1529 and soon began to preach the Evangelical gospel, and did so with even greater enthusiasm after a journey in 1531 which took him to Wittenberg and to Strasbourg. At the Emperor's request, the bishop dismissed him from his post, but the merchants' guild put a house at his disposal in the city. When he was again ordered to leave he replied by submitting an Evangelical confession. Early in 1532 his adherents took over the *Lambertikirche* by force and drove out the Catholic priests. The city council gave way. By August 1532 Evangelical preachers had been appointed in all the churches of the city, and images and altars were destroyed. In November 1532 the citizens were obliged to declare on oath their allegiance to the reformed gospel,

---

[1] Köhler, *op. cit.*, II, 355; *CS* V, 1916, 152 ff., 167 ff., 249 ff.
[2] 28 May 1535. Bucer, Blaurer and Frecht took part; cf. *CS* V, 330 ff.
[3] Richter, *Kirchenordnungen I*, 265 ff.; A. L. Reyscher, *Sammlung der Württembergischen Gesetze*, 1841 ff., vol. VIII. Brenz's Preface in Pressel, *Anecdota* No. 56.
[4] The standard older work is C. A. Cornelius, *Geschichte des Münsterischen Aufruhrs I*, 1855, II, 1860, and his collection of eye-witness reports in *Geschichtsquellen des Bistums Münster II*, 1853. See also H. Kerssenbroch, *Anabaptistici furioris . . . historica narratio*, ed. H. Detmer in *Geschichtsquellen des Bistums Münster V/VI*, 1899–1900. Also F. Blanke, 'Das Reich der Wiedertäufer zu Münster—die äusseren Vorgänge', *ARG* 37, 1940. See II n. 1. A survey in R. Stupperich, 'Das Münsterische Täufertum, Ergebnisse und Probleme der neueren Forschung', *Schriften der historischen Kommission für Westfalen 2*, 1958.

and in February 1533 the bishop himself consented and leased the parish church to the citizens under contract 'until the Council'. Thus Münster became an Evangelical city. But Luther and Melanchthon, disturbed by rumours of what had happened, issued a warning both to the council and to Rothmann himself. 'The devil is a rogue and is quite capable of leading even fine, devout and learned preachers astray.' They saw clearly in Rothmann's activities the danger of fanaticism; they detected the spirit of rebellion and pointed to Zwingli's example as a warning.[1]

Rothmann himself is an enigmatic figure. His rapid development is virtually incomprehensible. It appears that Schwenckfeld made a deep impression on him in Strasbourg and confirmed the spiritualist tendencies in him. From the summer of 1532 onwards the so-called 'Wassenberg Preachers' appeared alongside him. Until then they had lived under the protection of the Droste, the local lieutenant of the duke of Jülich, but under pressure from duke William they had to leave.[2] They were 'Lutherans' who had not yet actually become Anabaptists, though they were certainly 'disparagers of the sacraments'. So throughout the summer of 1533 there were controversies between the conservative elements, led by Johann von der Wyck, who was one of the city trustees, and the 'fanatical spirits'. At a disputation in August Rothmann declared his conviction that infant baptism was contrary to Scripture.[3] The guilds foiled an attempt to depose Rothmann and the preachers; those who had been banished had returned to the city before the end of the year. It was during these critical months that Anabaptists from Holland made their influence felt—an influence which was to determine the future outcome.

> The arrival of the Anabaptists from Holland is in the nature of the case difficult to explain.[4] Certainly Melchior Hoffmann had a lot to do with it.[5] After one of his colleagues had been put to death at Amsterdam in May 1532, Hoffmann prohibited all baptisms for a period of two years. But when he was imprisoned, the leader of the Anabaptists in Amsterdam, Jan Mathys, took his place and proceeded to lift the ban on baptisms and to send out 'apostles' commissioned to spread the doctrine and practice of believers' baptism. Before very long he was advocating the use of force as the means of establishing the kingdom of God.

The first two envoys of the new prophet were in Münster from 5 to 7 January 1534, and Rothmann was won over immediately. All his associ-

[1] *WAB* 6, 398.
[2] K. Rembert 'Die Wiedertäufer im Herzogtum Jülich', *Studien zur Geschichte der Reformation besonders am Niederrhein*, 1899. Another view in J. F. G. Goeters, *Rheinische Vierteljahrhefte* 24, 1959, 217 ff.
[3] Stupperich, *Münster. Täufertum*, 9; F. J. Wray, *ARG* 47, 1956, 243 ff.; Krebs-Rott II, No. 471 (Bucer's defence of infant baptism against Rothmann).
[4] A. F. Mellink, *De Wederdopers in de Noordelijke Nederlanden 1531–1544*, 1954.
[5] See II. 1.

ates were baptised and actively sought further candidates for baptism. Those who were baptised laid down their weapons—at this stage the new 'gospel' still demanded the renunciation of force. But immediately afterwards, on 13 January, two new 'apostles' arrived—Johann Bockelson of Leyden and Gert tom Kloster—who proclaimed belligerently that the city must be purged of the godless. Having got support from Knipperdolling, the leader of the city's democrats, the Anabaptists demanded full freedom for the exercise of their faith and called for a separatist church of the righteous. Their opponents began to leave the city as more Anabaptists from Holland came in, and the bishop, Francis von Waldeck, took counter-measures in terms of the imperial Edict.

Then began the breathtaking spectacle of the establishment of the new Jerusalem. In February 1534 Jan Mathys came in person to Münster and began to rule the city with his revelations. He preached that the godless should be wiped out—though in the event people were content merely to expel them (on 27 February). Next, absolute community of possessions was introduced, and the Bible was declared to be the city's law-book. Rothmann declared that the five books of Moses are 'the very sum of all divine wisdom'.[1] The Amsterdam congregation provided assistance. When the latter had tried to take control of their city they were put down with much shedding of blood.[2] When Jan Mathys met his end in an unplanned sortie on Easter Sunday, Johann of Leyden took his place and carried on the work of building the kingdom. Knipperdolling, the former burgomaster, became his 'sword-bearer' (i.e. hangman). In the middle of July polygamy was introduced, its opponents being brutally slaughtered. But it was not merely over the city that the Anabaptists purposed to rule. A prophet declared Johann to be the 'king of Israel', i.e. the apocalyptic world-ruler. To fail to take this claim seriously is to fail to understand the whole enterprise. Rothmann gave the reasons for it in a pamphlet on the *Restitutio*.[3] It found expression in the adoption of Old Testament ceremonial. In October, 27 'apostles' were sent out—most of them Wassenbergers —to present this claim to the world. They were seized by the besiegers and executed. The bishop had got the siege going in February, collecting allies with all diplomatic formality. He began with Cleves, Cologne, Hesse and Electoral Saxony, and gradually enlisted support almost from the whole Empire. Slowly the circle closed around the city; but Johann was not only an expert in defence but also a master of propaganda, and in spite of hunger he maintained his command. Eventually, early in 1535, he was obliged to let the women, the old people and the children out of the

---

[1] "Von verborgenheit der Schrift", 1534, 16. [2] Mellink, *op. cit.*, 106.
[3] A. Knaake, 'Restitution rechter und gesunder christlicher Lehre', *Neudrucke deutscher Literaturwerke des 16. u. 17. Jahrhunderts*, No. 77 f., 1888.

city. They wandered about in the no-man's-land, and the besiegers neither gave them refuge nor executed them. Even in the end the city was only taken by treachery on 25 June 1535. The king, the queen and others were taken prisoner. Rothmann seems to have been killed during the conquest. A 'disputation' was held with the prisoners, at which Johann gave a partial admission of his error. They were subsequently executed with the barbarity characteristic of the age. Münster became Catholic once more, a territorial city under the bishop.

The effects of the catastrophe were felt far beyond Münster itself. Not only had the region been lost, from the Reformation point of view, but also there was no longer any question of Anabaptists being tolerated anywhere. The theologians on both sides appeared to have been cruelly justified. Yet in spite of this the movement persisted. It was restored by Menno Simons[1] and David Joris,[2] who looked back to the tradition of the earlier Anabaptists and rejected the Münster inheritance altogether.[3] Characteristic features of Anabaptism became once more the renunciation of force and the refusal to make any oath of allegiance. From this point onwards it occupies a position on the periphery of Reformation history, and it is only in recent years that scholars have drawn attention to it again.[4] In Hesse, admittedly, things were better than in the other territories, for although the visitation ordinance of 1537 was harsher than the previous one, the aim was still to win over the Anabaptists and to convince them.[5] In October 1538 Bucer was called in to help in a disputation with them, and he recommended that they should continue to be treated with patience.[6]

The Münster uprising had an unexpected consequence in the archbishopric of Cologne.[7] In the course of discussions about giving military assistance to the bishop of Münster, Cologne and Jülich-Cleves held joint discussions in March 1534 on the principals of a Catholic reform, 'in order that the common man might the better be kept in obedience to authority and that rebellion might be avoided'. Gropper worked out a proposal for statutes of reform, and at the end of 1535 this was delivered to the councillors of the duchies. On the extent to which the proposal

[1] K. Vos, Menno Simons, 1914; C. Krahn, Menno Simons Lebenswerk, 1951².
[2] R. H. Bainton, 'David Joris', ARG supplement 6, 1937.
[3] Significant evidence of this is Pilgram Marbeck's alterations to Rothmann's 'Confession' 1542; see J. F. Wray, ARG 47, 1956, 243 ff.
[4] Franz, Wiedertäufer (see p. 87 n. 1).
[5] Details in P. Wappler, Die Stellung Kurhessens und des Landgrafen Philipps von Hessen zur Täuferbewegung, 1910. See also M. Lenz, Der Briefwechsel Landgraf Philipps mit M. Bucer I ,1880, 317 ff.
[6] Franz, Wiedertäufer, No. 72 and 73; W. Lipgens, Kardinal J. Gropper, 1951; O. Redlich, Jülich-Bergische Kirchenpolitik I, 1907, 293 f.
[7] ARC II, 42-73.

was applicable in each of the duchies there was disagreement. The provincial synod of Cologne (3–10 March 1536) approved the draft with slight emendations. Another meeting in May 1538 was to occupy itself with implementing the proposals, which were published together with Gropper's *Enchiridion*. But this attempted reform got no further, and it had no effect upon the archbishopric itself. As early as 1536 the archbishop had travelled to Brandenburg and Saxony, and when he returned he gave it as his opinion that as far as Cologne was concerned the proposed scheme was insufficient.[1] Nevertheless the Cologne statutes for reform remain 'one of the best formulae for reform' to emerge from the Catholic side.[2]

3. THE CONCORD ON THE LORD'S SUPPER[3]

The Württemberg Reformation had shown up once more how dangerous were the unresolved differences over the Lord's Supper. The Stuttgart Concord was too flimsy, and it was clearly only as an interim measure that assent to the Augsburg Confession had been required. So the responsible theologians sought to resume discussions on the Concord. Philip of Hesse was again the natural mediator, and he was approached by Bucer and Melanchthon. It was decided to have a small gathering of theologians, and this was eventually whittled down to a meeting of Bucer and Melanchthon alone, at which Bucer would represent the Southerners' point of view and Melanchthon would speak for Luther.

So in November and December 1534 Bucer made a round trip through Upper Germany and invited South Germans and Swiss to a secret conference at Constance (15–18 December). Not even Sturm was told about it at that stage. Bucer's intention was to get those who were invited to subscribe to the Stuttgart formula and to commit themselves to the Augsburg Confession. Basle and Bern, Blaurer and Grynäus did not appear, and Bullinger merely sent in a confession in which he sought to go beyond the idea of the Lord's Supper as nothing more than a memorial feast and to assert that there is a distribution of the body of Christ. However, he then went on to explain 'eating' in terms of 'believing', and he would not admit the presence of Christ in the material elements but only that it is effected by faith.

The entire conference approved Bullinger's exposition, but alongside it they accepted ten of Bucer's theses which, according to W. Köhler,[4] represent a total capitulation to the Lutherans and a parting company

[1] Lipgens, *op. cit.*, 117.
[2] *ARC* II, 121.
[3] E. Bizer, *Studiem zur Geschichte des Abendmahlsstreites im 16. Jahrhundert*, 1962²; W. Köhler, *Zwingli und Luther II*, 1953, 358 ff.; *ARG* 35, 1938, 203 ff.
[4] Köhler, *op. cit.*, 375.

with the Swiss: 'At the hands of the minister Christ the Lord gives himself to all his disciples with bread and wine as signs. The Lord's gift is not bread and wine but the true body and the true blood of the Lord, given as food for eternal life.'[1] So there is a commitment here to the distribution and to the elements. This is admittedly to be understood 'sacramentally', and the fact that the distribution is to the disciples obviously leaves open the possibility of a 'spiritualist' interpretation. Nevertheless it is difficult to understand how Bucer can here assert the presence of Christ 'with the signs' and at the same time, with Bullinger's confession, reject it.

Luther's judgement[2] offered little prospect of success, because he could not deviate from his own opinion and felt that a matter of this sort could not be decided by a mere handful of theologians. All the same, his instruction to Melanchthon was pacific:[3] he was ready to concede the personal integrity of his opponents, while counting on the same concession for himself. He took the view that there should be mutual tolerance, even if actual fellowship proved impossible. In such an eventuality it would still be possible to reach political agreement. At the end he gave his own opinion: 'The body (of Christ) is with the bread or in the bread in such a way that it is truly eaten with the bread', and that what is done or performed with the bread also affects the body, so that it is correct to say that 'the body of Christ is carried, received and eaten when the bread is carried, received and eaten.' Melanchthon, too, submitted a statement to Philip:[4] for him, the Lord's Supper is a token that Christ is 'essentially' present with us and in virtue of his divinity gives 'his life' as food. 'Therefore I conclude that the body and blood of Christ, that is, the real Christ, is truly and not figuratively present with the bread and wine.' The biblical passages other than the narratives of the Lord's Supper which speak of the presence of Christ indicate to Melanchthon that his view is by no means an absurd one. In so far as he speaks of a personal presence, Melanchthon is close to Bucer, but unlike Bucer he does not speak of a presence in the Spirit or in faith.

The Conference took place at Kassel on 27–29 December 1534.[5] The result was an agreement[6] which took as its basis a confession drawn up by some Augsburg preachers, because the elector was particularly suspicious of the city of Augsburg, which at that time was seeking admission to the League of Schmalkalden. It is therefore stated that the Augsburgers are willing to take 'the Confession and the Apology' as the basis of their teaching. Of the Lord's Supper it is stated that 'when we receive the sacrament, the body of Christ is truly and essentially received'; bread and

[1] Köhler, op. cit., 375.
[2] WAB 7, 127, 128; WAR 38, 294 ff.; ARG 35, 1939, 73 f.
[3] WAR 38, 298 ff.
[4] CR 2, No. 1229.
[5] ARG 35, 1938, 224 ff.; W. Köhler, Zwingli u. Luther II, 376 (note).
[6] ARG 35, 1938, 228.

wine are 'signs', '*signa exhibitiva*', 'so that whenever they are distributed and received, the body and blood of Christ are received at the same time'. Bread and the body of Christ are so linked that their essence is not confused, but both are given at the same time. Bucer's concern seems to have been simply to guarantee the supernatural character of the body of Christ. Difficulty arose, not over the fact of the link between bread and Christ's body, but over the manner in which the link is achieved. Thus Bucer preserved for the sacrament the character of a true encounter with Christ. Melanchthon wanted to make sure that all this was approved by Luther, whereas Bucer asserted that it had already been agreed by the South Germans at Constance. In addition, Bucer drew up a statement of his own[1] in answer to Luther. In it he said that he had previously misunderstood Luther to be advocating a crudely materialist conception of the sacrament. He had no desire to set out a middle position. He was concerned simply to exclude both the idea of a *coniunctio physica* and the idea of a merely natural food, and to safeguard the sacramental union against misinterpretation—particularly against the idea that the food as such effects salvation. If Luther could not see that they were at one, then at least he might be prepared to be patient for a little while, until one day— as Bucer hoped—they might be able to satisfy him completely. On 2 January he wrote to his South German brethren from Frankfurt,[2] saying that what mattered was the *vera vivi Christi per ministerium ministralis exhibitio*. 'Never has there been greater hope of a sure and honest concord.' Even Luther reacted with surprising magnanimity. If hearts meant what the words said, he would be content with the confession. All that remained for him to do—so it seemed to him—was to let time tell 'whether they were hiding anything'.[3] On 27 January 1535 the elector wrote to Philip,[4] informing him that Luther wanted a great conference of the leading Lutherans and the South Germans, in order to determine 'whether they will hold fast to this confession until further action can be taken, as is greatly to be hoped'.

Luther appears to have regarded the matter thus: he had already reached a tolerable agreement with the Strasbourg theologians. Now, on account of the meeting at Constance, the circle had widened. The South Germans would have to give their consent themselves, and even then there would still have to be a final meeting in order to formulate an agreement which all could approve and abide by. The importance of the discussions at Kassel lay in the fact that Bucer had made a crucial issue of the *ministerialis exhibitio*—an issue

[1] Enders, *Briefwechsel* (see n. 29 above), 10, No. 2228.
[2] Vadian, *Briefsammlung*, No. 808.
[3] *WAB* 7, 149 f., No. 2169.
[4] Enders, *Briefwechsel* 10, 125.

I

which Luther, as well as the South Germans, would have to face: the elements and the body of Christ are connected in such a way that wherever the sacrament is put, there the body of Christ is put also—*quo posito alius ponitur.*

It soon transpired that Luther's question, whether the South Germans were really of the opinion which Bucer had put forward, was amply justified—and not only with regard to the Swiss. Bucer's friends in Constance suddenly began to have reservations.[1] The situation in Augsburg became very difficult indeed. From July 1534 onwards, the Council took action against Catholicism and summoned Bucer to help them. In spite of this, Electoral Saxony was still very hesitant about admitting Augsburg to the League of Schmalkalden. Since the Württemberg affair the elector seemed to be setting his political hopes on the Habsburgs once more, and it looked as though he himself was not certain whether the League of Schmalkalden ought to continue.[2] Duke Ulrich of Württemberg thought that the elector would rather 'let the League die of its own accord' than accept new members, and so Ulrich was considering forming a South German alliance of his own.[3] The cities, however, supported Augsburg, so the question of Augsburg's acceptance seemed to decide the League's future.[4] But it was not without good reason that the elector regarded the city as Zwinglian. So at the end of February 1535 Bucer was called back yet again, in order to 'pacify the preachers and to restore unanimity among them'.[5] Here he did what the Wittenbergers had long waited for him to do: from the chancel he confessed 'that concerning the sacrament, what he had understood and expressed had been insufficient; he had taught nothing about the distribution of the body and the blood, nor had he sufficiently understood it. Therefore, for the honour of God, he willingly confessed it . . . and also on behalf of his colleagues, the other preachers.' These then made similar declarations.[6] Another confession of faith was drawn up, and its article on the Lord's Supper read: 'The true body and the true blood of our Lord Jesus Christ are distributed, given and received, in order to strengthen our faith'.[7] The commentary on this article states that 'in the Lord's Supper it is not mere empty signs, but the Lord Christ himself who is given to us', though without faith it is impossible to attain salvation. Certainly there were terrible quarrels about it. Keller, a Zwinglian, said that to sign it would be to deny his own conviction. Others, more like Schwenckfeld in their thinking, were simply indifferent to the whole

[1] Köhler, *Zwingli u. Luther II*, 381 f.
[2] *Pol. Corr.* II, No. 276.
[3] Ibid., No. 287, 290, 292, 297.
[4] Köhler, *Zwingli u. Luther II*, 385; Roth II, 284 f.
[5] Roth II, 241 f.
[6] Roth II, 242.
[7] Köhler, *op. cit.*, *II*, 386. Text of the Confession in Roth II, 275 ff.

question. The council had to restore peace and concord, and the preachers were told that the Council might have to use against them the very right to effect reform which they themselves had proclaimed with such emphasis.[1] So the agreement remained a highly unstable affair, based on a purely external ordering. Nevertheless, it meant that the Zwinglian monopoly which had existed in Augsburg for more than four years had been brought to an end.

A messenger was sent to Luther with a request that he send one of his own clergy. Luther received the request on 2 July and was delighted, saying that it had taken a great load from his mind and that he would be able to die in peace. Let bygones be bygones and let everyone have patience, 'for when a man has broken a bone he cannot straightway leap up or dance and skip—he must be allowed time'.[2] He sent a man in whom he had complete confidence, Johann Forster, whose birthplace was in fact Augsburg.[3] The clergy in the other cities went out of their way to ensure that nothing incur Luther's displeasure, which meant that on 28 September Luther was able to give a pleasing report to the elector.[4] By the end of the year plans were already being drawn up for convening the new assembly which Luther so much hoped for. The proposed Diet of Schmalkalden was twice postponed and then called off, so the Augsburg affair was delegated to a committee, and the only condition laid down was that the city should abide by the Augsburg Confession. On 26 April 1536, together with Kempten, Augsburg was admitted to the League.[5]

On 5 October Luther had written a series of letters suggesting to the cities that a conference of the clergy might be held either in Hesse or in Saxony. On 25 March[6] in the following year he invited them, through Bucer, to come to Eisenach on the fourth Sunday after Easter. Meanwhile in Augsburg Forster had laid bare the sheer fragility of the 'unanimity' which had been established there by decree. The Swiss remained completely aloof.[7] Bucer had tried to gain Bullinger's support for what Bucer regarded as the decisive point, namely that in the sacrament the minister displays or 'exhibits' the body of Christ. But it was precisely this that Bullinger would not accept. He declared that Bucer was ascribing too much to the minister's office, that it is Christ alone who can 'exhibit' his body. 'The minister exhibits only *ministerialiter*; he exhibits only the sacrament', 'only the sign'; Christ is present only *beneficio fidei*, for the wor-

[1] Roth II, 242.
[2] *WAB* 7, 210 ff., No. 2211 f.
[3] W. Germann, *D. Joh. Forster*, 1894.
[4] *WAB* 7, 277 ff., No. 2247.
[5] Roth II, 285 ff.; Köhler, *op. cit.* II, 394 ff.
[6] *WAB* 7, 286 ff., No. 2251 ff. and 378 f., No. 3001.
[7] Köhler, *op. cit.* II, 395 ff.

shipper receives only in proportion to his faith.[1] Bern maintained a viewpoint which was Zwinglian pure and simple, and was therefore aware that even Bullinger's position differed from its own. Constance was unable to overcome its suspicions, which were revived when Bucer and Melanchthon discussed with France the possibility of a concord with Catholics,[2] and also when Luther's commentary on Galatians was published.[3] On 1 December the Swiss met at Aarau and drew up a confession of their own with regard to the Lord's Supper. In it they did indeed assert that the true body of Christ is truly eaten, but they wanted this to be understood solely as something brought about by faith, for it is the 'essence' of the body of Christ which passes into the mind and the soul of the believer. Bern's representatives felt that even this was obscure and liable to misinterpretation.[4] At a further meeting in Basle (from 30 January to 4 February 1536)[5] representatives from Strasbourg took part uninvited. The result was the *First Helvetian Confession*,[6] which (according to W. Köhler) was to count as preparatory material for the Council. The doctrine of the Lord's Supper given in this Confession is poised delicately between the idea of a real presence on the one hand and the idea of symbolic signs on the other. It speaks of 'signs and real (*wesentlich*) things'; something is 'offered to us and supplied for us' by God 'through his power'. This is something in which the ministers do indeed have a part, but nevertheless the resultant 'objectivity' is nothing more than the objectivity of a sign. The Swiss imagined that Luther would approve this Confession. The only opposition to the Confession came from the Constance delegation, who made it quite clear that they rejected the idea that the minister 'co-operates' by means of any actions he may perform. They also insisted that forgiveness cannot be offered in the Lord's Supper, for it would then no longer be a *remissionis memoria* but a *remissionis opus*.[7] At a third meeting on 27 March the Confession, in a revised form prepared by Bullinger, was accepted.[8] After the February meeting Bucer and Capito wrote to Luther about what had happened,[9] but they gave such prominence to what was said in the Confession about the 'objective' aspect of the sacrament that Luther was bound to get a false impression. 'They made him a present of Protestant Switzerland in its entirety.'[10]

[1] Köhler, *op. cit.* II, 397.
[2] G. Ellinger, *Philipp Melanchthon*, 1902, 318 ff.; G. Kawerau, *Die Versuche, Melanchthon zur katholischen Kirche zurückzuführen*, 1902; W. Baum, *Capito und Butzer*, 1860, 496 f.; Köhler, *Zwingli u. Luther II*, 399 f.
[3] Köhler, *op. cit.* II, 400. The commentary in *WAR* 40, I and II.
[4] Ibid., 407 ff.   [5] Ibid., 412 ff.
[6] E. F. K. Müller, *Die Bekenntnisse der reformierten Kirche*, 1903 (text).
[7] Köhler, *op. cit.* II, 420.   [8] Ibid., 421; *Eidgenössische Abschiede IV*, 1, c, 670 f.
[9] *WAB* 7, 357, No. 2293.
[10] Köhler, *op. cit.* II, 416.

However, soon afterwards three publications made it perfectly clear that the Swiss had views of their own. There appeared in quick succession Vadian's *Aphorisms*,[1] which Bullinger regarded as the ideal basis for an agreement, then letters by Zwingli and Oecolampad, edited by Bibliander of Zürich with a preface by Bucer,[2] and finally Zwingli's *Fidei expositio*,[3] which he had written for the king of France and which presents his sacramental doctrine with exemplary clarity. Presumably Bullinger's wish, in having these books published, was to show that he respected Zwingli, even though his own views went beyond Zwingli's. But the Swiss did not go to the conference which Luther had planned. They merely charged the Strasbourg representatives with the task of presenting their Confession to Luther.

So the very carefully selected South German delegation made its way via Frankfurt to Eisenach, nervously awaited by Melanchthon,[4] who by this time had begun to have doubts himself. In Eisenach they were bidden to come to Grimma,[5] and shortly afterwards made their way to Wittenberg, where they arrived on Sunday, 21 May, and stayed until the Monday of the following week.[6] Luther, whose health was constantly causing anxiety, did not make discussions easy for them. It transpired that the main problem was that of faithless reception of the sacrament, for Bucer and his colleagues, who preserved their fundamentally 'spiritualist' convictions, denied that Christ's body was truly received by a faithless recipient of the sacrament. But Bucer did acknowledge that the bread is truly Christ's body and is given by the hands of the ministers to all who receive, provided that the words of institution are not debased—which can happen if the recipient is without faith. A solution was found by Bugenhagen, who suggested that instead of speaking of 'faithless' reception they should speak of 'unworthy' reception. Bucer accepted this. Luther then asked each one in turn for his opinion, and after a brief consultation with his colleagues expressed himself satisfied. He then accepted his guests as brothers, 'and Capito and Bucer began to weep, and on both sides—with folded hands and reverent demeanour—we gave thanks to God the Lord'.[7] They then shook hands and parted. Subsequently there were discussions on baptism and on the power of the keys. On Ascension Day (25 May) they celebrated the Lord's Supper together. The following day Melanchthon put before them the draft of an agreement which was signed by all present. Luther declared that the Concord was a matter which must con-

---

[1] Köhler, *op. cit.* II, 424.   [2] Ibid., 428.   [3] Ibid., 429.
[4] Ibid., 441–442.
[5] *WAB* 7, 409, No. 3021.
[6] Myconius' account, Walch 17, 2534 (see p. 105 n. 4); Bucer's in *ARG* 35, 1938, 97 ff.; Köhler, *op. cit.*, 443 ff.
[7] Myconius, in a letter to Baumgarten, said that he was suspicious of the agreement.

cern the princes, the churches and other persons, and their approval must be sought before anything could be done 'in the name of everyone'. It was not until 27 May that Bucer handed to Luther the Swiss Confession. Luther found it 'all right in itself', but there were parts which he considered unsatisfactory. He thought that discussions should take place with the Swiss, with the aim of getting them to accept the Concord.

This *Wittenberg Concord*[1] is not a compromise, for the aim was not to reach a 'half-way' position by means of concessions on both sides. The fact that the Lutherans put their signature to it does not mean that they regarded it as their own 'confession', but that it confirms the agreement they had reached with the South Germans. After the kind of discussions which they had just held, it would have been impossible for anyone to overlook the fact that there were still differences. It is for this reason that W. Köhler has described the whole Concord as a sham, for each side placed a different interpretation on the word 'unworthy'.[2] It is quite true that the interpretation which Bucer put upon the agreement showed immediately that in spite of all the precautions taken there was an ambiguity in the agreement. But what is far more important is that Luther had seen these differences and had nevertheless concluded the agreement. For from Luther's point of view the agreement satisfied his own religious concern that the words of the Bible should be taken in their natural sense, and that therefore anyone coming to the Lord's Supper might be certain of receiving the whole gift.[3] Once he was satisfied about this, he could leave other matters to take care of themselves. The effect of the Concord was to build for the South Germans a bridge towards Lutheranism. In Switzerland, however, the Concord failed on account of Zwinglian opposition, so that later on Luther felt obliged once again to draw a sharp line of division.

[1] Bizer (see p. 115 n. 3) gives the text, 116 ff. See *BSLK* on art. X of the CA.
[2] Köhler, *op. cit.* II, 453.
[3] Pressel, *op. cit.*, 238, No. 108 (letter by Brenz of 7 Nov. 1543).

CHAPTER IV

THE SUMMONING OF THE COUNCIL AND THE DIET OF SCHMALKALDEN, 1537[1]

THE papal Bull of 2 June 1536 required all ecclesiastical prelates, as a matter of obligation, to attend a Council at Mantua. But the Emperor and the princes were also requested to attend, for although they could have no voting rights their participation—so the ecclesiastical lawyers felt—was necessary. The Bull was delivered by a papal legate, on this occasion van der Vorst of the Netherlands. Its delivery by this means constituted a legally valid summons. On 11 November he arrived in Vienna to see king Ferdinand.[2]

Matthäus Lang of Salzburg was the only German bishop who saw fit to make active preparations.[3] After preliminary discussions with his suffragans and the local princes he arranged a meeting of his provincial Synod for 15 May 1537. Here the question of reform was combined with a series of protests against the secular authorities, for the priesthood, reduced and impoverished, 'is unlikely to be persuaded to offer its earnest obedience or to accept the novelties of reformation, unless something is done in return to remove their own wants'.[4] Experience was showing that no one wanted to be a priest as long as these wants persisted. The Synod therefore drew up a catalogue of complaints, which included interference by the secular powers in ecclesiastical matters (such as the remuneration of the clergy), as well as in clerical rights of jurisdiction and in 'clerical liberties' (i.e. immunities, etc.). But the king refused to discuss

[1] Sources: H. Voz, *Urkunden und Aktenstücke zur Geschichte von Martin Luthers. Schmalkaldischen Artikeln* (1536–1574), 1957, Kleine Texte 179 (cit. Volz, *Urk.*); E. Bizer, 'Die Wittenberger Theologen und das Konzil 1537', *ARG* 47, 1956, 77–101. Expositions: E. Bizer and H. Volz in *ZKG* 67, 1955–1956, 61 ff.; 68, 1957, 259 ff. and 287 ff. Text of the Schmalkaldic Articles in facsimile by K. Zangmeister, 1883; cf. also *WAR* 50, 160 and 192 ff. Three Catholic writings in *CCath* 18, 1932, ed. H. Volz.
[2] *Jedin* I, 253 ff.; *CT* IV, 42 ff.
[3] *ARC* II, 322 ff. (Salzburg Synod, *ibid.*, 319–506); *SVRG* 77, 1903, 29 ff.
[4] *ARC* II, 433, 30 ff.

these protests. So the Reform Constitutions which the Synod had decided upon were never published. Indeed, so alarmed was the Curia by the reports of the Synod which it had received from the papal nuncio in Vienna that on 5 August a formal reprimand[1] was sent to the cardinal archbishop, reproaching him because his Synod *speciem quandam nationalis synodi referre visa set et ad nationalem quodammodo tendere*; and also because unauthorised persons had been admitted (i.e. the representatives of the king!) and those present had been allowed to deliberate freely and un-reproved about matters which had been definitively settled long ago. The reprimand apparently took no account of the fact that the Synod's final recess had included the decision to go to the Council, though admittedly there were reservations about matters of detail. This reprimand 'made such a deep impression and had such a lasting effect that even ten years later it cropped up again amidst the arguments used against the demand for reform by the territorial overlords'.[2]

On 6 July the elector of Saxony received from George of Ansbach the text of the Bull.[3] By 24 July he had got Brück, his chancellor, to put before the theologians and lawyers of Wittenberg a series of questions about it.[4] He objected that nothing was said in the Bull about either the freedom, the 'christianity' or the impartiality of the Council; that it was to be held on Italian soil at Mantua; and that it would be linked to earlier Councils in such a way that their validity could not be called into question but would indirectly be confirmed. He therefore wanted to know whether the invitation could possibly be accepted by any who were bound to regard the Pope as an opponent, or, on the other hand, whether there was any way in which the invitation could be refused without affronting the Emperor. He also asked what steps might be taken to safeguard Protestants against any decisions of the Council which might arise. In a memorandum[5] written a few days later he gave it as his opinion that the invitation ought not to be accepted, for if he accepted it he would be putting himself under obligation to the Pope. He therefore asked for the text of a protestation to be drawn up, in which it was to be clearly stated that the Pope cannot be the master and judge of all Christendom. He hoped to be able to give an explanation to the Emperor which would justify his position. In the end he would appeal to public opinion. The Wittenberg theologians and lawyers gave their considered judgement[6] on this, but the elector was dissatisfied with it, for he felt that it failed to get to the heart of the matter. On 30 August he sent Brück to Wittenberg to explain his position. In his view, the Council would be a court of

[1] *ARC* II, 460 ff.   [2] *ARC* II, 321 ff.   [3] Volz, *Urk.*, 17 f.
[4] Virck, *ZKG* 13, 1892, 487 ff. (for dating of the documents).
[5] *CR* 3, No. 1449.   [6] *CR* 3, No. 1456 (mid-August).

arbitration. If he were to accept an invitation to attend it, he would have recognised the authority of the arbitrator and committed himself irrevocably to his judgement.[1] That is why he asked for a 'protestation' which would enable him to reject the notion that the Council represents a kind of arbitration tribunal. A few days later the elector was informed by Brück that Melanchthon had drawn up the text of a protestation.[2] He demanded that in addition to the protestation there should be a proposal which might form the basis of negotiations with his allies.[3] He also raised the question whether steps might be taken to defend Protestants against any adverse decision of the Council and against the Emperor if he sought to give effect to the Council's decisions. But despite the prince's pressure, further consultations were deferred until Melanchthon returned from his travels in South Germany.

At the beginning of December the elector furnished another memorandum, asking 'which articles require to be discussed, both with regard to the Council and to other matters'.[4] It was not likely that arguments from Scripture would be acceptable to the Council, and so it would be necessary to prepare for an adverse judgement and subsequent enforcement. Luther was therefore bidden to make a summary of those articles, from among all that he had taught until then, 'on which he took his stand and would not yield'. These articles were then to be approved by the other theologians and put before the other members of the League. But in addition, the elector had devised a plan for an Evangelical 'Counter-council' and worked it out to the last detail. The Wittenbergers then[5] suggested that a written declaration should be drawn up which could be presented to the Emperor, the princes and to the public at large 'in order to establish a correct procedure'. They rejected the idea of a Counter-council, and for good reasons: it would give the impression 'of a dreadful and deliberate schism'; it would require complete agreement among all the estates, in order that they 'might come together in harmony', and it would also require elaborate preparations. They affirmed the right of self-defence against any possible implementation of adverse judgements by the Council. Indeed Luther added, 'I will do my part in this with prayer, and (if necessary) with my fist'. The elector then[6] took up again the first request in his memorandum and gave Luther the task of stating 'for the sake of christian doctrine and religion', 'to what extent, and in which particular articles, it would be possible to yield and give way for the sake of peace and unity, or not.' He was then to show this statement to the other

[1] CR 3, No. 1464; Volz, Urk. 3, p. 18 ff.
[2] On 3 September.   [3] CR 3, p. 154 ff.
[4] CR 3, p. 139 ff.; Volz, Urk., No. 4.
[5] CR 3, No. 1458; WAB 7, 604 ff.; Volz, Urk. 27 n. 7.
[6] 11 December. WAB 7, 612 ff., No. 3116; Volz, Urk. 26 ff.

theologians in Saxony, and any who differed from Luther's statement were to record the fact and give their reasons. Luther was to regard himself as free to 'draw up something himself on all this in preparation for this Council' and to 'attack the Pope more strongly'. Meanwhile the theologians of Hesse had prepared their own statement,[1] in which they came to the conclusion that the Council was not what they had asked for and should therefore not be attended. If, in spite of this, people were going to attend, they would have to provide themselves with a new Confession 'in order not to give way so apathetically'. Subsequently on S. Thomas's Day the two heads of the League of Schmalkalden met at Eisenach to prepare for a Diet of members of the League. They decided that the estates were to make their own proposals about the Council and were to bring the theologians with them for consultation.[2] In response to this, Saxony drew up a statement which simply repeated the views of the elector: to go to the Council would amount to recognition of the Pope, and since to protest at a later stage would be pointless, it were better not to go at all.[3] The theologians of Wittenberg[4] judged the Council no more kindly, but they came to the opposite conclusion, saying that it was necessary to go in order to give account of their faith. Melanchthon complained at that time of the prince's 'lack of understanding of the theologians' 'philosophy'.[5] Hesse, too, was wholly negative in its attitude towards the Council. The Landgrave demanded a new Confession and an Evangelical Counter-council.[6] Ulm and Constance, however, feared new doctrinal controversies and felt that some yielding might be possible in externals. So there was little unity in the outcome. At Wittenberg the theologians opposed the elector, and the cities had views which differed from those of the princes. Meanwhile Luther had prepared his articles. A conference of theologians on 28 December[7] asked for a few points to be added, but only the article about the invocation of saints was incorporated *de novo*. Melanchthon felt that what was said about the Pope was too fierce. As the prince had requested, he added a note to the effect that the Pope's superiority over the bishops *iure humano* ought to be recognised, for the sake of peace and unity, 'if he will allow the Gospel'.[8] This twofold reservation is not to be overlooked, for presumably it was simply Melanchthon's wish that negotiations should not be made impossible from the start. But here he encountered rigid opposition from the elector, who accepted Luther's articles gratefully,[9] though they seemed to him 'a little short'.[10] He wanted these articles to be

---

[1] Not printed.   [2] Volz, *Urkunde* 79 ff.   [3] *CR* 3, No. 1521.
[4] *ARG* 47, 1956, 77 ff.   [5] *CR* 3, No. 1524; Volz, *Urk.* 101.
[6] *ZKG* 67, 1955, 70 ff.   [7] Volz *Urk.*, 69 ff.   [8] *BSLK²*, 463 f.; Volz, *Urk.*, 75.
[9] *WAB* 8, 4 (No. 3125); Volz, *Urk.*, 83 ff.   [10] Volz, *Urk.*, 87.

signed by the theologians of Erfurt on the way to the Diet of the Schmalkaldians, but this did not happen. The preparations for the Diet were now
complete. In a sermon on 28 January 1537[1] Luther summoned the congregation to intercessory prayer and warned them against trying to settle
the matter better than God would have it settled. 'It is neither the devil,
nor the world, nor gracious princes that I fear, but ourselves.' 'Remember
that this is no children's game, for what is done there will resound throughout the world and into posterity. God grant that we may not be the only
ones to know this. But you are to pray.' Melanchthon viewed the Diet
with the greatest possible trepidation.[2]

The importance of this meeting was underlined by the numbers who
attended it. The Evangelical princes attended in person, together with the
representatives of the cities and their theologians. The imperial Vice-
chancellor, Dr. Held, and the papal legate were also expected. 'Deus det,
ut sit legitimum concilium', remarked Luther. The decision about the invitation to the Council was far-reaching in its consequences. All the members
of the League expressed their rejection of the Pope in a 'confessional
document', and most of the theologians signed the articles by Luther
which were from then onwards to be known as the Schmalkaldic Articles.
After so much politics, these were clerical acts of lasting significance.

There is hardly any trace, in the records, of the most important decision
taken at the Diet, namely the decision to refuse the invitation to the
Council.[3] The assembly began on 10 February with a speech by Brück,
in which he presented the 'reservations' of the two heads of the League.
In the consultations which followed, the princes were quick to support the
elector's view and made their decision known to the plenary session
which voted its agreement. The representatives of Ansbach[4] stated in their
report that since it was clear that no one would be admitted to the Council
who did not submit to its decisions beforehand, then God should prevent
the members from submitting. The theologians and all the expert
judgements which they had brought with them played no part at all in
this. They were merely formed into a committee. After the invitation to
the Council had been rejected, there was little for them to do, except to
look over the Augsburg Confession and 'remove all references to the
papacy', for it was only in deference to the Emperor that this had not
been done in 1530.[5] On 14 February Dr. Held arrived and on the following day made a long speech to the estates.[6] He dealt first with proceedings

---

[1] WAR 45, 8 ff.   [2] Volz, Urk., 92 ff.; CR 3, No. 1517 f.
[3] ZKG 68, 1957, 291.   [4] Volz, Urk., 145 ff.   [5] Ibid., 164 ff.
[6] SVRG 77, 1903, 81 ff.; Rassow, Kaiseridee 393 ff. and Brandi, Quellen 276 f. The
instructions (in French) are given in K. Lanz, Correspondenz de Kaisers Karl V. (3
vols., 1844–1846) II, 268 ff. For the reconstruction of the German version see HPBl
102, 1888, 718 ff. It is a question whether Held's conduct really corresponded with

at the Imperial Cameral Tribunal, particularly at those points where the demarcation of religious matters and the extension of the Emperor's promise to new members of the League were in dispute. The question was one of great importance for the position of Protestants before the law. Held explained that the court must be allowed to decide which matters were to be regarded as religious ones. With regard to new members of the League, the Emperor could make no concessions.[1] He then said that the Council should be attended, for it was the only means of overcoming religious division. Consultations then took place, in order to give an answer to Held's speech. The reply was given on 24 February.[2] It repeated the complaints about the Religious Standstill and the Imperial Cameral Tribunal, summarised all the arguments for the Protestant view and declared 'that according to the view expressed by Held the Religious Standstill is void of all meaning for the Imperial Cameral Tribunal',[3] since there is no such thing as a purely religious matter. The Religious Standstill had been suspended rather than confirmed, and Protestants were therefore not in a position to give assistance against the Turks or to contribute towards the costs of the Imperial Cameral Tribunal. The reasons for refusing the invitation to the Council were listed with great thoroughness. To consent to go to the Council would be to consent to their own condemnation, since the Pope was to be judge in his own cause. Therefore there was no choice but to ask the Emperor for a different kind of Council. And there, despite speeches for and against, the matter stood.[4] In the end, Held confined his efforts to getting support against the Turks.

On Sunday, 25 February, came the celebrated scene between the elector and the papal legate. Jedin[5] has described it as 'the greatest humiliation ever suffered by a papal envoy on this side of the Alps'. The legate wished to hand over the papal Bull of invitation, but the elector withdrew from the room without so much as taking it from the table. The legate, for his part, would not take the Bull back again and let his position be known, 'for as long as the elector keeps silence about it he has tacitly accepted it, etc. But the prince's councillors did not take it either, but let it lie there, and the legate rode to his lodgings after a great deal of argument.'[6] Melanchthon took part in the proceedings as interpreter. What happened was naturally not the result of any premeditated humiliation of the legate, but rather of the Protestant view of the legal significance of the delivery

---

the Emperor's intentions, which must have been to reach an understanding with the Protestants. On Held see *Schl* 8138–8143. See also *CT* IV, 71; Lanz, *Staatspapiere* 238 f.
[1] R. Smend, *Das Reichskammergericht* I, 1911, 144 f.
[2] *CR* 3, No. 1540b; *CT* IV, 73 ff.; *Ursachen* I, 26.
[3] Smend, *op. cit.*, 154.   [4] *Ursachen* I, 27 f.   [5] Ibid., 256.
[6] *Pol. Corr.* II, 424, No. 439; *CT* IV, 89–92.

or the acceptance of the Bull. Melanchthon was very unhappy about the whole course of events. The Wittenberg standpoint was that it would be wrong to refuse to attend simply on the grounds that the Pope ought not to be judge; for the Pope does have the right to summon the Council, and only the Council can decide who is to be appointed judge. But the others felt that this was far too dangerous, 'for the Pope's tyranny is so great that if we agreed to come to the Council our acceptance would be taken to mean that we had acknowledged the Pope's judicial office'. This latter view prevailed 'after a long and acrimonious conflict', and thereby the danger of war had once again become acute.[1]

At a meeting of the theologians[2] Melanchthon proposed that a committee be formed which would go through the Augsburg Confession and draw up new articles about the power of the Pope which would then be put before the plenary session. At the first session of this committee in Luther's lodgings Luther declared his own allegiance to the Augsburg Confession, which was evidently taken to mean that he regarded a new confession as unnecessary. So only the first nine articles were discussed, the remainder of the work being left to a sub-committee and finally to Melanchthon himself.[3] On 17 February Melanchthon's *Tractatus de potestate papae* was submitted to the plenary and was approved by everyone, but written comments on it were to be sent to Wittenberg.[4] On this occasion everyone present received as a handout a copy of Luther's articles, presumably as material for further study. It was expressly indicated that they were Luther's own private work. At a further session on 23 February there was a discussion of the answer to be given to Dr. Held. It is probably to this session that Melanchthon was referring when he mentioned the 'long and acrimonious conflict'. The leading theologians acquiesced in the decision of the princes, even though they held a different opinion.[5] At the request of Amsdorf and Bugenhagen the committee met again that same afternoon in order to continue the task of working through the Augsburg Confession.[6] They had now reached the article on the Lord's Supper, and since they had Luther's articles in front of them they naturally referred to them. A heated discussion arose between Bucer and Osiander, and Ambrosius Blaurer expressed reservations. The princes, at Bucer's suggestion, prevented further discussion. On the following day the meeting was told that Luther had presented his articles in an entirely private capacity and no one should feel obliged to sign them. Melanchthon's *Tractatus*, on the other hand, was signed by everyone. There is

[1] CR 3, No. 1534.   [2] Volz, *Urk.* 167ff.
[3] Ibid., 170.   [4] Ibid., 171.
[5] Ibid., 134 n. 14; CR 3, No. 1535; Volz, *Urk.*, 130.
[6] Volz, *Urk.*, 171.

no indication that the elector, having asked for Luther's articles, actively sought to promote them.[1]

Luther himself was able to take little part in the discussions, for on 16 February he took ill with a calculus and was in acute pain. On 7 February he had written to Burgomaster Jakob Meyer of Basle about the Wittenberg Concord,[2] saying that he wished the mutual suspicion on the question of the Lord's Supper might disappear. Now was the time to show christian love and seek for unanimity, even though this was likely to take some time. Bucer, together with Wolfhard of Augsburg, would have been glad to have from Luther an unequivocal and final answer to the letters sent to him by the Swiss, and so when Luther was recovering they travelled to Gotha to visit him. Luther was able to receive them on 1 March.[3] He saw clearly enough that there were still difficulties and he warned them against the kind of 'cloaking about' which his friends found intolerable and could never satisfy the conscience. The distinction which Blaurer made (presumably on 23 February) between bread and wine as objects of the senses and the body of Christ as the object of faith was particularly repugnant to Luther. 'Even over the border Karlstadt is no use. He is neither *Dialecticus* nor *Rhetoricus*, and even if he knew anything he would be incapable of teaching it.' 'If I die, then refer to what I wrote to Meyer.' He finally said that he would dearly like to write kind replies to 'the good people' who had written to him. Luther's exhortation to patience and uprightness was his last word, for the time being, on the whole question of the Concord.[4] On 14 March he was back in Wittenberg.

On 24 February Luther's articles had been signed at Schmalkalden by a large number of theologians.[5] Melanchthon's *Tractatus* was approved by everyone and was incorporated in the final recess of the Diet, thus becoming an official document of the League. In the preface written by Luther he expressed the opinion that his articles also were universally accepted, but this was an error on his part. Afterwards Bugenhagen pronounced a blessing upon everyone, 'all acknowledged as brothers in the Lord, and to each he offered his hand, briefly exhorting every one to hold fast to the doctrine of the holy Gospel which had been recognised and accepted, and to teach it and preach it with one accord in every

[1] Volz, *Urk.*, 173 f. In *ZKG* 68, 1957, 259 ff., Volz states his opinion that the elector intended to use Luther's articles as material for a confession, without regard to the Council question, but was prevented from doing so by Melanchthon's intrigues. Against this view see E. Bizer, *ibid.*, p. 287 ff.

[2] *WAB* 8, No. 3137, p. 43 ff.

[3] *WATR* 3, No. 3544; *CR* 3, 313.

[4] Luther's 'Testament', *WAB* 8, 54 ff. Luther on Bucer and Osiander as preachers, *WATR* 4, 5047.

[5] Volz, *Urk.*, 173 f.

church, and to be faithful in praying for one another to the Lord.' On 3 March the papal nuncio departed.[1]

It then fell to Melanchthon to compose the official document of refusal with a commentary.[2] The latter is a short summary of the reasons why it was impossible to attend the Council: the papal Bull showed that there would be no genuine discussions, but merely confirmation of papal decisions which had already been taken. Further, the attempt had been made to bind the princes by the very acceptance of the Bull, so that by merely receiving it they were taken to consent to the Council's judgements. The document of refusal anticipates the criticisms which were liable to be made of the Protestants and offers a defence of their decision. The material arguments are based on the contents of the papal Bull. It is not permissible for the Pope to be judge in his own cause, particularly when he has anticipated the verdict. To agree to come to the Council would be to submit to that verdict in advance. This was the official outcome of the Diet of Schmalkalden. Both theologically and historically it was to have a determinative influence upon the succeeding generations.

The development of Church organisation

In all the territories belonging to princes the Reformation was implemented by means of visitations, for which the Electorate of Saxony provided the model. These were undertaken by specially appointed commissions of theologians and lawyers by order of the territorial princes. In the early stages there was no central ecclesiastical authority left, for the bishops refused to take part and the reformers were concerned only about the exercise of the preaching office. In 1527 the office of superintendent was introduced by Electoral Saxony in the towns which were centres of administration. From 1533 Bugenhagen was *Ober-Superattendent* at Wittenberg. As a result of his church ordinances—for Brunswick in 1528 (cf. Kleine Texte 88, 1912), for Hamburg in 1529 (cf. Sehling, vol. 5), for Lübeck in 1531 (ibid.), for Pomerania in 1534 (Sehling, vol. 6), for Denmark in 1537, Holstein in 1542, Brunswick-Wolfenbüttel in 1543 and Hildesheim in 1544—the superintendent's office, episcopal in character (in the sense that he was to be the responsible leader in the internal and external affairs of the churches) was introduced over a wide area.[3]

The difference between Luther's preface to the visitation articles for Saxony and the elector's 'Instruction' of 1527 highlights the theological

---

[1] *Jedin I*, 260.
[2] *CR* 3, No. 1543b; *Jedin I*, 553 n. 31; *Le Plat II*, 575 ff.; *Ursachen I*, 29.
[3] W. Elert, 'Der bischöfliche Charakter der Superintendenturverfassung', *Luthertum* 46, 1935, 353 ff.

problems occasioned by these visitations—problems which were to increase as development continued. Sohm, starting from the view that the Church can have no 'law', propounded the thesis in 1892 that Luther regarded the new ecclesiastical law as fundamentally a matter for the secular authorities, and that it was to those authorities that 'supremacy over the Church' (as distinct from the government of the Church or the powers of the Church) was to be ascribed.[1] Holl contested this strongly, claiming that Luther had 'defended the independence of the Church over against the state' and had a very clear concept of Church organisation.[2] Recent research on the whole has followed Holl.[3] It is true that Melanchthon also charged the secular authorities with the task of guarding the 'first table' (*custodia utriusque tabulae*) and gave them specific functions in the church as *praecipuum membrum ecclesiae*; but he did not allow them rights over the preaching office or over the administration of the sacraments or over the power of the keys. The *custodia primae tabulae* does not give the territorial prince any right as such, but merely binds his person and his office to the preaching office, and from his public assent to the faith draws the conclusion that he is under obligation, for example, to suppress any open propagation of false doctrine. How could any avowedly Evangelical territorial prince tolerate any public challenge of 'pure doctrine' in his own territory? Moreover his status as *praecipuum membrorum* obliges him to give assistance to the Church in instances where it cannot help itself, as for example in carrying out visitations. In such a case one is dealing with an emergency law which ceases to operate when the emergency no longer exists. From such rudiments it is quite possible for a system of Church government by territorial princes to develop, but such a system is by no means inherent in them. 'Luther is not to be numbered among the spiritual ancestors of Church government by territorial princes'.[4]

The first step towards the establishment of a central ecclesiastical authority came in 1537, when the 'great committee' of the territory proposed that the elector set up 'consistory courts' intended to deal with matrimonial and disciplinary matters.[5] Justus Jonas prepared a report on this[6] and declared that 'Church affairs and matrimonial matters'

---

[1] Kirchenrecht I, 1892, 582; cf. Sehling, 'Geschichte der protestantischen Kirchenverfassung', *Grundriss der Geschichtswissenschaft II*, 8, 1914².

[2] *Holl. I* (Luther), 1932⁶, 375 f.

[3] J. Heckel, 'Cura religionis, ius in sacra, ius circa sacra', *KRA* 117–118, 1938, 224 ff.; and 'Initia iuris ecclesiastici Protestantium', *SAM* 1949, bk. 5.

[4] *RGG³* III, 1574 (Grundmann).

[5] O. Mejer, 'Anfänge des Wittenberger Konsistoriums', *Zeitschrift für evangelisches Kirchenrecht* 13, 1876, 28 ff.; K. Müller, 'Die Anfänge der Konsistorialverfassung im lutherischen Deutschland', *HZ* 102, 1909, 1 ff.

[6] A. L. Richter, *Geschichte der evangelischen Kirchenverfassung*, 1851, 82 ff.

required a separate forum, because neither the prince's court nor the superintendent were as yet equipped to deal adequately with such things, and without the consistory courts 'much vice and wantonness' would go unpunished. Such a court was in fact instituted at Wittenberg in 1539 to deal with cases in the *Kurkreis* and *Kreis Torgau*.[1] An attempt was made in 1542 to extend its competence, but nothing came of it.[2] At first Spalatin feared that the new authority would supersede the visitors, but Luther pacified him by pointing out how limited was its sphere of competence.[3] Soon however, Luther became involved in the question of secret betrothals, which Luther wanted to have forbidden, but which the consistory court treated and recognised according to canon law. Luther felt that despite the new authority people's consciences would still be confused.[4] The lawyers 'must know that the consistory court ought not to be under their sole jurisdiction, but ought to be under the clergyman'. In the newly founded Evangelical bishopric of Naumburg the establishment of a consistory court never came about, despite Luther's efforts.[5] In a celebrated letter and in one of his table conversations[6] Luther protested against the intervention of secular officials in ecclesiastical disciplinary proceedings, and also against the setting up of a consistory court by duke Moritz to deal with 'the teaching of God's Word, christian ceremonies, matrimonial matters and whatever else we shall refer to you' (Mandate of 22 September 1543). A conference of theologians at Lätare in 1544 asked the duke to set up a consistory court which they envisaged would deal also with administrative tasks relating to the clergy, such as examining ordinands, examining and ratifying the appointment of superintendents, but this again came to nothing.[7] But soon afterwards prince George of Anhalt succeeded to the Evangelical bishopric of Merseburg (the previous bishop died in January 1544), and from then until his resignation after the Schmalkaldic War he had a consistory court.[8] When the elector August then reorganised the administration, three consistory courts were set up, but all

[1] A. L. Richter, *Geschichte der evangelischen Kirchenverfassung*, 1851, 116 f.

[2] Sohm, *Kirchenrecht* I, 1892, 626 f.; *Sehling* I, 200 ff.

[3] *WAB* 9, 305 f., No. 3568.   [4] *Holl* I, 323; *WAR* 49, 294 ff., 316 f.

[5] P. Brunner, 'N. von Amsdorf als Bischof von Naumburg', *SVRG* 179, 1961, 93.

[6] *WAB* 10, 436 f. and *WATR* 5, 6407.

[7] E. Sehling, *Die Kirchengesetzgebung unter Moritz von Sachsen 1544–1549 und Georg von Anhalt*, 1899, esp. 121 ff.; E. Brandenburg, 'Zur Entstehung des landesherrlichen Kirchenregiments in Sachsen', *HV* 4, 1901, 195 ff.; K. Müller, *HZ* 102, 1909, 23 ff.; H. Bornkamm, 'Das Ringen der Motive in den Anfängen der reformatorischen Kirchenverfassung', *ARG* 41, 1948, 93 ff., and in *Das Jahrhundert der Reformation*, 1961, 203 ff.

[8] *Sehling* (as n. 65). E. Körner, 'Fürst Georg v. Anhalt, der erste evangelische Dompropst zu Meissen', *Neues Archiv für sächsische Geschichte* 43, 1922, 221 ff.; F. Lau, Georg III. von Anhalt (1507–1553), erster evangelischer Bischof von Merseburg', *Wissenschaftliche Zeitschrift der Karl-Marx-Universität Leipzig* 3, 1953–1954, 139 ff.

K

remained essentially disciplinary and matrimonial courts. In other territories in Central and North Germany consistory courts to some extent had other functions allocated to them, though they did not thereby become superior authorities having powers of Church government. In Württemberg[1] duke Ulrich created a central administration after the Austrian pattern, organised on collegiate lines with a central exchequer, but this system was not adopted for the Church. Church government was done by superintendents and by visitation commissions specifically appointed at certain times. Only after the treaty of Passau did duke Christoph, in his 'Visitation Ordinance' of 26 May 1533, make the visitation commission a permanent authority which in the Great Church Ordinance of 1559 came to be described as the 'ecclesiastical court' or council (Kirchenrat). But in addition to this, there were from time to time particular visitations at the duke's instigation. A 'theological department' of the Kirchenrat, which included some lay members, dealt with the personal affairs of church and school employees (their examination, appointment, discipline and dismissal); while the 'economic department', under one of the duke's officials, dealt with patronage rights, actions on behalf of ecclesiastical bodies corporate, stipends and maintenance of parsonages, and above all with funds accumulating from benefices which had been pooled in the 'common chest'. The individual congregations were left with only those resources which were not allocated to the maintenance of the clergyman. The responsibility of immediate oversight and regular visitation rested with the 'special' superintendents or the 'general' superintendents, whose reports were discussed twice yearly by the 'synod', which was made up of the Kirchenrat and the general superintendents. The decisions of the synod had to be put before the supreme council (Oberrat) of the duchy. In the dispute with C. Leyser and Jakob Andreä[2] in 1554 the synod claimed the power to excommunicate, but was not able to exercise it at first. The final decision in every instance lay with the duke. This system of church organisation came to be regarded as an ideal model and it influenced other churches also (e.g. Electoral Palatinate, Brunswick-Wolfenbüttel, Lippe, Henneberg, Baden-Durlach) and finally in 1580 Jakob Andreä introduced it to Electoral Saxony,[3] though the

[1] W. Lempp, 'Der württembergische Synodus 1553–1924', BWKG 1959, 15 ff. and 310 ff.

[2] Theologische Studien aus Württemberg III, 1882, 267 ff.; Pressel, Anecdota, No. 208; CR 43, 49 ff. (Leyser to Calvin).

[3] Bornkamm, Das Jahrhundert der Reformation, 216; cf. H. Roller, 'Vorreformatorische und reformatorische Kirchenverfassung im Fürstentum Braunschweig-Wolfensbüttel', Studien zur Kirchengeschichte Niedersachsens 10, 1959, 61 ff.; C. Mahrenholz, 'Die Verfassungs- und Rechtsgestaltung der Evangelischen lutherischen Landeskirche Hannovers in Geschichte und Gegenwart', Zeitschrift für evangelisches Kirchenrecht 8, 1961, 113 ff.

'synod' quickly fell into disuse. In Hesse (Marburg 1610) the two functions of the central authority continued to be expressed in the name which was given to it, for it was described as *Kirchenrat und Konsistorium*. But the astonishing fact which emerges from this brief survey of the development of church organisation is that the churches of the Reformation managed for a whole generation without any central church government.

CHAPTER V

THE PROROGATION OF THE COUNCIL, LUTHER'S POLEMIC AGAINST THE POPE, AND THE FRANKFURT STANDSTILL[1]

I. THE PROROGATION OF THE COUNCIL

EVEN in 1537 the calling of the Council was prevented, not by the attitude of the Protestants, nor on this occasion by resistance within the Curia itself, but by the attitude of France and of the duke of Mantua. King Francis I had at first agreed, but when the invitations had gone out he declared that as long as the war with the Emperor continued it was impossible to meet at Mantua. A papal legate who was sent to France achieved nothing. 'Not a single copy of the Bull of invitation reached any French bishop.'[2] Then, in the middle of February, when detailed arrangements were being made in Rome, the duke of Mantua declared that he would require a strong military guard under his command for as long as the Council was in session. He was prepared to enter negotiations about the strength of the force, but his demand would have made nonsense of the canonically necessary 'freedom of the Council'. This meant that Mantua could no longer be considered as a possible venue for the Council.[3] Obviously it was not the Pope's fault that this happened at such a late stage, but it meant that he had to postpone the Council. The postponement was announced on 20 April 1537 in the Bull *Decet Romanum Pontificem*, in which it was stated that an 'armed' Council was an impossibility. The French refusal, which was far more important, was not even mentioned in the Bull. A new date,

---

[1] A. Korte, 'Die Konzilspolitik Karls V. in den Jahren 1538–1543', *SVRG* 85, 1905; W. Friedensburg, Kaiser Karl V. und Papst Paul III. (1534–1549), *SVRG* 153, 1932; H. Jedin, *Geschichte des Konzils von Trient*, 2 vols., 1949 and 1957; G. Müller, 'Zur Vorgeschichte des Tridentinums. Karl V und das Konzil während des Pontifikats Clemens VII. *ZKG* 74, 1963, 83 ff.

[2] *Jedin I*, 262.

[3] Ibid., 263 f.

1 November 1537, was proposed.[1] Diplomatic activity began all over again, and the search was on for a suitable meeting place. This time only the cities in Venetian and Papal territories were mentioned as possibilities —a sign that the Protestants' demand for a Council on German soil was already being disregarded. In Germany, too, a different view of the Council and its function was beginning to emerge. Aleander's opinion was that the emphasis should no longer be on winning back those who had fallen away, but rather on strengthening the waverers and preserving what was left.[2] Once again Francis I rejected all the places mentioned, insisting that the Council should take place in Germany or in France. Since the first seemed intolerable to the Pope and the second intolerable to the Emperor, Francis' demands put back the Council for a second time. With Venice's agreement the Pope decided for Vicenza, but this happened so late that on 8 October a new postponement had to be announced until 1 May 1538.[3] The effect of this on German Catholics—as Eck, Held and king Ferdinand testified—was crushing, and it gave support to those who were convinced that this Pope, too, did not really want a Council. This suspicion was by no means confined to Protestants.[4] Meanwhile at the Curia preparations were made, but the only person to arrive on the date which had been announced was the exiled bishop of Upsala.[5] The Pope had taken no steps to prevent this happening. He himself was on the way to a meeting at Nice with the two monarchs, and on 25 April 1538 he postponed the Council again for an indefinite period, since no participants had appeared.[6] It was indeed his hope that at Nice he might be able to mediate in establishing a peace which would make it possible to hold the Council later in a better atmosphere. But all that emerged from that meeting was a ten-year armistice, and France rejected the idea of a Council once again.[7] After the Pope's return, a new Bull, backdated to 28 June, was published, deferring the Council until Easter 1539[8]. But the forces of opposition were not to be overcome so quickly. New enmities and new problems arose, this time caused by the Emperor's policies which were directed towards unification within the Empire. He was reaching the point at which he did not need a Council any more than Francis. The Pope evidently made strenuous efforts to avoid a further postponement, but despite his efforts the proposed opening date, 21 May 1539, proved im-

---

[1] CT IV., 104 ff., 111 f.; NBD I, 2, 438 and 440.
[2] CT IV., 114; NBD I, 2, 440 (cf. ibid., 154); Jedin I, 266.
[3] CT IV, 135 ff.
[4] Jedin I, 270; NBD I, 2, 220 and 166.
[5] Jedin I, 274.
[6] CT IV, 161 f.
[7] A. Korte, op. cit., 15 ff.
[8] Jedin I, 274 f.

practicable, and he was obliged to defer again, this time *ad beneplacitum*, for 'he quite rightly feared that if he were to fix a new date which then had to be altered again, he would be exposing himself to ridicule.'[1]

Certainly the conditions prevailing at the time accounted adequately for the Council being deferred no less than five times. Nevertheless, even the most loyal Catholics were now convinced that the Pope did not really want a Council any longer. Jedin has sought to trace the reasons:[2] from the start, the Pope had either not recognised the difficulties or he had made light of them. He ought to have seen that a great deal of serious theological discussion was required, for which inadequate preparations had been made, and which would take up more time than had been anticipated. He was quite prepared to countenance a reformation in the 'members', but was slow to appreciate that the 'members' would insist on a reformation of the 'head' and of the practices of the Curia, particularly the practice of dispensations. As head of the Vatican state the Pope feared the power of the Emperor. Charles's serious illness in 1540 allowed him to breathe more freely, for it seemed to spell the end of political pressure.[3] How could the Pope possibly wish for the Emperor's power to be strengthened as a result of the Council? Finally, all hope of winning England back by means of a Council had now disappeared. Even after Henry's excommunication on 17 December 1538 the Catholic rulers regarded trade with England as far more important than any return on his part to the Roman Church. All this did not mean that the Pope had no desire for a Council at all. It meant merely that he would not pursue it without regard to the cost or to the circumstances. Even after 1538 papal conciliar politics were 'no two-faced game, but were conducted along two lines with the skill of a virtuoso, the only fault being that they were nothing more than politics.'[4]

2. LUTHER'S POLEMICS AGAINST THE POPE

Bugenhagen noted these statements in Luther's 'Testament': 'God be praised, I know that I have done right in storming the papacy with God's Word, for the papacy is an insult to God, to Christ and to the Gospel.' 'And now I am ready to die, if the Lord will. I would like to have lived until Whitsuntide, in order to attack even more vigorously in the sight of all the world the Roman beast and its empire. That is what I shall do, if I live.'[5]

---

[1] *CT* IV, 178; *Jedin* I, 278 f.
[2] *Jedin* I, 280 ff., who thus defends the Pope against the strictures of Friedensburg, Cardauns and Korte, who think that he did not in fact want a Council.
[3] *Jedin* I, 284.
[4] Ibid., 286.
[5] *WAB* 8, 55, 1 ff. and 56, 29 ff.

In the period following the Diet of Schmalkalden Luther conducted violent polemics against the papacy and published a series of small pamphlets.[1] Of greater weight is his 'The three symbols or confessions of christian faith',[2] which is designed to thow that Evangelicals did not reject the ancient creeds of the Church. In March 1538 Luther published the memorandum *Consilium de emendenda ecclesia*, which had been produced by a commission of Roman cardinals in preparation for the Council and which Contarini (who had been a cardinal since 21 May 1535) delivered to the Pope on 9 March 1537.[3] This document is a notable indication of the number of Roman cardinals who were anxious for reform. With astonishing freedom the document states that the root of all evils lies in the exaggerated view of the papacy. The view put forward by certain flatterers that the Pope is the absolute ruler of the Church is the Trojan horse from which the innumerable abuses in the Church have come. The only way of overcoming these abuses is to undertake a relentless reform of the Curia itself. Luther, however, did not see in this document the desire for reform but only its loyalty to what remains after abuses have been removed. Even in this form, it was still unacceptable to Luther. And indeed, the things which really mattered to Luther are nowhere stated in this document. For these Roman reformers questions of the power of the papacy or of right doctrine and administration of the sacraments were naturally not open to discussion. So this programme of reform, for all its seriousness, merely illustrates again how much could have been expected of a Council. At the most it would have achieved merely a reform of externals and of blatant abuses, and to that extent Luther was justified in saying that Rome was not interested in a genuine Council but wished to remain 'unreformed' as before. Even the programme of reform contained in the cardinals' memorandum was in fact stifled by the Roman bureaucracy.[4]

Early in 1539 Luther wrote a pamphlet *On Councils and Churches*, in which he took issue with the Roman view of the Council.[5]

> The extended prorogation convinced him that the Pope had no genuine desire for a Council. To Luther this was an indication of the wrath of God, and it terrified him. Rome demanded that the Council should be guided according to tradition and the fathers. Luther finds this demand dishonest and impracticable. It is dishonest because the Roman Church itself does not keep to tradition—the Pope could not even tolerate a reform which put the Church

[1] Collection in *WAR* 50.
[2] *WAR* 50, 255 ff.
[3] *WAR* 50, 284 ff.; *CT* XII, 131 ff.; W. Friedensburg, *ARG* 33, 1936, 1 ff.; *Jedin I*, 339 ff.
[4] *Jedin I*, 341 ff.
[5] *WAR* 50, 488 ff.

back to the position which it occupied fifty or sixty years ago, let alone a reform based on the ancient Councils. The Roman Church is not even at one with the papal claim to be 'above councils, above the fathers, above kings, above God and above the angels', for it is not possible to make such claims and at the same time to call for a Council. 'Show whether you will bring him down and make the fathers and the councils his masters! If you do that, I will gladly take your part and support you' (519.9). But even if the demand is being made honestly, it is impracticable. Luther has studied the ancient councils and can affirm that they, like the fathers, contradict one another and are not unanimous. On this ground alone it is impossible to turn tradition into a canon. 'Who is to arbitrate in all this ?' (520.21). Luther takes Augustine and the early councils as examples which show how the Church was unable to live with their directives and was thrown back upon Scripture. Thus he arrives at his own view of what a council should be. It is not the function of councils to regulate the Church by means of laws, but simply to defend the ancient faith over and over again on the basis of Scripture. Councils are therefore not 'judges according to their own good pleasure' (625.23), but are bound to Scripture as the Church's 'law'. The judge is 'the Church, in so far as it preaches, believes and confesses holy Scripture'. Thus Councils are useful in times when the Church is under attack, when an individual clergyman or bishop cannot cope alone with the onslaughts of opponents (616.12), but they do no more than clergy and schoolmasters are doing all the time. A Council is thus necessary now, for Evangelicals are asking the help of all Christendom against the Pope who is destroying the Church, and to restore to its original purity and completeness 'S. Peter's article', i.e. the doctrine of justification. This is a task in which Emperor, king and all learned men who take the faith seriously should assist. But if it is not the intention to have a Council of this sort, it were better to have none at all. As long as there is doubt whether such a Council will be granted, men must commit the matter to God and in the meantime make do with 'little councils' in every church and school. In the latter part of the document Luther expounds the Evangelical idea of the Church. The Church is constituted by preaching, baptism, the Lord's Supper, the power of the keys, ministries, prayer and the Cross. Admittedly the devil, aping God, has built up alongside this Church a church of his own, the papal church which is entirely engrossed in mere externals, and also the church of the fanatics which despises and rejects even the external Word. But the external ordering of the Church must be free, though care must be taken in making any changes to ensure 'that the mass of people are not confused but enabled to co-operate' (649.33). The Church is nothing more than the shawl in which a child is brought to its baptism (651.1). The only 'hierarchies' necessary to the christian life are the hierarchies of home, state and church—there is no room left for any other sort.

Luther's pamphlet shows clearly that the difference between his view of the Council and the Roman view is not merely a matter of ecclesiastical politics. His view is based on a totally different conception of the Church, a conception which results from his doctrine of justification. It was fundamentally impossible for Luther to agree to the Council as planned, even though it purported to be a Council of reform. Certainly it was not possible for him to submit to its decisions. But this does not mean that Luther was not anxious that something should be done which would be helpful to Christendom as a whole. Nor does it mean that he would not have gone to a papal Council to give an account of his faith, even though this might have led to a renewed split or to martyrdom. In rejecting the notion of a papal Council which set itself up as the arbiter of faith Luther was following the dictates of his theological conscience or his theological awareness.

3. THE TURNING-POINT IN IMPERIAL POLITICS—THE FRANKFURT STANDSTILL[1]

At Schmalkalden no one could have known how the Emperor would react to the Protestants' refusal. Dr. Held had presented his demands as very urgent ones, and Melanchthon clearly saw a danger of immediate war. On 12 August the elector of Saxony summoned the League's war ministers to Coburg, in order to take precautions against possible attack. At a meeting of the League in Brunswick on 24 March 1538[2] a nine-year alliance in religious affairs was concluded with Christian of Denmark, and a number of princes extended this to cover secular affairs as well.[3] Both at Brunswick and Eisenach[4] consultations were held on the subject of defying the Imperial Cameral Tribunal, but all that emerged was a document in which the Tribunal was attacked, the complaints against it summarised, with the threat of counter-measures in the event of any judgement by the Tribunal being executed.[5] The document appeared on 13 November 1538. Meanwhile the Vice-chancellor was doing all in his power to intimidate the Protestants. He actively promoted the formation of the Catholic *Nuremberg Alliance*, which came into existence after a great deal of negotiation on 10 June 1538 'for the preservation of our christian faith, and the maintenance of peace, unity and good manners in the holy Empire'.[6] But for the Emperor the Turkish War, which on 9 October 1538 led to the defeat at Esseg, and the war with France were far more urgent than a military conflict with the Protestants, who before anything else had to be prevented from forming an alliance with Francis I. With the prorogation of the Council and the growing doubts about the seriousness of the Pope's intentions, a Protestant war was a possibility which

[1] H. Baumgarten, *Geschichte Karls V.*, 1885–1892; W. Rosenberg, 'Der Kaiser und die Protestanten in den Jahren 1537–1539', *SVRG* 77, 1903; R. Stupperich, 'Der Humanismus und die Wiedervereinigung der Konfessionen', *SVRG* 160, 1936.
[2] Rosenberg, *op. cit.*, 21.
[3] *Ursachen* VIII, 13 (text).
[4] Rosenberg, *op. cit.*, 55
[5] *Ursachen* VII, 19. (The various 'reservations' listed in VII, 9–16.)
[6] Ibid., VIII, 14 f.

the Emperor seems not even to have considered. Certainly he did nothing to pacify them and he let Dr. Held remain in Germany.

But in the (German) instructions given to Held for the Diet of Schmalkalden he had been told to get expert opinion in Nürnberg about 'what might happen if a Council were not held',[1] which means that the Emperor had been preparing himself for that possibility at quite an early stage. At the discussions in Nice in June 1538 king Francis refused to declare himself against the Lutherans if he did not receive Milan forthwith—a declaration which could not fail to make the Emperor acutely aware of the danger of a Franco-Protestant alliance, and which made a war against the Protestants virtually impossible at that moment. Immediately after this conference the Emperor and the Pope went together to Genoa. There, on 24 June, letters arrived from king Ferdinand and from Morone, the papal nuncio at Vienna, which offered a fresh possibility.[2] Ferdinand had met the elector Joachim II of Brandenburg at Bautzen for political negotiations, and he reported that the elector had offered to attempt a settlement of the religious dispute by conducting amicable discussions and without touching the substance of faith. As a result of his political worries, particularly the need for aid against the Turks, Ferdinand had given him authority to initiate discussions and he recommended that his imperial brother should do likewise. In fact the Emperor got the Pope to agree to peaceable discussions being held with the Protestants before the Council began,[3] and the Pope appointed Aleander as his legate to deal with the matter,[4] deferring the Council—as we said earlier—until Easter 1539.

The elector Joachim now went to the Schmalkaldians and asked them to tell him 'what was wanting and on what basis peace should be established'.[5] He made no mention of a religious agreement. Meanwhile the king put pressure upon the papal nuncio to hasten the Council or to get concessions from the Pope, and he asked Joachim to let him know what the Protestants were demanding. On 2 July[6] Joachim was able to inform him, on the basis of information received from Saxony and Hesse, that the Protestants were willing to assist against the Turks, provided that a permanent religious peace were guaranteed to them and that their grievances about the Imperial Cameral Tribunal were remedied.[7]

At the July meeting of the Schmalkaldians in Eisenach consultations

[1] G. Heide, *Geschichte der Stadt Nürnberg VIII*, suppl. 5 p. 189 ff.
[2] *NBD* I, 4; cf. ibid. I, 2, No. 96 and Rosenberg, *op. cit.*, 40 ff.
[3] Rosenberg, *op. cit.*, 43 and 44 f.
[4] *NBD* I, 3, No. 1b ff.
[5] Rosenberg, *op. cit.*, 46.
[6] Ibid., 48; *NBD* I, 4, suppl. 29.
[7] Rosenberg, *op. cit.*, 51; Lanz, *Correspondenz* II, 291.

were held about the offer, and because the Imperial Cameral Tribunal threatened to put Goslar under the ban the war ministers were invited to attend once again. They demanded that their negotiators should be granted the full authority of the Emperor 'in a satisfactory form'. A committee worked out a list of very far-reaching demands, but these were not given to Joachim. He received merely an indication of their readiness to take part in discussions, which should be held in Frankfurt am Main. Ferdinand was not informed of this until the end of September, when a Brandenburg official visited him. The negotiators appointed to assist Joachim came from the Palatinate. Like Joachim they had Evangelical leanings and so Ferdinand in fact trusted none of them. So on 2 October he asked the Emperor to authorise two other negotiators, so that the two electors would function only as mediators.[1] Meanwhile Aleander had arrived at Ferdinand's court[2] and stated with some consternation that the king was evidently no longer interested in discussions about unity, but only in getting peace and assistance against the Turks. It seemed therefore that he had no need of the services of a legate.[3] The Emperor continued to regard religious unity as the goal to be pursued, but he was prepared to defer this, and so would not authorise anyone to negotiate until more was known about Protestant demands.[4] So Joachim drew up a list of these himself and got Saxony and Hesse to approve it. On 26 December he sent it to Vienna.[5] Meanwhile, the Protestants had given up all hope of the enterprise achieving success, and the activities of the Imperial Cameral Tribunal gave rise to new fears. Proceedings had been initiated against Electoral Saxony, Hesse and Hamburg, and the ban upon Goslar and Minden[6] seemed to the members of the League to make it essential that they prepare to defend themselves by force of arms. On 20 November notices were sent out convening a further meeting of the League at Frankfurt on 12 February. It is not difficult to understand why the Curia quickly lost interest in the efforts to reach agreement.[7] The Emperor, on the other hand, went ahead and appointed as his authorised negotiator the exiled archbishop of Lund, John of Weeze. He arrived in Vienna on 28 December.[8] He had authority to negotiate with the

[1] NBD I, 4, app. 14; Rosenberg, op. cit., 60 and 76 f.
[2] 7 September; Rosenberg, op. cit., 53.
[3] NBD I, 2, No. 112; I, 3, No. 26 and 39.
[4] NBD I, 3, p. 204.
[5] NBD I, 4, app. 40.
[6] 9 October 1538; Pol. Corr. II, No. 549; for later developments see vol. III.
[7] NBD I, 3, No. 47.
[8] NBD I, 4, app. 16; H. Baumgarten, Deutsche Zeitschrift für Geschichtswissenschaft 6, 1891, 293; Enders, Briefwechsel 12, 108, No. 5; WAB 8, 385 n. 4; E. Issel, Die Reformation in Konstanz, 1898, 134; Lanz, Staatspapiere, 1845, 277; NBD I, 4, app. 17; Rosenberg, op. cit., 73.

estates to whom the Nuremberg Standstill did not apply, and a letter from the Emperor to the king expressly authorised discussions to proceed without papal legates being present. However, when the Protestants' demands became known in Vienna, Ferdinand was filled with indignation and recommended that all policies aimed at concord should be given up. Aleander declared again that the use of force seemed to be the only possible way out.[1] In any case, the instructions which Ferdinand had given to his representatives, if they had been acted upon, would have made all further negotiation pointless.[2] So at the end of 1538 the situation was about as menacing as it could possibly be.

But what was decisive at this moment was the presence of John of Weeze and also the Emperor's desire 'to restore unity of faith by means of concessions which left the essentials of religion untouched', and with this in view to arrange a standstill 'for the shortest possible period and under the least damaging conditions', in order to get help against the Turks.

Among the Schmalkaldians the fear of military attack had risen to such proportions that the heads of the League were set upon arming themselves for war. The proposition which was put to the Frankfurt assembly painted a gloomy picture of the situation.[3] It was considered necessary, before the Emperor's spokesman arrived, to consult about defensive measures. The Landgrave, and even the elector of Saxony, declared themselves in favour of an offensive, should negotiations for peace fail. Francis of Lüneburg used Lutheran arguments against this proposal. Saxony then recommended that the League should adopt a common and comprehensive policy and enlist men for military service, paying them a waiting wage. Saxony also got a statement from the theologians to the effect that if one or more members of the League should be put under the ban, this would justify military action in their defence.[4] The Landgrave declared that to wait would be to tempt God. Yet in spite of this, the decision was put off until after the end of peace negotiations, and the members simply accepted the request for payment of special fees for armament purposes. In the peace negotiations[5] the Emperor's representative set his sights merely on achieving a religious standstill. He asked for suggestions about ways in which the Nuremberg Standstill could be improved. The principal demands of the Evangelicals were for a permanent peace, whether or not a Council took place, and the suspension

[1] NBD I, 3, No. 123.
[2] NBD I, 3, p. 77; H. Baumgarten, Geschichte Karls V, III, 356.
[3] O. Meinardus, 'Die Verhandlungen des Schmalkaldischen Bundes', Forschungen zur deutschen Geschichte 22, 1882, 636 ff., app. 5; Mentz II, 181 f.
[4] Enders, Briefwechsel 12, 70, No. 2674; WAB 8, 356 (app.); Mentz II, 180.
[5] 25 February–19 April; Mentz II, 184; Pol. Corr. II, 560 ff.

of all sentences imposed by the Imperial Cameral Tribunal in religious matters, including disputes over church properties.[1] Their position was strengthened by the arrival of envoys from Denmark, England and Jülich-Cleves, and by the news that William of Fürstenberg, who had a veritable army of mercenaries at his disposal, was ready to offer them his services. Nevertheless their demands were rejected by the Emperor's representative on the grounds that to grant them would be to destroy the order of the Church and of the Empire, and also the normal and proper processes of justice. Instead he proposed a religious conference, and in the meantime a standstill of one year's duration. Some incredibly tedious negotiations then followed, which were saved from collapse only by the zeal of the mediators and the desire for peace on the part of the members of the League. The end was not reached until 19 April.[2] The result was that the Emperor granted to all who were at that time adherents of the Augsburg Confession a standstill from 1 May for a period of fifteen months. Within that period no Evangelical estate was to be attacked or otherwise violently treated on grounds of religion. At the same time the Nuremberg Standstill was to remain in force, and when it expired those who were adherents of the Augsburg Confession on 19 April would continue to be protected until the next Imperial Diet. For the duration of both the Frankfurt Standstill and the Nuremberg Standstill all legal proceedings specifically named, including the ban imposed upon Minden, were to be suspended. Meanwhile, for their part, the Schmalkaldians were to attack no one in the cause of religion, they were to accept no new members into the League, and no further secularisation was to take place. The Emperor would use his influence to see that the Nuremberg Alliance was not extended during this period. He would also call a meeting at Nuremberg on or about 1 August to which the estates on both sides should send conciliatory theologians of their choice for the purpose of negotiating a concord. The Protestants declared that they would not tolerate the participation of the Pope in such negotiations. Both sides were to discontinue armaments and were to keep the peace. Finally the Protestants promised to attend a meeting at Worms on 18 May and to give assistance against the Turks according to the decisions which would be reached there.[3] There were two points on which it proved impossible to reach agreement, and these were referred to the Emperor for his decision. The first was the Protestant demand that the Standstill should not be confined only to those

---

[1] *Pol. Corr.* II, p. 560 n. 3.

[2] *Ursachen* I, 32 (text); *Walch* 17, 396; *Le Plat* II, 625 ff.; cf. *Pol. Corr.* II, No. 608 (app); P. Fuchtel, 'Der Frankfurter Anstand', *ARG* 28, 1931, 145 ff.; E. Ziehen, 'Frankfurter Anstand und deutsch-evangelischer Reichsbund von Schmalkalden', *ZKG* 59, 1940, 324 ff.

[3] *Pol. Corr.* II, p. 614 n. 1.

who were adherents of the Augsburg Confession at that time; and the second was their request that the Nuremberg Alliance should be prohibited from accepting new members. If the Emperor could not agree to these requests, then the Frankfurt Standstill should be limited to a period of six months' validity, after which the Nuremberg Standstill would continue in force.

After so much effort and such lengthy preparations the outcome must appear slender indeed. But the significance of the agreement lies firstly in the fact that the Emperor actually entered into discussions with the Protestants again and showed that he was prepared to seek a new way out. For the time being, therefore, tension had been relieved. The agreement also went beyond the Nuremberg Standstill in so far as the suspension of legal proceedings had been conceded publicly and universally. Johann von Weeze had expressly committed the Imperial Cameral Tribunal to observe the Standstill.[1] Moreover, the extension of the Standstill to cover those who adhered to the Augsburg Confession at the time of the agreement amounted to a recognition of the Reformation's progress. The most important achievement, from the Emperor's point of view, was that the Standstill made religious conversations possible. The final recess named those who were to take part.

Bucer was one of the Evangelical theologians who criticised the agreement most vehemently.[2] To accept the clauses about the extension of the League and secularisation seemed to him to be a betrayal of the Evangelical cause. Landgrave Philip, on the other hand, thought the opposite, for it was 'ridiculous enough' for the Emperor 'to stop up the law, for in truth half of our "religious matters" have about as much to do with religion as a hare to a drummer'.[3] The Catholics, particularly duke Henry of Brunswick and the Bavarian dukes, felt that they had been betrayed, and Henry soon began to threaten Goslar with the ban again. But the person who was really embittered was the papal legate, who had not only been excluded from the discussions but was now faced with the immediate prospect of religious conversations from which the Curia was to be excluded, a step which could easily lead to the formation of a council for the German nation, which would be all the worse if the Curia—which had struggled so hard to prevent it—really was denied participation. He was so angry that at Held's suggestion he made a formal complaint against John of Weeze, reproaching him with having allowed himself to be corrupted, so that he had betrayed the Catholic cause.[4] The Curia

[1] Smend, *Reichskammergericht* I, 156.
[2] Lenz, *Briefwechsel* I, 70 ff., 77 n. 8; *WAB* 8, 413 ff., No. 3324.
[3] Lenz, *Briefwechsel* I, 87.
[4] *NBD* I, 4, app. 48.

sent an instruction to the Emperor, warning him not to implement the terms of the Standstill and bringing a whole series of accusations against the negotiators, and rejecting the policy of negotiation altogether. The Emperor would have to bring up the religious question again at an Imperial Diet.[1] But the Emperor continued along the path that he had chosen. Naturally he took no action on the requests which had been referred to him, and so the Frankfurt Standstill expired after six months instead of fifteen, and at the end of the six months the Imperial Cameral Tribunal began legal proceedings again.[2] On 5 July the Emperor wrote from Madrid postponing the proposed meeting at Nuremberg which was due to have taken place in August. In fact it never took place. From February 1540 onwards the Emperor stayed in the Netherlands. There Ferdinand met him and received a deputation from the Schmalkaldians on 24 February, reminding him of the promised religious conference. He gave them no information. The barons of Manderscheid and Neuenahr sent a proposal to the Schmalkaldians, suggesting that they should leave to the Emperor the task of achieving unity, for he would appoint a body of learned men to work out an agreement. This proposal was entirely unacceptable to them. At their next meeting on 3 March 1540 they set themselves to make preparations for the religious conference, but they showed no inclination to make concessions in matters of doctrine.[3] The Nurembergers, who in the opinion of the elector were too ready to make concessions, were called to order by the Wittenbergers.[4] From the Emperor's point of view, the collapse of peace talks with the French and the end of the armistice which he had arranged with the Turks finally settled the matter. Under such pressures he announced on 18 April that a religious conference—regardless of the Frankfurt Standstill—would take place at Speyer on 6 June.[5] When the Curia protested, he replied that political necessities dictated his action.[6]

---

[1] *NBD* I, 6, 162 n. 4.

[2] On 8 December J. v. Weeze gave an inconclusive reply, *NBD* I, 6, app. 27 and p. 308 n. 2; cf. *Mentz* II, 212; *WAB* 8, 647. On what follows see Stupperich, *Humanismus* 61 f.

[3] *CR* 3, 926 ff.; *WAB* 9, 20 ff.; C. G. Neudecker, *Merkwürdige Aktenstücke aus dem Zeitalter der Reformation*, 1838, 177 ff.; *WAB* 9, 129 f. Luther's rejection of the idea of holding a large conference of theologians, *WAB* 9, 17 f.

[4] *WAB* 9, 50; Bibl. Buceriana No. 79c (*SVRG* 169, 1952); Cardauns, *op. cit.*, 85–108.

[5] *Ursachen* I, 32; *Walch* 17, 453 ff.

[6] *NBD* I, 5, 184, 190; I, 6, 257.

CHAPTER VI

THE ERA OF THE RELIGIOUS CONFERENCES

I. REFORMATION AND REFORMS

(a) From the Catholic point of view, an open breach of the Frankfurt Standstill occurred when the Reformation was introduced into the duchy of Saxony.[1] Duke George ('the bearded')[2] died on 17 April 1539. The duchy fell to his brother Henry, who since 1536/37 had been a member of the League of Schmalkalden.[3] The other members of the League had decided to protect him against possible attack, and they did not dismiss the troops which they had recruited before the Standstill until Henry had received his inheritance.[4] King Ferdinand expressly reminded Henry of the terms of the Standstill agreement in order to dissuade him from undertaking reforms.[5] But even while he was on his way to receive homage, Henry embraced the Reformation. On Whitsunday, 25 May, a service according to the Evangelical pattern was held in Leipzig, at which Luther preached.[6] The territory was then hastily visited by Cruciger, Myconius and Jonas.[7] The church in Leipzig was newly ordered by Johann Pfeffinger.[8] On 19 and 20 July disputations were held at the university between the visitors and the Catholic theologians on the subject of the Lord's Supper and the Mass, on monasticism and vows, and on the papacy. On 12 and 13 August the university senate accepted the Augsburg Con-

[1] E. Brandenburg, 'Herzog Heinrich v. Sachsen und die Religionsparteien im Reich', *Archiv für sächsische Geschichte* 17, 1896; F. Seifert, *Die Reformation in Leipzig*, 1883; S. Issleib, 'Herzog Heinrich als evangelsicher Fürst', *BSKG* 19, 1906, 143 ff.; Bornkamm, *Das Jahrhundert der Reformation*, 1961, 158 ff.
[2] O. Vossler, 'Herzog Georg der Bärtige und seine Ablehnung Luthers', *HZ* 184, 1957, 272 ff.
[3] *Ursachen* VIII, 10; *Mentz* II, 492.
[4] *Mentz* II, 195.
[5] *Pol. Corr.* II, No. 617, p. 612 n. 3.
[6] *WAR* 47, 772 ff.
[7] *Sehling* I, 1, 257 ff.; *WAB* 8, 505 ff., 524, 551, 553, 610.
[8] F. Seifert, *BSKG* 1, 1882, 125 ff., and G. Lechler, *ibid.* 3, 1885, 1 ff.

148

fession and the Apology as the doctrinal norm for the future.[1] On 19 September the new church ordinance—the so-called *Heinrichs-Agende*—was issued, regulating the ordering of services.[2] In December a second visitation began, this time conducted by officials of the duke.[3] Relationships with Electoral Saxony were at first very close, but they soon began to be clouded.[4] Luther watched the implementation of the duke's Reformation with growing disquiet. On 18 August 1541 the duke died, and his son and successor, Moritz, completed the task of Reformation but remained politically independent.[5]

(b) The beginnings of the Reformation in Mark Brandenburg were of a totally different kind.[6] Joachim I was a passionate adherent of the old faith and a firm protagonist of the Emperor and opponent of the Protestants. It was over the religious question that he parted from his wife Elizabeth, who in 1528 sought refuge in Saxony and lived there in straitened circumstances. After his death in 1535 the territory was divided between his sons, the elector Joachim II and the Margrave John of Küstrin. By his testament and by a personal oath he had bound them to Catholicism. Nevertheless at Easter 1538 during a service of the Lord's Supper at which the sacrament was administered in both kinds Margrave John confessed his allegiance to Lutheran doctrine, joined the Schmalkaldians and summoned Evangelicals from Ansbach to conduct a visitation. An 'Ordinance concerning the funds of churches, hospitals and other properties' assured the Church of its possessions and of their orderly administration, gave to the city councils the right to supervise the clergy, and introduced the office of superintendent. In the course of the next decade a church order developed which was strictly Lutheran and strictly territorial. The elector Joachim, who had been influenced by Luther in his youth but who was bound by his father to the old Church and bound politically to the Habsburgs, set his hopes on a Council and searched for a way which would allow of reforms without at the same time breaking the link with the traditional Church. Under pressure from the nobility and from the cities he made contact with Melanchthon and George of Anhalt. His first aim was to further church unity and he found an able

[1] H. Helbeg, 'Die Reformation der Universität Leipzig im 16. Jahrhundert', *SVRG*, 171, 1953.

[2] *Sehling* I, 88 ff. and 264 ff.

[3] 20 December–7 July (Meissen), 20 Dec.–11 Oct. (Thuringia); *WAB* 8, 551; Issleib, *op. cit.*, 179.

[4] *Mentz* II, 492.

[5] Ibid., 497 ff.

[6] P. Steinmüller, 'Einführung der Reformation in die Kurmark Brandenburg durch Joachim II', *SVRG* 76, 1903; L. Zscharnack, *Das Werk M. Luthers in der Mark Brandenburg*, 1917; W. Wendland, 'Einführung in die Quellen u. Literatur zur märkischen Reformationsgeschichte', *JBrKG* 34, 1939, 131 ff.

L

assistant in George Witzel. Before his meeting with king Ferdinand at
Bautzen, at which he was instrumental in establishing the new approach
to Protestants, he summoned Melanchthon to Berlin (in April/May 1538)[1]
and proposed for his own territory from Easter 1538 the kind of Reformation which he expected from the Council. Melanchthon was presented
with a draft scheme which admittedly failed to satisfy him because it
contained 'a great deal of unsound doctrine'. At the consultations which
led to the Frankfurt Standstill Joachim apparently lost all hope of a lead
from the Emperor in undertaking a Reformation. In the following August
he submitted a new church ordinance for discussion, which like the
Nuremberg Ordinance of 1533 was basically what had been worked out
by prince George. In October Melanchthon was once again in Berlin.[2]
Then on 1 November 1539 in Spandau and in Berlin services were held
at which the bishop of Brandenburg, Matthias von Jagow, administered
the sacrament after the Evangelical pattern and thus gave his sanction to
the work of reform. Which of the two services was attended by the
elector is a matter of debate.[3] In letters to his father-in-law, the king of
Poland,[4] and to king Ferdinand[5] he justified the step he had taken, and
explained that it by no means indicated any desire on his part to separate
himself from the Catholic Church. It meant simply that with the benefit
of 'good and timely advice', including advice from 'the most distinguished
prelates', he had taken steps 'to remove those obvious and crude abuses
which it would be scandalous not to deal with'. His church ordinance[6]
was approved by the Wittenbergers, despite their thoroughly conservative attitude. Luther protested only against carrying the sacrament about,
and found a few other things 'typical of Witzel'.[7] In March 1540 it was
accepted by the estates of the territory, though the clerical estates protested,[8] and it was printed in the summer of 1540. It contained the Lutheran
catechism, but kept virtually the whole of traditional ceremonial. Luther
was able to comfort his Berlin correspondents by pointing out that
despite this the article on justification by faith had been included and right
preaching had been guaranteed.[9] At the Imperial Diet of Regensburg

---

[1] N. Müller, 'Die Besuche Melanchthons am kurf. Brandenburgischen Hofe 1535
und 1538', JBrKG 2/3, 1906, 10 ff., 550; cf. ibid. 4, 1907, 127 ff.
[2] CR 3, 803.
[3] W. Dürks, 'Der Beginn der märkischen Reformation im Jahre 1539, JBrKG 34,
1939.
[4] F. Holtze, Forschungen zur brandenburgischen und preussischen Geschichte II, 2, 98 ff.
[5] N. Müller, JBrKG 5, 1908, 45 ff.
[6] Sehling III, 1909; P. Kalkoff, Wartburg 38, 1939, 261 ff.
[7] WAB 8, 620, No. 3420.
[8] Kurmärkische Ständeakten I, No. 16, p. 84, and No. 19, p. 103 f.
[9] WAB 8, 624, No. 3421; CR 3, 844; P. Kawerau, Der Briefwechsel des Justus
Jonas I, 375 f. and 377 f.

the ordinance even won the approval of the Emperor 'until the Council'. The elector's own position remained somethat obscure for a considerable time, for at the religious conference at Worms he took his seat on the Catholic side, and in all 'temporal' matters he remained loyal to the Habsburgs. His relationship to Luther suffered from the embarrassment caused by Agricola, who on 15 August 1540 had left Wittenberg for a post in Berlin.[1] Joachim's ordinance, taken as a whole, was an attempt at Reformation which gained the approval of the bishop and the Emperor, and from which anti-papal polemics were absent. It was an attempt to be fair to both sides and to steer a course between the two extremes.

(c) The efforts made in the archbishopric of Salzburg[2] to continue the work of reform give us a vivid insight into the difficulties against which the Catholic movement for reform had to contend. From April 1539 the Bavarian dukes had been tackling the situation caused by the catastrophic lack of priests, and they ordered a general survey of benefices and assistant curacies. Subsequently the archbishop also occupied himself with the matter, though with the modest aim of getting a plan of appointments adapted to the diminished number of priests, so as to regulate incomes and thereby make the priest's office more attractive and to encourage improved recruitment in the future. But the dukes wanted to look at the matter more closely and deal with the problem at its roots, for otherwise the reasons for the decline in vocations would remain undiscovered. They therefore demanded that the general visitation which had been promised twenty years previously should now take place, and that whatever grievances were brought to light should be dealt with. But this was precisely what the bishop was most anxious to avoid, for he feared that it would lead to interference by the princes in every aspect of church life. Nevertheless, it was decided to carry out the dukes' proposal. On 14 March 1541 a general visitation was begun in Reichenhall by two commissions—one appointed by the princes and the other appointed by the archbishop—each of which had been given separate instructions. It soon became apparent that it was impossible for the two commissions to work together. In January 1542 the bishops discussed the report of the visitation in the Bavarian part of the diocese of Salzburg, and they found themselves asking whether it would not be better to shelve the visitation of the rest of Bavaria. To implement reform might lead to even greater difficulties, and in any case visitations gave the princes an opportunity to see things which might lead them to make even more stringent demands for reform than those they had already made—and they were stringent enough, from the bishops' point of view. No one disputed that the clergy were

[1] G. Kawerau, 'Joachims II. Verhältnis zu Luther, JBrKG 7, 1911, 243 ff.
[2] ARC II, 609–725 (for the visitations see 697 ff.).

demoralised and everyone was convinced that this was an intolerable state of affairs. But if demands for reform were made which were too far-reaching, then even more clergy might leave and the situation would be even more desperate than before. If this happened, the dukes would certainly have good reason to intervene. So there was a discussion of ways in which the work of visitation might be avoided, and it appears that both sides agreed amicably to let it drop. The bishops were very occupied by the serious situation in their dioceses, but their hands were tied, not only by opposition from the clergy, but also by the covetousness of the territorial princes.

(*d*) It was much the same in Rome itself.[1] The group of cardinals around Contarini had made a first attempt at reform by drawing up their memorandum of 9 March 1537 which was mentioned earlier. Although this came to nothing, neither these cardinals nor the Pope himself wanted to give up the task of reform. At the beginning of 1539 Paul III's efforts for reform 'entered their second stage in an attempt to effect a general reform of the Curia on conservative lines'.[2] Two cardinals were appointed to each of the most important departments and given the task of reforming them. But they encountered stiff and skilful resistance from the officials, who knew exactly how to defend their positions (which for the most part had been purchased honestly) and who justified their way of doing things either by appealing to tradition or by pointing out their own rights (which they had bought and paid for). In the end the Pope himself demanded that the cardinals and bishops be treated with consideration, for they themselves occupied important offices.[3] So after all the fuss, the outcome was meagre. Only small details were improved,[4] and for the rest, everything went on as before. However, it was a sign of progress that the Pope himself was now actively engaged in reform, and that he had appointed as cardinals a whole series of devout and learned men like Contarini, Carafa, Pole, Cervini, Morone and others. Moreover, on 13 December 1540 the Pope addressed an assembly of over eighty bishops and demanded that they fulfil their obligation to reside in their own dioceses and leave Rome.[5] We do not know how many complied. But it is significant that the bishops replied with a memorandum[6] in which they listed all the things which prevented them from exercising their pastoral duties and which made them feel that it was virtually pointless to reside

---

[1] K. D. Schmidt, *Studien zur Geschichte des Konzils von Trient*, 1925, 19 ff.; *Jedin I*, 347 ff.

[2] *Jedin I*, 347.

[3] Ibid., 349 (5 January 1543).

[4] Ibid., 349 and 587 n. 88 (correction of earlier theories).

[5] *CT IV*, 454; cf. *CT I*, 113 ff.

[6] *CT IV*, 481 ff.

in their dioceses. Exemptions, reservations and patronage rights prevented them from seeing that proper appointments were made; preachers and confessors from the mendicant orders impeded the regular care of souls; appeals to Rome and interference on the part of secular courts destroyed the bishops' judicial authority. All these were things which the Pope either could not alter or did not wish to alter. In fact he himself allowed, practised and confirmed such things.[1] But without doubt the greatest achievement of the reform movement in Rome was the ratification of the Jesuit order by the papal Bull *Regimini militantis ecclesiae* on 27 September 1540.[2] Contarini had been instrumental in getting this through against opposition from two 'conservative' cardinals. No one could have guessed at that time what the future significance of the Jesuits was to be for the Catholic Reformation.

2. THE ERASMIANS' EFFORTS TO ACHIEVE UNITY

The fact that it had proved impossible to hold a Council produced an embarrassing political situation. The two heads of Christendom felt that the only way out was to pursue policies aimed at achieving unity in religious matters. The Wittenberg reformers, to judge from their statement on 18 January 1540,[3] considered that this was attempting the impossible. Nevertheless, there were intellectual and political forces at work which favoured the policies which Pope and Emperor had decided to pursue and which gave them an appearance of viability, namely the ideas of Erasmus and his followers about reform and unity.[4]

Erasmus died in 1536. His *De amabili ecclesiae concordia* of 1533[5] gives us a summary of his later theological thinking. The central question for him is about the kind of church in which alone God is to be found, for only such a church can be the 'right' church. It is faith which gives access to the Church, and faith is a gift bestowed upon man by God, though man must naturally be open to receive it. 'Salvation is effected freely by Christ, if we come worthily to his house.'[6] Worthiness, in its turn,

[1] *CT* IV, 489 ff.; *Jedin I*, 354.

[2] *Arch. hist. soc. Jesu* 10, 1941, 325 f.; H. Böhmer (ed. H. Leube), *Ignatius von Loyola*, 1941; F. Wulf, *Ignatius von Loyola—seine geistige Gestalt und sein Vermächtnis*, 1956.

[3] *WAB* 9, 19.

[4] R. Stupperich, 'Der Humanismus und die Wiedervereinigung der Konfessionen,' *SVRG* 160, 1936; K. H. Oelrich, 'Der späte Erasmus und die Reformation', *Ref. Studien und Texte* 80, 1961.

[5] *Opera* (ed. Clericus) V, 469–506. Letter No. 2853 in *Opus epistolarum* 10, 1941, 282 (ed. H. M. Allen/H. W. Garrod) offers a convenient summary. Cf. also O. A. Hecker, *Religion und Politik in den letzten Lebensjahren Herzog Georgs des Bärtigen v. Sachsen*, 1912, 33 ff.

[6] Stupperich, *Humanismus* 8.

comes about by means of *mortificatio*, the renunciation of fleshly lusts, and God's grace bestows *vivificatio* in consequence. Faith lays hold on Christ himself, bringing righteousness and giving assurance to the conscience. This is not the result of any merit on man's part, but rests solely on the merits of Christ, and it issues in works of love which are necessary if salvation is to be attained. Erasmus makes a distinction between innocence, which is purity of heart, and righteousness, 'which is an adornment, enabling man to do good works'. Thus Erasmus arrives at a twofold righteousness: 'the first is innocence, to which we are restored through faith and through baptism, and the second is the righteousness of faith which is made effective in love'. A Protestant, Antonius Corvinus, wrote a 'dialogue' on it which 'steered a middle course between approbation and rejection',[1] but when Luther had supplied a preface[2] it became an outright rejection. Luther thought that Erasmus would do better to keep off theology altogether and employ his talents on other things. 'Theology demands an intellect which will seek earnestly for the Word of God and will love that Word in all simplicity.'[3]

Erasmus' disciples then adopted the terminology of the reformers and described Erasmus' 'first righteousness' as *iustitia imputata*. Their leader was Julius Pflug, who in 1532 became provost of Zeitz, then dean of Meissen. Erasmus dedicated the work to him.[4] He expounded these ideas in the duchy of Saxony and coupled with them the proposition that reform should be carried out by a Council 'of men of goodwill like Erasmus on the one hand and Melanchthon on the other, who should try to bring the opposing parties closer to one another and by means of mutual concessions restore peace to Germany.'[5] The concessions he had in mind were the restoration of the chalice to the laity and the right of priests to marry, and he also called for better discipline of the clergy. He was supported by the restless convert George Witzel,[6] who in 1535 published the first Catholic catechism to be written in German. In 1537 Witzel presented his programme for Catholic reform, *Methodus concordiae ecclesiasticae*, which he had written in 1532. On the doctrine of justification he, too, follows Erasmus, to such an extent that Amsdorf accused him of plagiarising Erasmus.[7] Like Pflug, Witzel was convinced that the Catholic Church, too, must make concessions and undertake reform,

[1] *WAR* 38, 273.
[2] *WAR* 28, 276 ff.
[3] *WAR* 38, 278, 25; cf. 277, 23 ff.
[4] Stupperich, *Humanismus* 11.
[5] *RE*³ XV, 260 ff.
[6] *Opera* (3 vols.), Cologne 1559–1562; G. Richter, *Die Schriften Georg Witzels bibliographisch bearbeitet*, 1913; G. Kawerau, *RE*³ XXI, 399 ff.; E. Amann, *DThC* XV/2, 1950, 3577 ff.; P. Vetter, *ZKG* 18, 1932, 65 ff.
[7] Stupperich, *Humanismus* 14.

and for that reason he ardently advocated a Council. For him, the ancient Church should be the pattern for reform. Johann Gropper[1] in Cologne is often regarded as a member of this group, even though he had n) contact with Erasmus. For a long time it was thought that Gropper was dependent upon Albert Pigge (Pighius) of the Netherlands, who died on 26 February 1542, but there is little to substantiate this. In 1538 Gropper published his Enchiridion, *Institutio compendiaria doctrinae Christianae*,[2] which was immediately adopted in the archbishopric of Cologne as the official handbook of dogmatics. Its treatment of the doctrine of justification extends over 550 pages. For Gropper, the heart of the matter is the doctrine of twofold righteousness. Man's permanent imperfection is made good by faith in Christ, 'if you believe that the righteousness of Christ (of whom you have become a member) supplies what is lacking, provided that you strive constantly, in the power which the Lord gives you, to develop the grace which you have received'.[3] This reveals clearly the difference between Gropper's view and Luther's, for the 'imputation' of righteousness is conditional upon individual effort, which in turn is based upon grace, free will, and the given fact of membership in the body of Christ. On this view, a special 'promise' is rendered unnecessary.

But Erasmians were by no means only to be found in the ranks of the theologians, but among the bishops, too.[4] Bishop Stadion of Augsburg said that it was Erasmus who led him to true Christianity and he placed him above the great theologians of the past. A similar view was held by Cardinal Sadolet, archbishop Krzycke of Gnesen, Stanislaus Thurzo of Olmütz, John Danticus of Kulm and Tunstall of Durham. Erasmians were also found among the diplomats in the service of the Emperor, such as the brothers Alfonso and Juan Valdés, Louis de Praet, and even Granvella,[5] who was in charge of foreign affairs. These men were united 'in a common pattern of thinking, just as the leaders of the churches in the Age of Enlightenment were united two centuries later'. 'They searched the Bible and the early fathers for answers to those questions which concern men most deeply.' They asked the same kind of questions, even though their answers and their political and ecclesiastical decisions give an impression of such variety 'that it seems quite inappropriate to stick a single label on such a multiplicity of individual traits'.[6]

[1] Stupperich, *Humanismus* 15 ff. (following Jedin); Cf. *ARC* II, 121 n. 9.
[2] Ed. Lipgens, 225; H. Jedin, *G. Seripando* II, 1937, 264; *CR* 3, 652; *WAB* 9, 52, 49 ff.
[3] *Lipgens*, 100.
[4] *Jedin* I, 294.
[5] M. van Durme, 'A propos du quatrième centenaire de la mort de N.P. de Granvelle', *BHR* XIII, 1951, 270 ff.
[6] *Jedin* I, 295.

This explains why the Emperor stated several times before the Frankfurt Standstill was negotiated that he would need to know more exactly what the Protestants were demanding. Would it trasnpire in the end that Wittenbergers were no more than a few extremists who by no means represented Protestant feeling in its entirety? Had not changes in the situation occurred since 1530? Had not Melanchthon shown astonishing 'moderation' at the Imperial Diet of Augsburg? Had he not said to Du Bellay, when the French king was trying to mediate a settlement, that he considered agreement to be possible?[1] It is understandable that to outside observers the line of distinction between Erasmus and Melanchthon no longer appeared to be very clear, if even Cordatus could say of the 1535 edition of the Loci that they might have been written by Erasmus.[2] Had not Bucer also, in his commentary on Romans in 1536, propounded a doctrine of twofold justification[3] and spoken, like Erasmus, of mortificatio and vivificatio? Did not he also say that faith without works cannot give life? And had he not been prepared to take action on Francis I's proposals?[4] Was there not then good reason for thinking that the breach might be healed by means of a skilful formulation of what both sides held in common, and by granting concessions on externals such as the ordering of worship and the churches' rights?

As early as 1532/33 Erasmian attitudes had found expression in the Church ordinance of duke John of Jülich-Cleves. It was produced by a disciple of Erasmus, Konrad von Heresbach, and it had been shown to Erasmus for his approval.[5] Again, Witzel's thinking had influenced Joachim II's Reformation in Brandenburg. There were similar tendencies even in Electoral Saxony.[6] On 29/30 April 1534 Pflug and some theologians from Mainz held a discussion at Leipzig with Melanchthon and the elector's chancellor, Brück, though these had broken down over the question of the Mass.[7] Later, Carlowitz had gone behind his prince's back and arranged the religious conversations at Leipzig which took place on 1 and 2 January 1539, at which one side was represented by Bucer, Melanchthon and Brück, and the other side by Fachs, Carlowitz and Witzel.[8] On that

[1] CR 2, 742 f.
[2] CR 21, 420 f.; Stupperich, Humanismus 21.
[3] Stupperich, Humanismus, 25 f.
[4] Ibid., 34 ff.
[5] J. P. Dolan, 'The influence of Erasmus, Witzel and Cassander in the Church Ordinances and Reform Proposals of the United Duchies of Cleve, etc.', RST 83, 1957.
[6] O. A. Hecker, op. cit. (see n. 36 above).
[7] Stupperich, Humanismus 39 f.; CR 2, 722 ff.; Seckendorff, Hist. Luth. III, 8, para. 31 (criticism in Hecker, op. cit., 49).
[8] Lenz, Briefwechsel I, 63 ff.; Hecker, op. cit., 92 ff.; Enders, Briefwechsel 18, 23 n. 2; E. Brandenburg, Neues Archiv für sächsische Geschichte 17, 1896, 170; Hecker, op. cit., 82 ff.; Stupperich, Humanismus 42.

occasion Carlowitz had wanted to take the Church as it was in the time of Gregory or of Augustine as the model, but he was told—on the basis of arguments such as Luther used in his essay on Councils and Churches— that this was impossible. The representatives of Electoral Saxony withdrew from further discussions, but Bucer and Witzel went on and managed to reach agreement on fifteen articles. These were applauded by Landgrave Philip, who suggested at the Frankfurt negotiations that they should form the basis for discussion,[1] but they were rejected by the Wittenbergers, who described them as a dangerous patch-work of sophistries.[2] Carlowitz, on the other hand, was convinced that a week of discussions with Bucer would be sufficient to get agreement,[3] for he felt that the difference between the two sides could be reduced to questions about worship and church order, and continued separation over such questions could no longer be justified.[4] Early in April 1539 the two bishops of the duchy, under pressure from the territory itself, sought permission in Rome to administer communion in both kinds.[5] After the death of duke George, the theologians of Meissen, led by bishop John of Maltitz, handed to the new duke a copy of the *Liber Misnicus*, 'Common christian teaching which every christian should know'. In Wittenberg this was rejected out of hand.[6]

3. LANDGRAVE PHILIP'S BIGAMOUS MARRIAGE

The political situation of the Protestants was disastrously affected by Philip's bigamous marriage.[7] Philip had contracted a loveless marriage with the daughter of duke George of Saxony. He had lived like many of his contemporaries and equals and had contracted syphilis, which in 1539 led to a complete breakdown in his health and forced him to retire early from the negotiations at Frankfurt. His sister, the 'duchess of Rochlitz',[8] advised him to embark on a permanent extra-marital relationship.

---

[1] Cardauns, *op. cit.*, 14.

[2] *WAB* 9, 9, No. 3431; Bibl. Buceriana No. 79 (*SVRG* 169, 1952); Cardauns, *Geschichte* 85 ff.; *WAB* 8, 652 n. 1; Hecker, op. cit., 96 ff. Luther showed surprising tolerance with regard to the daily Mass without communicants. He merely complained that people were showing greater concern about ceremonies than about preaching.

[3] C. G. Neudecker, *Urkunden aus der Reformationszeit*, 1836, 334 ff.

[4] *CR* 3, 1047 and 1050; *Mentz* II, 279 f.

[5] Hecker, *op. cit.*, 120 ff.

[6] *WAB* 8, 460, No. 3348 and 496, No. 3352; *Mentz* III, 436; Stupperich, *Humanismus* 40 f.

[7] W. Köhler, *HZ* 94, 1905, 385 ff. and 'Luther und die Lüge, *SVRG* 109 f., 1912, 109 ff.; H. Eells, *The Attitude of Martin Bucer towards the Bigamy of Philip of Hesse*, 1924.

[8] E. Werl, 'Herzogin Elisabeth von Sachsen (1502–1557)', *Hessisches Jahrbuch für Landesgeschichte* VII, 1957, 199 ff.

Philip's choice fell upon one of his sister's ladies in waiting, Margaret of Saale. Her mother, however, insisted on a proper marriage, or at least a secondary marriage which a few princes at least would have to know about, and about which expert opinion would have to be sought, in order to be certain of its legality. So Bucer was charged with procuring expert advice from the scholars. He undertook the task on condition that the matter should remain secret until such time as the clergy might 'discreetly and at the right moment' inform the people about it.[1] His first step was to consult the theologians of Wittenberg. He gave great emphasis to the conscientious difficulties which Philip found himself in, and also the extent to which his manner of life impeded his activities on behalf of the church. Now Philip sought a means which Scripture allows, which the Pope has also on occasion allowed, and which the reformers themselves had suggested to the king of England. Their judgement should show publicly 'what is right in this case', or at least give secret support to Philip's decision. At this point a mild threat crept in, for Bucer pointed out that the prince could go to the Emperor and apply for a papal dispensation. On 10 December Luther and Melanchthon gave their considered judgement.[2] They distinguished between a general law and a possible dispensation. To make a public judgement in this instance which purported to be a general law would not only be contrary to Scripture but would also cause scandal and give the impression that Evangelicals were advocating the kind of freedom which is found among the Turks and the Anabaptists. On the other hand a dispensation, granted 'under the seal' and known only to a few trusted people, was a possible solution. Accordingly this second marriage took place on 4 March 1540 in Rothenburg an der Fulda in Melanchthon's presence. But the matter was not kept secret. The duchess of Rochlitz heard of it, was horrified and began to talk.[3] Duke Henry of Saxony interrogated the bride's mother and requested information from the elector of Saxony. At the Hagenau Conference king Ferdinand had already heard of it. So the Landgrave was in a very difficult position. He had transgressed imperial law, for bigamy was forbidden by the penal code of the Empire (the *Carolina*) which he himself had proclaimed. His first thought was to defend himself by having Luther's considered advice published. Luther, however, resisted this. To the elector he justified quite openly and frankly the advice he had given,[4] saying that he had given counsel as a confessor to a penitent, and such counsel cannot be judged by a secular court,

[1] Lenz, *Briefwechsel* I, 354.
[2] *WAB* 8, 638, No. 3423.
[3] Rockwell, *op. cit.*, 51.
[4] *WAB* 9, 131 ff., No. 3493.

'for by the world's laws and the laws of the Empire it would be inde-fensible'.[1] For that reason it was not to be made public.

> 'Both before I broke with the papacy and since, I have heard many things in confession and have given counsel which, if it were made public, I would have to deny, or alternatively reveal the contents of the confession.'[2] Luther had advised a number of clergy under duke George, for example, to marry their housekeepers in secret. He considered that such a marriage bound both partners in the sight of God, but was not valid in law. To the extent that Luther took seriously the 'conscientious difficulties' of prince Philip he was deceived, for he discovered afterwards that Philip had a concubine in any case who evidently caused him no qualms of conscience. Luther wrote that if he had known that, 'not even an angel would have persuaded me to give the advice I gave',[3] and he had certainly never suggested that the woman should be raised to the rank of princess, for the entire Empire would have regarded that as intolerable. He went on[4] to resist any attempt on the prince's part to make a universally valid law out of the particular advice given under the seal or to appeal to that advice before the secular court of the Emperor. He, Luther, as a confessor, was not in a position to make public law. He was con-cerned to deal only with private and secret distress of conscience, and for that he could get no assistance even from the law of Moses. 'Such distress goes beyond law and precedent, and yet it does not make law or precedent.'[5] He could defend his case before God, but not before the world or its laws, and such a defence would hardly be of use to the prince. People would be right if they said that Luther and Melanchthon have no right to make changes in existing laws, 'but at the same time, in order to relieve distress of conscience, they may be obliged to give secret counsel which differs from the dictates of the law.'[6]

If a man presents himself before God's judgement, he cannot then present himself before a human court without exposing himself to the penalties which human law requires. It was on the basis of considerations such as this that at a conference in Eisenach in July 1540 Luther recom-mended that the affair should be put out of the way by a 'good, strong lie', i.e. by simply disavowing the whole thing and regarding the new bride as a concubine.[7] The political repercussions of the affair evidently made no impression on Luther. In fact the Landgrave followed Luther's advice and gave evasive replies to all who questioned him.[8] But he dis-

---

[1] WAB 9, 133, 28.
[2] Ibid., 35 ff.
[3] Ibid., 134, 47.
[4] Ibid., 176, No. 3513.
[5] Ibid., 178, 37 f.
[6] Ibid., 199, 43 f., No. 3518.
[7] As n. 6 (esp. lines 132 ff.).
[8] WAB 9, 225, No. 3531.

covered that as a result of the affair he would get no assistance from other members of the League in the event of his being brought before the Imperial Cameral Tribunal or of his being attacked by the Emperor. From that moment onwards he tried to effect a rapprochement with the Emperor and offer him his services in return for consideration on the Emperor's part. We shall soon see that the Emperor was happy to oblige.

CHAPTER VII

THE RELIGIOUS CONFERENCES[1]

I. THE HAGENAU CONFERENCE[2]

THE Catholics were invited to a preliminary conference on 23 May, the Evangelicals on 6 June 1540 at Speyer,[3] but the meeting was transferred to Hagenau. The Emperor was represented by king Ferdinand, and despite urgent pleas from Bucer and Osiander the elector of Saxony and the Landgrave Philip declined to appear in person, because the conversations had not been arranged according to the terms of the Frankfurt Standstill.[4] So although the king presided, it was essentially a conference of theologians. Calvin came with the theologians of Strasbourg. Melanchthon had set out full of misgivings, had been taken ill on the way and had stayed in Thuringia,[5] so that Wittenberg was represented only by Cruciger, Myconius and Menius. The papal nuncio Morone had come with king Ferdinand,[6] but his commission was simply to advise the Catholics. He was to take no part in the discussions and he was to make no promises.[7] Opinion among the Catholics was divided, although no one thought of

[1] See Brandi, *Quellen*. R. Moses, *Die Religionsverhandlungen in Hagenau und Worms*, 1889; L. Cardauns, 'Zur Geschichte der kirchlichen Unions- und Reformbestrebungen', *Bibl. d. Preuss. Hist. Institut* V, 1910; R. Stupperich, 'Der Humanismus und die Wiedervereinigung der Konfessionen, *SVRG* 160, 1936; A. P. Brück, 'Instruktion Kardinal Albrechts von Brandenburg für das Hagenauer Religionsgespräch', *Archiv für mittelrheinische Kirchengeschichte* IV, 1952, 275 f.
[2] *NBD* I, 5, 421.
[3] *Ursachen* I, 33; *Walch* 17, 453 ff.
[4] *CR* 3, 1022 ff., No. 1959.
[5] *WAB* 9, 138 f., No. 3497; *CR* 3, 1050 and 1051. Melanchthon had written two documents in preparation for the conference: *De ecclesiae autoritate et de veterum scriptis*, and *De officio principum, quod mandatum Dei praecipiat eis tollere abuses ecclesiasticos*. Details in *WAB* 9, 139 n. 6. For the elector's recommendation that Luther should not take part, see *CR* 3, 1052.
[6] *NBD* I, 5 XV.
[7] Lanz, *Staatspapiere* II, 583 ff.

yielding. The intention of some was to get an immediate restitution of the old church, while others sought to get conversations adjourned until the Council.[1] Bishop Fabri suggested that they should proceed by taking as their starting point the Augsburg discussions, but that the final decision should be left to the Council. Cochläus declared that the doctrine of justification and the doctrine of the Church should be discussed as matters of urgency. Friedrich Nausea, with the aid of the Augsburg compromise articles, gave a Catholic interpretation to the Augsburg Confession, but is said to have recommended that the administration of the chalice to the laity and the right of priests to marry should be conceded.[2] King Ferdinand decided that the Augsburg articles should be taken as the basis for discussion.[3]

Right at the beginning of discussions, when the moment came for the participants to be sworn in, a problem arose. Upon what criteria were decisions to be based? The Protestants were prepared to be bound to Scripture as interpreted by the 'apostolic and christian church' but not to the fathers or to the councils.[4] They refused to take the Augsburg compromise articles as the starting point for discussion, and demanded instead the Augsburg Confession, in order to demonstrate that 'in all things they hold fast to the one, ancient, true and apostolic church and doctrine'. They requested 'free discussion', and when the king spoke of the Pope's rights to ratify any conclusions which the conference might reach, they protested. So the king had no alternative but to declare on 16 July that it had proved impossible to reach agreement on a *modus conciliandi*. The decision on this had therefore to be left to the Emperor and the Pope, and further discussion of the religious question would have to be deferred until another conference could be convened. The final recess, dated 28 July,[5] fixed the date and place of the next conference: it was to be held at Worms on 28 October. Certain details were fixed in advance. Each party was to have eleven votes, and the negotiators were to be bound to 'Scripture, as truly, plainly and commonly understood by the apostolic and christian churches'. The elector of Saxony said that he would accept this obligation 'only if it is rightly understood'.[6] It was further stated that any results achieved were to be subject not only to the approval of the Emperor but also to ratification by the Pope. The Wittenbergers recommended that 'a short protestation' should be made against this, for 'since he is a persecutor of the Gospel, we cannot expect him to

[1] *CR* 3, 1055; Stupperich, *Humanismus* 66.
[2] Cardauns, *Geschichte*, 160.
[3] *NBD* I, 5, 431.
[4] Raynald, *op. cit.*
[5] *Ranke* VI, 160 ff.
[6] *WAB* 9, 181.

ratify anything'.[1] Finally the Emperor was asked to call an Imperial Diet at which he would be present in person, and at which reports would be submitted on the discussions.

So the Hagenau conference remained simply an attempt, and it reveals clearly the fundamental difficulties which barred the way to achieving agreement. How could conversations on the religious question take place at all, as long as one side stuck rigidly to the authority of Scripture, and the other side stuck equally rigidly to the authority of the Pope, neither side being in a position to free itself?[2]

2. THE CONFERENCE AT WORMS[3]

The Hagenau recess was confirmed by the Emperor on 15 August, and he invited the Protestants to come to Worms on the appointed day. They met at Gotha for preliminary discussions[4] and declared that they could not possibly take the Augsburg compromise articles as a basis for discussion at Worms. They insisted that the basis must be the Augsburg Confession, and that in accordance with the decisions of the final recess at Frankfurt discussion should be centred on its doctrine. There were no other changes in the position of either party. The Emperor hoped for political advantages and on 14 September gave notice that an Imperial Diet would be held at Regensburg, at which the intended agreement should be finally decided. The Pope declared that it was a pious work to take trouble on account of those who had fallen away. Cardinal Farnese was as sceptical about achieving success as Luther was.[5] Granvella was deputed to represent the Emperor. Jakob Sturm had praised Granvella for his love of peace.[6] But Granvella kept the assembly waiting for almost a month, and did not arrive until 22 November. He clearly regarded his task in all this as a purely political one.[7] Thomas Campeggi came as papal legate,[8] and was simply to be an observer.

On 25 November Granvella opened the conference with a speech in which he blamed the Protestants for every ill.[9] The conference was to draw up a list of 'christian articles of genuine substance'—a task which the

[1] *WAB* 9, 181.
[2] *WAB* 9, 204 f., No. 3519.
[3] *Schl* 41404–41416; *Ursachen* I, 36; *Ranke* IV., 141 ff. and VI, 168 ff.; G. Kawerau, *ARG* 8 1910–1911, 403 ff.; O. Waltz, *ZKG* 4, 1881, 287; W. Friedensburg, *ZKG* 21, 1901, 112 ff.; *NBD* I, 6, 18 ff. and 218 ff.; M. Lenz, *Briefwechsel* I, 220 ff., 490.
[4] *CR* 3, 1043 ff; Seckendorff, *Hist. Luth.* III, 294; Stupperich, *Humanismus* 69.
[5] Stupperich, *Humanismus* 72.
[6] *Pol. Corr.* III, No. 112 and 127.
[7] *NBD* I, 6, 57.
[8] H. Jedin, *CCath* 15, 1958, 23 ff.; *NBD* I, 6, 5 ff.; *CR* 3, 1192 ff.
[9] *ARG* 8, 1919–1911, 406; Lenz, *Briefwechsel* I, 256.

Protestants performed by presenting the Augsburg Confession with its Apology. At that point discussions came to a standstill once more, and an argument developed about the method of voting. This seemed important to the Catholics, because three of their eleven voters—the representatives of Jülich, Brandenburg and the Palatinate—were uncertain on the question of justification, and they were not prepared to sign the articles which had been drawn up by Eck,[1] and which the Catholics were discussing amongst themselves. So the Catholics were anxious to prevent at all costs the casting of individual votes. On 5 January[2] they managed to get it agreed that each side should appoint only one speaker, thus ensuring that dissident minorities were prevented from making their voice heard. Mainz and Bavaria opposed even this,[3] but their concern was evidently to prevent any discussion taking place at all. It was not until 14 January that the real business of the conference was reached.[4] Eck and Melanchthon debated and reached agreement on the doctrine of original sin. Eck apologised for the long delay, and said it was due to the fact that it had taken him a long time to complete the comparison of the Augsburg Confession in its present form with the original version.[5] Granvella had already applied to the Emperor for an adjournment.

But the main business took place in secret.[6] Since the Hagenau conference Bucer and Gropper had become friends and were full of praise for one another. Both had agreement on religious questions at heart, and Gropper had been instructed by the archbishop of Cologne to make every effort to that end. They were now meeting very often, and the main topic of discussion was the doctrine of justification, which Gropper expounded along the lines of his Enchiridion. His concern was to link faith and obedience. Bucer was in full agreement with him in this, but simply wanted to guard against any attempt on man's part to make his obedience a claim upon God, and so Bucer laid great stress upon man's imperfection. Through Gropper and one of the Emperor's officials, Veltwyk, Granvella met Bucer and Capito. He invited them to a secret colloquy, which was to be entirely independent of the main discussions.[7] On the following day he gave greater urgency to his request by arguing 'that a secret discussion of this sort was the last means open to him of

[1] CR 3, 1254; WAB 9, 296, No. 3564.
[2] CR IV, 7 ff. and 10 ff.
[3] ZKG 21, 1901, 117.
[4] WAB 9, 307, No. 3569.
[5] CR 4, 33 f.; Melanchthon, Alle Handlungen die Religion belangend; Eck, Apologia; A. L. Herminjard, Correspondance des Réformateurs dans les Pays de langue française, 1878 ff., VI, 418; Pol. Corr. III, No. 168; H. Mackensen, 'Debate between Eck and Melanchthon', LQ 11, 1959, 42 ff.
[6] Stupperich, Humanismus 76 ff.
[7] M. Lenz, Briefwechsel I, 269, 274, 517.

getting a religious agreement in Germany', for 'it would be a serious matter if he were unable to bring to his imperial Majesty any hope of an agreement, for those who counselled his imperial Majesty to war would get their way'.[1] The two theologians from Strasbourg, on the advice of Feige, the chancellor of Hesse, and Jakob Sturm, accepted the proposal and subsequently received the written approval of the Landgrave.[2] On 15 December discussions began on the basis of a draft which had already been drawn up,[3] and on the doctrines of original sin and justification the two sides came 'very close'.[4] Nevertheless, there were times when Bucer did not know quite what to make of his partner, and he advised the Landgrave to be cautious.[5] Gropper, for his part, sought to balance Scripture and tradition and found that Bucer had similar ideas, for he also respected the customs of the ancient church. Gropper also wanted a reform in ceremonial, though he wished to preserve ceremonies as 'signs'. On the subject of the Mass, Bucer had to admit several times that Gropper could not simply do away with it. On 31 December, in spite of all the difficulties, it was possible to complete a draft agreement.[6]

Thus Granvella got what he had hoped for, namely a document to put before the Imperial Diet. He applied to the Emperor for an adjournment of the conversations, and in doing so he made great play of the difficulties caused by Mainz and Bavaria, saying that in such circumstances nothing useful could be expected in Worms. Charles replied speedily: on 18 January the conversations were broken off, almost before they had begun,[7] in order to be continued at the Imperial Diet of Regensburg.

3. THE IMPERIAL DIET OF REGENSBURG, 1541[8]

In the meantime an attempt was made to gain recognition for the draft agreement which had been concluded at Worms. Veltwyk pressed the Landgrave to give it his approval.[9] Philip asked Bucer to translate the text into German, and his notes on it show that he examined it with great

[1] Stupperich, *Humanismus* 83 f.
[2] Lenz, *Briefwechsel* I, 280, 282.
[3] Stupperich, *Humanismus* 87.
[4] Ibid.
[5] Ibid., 88.
[6] Ibid., 90 ff. and *ARG* 36, 1939.
[7] W. Friedensburg, *ZKG* 21, 127.
[8] Bibl. Buceriana No. 69 (*SVRG* 169, 1952); *Ursachen* I, 37; F. Roth, 'Zur Geschichte des Reichstags zu Regensburg 1541', *ARG* 2, 1904–1905, 250 ff.; 3, 1905–1906, 18 ff.; 4, 1906–1907, 65 ff. and 221 ff.; P. Heidrich, *Karl V. und die deutschen Protestanten am Vorabend des Schmal. Krieges* I, 1911, 7–53; L. v. Pastor, 'Die Correspondenz des Cardinal Contarini,' *HJG* I, 1880, 321 ff.
[9] Stupperich, *Humanismus* 94.

M

care, but he would not commit himself to it.[1] He sent it to the elector Joachim, who received it on 10 January.[2] He in turn sent it to Luther, describing it as an attempt by a few 'learned men on that side' which was worthy of support, even though it was necessary to recognise that 'on that side' the 'men of good will are in a weak position'.[3] Luther[4] acknowledged the good will of those who had drawn it up, but found their proposals unacceptable, because the Catholics 'would sooner countenance our Reformation than one based on the old canons and councils'—as duke George's Reformation had shown. He also felt that there was a great deal in the document which Evangelicals would find intolerable. His advice was to get 'devout and learned men' to discover 'where and what God's Word is'. If this were done, then the rest could wait 'until God's Word has taken root'. The elector John Frederick received some peace proposals from Philip, but he replied that he intended to stick to what had been resolved and to negotiate only on the basis of the Augsburg Confession.[5] His representatives at the Imperial Diet[6] were instructed to protest whenever the papal legate made an official appearance, even if the Landgrave did not support them in this. John Frederick thought that the best solution would be to get a permanent external peace. Should the Council be discussed again, his representatives were to refer to the Protestants' earlier refusal to attend, and were to demand a Council which would be 'honest, free, christian and non-partisan'. Finally, Melanchthon was not to be allowed to start private discussions with the Landgrave. The Curia, at the express wish of the Emperor, was represented by cardinal Contarini,[7] who was thoroughly acquainted with Protestant theology, and who based his own theology on Augustine and the Scriptures. He was passionately concerned to find a way of overcoming the religious cleavage. On the doctrine of justification he had arrived independently of Gropper and Pigge at conclusions which resembled theirs.

On 5 April the Emperor's 'proposition'[8] was read. It said that the Emperor regarded the religious question as the most important issue facing

---

[1] Lenz, *Briefwechsel* I, 303 and III, 36 n. 2.

[2] Ibid. I, 529 ff.

[3] *WAB* 9, 322, No. 3573, 4 Feb. 1541.

[4] *WAB* 9, 329, No. 3576 and 332, No. 3578, 21 Feb.

[5] P. Vetter, *Die Religionsverhandlungen auf dem Reichstage zu Regensburg 1541*, 1889, 11 f.

[6] *CR* 4, 123 ff.

[7] H. Rückert, *Die theologische Entwicklung G. Contarinis*, 1926; H. Jedin, *Kardinal Contarini als Kontroverstheologe*, 1949; and 'Ein "Turmerlebnis" des jungen Contarini', *HJG* 70, 1951, 115 ff.; and *Contarini und Camodoldi*, 1953; O. Ferrara, *G. Contarini et ses Missions*, 1956; H. Mackensen, 'Contarini's theological role at Ratisbon in 1541', *ARG* 51, 1960, 36 ff. (contests Rückert's view that Contarini was essentially a Thomist); V. Schulz, '13 Depeschen Contarinis', *ZKG* 3, 1879, 150 ff.

[8] *CR* 4, 152.

him, and he intended that new conversations should take place, this time by a few persons whom he would appoint personally. They would be asked to examine those points on which there was division of opinion, with a view to reaching agreement and then submitting a report, in order that decisions might be reached on it and the Pope consulted about it. The road from Worms had thus been left behind, and the Emperor had struck out on a new line of procedure. Despite some protests, this was accepted by the estates.[1] On 21 April the Emperor named the participants: Pflug, Eck, Gropper, and Melanchthon, Bucer and Pistorius (from Hesse). In addition, a few 'observers' were appointed, and the conversations were to be presided over by Granvella and count Frederick of the Palatinate. Then sealed copies (without title or heading) of the draft agreement worked out at Worms were put before the negotiators. It was made clear to them that the Emperor had chosen this as the basis for negotiations, on the grounds that the Augsburg Confession was unsuitable.[2] The papal legate took no part in the discussions, but Granvella allowed the Catholic negotiators to meet with him every morning to report on progress, thereby ensuring that Eck was made to toe the agreed line. Contarini perused the document beforehand and made alterations at one or two places.

Discussions began on 27 April.[3] The first four articles were dealt with quickly. The article on justification was rejected on the grounds that it lacked clarity, so on this point they had to leave the draft behind and attempt to draw up a new one. Eck, Melanchthon and finally Contarini all tried their hand, but each attempt was rejected. However, on 2 May they reached agreement on a new formula which according to Eck Granvella himself penned.[4] This result filled the negotiators with joy and new hope. The Emperor ascribed it to divine inspiration,[5] and Contarini described it as a miracle.[6] Even Calvin regarded it as a great triumph that the Catholics had consented to it, though he felt that at many points the formula could have been clearer.[7] Unfortunately, it soon became apparent that the formula was capable of more than one interpretation. John Frederick told his representatives that they were not to accept the article, because it obscured the *sola fide*. As discussions went on, everyone realised that in fact very little had been achieved. Melanch-

---

[1] *CR* 4, 159 ff., 163 ff.

[2] L. v. Pastor, *HJG* 1, 1880, 368; *CR* 4, 331.

[3] Vetter, *op. cit.*, 85 ff.

[4] *CR* 4, 198.

[5] *NBD* I, 7, XVI.

[6] F. Dittrich, *Regesten und Briefe des Cardinal G. Contarini 1483 bis 1542*, 1881, 177; Stupperich, *Humanismus* 100.

[7] Herminjard, *op. cit.*, VII, 111.

thon and Eck could not agree with one another, and the Emperor asked
Landgrave Philip to use his influence with Melanchthon. The Emperor
urged the negotiators to seek peace among themselves, assuring them
that he was willing to effect a Reformation even if the Pope opposed
it.[1] On 5 May they began work on the article which dealt with the Mass,
but transubstantiation proved to be an insuperable obstacle. On 10 May
the Protestants submitted a written statement of their position on this,
basing their case on the fact that this doctrine was unknown to the ancient
church, and complaining that too much time was being wasted in debating
this unprofitable matter, while 'nothing at all was being said about the
right use of the sacrament'.[2] But from the Catholics' point of view what
was at stake was a defined dogma which required assent. Behind this
particular doctrine lay the whole question of the Church's authority.[3]
The Protestant princes agreed 'with one accord' not to give way on this,
so the article had to be passed over without agreement. There were
'frequent disputes' over penance and absolution, because the Catholics
insisted that it was necessary to include a list of at least all the grave sins.
On the doctrine of satisfaction Bucer 'almost gave way', but Melanchthon
remained intransigent. But the article on which no agreement at all was
reached was the article on the Church—'into which the authority of the
Pope had been subtly introduced'. On 22 May the commission was required
to give an account of its progress. For the Emperor the result was disap-
pointing, for on 31 May the Protestants presented a summary of points
on which they were unable to agree with the articles included in the draft,
particularly the articles 'on the authority of the church and councils, on
the sacrament of the body and blood of Christ, on absolution or penance,
etc.'[4] So beside the draft agreement there was a short list of the articles
which had been agreed, and a long list of those on which no agreement
had proved possible. The Emperor tried to get help from Landgrave
Philip in an attempt to achieve a better result, but Philip steadfastly
refused. He felt that a purely external peace was the only possible solution.
John Frederick took an even tougher line and wrote to his representatives,
'If any man seek agreement, let him agree with God and God's Word.'[5]
So on 8 June the Emperor had to present this result to the estates for their
consideration.[6] Ten days earlier, on 28 May, Granvella and Morone
had met to consider what might be done in the event of total failure. On
15 June Contarini was told to inform the Emperor that the Pope was now

[1] CR 4, 295.
[2] CR 4, 273.
[3] Jedin I, 310.
[4] CR 4, 348–376.
[5] CR 4, 346.
[6] CR 4, 390 f.

determined to summon a Council without delay.[1] But while all this was going on the elector Joachim, with the approval of the imperial chancellory, made a quite unconventional attempt to get agreement, or at least mutual toleration. He sent a delegation to Luther, asking him whether he would be prepared either to accept the articles in the form in which the Catholic negotiators had put them, or if this were impossible, at least to tolerate them until the Emperor could implement a Reformation.[2] Luther refused the first request, saying that 'he could no more do that than Philip [Melanchthon] could', but 'for the sake of peace he would tolerate them for a time, provided that no changes were made in the articles which affected the purity of doctrine'.[3] Joachim and Weeze, probably at the instigation of the Emperor, made an attempt to formulate articles which both sides could accept, but the attempt was rejected by the Evangelicals, who said that any agreement would again prove to be to their own detriment.[4] The idea of temporary mutual toleration seemed still to be a hopeful one, and Contarini brought it up in Rome, only to be sharply rebuffed.[5] It was suggested to the estates that they might approve 'as an interim norm for the Empire those articles which had been agreed, and show toleration with regard to the others until the Council',[6] but they were unwilling to do so. Thus the Emperor's efforts to achieve unity collapsed because both sides proved unyielding. The final statement by the Catholics on 1 July[7] rejected the Worms draft on the grounds that it was incomplete, ambiguous, and full of errors. Eck disclaimed all responsibility for the failure of the attempt. Pflug and Gropper complained bitterly about his attitude.[8] On 12 July the Protestants gave their verdict on the proceedings.[9] Its tone was somewhat milder than the Catholics' statement, but not its substance.

So the religious question was back where it was before, and all the old problems reappeared. On 7 July Contarini did something which had never been done before at an Imperial Diet. He issued an urgent summons[10] to the assembled bishops to take seriously their spiritual obligations, to give no cause for scandal themselves, and to pay particular attention to preaching and the instruction of the young. The bishops pleaded with

[1] CT IV, 195 f.; ZKG 5, 1882, 595 ff.; Le Plat III, 118 ff.
[2] CR 4, 379 f., 385 f., 394 ff.; F. Roth, ARG 4, 1906–1907, 92; WAB 9, 433, No. 3628.
[3] WAB 9, 436, No. 3629; CR 4, 400, 406 f.
[4] CR 4, 584; Herminjard VII, 204 f.
[5] CT IV, 195 f.
[6] V. Pastor, HJG 1, 1880, 480.
[7] CR 4, 450 ff.
[8] CR 4, 459.
[9] CR 4, 476 ff.
[10] Le Plat III, 91 ff.

equal urgency for the summoning of the Council and drew attention to German grievances. Without the Council and reform from the top they evidently did not feel strong enough to comply with the cardinal's demands. The Protestants, too, submitted a document on reform.[1] The Emperor could do no more, at that point, than to leave further action to the papal legate, who on 12 July referred him officially to Rome, where the matter would be decided either by a general Council or by some other appropriate means. But when the Emperor, in his turn, referred the estates (on 12 and 25 July) to the Council, the old dispute about the nature of the Council flared up again. The Protestants drew attention to their earlier utterances on the subject and declined to recognise the authority of the Pope or of a papal Council.[2] The Catholics obviously welcomed the new efforts to summon a Council. Both sides were willing to accept either a Council for the German nation or an Imperial Diet, should a general Council fail to come to pass. But the Catholics declared once again that they were determined 'to maintain unswerving loyalty' to the old faith.[3] So no one had got a single step further, though everyone now appreciated more fully the difficulties which stood in the way of agreement. Melanchthon wrote, 'Our learned negotiators now realise that this kind of juggling is useless; but they would not have believed this if negotiations had broken down at the very beginning'.[4]

The agreement on the doctrine of justification which had been so loudly hailed and had given rise to such expectations soon turned out to be valueless. Luther rejected it,[5] and Contarini fared no better with it, for the consistory disapproved and rejected it on 27 May. He learned of this on 8 June.[6] He died on 24 August 1542,[7] shortly after the recess of the Imperial Diet.

The final recess of the Imperial Diet, dated 29 July,[8] confirmed the recess of the Diet of Augsburg and declared that the Nuremberg Standstill would remain in force for eighteen months. A general Council or a national Council was expected within that period. In case no Council were convened, an Imperial Diet was arranged to take its place. Another attempt to reach agreement would be made then. Meanwhile, the Catholic estates were put under obligation 'to establish a christian order and chris-

[1] *CR* 4, 541.
[2] *CR* 4, 517 f.
[3] *CR* 4, 528.
[4] *CR* 4, 586.
[5] *WAB* 9, 459, No. 3627.
[6] V. Pastor, *HJG* 1, 1880, 478–481.
[7] F. Hünermann, G. Contarini, *Gegenreformatorische Schriften 1530–1542*, vol. 7, 1932 (contains his *Epistola de iustificatione*).
[8] *CR* 4, 625 ff.; *Ursachen* I, 37, p. 454 ff.; *CT* IV, 200 (the draft); *ZKG* 3, 1879 (Contarini's report of 26 July).

tian reform' in their territories. Appended to the recess was an unofficial 'declaration' by the Emperor,[1] which assured the Protestants of their possessions, allowed them to undertake a 'christian Reformation' of churches and monasteries within their territories, and promised them religious equality at the Imperial Cameral Tribunal. All proceedings against them by that Tribunal would be suspended.[2] Similarly the Catholics were given an unofficial declaration,[3] which guaranteed that they would be able to keep the income they obtained from rents and dues, and that their territorial rights and privileges would be respected. That day the Emperor left, in order to return to Italy and Spain.

There can be no doubt that he took very seriously his efforts to achieve agreement. He sincerely desired a Reformation, and on several occasions he stated that he would be prepared to carry through a Reformation even against opposition from the Pope. His personal religious disposition and the political necessities of the time favoured such a course. For this reason the collapse of his efforts to achieve agreement was more than a mere diplomatic failure. It meant that an entirely new policy had to be found. What other course now remained open to him than one which would attempt a solution by force? Even at the Diet he had begun to seek the allegiance of a few princes from the enemy camp. The most important of these was the Landgrave of Hesse, who had by now been in touch with the Emperor for some time, and had offered to support his policies,[4] though without getting any promises in return. As late as 13 June in Regensburg a treaty[5] was concluded by which Philip was put under obligation not to make any foreign alliances. If Philip should renew any existing alliance, he was to ensure that it was no longer directed against the Emperor. He was to take steps to prevent the duke of Cleves from joining the League of Schmalkalden, and he was not to make a personal alliance with the duke. In return, Philip was to receive the Emperor's pardon and friendship, and 'whatever he had done or was suspected of having done previously, whether openly or in secret, against the Emperor or against the law and order of the Empire was now completely forgiven', except, however, 'if on account of religion a general war against all Protestants should break out'. The elector Joachim received a similar agreement which safeguarded his church reform until the Council.

---

[1] Text in *CR* 4, 623 ff.

[2] Brandi, *Quellen*, 306; Smend, *Reichskammergericht*, 157.

[3] Heidrich, *op. cit.*, 44 ff.

[4] Cardauns, *Von Nizza bis Crepy*, 1923, 58; Lenz, *Briefwechsel* I, 498.

[5] A. Hasenclever, 'Joh. von Naves', *MIÖG* 26, 1905, 296 ff.; Lenz, *Briefwechsel* III, 98 (text of the agreement).

CHAPTER VIII

TWO YEARS OF PEACE

I. THE IMPERIAL DIETS OF 1542 AND 1543

THE Emperor went from Regensburg to Italy, where he met the Pope at Lucca (12–18 September). There was a discussion of political problems and of the question of church reform and the summoning of the Council.[1] Afterwards he went on to Spain. In the summer he wrote to Mary, his regent in the Netherlands, that he would not be able to come to the Netherlands for two years.[2] The Turkish menace was the most urgent of his problems, made acute by the fall of Buda, which Sultan Soliman captured on 2 September.[3] Charles attempted to meet the challenge by a campaign against Algiers. The campaign was unsuccessful and he sustained heavy losses.[4] Spanish affairs occupied his attention throughout the following year. Ecclesiastical problems had to be pushed into the background. Their solution—if there was a solution at all—depended on the solution of political problems.

The final recess of the Imperial Diet of Regensburg had provided for a meeting of the estates on 14 January 1542 at Speyer, at which outstanding questions would be dealt with. But in view of the Turkish situation this meeting was turned into an Imperial Diet,[5] which was opened on 9 February 1542 by king Ferdinand. The sole item on the agenda was the question of getting help against the Turks. Although the Protestants recognised their obligations in this matter and were therefore not able to exploit the political situation, they were not prepared to reinforce

---

[1] W. Friedensburg, 'Aktenstücke zur Politik Kaiser Karls V. in Herbst 1541', ARG 29, 1932, 35 ff.; and 'Kaiser Karl V. und Paul III.', SVRG 153, 1932; Brandi, Quellen, 308.

[2] Lanz, Correspondenz II, 326; cf. Brandi, Quellen 309.

[3] Heidrich, op. cit., 54.

[4] G. Turba, AÖG 76, 1890, 1; Brandi, Quellen 309.

[5] Heidrich, op. cit., 54.

a power which could later be used against them. So in return for their assistance they demanded a permanent religious peace. Failing that, they requested that the Emperor's declaration which had been appended to the final recess of the Diet of Regensburg should be taken up into the recess itself and thus become part of the law of the Empire. The Catholic estates opposed this energetically. The Protestants also demanded that a commission be appointed to look into the affairs of the Imperial Cameral Tribunal, and that the membership of the Tribunal should be changed. After tedious negotiations,[1] in which the Schmalkaldians often failed to agree amongst themselves—the cities were frequently opposed to the princes—king Ferdinand hit upon the expedient which had been adopted at Regensburg. He gave the Protestants a written assurance[2] that the Emperor's declaration would remain in force and that the judges on the Imperial Cameral Tribunal would be bound to it on oath. On the same day (10 April) he issued a similar declaration to the Catholics, assuring them that they had 'no grounds whatever for fearing that the Regensburg recess is in any way altered by this declaration, or for thinking that other declarations were included with it'.[3] So the declaration remained, 'as the elector of Saxony aptly put it, a sword which could not be used'.[4] In the end the Protestants got a promise which was even more favourable than they had obtained at Regensburg, for they were promised a religious peace for five years from the 'start of the expedition against the Turks which is now proposed'. They were also assured that a commission would look into the affairs of the Imperial Cameral Tribunal.[5] This was actually appointed, but in June it was suspended again by order of the Emperor.[6]

The Imperial Diet of Nuremberg (24 July–26 August 1542)[7] had to tackle the same problems again. Admittedly the king was put at a disadvantage by the suspension of the commission of enquiry, but the Protestants had lost some freedom of manoeuvre as a result of the Brunswick affair. The chief question was that of assistance against the Turks, and the main opposition came from the cities, for they would have to provide the bulk of the cost. The religious question only came up because the papal legate asked leave to announce that a date (1 November) had been fixed for the Council.[8] The Protestants heard him 'only out of respect for

---

[1] Heidrich op. cit,., 60 ff.
[2] Ibid., 76 ff.
[3] Ibid., 83.
[4] Ibid., 88.
[5] Ibid., 84. (The Protestants declared that they accepted the final recess only on the basis of the Regensburg Declaration and the assurance which the king had just given.)
[6] Smend, op. cit., 158.
[7] Heidrich, op. cit., 88 ff.
[8] CT IV, 190 ff.

Ferdinand'.[1] When the final recess was read out, the Protestants repeated the protest which they had delivered at Speyer. But they were divided about the attitude they were to take towards the Imperial Cameral Tribunal. Some princes wanted to refuse to recognise its authority, but the cities did not wish to dispense with it altogether. However, on 4 December, because the Tribunal had initiated proceedings at duke Henry of Brunswick's instigation, they rejected its authority to try any disputes relating to members of the League.[2] Their refusal, even though the Tribunal dismissed it, was an act of enormous consequence, because it formally disrupted unanimity within the Empire on the question of the administration of justice.

The second of the Imperial Diets to be held at Nuremberg in this period[3] was summoned in November 1542, but did not begin until January 1543. It took place at a time when the Habsburgs were being pressed hard, not only by the Turks, but also by France and the duke of Cleves. The king asked for help against the Turks, and the Emperor, represented by Granvella, for help against France and Cleves. The Protestants were more determined than they had been at Speyer, and 'as one man' they insisted that they would enter no negotiations about this unless definite promises were made to them 'about peace and about rights'. After months of negotiation the final recess of 23 April 1543 ordered a commission of enquiry into the Imperial Cameral Tribunal and suspended the Tribunal's verdict in all cases in which Protestants were involved. The Protestants' demands that all the members of the Tribunal be replaced and that the Emperor's declaration at Regensburg be included in the recess were not met, and so the Protestants protested against this recess too. Granvella, however, was content, because they had at least not taken the part of the duke of Cleves. But he was now convinced, from the way things had gone at the Diet, that a religious war was necessary.[4] It was becoming increasingly evident that as Protestantism established itself, so all order within the Empire was being disrupted. If they had reached the point at which it was impossible to take concerted action against threats from outside the Empire, and if the highest court of the Empire was virtually prevented from functioning, then the Empire had ceased to be a state. This was not altered by the fact that the Schmalkaldians, at their next meeting at the end of June 1543, decided to offer help to the Emperor 'of their own free will', and only made their request for peace and for a guarantee of their rights in an appendix.[5] The commission of enquiry into the Imperial

[1] Heidrich, op. cit., 97.
[2] Smend, op. cit., 158 f.; Mentz II, 321; Ursachen VII, 21 (text).
[3] Heidrich, op. cit., 108 ff.
[4] Ibid., 153 f.
[5] Ibid., 155 f.

Cameral Tribunal was actually begun in October, but it could not complete its work, because the Protestant members of the commission resigned from it on the grounds that they did not receive the consideration which the declaration had promised them.

2. DEVELOPMENTS WITHIN THE EMPIRE

(a) The Brunswick Feud[1]

The feud which the two heads of the Schmalkaldic League conducted against duke Henry of Brunswick-Wolfenbüttel was not only a threat to the continued existence of the League but also made their relationships with the rest of the Empire very difficult.

The three princes had been enemies for years, campaigning against each other publicly in abusive literary exchanges of the coarsest kind. But when the Imperial Cameral Tribunal, at Henry's instigation, put the city of Goslar under the ban on 25 October 1540, this gave the pretext for a real battle.[2] The princes consulted the other members of the League, and as a result of pressure from the League the Emperor suspended the ban in January,[3] but the dispute between the princes went on. Luther, whom Henry had accused of calling his prince 'Hans Worst', replied with one of his coarsest writings, 'Against Hans Worst'.[4] In it he not only defends the elector of Saxony but also answers charges brought by Henry against the Evangelicals, so that in spite of its vulgarity the pamphlet is not without theological value. An attempt was made to have the dispute settled at the Diet of Regensburg, but the only result was that a renewed prohibition on engaging in, and printing, slander was included in the final recess. After the Diet, Henry continued hostilities against Goslar and Brunswick, and so Saxony and Hesse in July and August 1542 occupied the territory.[5] Duke Henry sought assistance from the Catholic alliance of which he was a leading member, but none was forthcoming. In an attempt to start a 'legal' war, Henry got the Imperial Cameral Tribunal to give judgement in his favour, but on 4 December the Protestants refused to recognise the authority of the Tribunal—as was mentioned earlier.[6] The two princes put the territory under the rule of a commissariat,

[1] *Schl* 29819–29824, 30339; *Ursachen* IV; Lenz, *Briefwechsel* III, 151 ff.; F. Koldewey, 'Die Reformation des Herzogtums Braunschweig-Wolfenbüttel unter dem Regiment des Schmalkaldischen Bundes 1542–1547', *Zeitschrift des hist. Vereins für Niedersachsen* 1868, 243 ff.; and 'Heinz v. Wolfenbüttel', *SVRG* 2, 1883.

[2] *Ursachen* IV, 4 and 14.

[3] *Ursachen* IV, 38, 1 (28 Jan. 1541).

[4] WAR 51, 461 ff.; WAB 9, 330, No. 3576. Luther considered it 'a short and sweet account of our cause'.

[5] *Ursachen* IV, 36.

[6] *Roth* III, 69 ff.

and the Church in the territory was reformed by Bugenhagen and Corvinus though it was treated as booty, and Luther soon was complaining about 'bad smells' and 'robbing our own'.[1] What was to be done with the territory was a question on which the members of the League were divided.[2] Ulrich of Württemberg urged strongly that the duke should be reinstated, but the Wittenberg theologians, anxious that the Reformation should be carried through in the territory, opposed this.[3] 'As David would have done wrong if he had willingly put one or two small places at the disposal of idolaters, knowing that they would pursue their idolatry there',[4] so it would be wrong to give the territory back to duke Henry, for this would perplex the conscience of the people and put the clergy and their families at his mercy. A proposal to put the territory under imperial administration met with opposition from the duke himself, for he feared that this would deprive him of it for ever. By the autumn he had won the territory back, but on 21 October 1545 he was taken prisoner by the Landgrave at Northeim,[5] and Philip had him brought to Ziegenhain. Shortly before Christmas 1545, at the request of the elector, Luther published his 'Letter to the Elector and the Landgrave', in which he advised against letting the duke go free.[6] 'A man ought not to show false love or false pardon towards his enemy, or he will bring the sins of his enemy upon himself.'[7] True mercy will be shown to the duke in preventing him from putting his blasphemous intentions into effect and in protecting the people from him. It was not until his opponents were defeated in the Schmalkaldic War that Henry regained his liberty.

(b) *The dispute over the bishopric of Naumburg*[8]

Electoral Saxony's intervention in the bishopric of Naumburg was as inconclusive an affair as was the Reformation in Brunswick. The bishop of Naumburg died on 6 January 1541. This created a vacancy which the elector saw as a 'convenient moment, in justice to religion as well as to the house of Saxony, to bring more certainty, peace and concord' to his

---

[1] *WAB* 10, 141, No. 3788.
[2] Rommel, *Die Reichsstadt Ulm in der Katastrophe des Schmalk. Bundes*, 1922, 6 f.; *Roth* III, 69 ff. (on Augsburg).
[3] *WAB* 10, 469, No. 3948 and app. 473.
[4] *WAB* 10, 470, No. 3948, lines 44 ff.
[5] *Ursachen* IV, 51 and 52; on the obscure details see Issleib, 'Philipp von Hessen, H. von Braunschweig und M. von Sachsen 1541–1547', *Jahrb. des Geschichtsvereins für das Herzogtum Braunschweig* 2, 1903, 1 ff.
[6] *WAR* 54, 374 ff.
[7] Ibid., 391, 21.
[8] P. Brunner, *SVRG* 179, 1961; *Ursachen* V, 12; F. Köster, *ZKG* 22, 1901, 278 ff.; E. Hoffmann, 'Naumburg a. S. im Zeitalter der Reformation', *Leipziger Studien aus dem Gebiete der Geschichte* VII/1, 1901; cf. *WAR* 53, 219 f.

territory.[1] Thus a political claim that the bishopric should be regarded as a part of his territory became intertwined with religious demands. With all possible speed the cathedral chapter elected Julius Pflug to the see, without consulting the elector. In the autumn of 1541 the elector replied by appointing a lay official from Electoral Saxony to take charge of the secular administration of the bishopric. The Wittenberg theologians, after prolonged discussions, gave their support to an even more ambitious plan to put an Evangelical bishop into the see. The Naumburg council had reservations about this, but these were eventually dispelled by Luther, who contested the chapter's right to make an election—'no matter what their duties or privileges may be'—because they had persecuted the Gospel; 'for the commandment to teach what is right and to hold the right kind of services is above all other commandments'. Since the estates and the patron (i.e. the elector) had the responsibility of seeing that worship was rightly ordered, it was appropriate that they should also have the right of appointment to the see and the right of control over the property attaching to the bishopric, for the secular rights must 'follow upon' the clerical rights.[2] So, according to Luther, the right to decide the appointment also included the right to control the property. The elector then had Nikolaus von Amsdorf elected bishop. He was consecrated[3] and given words of encouragement[4] by Luther, received the homage of his subjects and entered upon his office. It was inevitable that this procedure would be contested, as Luther pointed out in his sermon at the consecration.[5] Pflug could no more renounce his claim than the elector could recognise it.[6] Pflug continued to have supporters within the bishopric, which made difficulties for Amsdorf. He brought a complaint at the Diet of Speyer and was supported by the Emperor. Endless discussions merely sharpened the conflict, until eventually, at the Imperial Diet of Worms in 1545, the Emperor formally enfeoffed the bishopric to Pflug, treating the elector's procedure as an act of robbery. The issue was finally decided by the war, for Naumburg had to yield to duke Moritz, and Amsdorf fled with a few troops to join the elector's army at Gotha. What was worse, for the Reformation, was that Amsdorf in office had no opportunity to develop as an Evangelical bishop, for in secular affairs he was entirely at the mercy of the lay administrator, and in ecclesiastical affairs was wholly dependent on the territorial government of the elector, who moreover denied him even the most necessary support. Consequently

[1] *WAB* 9, 539 f., No. 3683; *Ursachen* V, 12.
[2] *WAB* 9, 596, No. 3706.
[3] *WAR* 53, 219 ff.
[4] *WAB* 9, 608 ff., No. 3709.
[5] *WAR* 49, XXVI.
[6] *Ursachen* V, 14 ff. and V, 21.

Amsdorf was unable to set up a consistory court or to undertake a visitation of the bishopric. He later managed to begin a visitation, but could not complete it.

It was in the bishopric of Meissen that serious political complications arose among the Evangelicals which troubled relationships between the two Saxon states. The cause was a difference of opinion between the bishop and the elector of Saxony over the payment of the tax levied in connection with the Turkish war. The elector attempted to decide the issue by assuming jurisdiction over Wurzen, where he immediately forbade the Mass. He was evidently convinced that he had the territorial rights there, and was simply concerned to make sure of getting the tax paid. But he came into conflict with duke Moritz who also laid claim to the territorial rights, and so far from being ready to renounce them was prepared to defend them if necessary by force. Landgrave Philip mediated and produced an agreement which was fair to both sides. But the dispute heightened the differences between the two houses and confirmed the duke in his dislike of the League of Schmalkalden.[1]

(c) *The Reformation in Cologne*[2]

We do not know what prompted the archbishop and elector of Cologne, Hermann von Wied, to continue along the path towards Evangelical reform after his attempt at reform in 1538 had failed. He was in frequent touch with Protestant princes and scholars after that time, but 'there are strong reasons for doubting whether he was even remotely capable of understanding the fundamental differences between Catholic and Protestant doctrine'.[3] But there can be no doubt that without any ulterior motive he made sincere efforts to understand the issues involved in the religious question. Contarini's exhortation to the bishops at Regensburg, followed by the final recess of the Diet which urged a 'christian ordering and reform', and finally a letter to the bishops written by Morone on 28 February 1542, all influenced him profoundly. In February 1542 Bucer was summoned for discussions with the archbishop and with Gropper and was given a friendly reception by the city council. Obviously all three still thought that a joint reform was possible. After Bucer had gone, the estates thanked Hermann for his reformist intentions and asked that at the next meeting of the estates of the territory a draft scheme for reform should be presented. Towards the end of the year Bucer was again summoned to undertake this task. On 17 December he preached in the minster

---

[1] *Mentz* II, 499 ff.
[2] C. Varrentrapp, *Hermann v. Wied u. sein Reformationsversuch in Köln*, 1878; and *ZKG* 20, 1900, 37 ff.; cf. Jedin, *HJG* 74, 1955, 687 ff.
[3] H. Jedin, *HJG* 74, 690.

at Bonn, where the archbishop had his residence, and afterwards began a series of lectures on the first epistle to the Corinthians. But then he encountered opposition from the cathedral chapter and from the city council of Cologne. Both these bodies protested vehemently against this 'foreigner' and requested that his sermons should cease. Then the friendship between Bucer and Gropper came to an end, though Gropper's motives for breaking it off remain obscure. He avoided private conversations with Bucer and refused a request from Bucer that they should hold a disputation. Everhard Billick, a Carmelite prior, and Gerhard Kalkbrenner joined Gropper in leading the opposition. On 27 January 1543 Gropper handed the archbishop a Catholic programme of reform, the text of which has not survived, but which Bucer described as a 'piece of patchwork'. The elector archbishop took sides with Bucer, who was also supported by Erasmus Sacerius, who was preaching in Andernach, and Hedio from Strasbourg. On 1 February 1543 the Pope exhorted both the chapter and the clergy to maintain their loyalty to the Catholic faith. But at a meeting of the estates of the territory in March the elector was once again given a free hand and asked to submit the draft of a Reformation ordinance. In a long written statement[1] Bucer defended himself in detail against the charges which had been levelled at him, and he was particularly hurt by the argument that no one should dispute with him because he was a heretic. Gradually he gathered assistants, chief among whom was Melanchthon, who together with Bucer drew up the draft which had been requested.[2] He added to Bucer's scheme a number of theological articles on matters which he felt it was essential to be clear about. The central idea of the ordinance was to link doctrine to Scripture, but traditional elements were spared to a very considerable degree, among them the hierarchy, the cathedral chapter, church property and the externals of worship. No mention was made of the Pope. The dependence of this document on the Nuremberg ordinance of 1533 is unmistakable. Afterwards Bucer and Melanchthon continued the literary controversy. Bucer defended himself against the charge of heresy and accused his opponents of having selfish reasons for not wanting a Reformation. He wrote letters defending himself against Latomus's accusations.[3] The cathedral chapter, the university and the city council joined in opposing Bucer, the city council apparently fearing for the city's freedom if a Protestant elector came to power.[4] But the forces of opposition were not confined to the city of

[1] Bibl. Buceriana, No. 75 (SVRG 169, 1952).
[2] Ibid., No. 74.
[3] Ibid., No. 76–78, 80; CCath 8, 1924.
[4] J. Greven, 'Die Kölner Cartause und die Anfänge der katholischen Reform in Deutschland', Vereinsschriften der Gesellschaft zur Herausgabe des CCath., No. 6/3, 1935.

Cologne. On 1 June Hermann received a note from the Pope, bidding him return to the bosom of the Church and expressing some doubt whether Hermann still was worthy of the name of bishop. Of greatest significance for the future was the arrival in Cologne of the Jesuit Peter Faber. He gained an adherent in Peter Canisius and in the following year founded a Jesuit house in the city. But in spite of all this, the estates of the territory, when they met in July 1543, again sided with the archbishop.

3. THE FATE OF THE COUNCIL BETWEEN 1541 AND 1543[1]

It was clear that the Council would have to be summoned within eighteen months from the end of the Imperial Diet of Regensburg, otherwise there was a risk that the Germans would have a Council of their own. The Pope was moved, not only by the general desire for a Council and by the fact that it was politically necessary, but also by the progress which the Evangelical movement was making in Italy. He now needed a clear basis on which to meet it, and so on 15 July 1541 he let it be known in the consistory that he was ready to end the suspension of the Council and to inform the princes accordingly.[2] At a conference with the Emperor at Lucca in September[3] it proved impossible to agree on a place. It was a real problem. The Emperor proposed Trent, but this was unacceptable to the French because it was an imperial city. If the French refused to come to the Council there would be doubt about its ecumenical character. On the other hand the Emperor, in view of his promises to the Germans, had to insist that the Council meet at a city of the Empire.[4] Nevertheless Morone (who was made a cardinal on 2 June 1542) was sent to Germany to persuade the bishops to support the work of church reform. The result was that the Catholic estates at Speyer on 4 April 1542 decided on Trent as the place for the Council, and the Pope—under protest—accepted the decision.[5] On 22 May 1542 the new Bull was approved and was published on 29 June. It stated that the Council would begin on All Saints' Day 1542.[6]

But on 10 July Francis I, supported by an alliance with the Turks,

---

[1] *Jedin* I, 356 ff.
[2] The same consistory took the first step towards setting up the Inquisition which came into being a year later—see *Jedin* I, 356. On Protestantism in Italy see *v. Pastor* V, 337 ff., 705 ff. and *Jedin* I, 590 n. 4. (D. Cantimori, Italien Härelsker der Spätrenaissance, 1949).
[3] *ARG* 29, 1932, 38 ff.; *CT* IV, 206 ff.; *NBD* I, 7, 165 ff.; *Jedin* I, 357 ff.; Cardauns, *Von Nizza bis Crepy*, 191 ff.; Brandi, *Quellen* 308.
[4] Contarini's memorandum, *CT* IV, 208 f.; Granvella's, *ARG* 29, 1932, 45 ff.
[5] *CT* IV, 214 f., 218 f.; *Jedin* I, 360 ff.
[6] *Jedin* I, 364; *CT* IV, 226 ff. (text); *Ursachen* I, 38.

declared war again on the Emperor.[1] The Pope's efforts to keep the peace
had been in vain. Equally vain were the Emperor's efforts to get the Pope
on his side. The Pope was afraid that the French might go into schism
and therefore he felt obliged to be neutral, however deeply the Emperor
resented this.[2] But Trent was now quite impossible for the French, and
Francis refused to allow the Bull to be published in France.[3] Otto
Truchsess of Waldburg went as papal legate to Germany and on 13
August appeared before the Imperial Diet of Nuremberg, where the
Catholic estates accepted the Bull but did not conceal their scepticism.[4]
But in Rome and in Trent preparations went ahead and three legates for
the Council were named, although not even Thomas Campeggi was
sure whether it was in earnest this time.[5] But what made failure inevitable
was that hardly any bishops followed up the invitation. On 7 January 1543
Granvella went through Trent on his way to the Second Imperial Diet
of Nuremberg, and on arrival in Trent he introduced himself as the Emperor's representative. This was nothing more than a demonstration and
it caused not a little embarrassment to the legates present, because no
Council was in fact taking place.[6] The Pope sent urgent summonses which
in France had no effect at all and in Italy and Germany achieved little.
Waldburg was sent again to the second Imperial Diet of Nuremberg.[7]
King Ferdinand would not allow Nausea, the bishop of Vienna, to go.[8]
Seven months after the appointed time there were no more than ten
bishops assembled in Trent. So the Pope recalled two of the legates to
Rome for consultations. Then the Emperor, returning through Italy to
Germany, met the Pope at Busseto near Parma on 21 June 1543.[9] The
Pope proposed that the Council should either be suspended or trans-
ferred to a town inside Vatican territory. Looking at the matter from the
Germans' point of view, the Emperor inevitably found both proposals
unacceptable. However, the Pope made his decision on 6 July and published it on 29 September. The Council was suspended on the grounds
that prevailing conditions made it impracticable, and that a further
period of waiting would merely be harmful to the Church's dignity.[10]
This was an inevitable decision, but one which the Emperor found hard

[1] Cardaunus, *Von Nizza bis Crepy*, 203 ff.
[2] *CT* IV, 238 ff.; Brandi, *Quellen* 327 f.; *Jedin* I, 366 f.
[3] *Jedin* I, 368.
[4] *NBD* I, 7, 566 ff.; *CT* IV, 234 ff.; *Jedin* I, 368 f.
[5] *Jedin* I, 372 f.
[6] Ibid., 375 f.
[7] *CT* IV, 309 ff.; *NBD* I, 7, 317 ff., 327; *CT* IV, 319 ff.; *NBD* I, 7, 572 ff.; *Jedin* I, 380 ff.
[8] *Jedin* I, 382; *CT* XII, 364 ff.
[9] *Jedin* I, 385; *NBD* I, 7, 370 ff.; Brandi, *Quellen* 333.
[10] *CT* IV, 352–355.

N

to bear. How was he to meet the Germans' demands now? Quite apart from the religious aspect of the matter the Emperor was deeply resentful of a papal policy which prevented the Pope from supporting him decisively against the Turks, and he suspected that everything that the Pope had done in connection with calling a Council had never been intended as more than an outward show.[1] Thus Charles came to Germany. It is small wonder that in the following period his religious policies appeared to lack assurance.

[1] *Jedin* I, 390.

CHAPTER IX

ON THE EVE OF WAR

I. THE GELDERN CAMPAIGN

THE Emperor's first task on arriving in Germany was to settle the dispute over Geldern, which had been smouldering for five years.[1] In 1538 the duchy of Geldern had been sold by duke Egmont to duke William of Jülich-Cleves, and after Egmont's death (June 1538) William took possession of it. But the Emperor, too, laid claims to the territory which were contested by William. Duke William declined (in February 1540) to join the League of Schmalkalden, and in April 1540 he declined an offer from the Emperor. But in July he sought to secure his position by making an alliance with France which was confirmed by a purely formal betrothal with the twelve-year-old Jeanne d'Albret of Navarre. Since, moreover, Henry VIII of England had married the duke's sister Anne of Cleves on 6 January 1540, and since he could also count on support from some German princes, he felt safe enough. In 1542 the alliance with France led to an ugly incident, for while French troops were advancing on the Netherlands from the south, Martin von Rossem, in command of the Geldern army, stormed through the Netherlands[2] as far as Antwerp and Louvain, and with his motto, 'Burning is the Magnificat of war', caused terror on all sides. Fighting was later confined to the territory of Jülich and continued as frontier warfare, with varying fortunes, until 1543. At this point duke William sought entry into the League of Schmalkalden. He received communion in both kinds, hoping that this would facilitate his acceptance, but Philip of Hesse, in accordance with the terms of his treaty with the Emperor, prevented this.[3] The Emperor then acquired the

[1] On the Geldern question see Brandi, *Quellen*, 282 and 293, and *Schl* 37186–37201; also P. Heidrich, *Der Geldrische Erbfolgestreit 1537–1543*, 1896; O. Redlich, 'Staat und Kirche am Niederrhein in der Reformationszeit', *SVRG* 164, 1938.
[2] *Brandi* 409 ff.
[3] Heidrich, *Erbfolgestreit* 35 ff.

assistance of troops which Granvella had recruited in South Germany and which had assembled at Bonn. The Emperor joined them there, and Düren, Jülich and Roermond submitted to him in quick succession.[1] Afterwards duke William appeared at the Emperor's camp outside Venlo and made his personal submission. In the treaty of Venlo of 7 September 1543[2] he renounced his claim to Geldern and Zutphen, promised not to enter any foreign alliance, and agreed not to initiate ecclesiastical reform. The Pope declared his marriage invalid. His subsequent marriage to one of Ferdinand's daughters bound him to the house of Habsburg. So this dispute which had caused such unrest for so long a time had been brought in less than three weeks to a conclusion which was all that the Emperor could desire. Looking back on it he remarked that 'this experience had opened the Emperor's eyes and had impressed on his mind that it is not impossible to restrain such arrogance by force. On the contrary, it is very easy, given the right circumstances and the appropriate means.'[3] He went on with the campaign, advancing on the French frontier, occupying Cambrai and establishing Metz more firmly within the Empire. In January he went up the Rhine to the Imperial Diet of Speyer. On the way he was met at Kreuznach by Farnese, the papal legate, who had instructions to mediate between Charles and the French with a view to getting at least an armistice, in order to make a Council possible. He urged Charles to give way and to renounce his claim to Milan and Savoy. This so infuriated Charles that he threatened to take the Reformation of the Church into his own hands.[4] So the legate returned home, even before the Imperial Diet had begun. All this naturally had a favourable effect upon the Protestants. Other things also augured well for the Diet, even though, as was mentioned earlier, it had proved impossible to carry out the commission of enquiry into the affairs of the Imperial Cameral Tribunal.

2. THE IMPERIAL DIET OF SPEYER, 1544[5]

The Diet was opened on 20 February, and the Emperor requested assistance against France and against the Turks. The Protestants were impressed by the Emperor's victory and were aware that the Brunswick affair had put them in a weak position. So they were disposed to meet the

[1] Brandi, *Quellen*, 338.
[2] Ibid., 339.
[3] *Commentaires*, ed. K. de Letthove, 1862; Brandi, *Quellen*, 339.
[4] *Jedin* 1, 395 ff.; Lanz, *Staatspapiere*, 346–358.
[5] P. Heidrich, *Karl V.*, 1912, 3 ff.; A. de Boor, 'Beitrag zur Geschichte des Speyrer Reichstags v. 1544', *Diss. Strassburg* 1878; F. Roth, *ARG* 1, 1904, 101 ff.; *NBD* I, 7, XXXI.

Emperor's request, though still putting forward their demands for 'peace and rights'. All the same, consultations about assistance for the Emperor were taken first on the agenda, though 'without obligation'. The Rhenish electors and the cities were hesitant, but the Landgrave advocated assistance with such enthusiasm that in the end it was conceded. Thus the Protestants had parted company with their natural allies, and did so apparently light-heartedly. In the consultations about peace and rights which then followed, they asked for public recognition of the declaration and requested that its provisions should be extended to cover any who in future might adopt the Augsburg Confession. But neither the Emperor nor the Catholic estates would allow this. It was no longer possible to adopt the expedient of giving a private assurance. In the end the Catholics agreed that in the final recess it should be stated that the Emperor had given his assurances on his own authority, though they were not to be taken as decisions of the estates as a whole—'they did not decide, they submitted'.[1] The final recess was dated 10 June and it promised assistance to the Emperor against the French as well as against the Turks. The settlement of the religious question was left until a 'general, christian and free Council' (note that Protestant wording has been adopted) could be convened. But since recent events made such a Council highly unlikely—at least in the near future—it was decided that another Imperial Diet should be held in the autumn or the winter for the purpose of discussing a 'christian Reformation'. Meanwhile, the religious standstill was renewed and all legal proceedings against Protestants suspended. Preparations were also to be made for reforming the Imperial Cameral Tribunal. The recess expressly stated that the religious cleavage would be overcome 'by no other means than by christian and peaceable agreement'. A long series of instructions relating to ecclesiastical possessions stated that they should be used for churches, parsonages, schools, alms and hospitals—'no matter what religion they are'. The Protestants made a declaration to the effect that they stood by their earlier protestation against the Council, and they repeated their demand that all the directives incorporated in the final recess should apply equally to all future adherents of the Augsburg Confession. They also decided to prepare and exchange 'considered statements' to be submitted at the next Imperial Diet, and to prepare a list of suitable candidates for appointment to the Imperial Cameral Tribunal.

Thus the Emperor had achieved his political goals. He had parted the German princes from France and even got their active support against their former ally. But on the religious question he had completely changed his position and had conceded that if no Council took place a Reformation would be undertaken in the foreseeable future by an Imperial Diet

[1] *Brandi*, 440.

which would have to be regarded as a Council for the German nation. On 24 August the Pope replied with a note[1] in which he accused the Emperor of having exceeded his competence, and demanded that he should withdraw the concessions granted to the heretics. The Pope finished by emphasising how great was his own desire for a Council and for peace. The note was intended to express 'the Pope's opposition in principle to the Emperor's policies on the religious question in general and the Council in particular',[2] and although it was never published, it prompted Calvin to defend the Emperor,[3] and stirred Luther—who possibly had access to it through Granvella[4]—to write his pamphlet *Against the Roman Papacy, the Invention of the Devil*.[5] This was Luther's last great onslaught on the papacy. There is no point in posing the question whether the Emperor's concessions to the Protestants represented a change of heart.[6] There are many statements of his which seem to prove the opposite, and they are largely confirmed by his later conduct. On the other hand, Charles's relations with the Pope—who evidently took the Diet's decisions very seriously—had become so bad and the prospects of a Council had become so remote that Charles had little room for manoeuvre. He now had to play a political game, his actions being determined by what was possible and what was expedient. No doubt he hoped that the next Imperial Diet would present him with favourable opportunities.

After the Diet he went straight back to Metz where his troops were assembled. He led a campaign which penetrated very quickly to the heart of France.[7] After only fourteen days efforts were made to get a peace treaty. Serious negotiations soon followed, and on 14 September 1544 the Peace of Crépy was signed. The political problems were settled by the customary expedient of rearranging territorial boundaries and organising dynastic marriages. The Emperor was promised considerable assistance against the Turks.[8] But more important than this was a secret treaty of 19 September[9] which affected the religious question. Francis promised to lend his support in removing ecclesiastical abuses and in bringing back to the Church those who had fallen away. He also acknow-

---

[1] *CT* IV, 364; A. v. Druffel, 'Kaiser Karl V. und die römische Curie 1544–46', *AMA*, Hist. Klasse XIII/2, 145 ff., XVI/1, 1 ff., XVI/3, 181 ff., XIX/2, 445 ff., 1877–1891; J. Müller, *ZKG* 44, 1925, 399.
[2] *Jedin* I, 399.
[3] *CR* 35, 253–288.
[4] Druffel, *op. cit.*, 220 ff.
[5] *WAR* 54, 206 ff.
[6] Heidrich, *Karl V*, II, 46.
[7] In the Emperor's army was the young prince of Orange, who fell outside St. Dizier. His inheritance passed to William of Nassau.
[8] Brandi, *Quellen*, 349.
[9] A. Hasenclever, *ZKG* 45, 1927, 418 ff. (text).

ledged that this was a task which the Emperor, in virtue of his authority and dignity, had the right to undertake. He promised to send representatives to a Council, either in Trent, Cambrai or Metz, and agreed that the assistance which he provided against the Turks might be employed against the German Protestants, if the use of force were to become a necessity. If the Emperor required it, he would declare himself to be an enemy of the Protestants, and he would take any steps against them which Charles might wish. Finally, Savoy and the imperial city of Geneva were to be returned to the duke of Savoy and the inhabitants restored to the true faith. These treaties are a recognition of the Emperor's complete triumph, and the secret treaty shows beyond all shadow of doubt that the Emperor had definitely decided on a religious war, though the time had as yet not been fixed.

3. THE REFORMATION'S PROGRESS AND THE STRUGGLE FOR COLOGNE

(a) Protestantism continued to make progress during this period. These are only a few of its most important conquests: In Neuburg, 1543, duke Ottheinrich announced a new church ordinance[1] which Osiander had drawn up. In the Electoral Palatinate the new elector, Frederick II (1544-1556) allowed the Protestant movement free course, and in the Upper Palatinate the German Mass was introduced in 1544 and the chalice administered to the laity. Priests were allowed to marry. From 1543 duke Moritz appointed Evangelical clergy in the bishoprics of Meissen and Merseburg. In 1544 Merseburg was given to duke August of Saxony and its ecclesiastical affairs were entrusted to George of Anhalt. The Reformation in duke Henry's territory influenced the city of Hildesheim, which received an Evangelical church order in 1544. In the seecities of Worms and Speyer the Evangelicals received during the forties a number of churches and schools, and in 1542 a church was granted them in Regensburg. Rothenburg ob der Tauber was reformed in 1544 and Donauwörth in 1545.[2]

(b) But in Cologne, Hermann's efforts came virtually to a standstill. While the Emperor was staying in Bonn he requested that the reformers from Strasbourg should be sent away from Cologne and that all reforms should be postponed until a Council could be held. The elector, however, would not be deterred. The cathedral chapter replied to Bucer's draft order by getting Gropper to draw up a 'Counter-proposal' which was

---

[1] Richter, *Kirchenordnungen* II, 146; B. Kurze, 'Kurfürst Ottheinrich', *SVRG* 174, 1956.
[2] K. Müller, *Kirchengeschichte* II, 1, 414 ff.; R. Bollinger, *Das Evangelium in Regensburg*, 1959, 156 ff.

designed to prove that Bucer's 'Reformation' was not consistent with Catholic faith.[1] Melanchthon considered that Gropper's presentation of the doctrine of justification was almost identical with that of the reformers, but he regarded it as intolerable that Gropper should defend abuses.[2] In January 1544 the archbishop said that he would be willing to limit himself to four points of reform: Evangelical preaching, the administration of the chalice to the laity, a German service of baptism and German hymns. But the cathedral chapter and the city council refused even these innovations and were commended by the Emperor for doing so. He had returned to the city on his way to Speyer.[3] But what was more important was that Luther found the doctrine of the Lord's Supper which was given in Bucer's draft quite unacceptable, and he began to regard its author with suspicion. In Luther's opinion the draft would be 'not only tolerable but positively reassuring to the fanatics, for it contains their doctrine rather than ours'. In September Luther wrote his *Short Confession on the Lord's Supper*,[4] which returned to the old controversy with the Swiss, though without making much impression. However, he said nothing in it about Bucer's draft order for Cologne. On 10 October Melanchthon wrote, saying that he thought he had managed to pacify Luther. If he had not, he had better think of packing his bags again. In the autumn new protests were made against the elector. The cathedral chapter and the city council sent a delegation demanding that the innovations be done away with, and threatening to use 'all lawful means' in opposing him and taking the matter to his superiors.[5] On 9 October they appealed to the Pope and to the Emperor. The archbishop proposed that a body of devout and learned men should examine his preachers, but this was refused on the grounds that these preachers had a view of the Church which was quite different from the view held by those who opposed them.[6] Again the Emperor supported the opposition, first of all sending the archbishop a letter, then Naves the vice-chancellor, and finally a summons.[7] The elector archbishop protested against the appeal to the Pope and a meeting of the estates of the territory on 2 December tried to mediate. They suggested that communion in both kinds should be allowed and that from time to time a sermon should be given before the service, but Gropper challenged this. The elector appealed to his conscience, saying that in his old age and so near to the grave he could not depart from what he believed to be true. Two of his

---

[1] *Varrentrapp*, 223 (see VIII n. 40 above).
[2] K. and W. Krafft, *Briefe aus der Zeit der Reformation*, 1875, 171 ff.
[3] *Varrentrapp*, 225 n. 3.
[4] *WAR* 54, 119 ff.
[5] *Varrentrapp*, 233.
[6] Ibid., 234 f.
[7] Ibid., 237.

suffragans, the bishops of Liége and Utrecht, and also the university of Louvain joined with Cologne in the appeal to the Pope. Mainz, Trier and Rome all brought pressure to bear upon the elector. The estates sent a delegation to the Emperor, but Naves, who was in Bonn on 1 March, dismissed it,[1] and so it achieved nothing. So this was the situation as the new Imperial Diet was about to begin—the Diet which was supposed to have been a Council for the German nation. Melanchthon and Bucer prepared for it as though it were to be a national Council, and they drew up submissions which in the event turned out to be of purely academic value.[2]

4. THE SUMMONING OF THE COUNCIL

But meanwhile the increased power of the Emperor and the Pope's reaction to the peace treaty had brought about a new situation. He sent out legates with the message that he had decided to call a Council in Trent without delay, and that therefore it would be superfluous for an assembly of the Empire to discuss the religious question.[3] The announcement came just as the two monarchs, Charles and Francis, had petitioned for a Council.[4] On 30 November the Bull *Laetare Jerusalem* was published, summoning a Council for '*Laetare*' Sunday, 15 March 1545 at Trent.[5] Its business was to overcome the religious cleavage, to reform Christendom and to set Christians free from the infidels. Invitations were sent to all the clergy who were qualified to attend, and also to the princes. This was a new development which at Speyer could not possibly have been foreseen, and which now began to have its effect upon imperial politics, even though the Emperor was not disposed to take it entirely seriously. Previous experience suggested caution. For this reason he had to develop his policies along two quite separate lines. 'On the one hand he took steps to further the Council, and instructed king Ferdinand to tell the estates on 24 March 1545 that they should refer the religious question to the Council; while on the other hand . . . he seemed to continue the policies which he had adopted at Speyer.'[6] Further preparations for the Council in fact proceeded slowly. It was not until 22 February that the Pope appointed cardinals Del Monte, Cervini and Pole as presidents of the Council. He secretly gave them authority to dissolve or postpone the

[1] *Varrentrapp*, 243.
[2] *CR* 5, 578 ff.; *Sehling* I/1, 1902, 209 ff.; cf. *WAB* 11, 13 f.; Neudecker, *Urkunden* p. 713 ff.; *Seckendorff* III, 539 ff.; *WAB* 11, 42; *CR* 5, 671 f., 674 ff., 686 ff.
[3] *CT* IV, 380 ff.
[4] *Jedin* I, 403 and 604 n. 32.
[5] *CT* IV, 385–388; *Jedin* I, 604 n. 34.
[6] *Jedin* I, 406.

Council again, if this should be necessary.[1] On 13 March Del Monte and Cervini arrived in Trent, only to find that no participants had turned up.[2] Only in May was it possible to assemble the bishops, and then only to discuss with them the reasons for the delay and a few other incidental matters.[3] It was the Imperial Diet and the policies of the Emperor which constituted the chief reason for delay, for by that time the Imperial Diet had started.

5. THE IMPERIAL DIET OF WORMS, 1545[4]

The Imperial Diet had originally been announced for 1 October 1544, but the Emperor was prevented by sickness from leaving the Netherlands, so that it was not until 24 March that Ferdinand began the proceedings. News from the Netherlands that Protestants were being persecuted there caused Protestant morale to sink so low that the Landgrave declared that they would have to start recruiting troops. The chief issue at the Diet was its relationship to the Council. The king, acting on the Emperor's instructions, proposed that the religious question should be referred to the Council and that the Diet should deal only with political questions.[5] But the Protestants first sought an assurance that they would not be required to recognise the Council's authority, and that the Speyer resolutions about religious peace and rights would be put into effect. It was clear to them that the Emperor regarded the Council as the end of religious standstills. News kept reaching them about the preparations which were being made for war, and in their disquiet they repeated with monotonous regularity their protests against the papal Council and their demands for security. Assistance against the Turks, which king Ferdinand had described as a matter of extreme urgency, was not even discussed. In any case, news came in of an armistice with the Turks, which suggested that the king was not very serious about his demands. When the Emperor eventually arrived on 16 May, he had already made up his mind on war. Evidence for this is a letter which he sent to the king of Poland, asking for his support.[6] But he still needed an alliance with the Pope. A few days

[1] CT IV, 393 ff.
[2] Jedin I, 408.
[3] Ibid., 415.
[4] Heidrich, Karl V, II, 84; P. Kannengiesser, Der Reichstag zu Worms vom Jahre 1545, 1891; F. Hartung, Karl V. und die deutschen Reichsstände von 1546 bis 1555, 1910. Kannengiesser and Janssen (III, 590) think that Charles was still ready to mediate. Certainly the documents of the Imperial Diets give this impression, though Charles's policy as a whole proved otherwise. The letter he wrote to the king of Poland only two days after arrival in Worms is decisive.
[5] Bibl. Buceriana, No. 83 (SVRG 169, 1952).
[6] Lanz, Correspondenz II, 434; NBD I, 8, 34 n. 1; Heidrich, Karl V., II, 83 ff.

later the papal legate, Farnese, appeared and negotiations with him were completed with such speed that after ten days he was on his way back to Rome to get the agreement of the Pope. He arrived in Rome on 8 June and was promised 12,500 men and 200,000 ducats. In addition, Charles would receive a half of the income of the Spanish church over a period of four months, with permission to raise even more by selling Spanish church properties.[1] If, in spite of this, discussions at the Imperial Diet were allowed to continue, this could only be because the Emperor wanted to gain more time, and to make sure that the decision about the timing of the war remained in his own hands. The Emperor was no more able than Ferdinand to bring about a change in the attitude of the Protestants. For them, everything hung upon the Council issue, in which neither side could give way. Finally the elector of the Palatinate attempted to mediate by proposing that the Protestant request for a national Council should be granted. The Emperor amended this proposal and suggested yet another religious conference. The Protestants continued to reject the Council's authority but accepted the proposal for a religious conference, which the Emperor now seemed to be pursuing with some enthusiasm. He had decided, in the meantime, that he would not attempt a war during that year. He had heard, presumably through Ferdinand, that there was doubt about duke Moritz's attitude. The final recess of 4 August[2] set dates for the religious conference and for the next Imperial Diet. Once again the Protestants declared that they did not recognise the authority of the Council or the authority of the Imperial Cameral Tribunal, and that they stood by the final recess of the Imperial Diet of Speyer. Throughout the Diet they had been well informed of all developments and were under no illusions. A meeting of the members of the League of Schmalkalden had been held simultaneously, and in its recess the Protestants stated quite openly that the religious conference would bring them no benefit, because the Catholics had not given it their consent and regarded the Council as the place where the religious question should be settled. They arranged another meeting of the League, which would take place at Frankfurt in December, and at which further consultations would be held. The result of the Imperial Diet, in so far as imperial politics were concerned, was catastrophic. None of the problems presented to it had been solved. The machinery of the Empire was virtually at a standstill, crippled by the religious cleavage. But it had at least made everyone aware of what was to come, even though no hint of this was given in the final recess.

It had not been possible to open the Council while the Imperial Diet

[1] *Jedin* I, 417 and 610 n. 98.
[2] Text in Lünig, *Reichsarchiv*.

was meeting, for fear of Protestant reaction. On 2 June, while he was on the way from Worms to see the Pope in Rome, Farnese called briefly at Trent to inform the legates of the negotiations he was conducting with the Emperor, so that they could give encouragement to the twenty or so bishops who were there at the time.[1] It is significant that even at that stage someone proposed that the Council should be replaced by a Roman reform commission.[2] There were still people who would have preferred to avoid a Council if possible, but the Pope was insistent. When it became apparent that the war had been postponed, the Pope deferred the opening of the Council—to the annoyance of the legates—until the time of the Emperor's departure from Worms.[3] The legates were fast beginning to believe that they would never be able to open it.[4] The Pope considered moving it to Italy, but the Emperor would not have that at any price.[6] Del Monte was so angry that he became ill.[7] From the Emperor's point of view, the opening of the Council and certain condemnation of the Protestants were of no immediate use to him. The ecclesiastics, for their part, found it an intolerable imposition that they should be so bound to him and that he should maintain such a hesitant attitude. Eventually it was decided in Rome that no matter what else happened, the Council would be opened on the third Sunday in Advent.[8] The opening in fact took place at a solemn service on 13 December 1545.[9] The only German bishop present was Helding, the suffragan of Mainz. The few bishops to arrive from France had already been recalled by Francis,[10] though two remained to attempt obstruction, even at the first general congregation on 18 December—a sign that the unity between the two monarchs was not absolutely reliable. In fact, when the duke of Orleans died on 9 September 1545, the Peace of Crépy became a fragile thing, for the duke of Orleans was to have played the principal role in effecting a reconciliation of the dynasties. However, this uncertainty had no influence on the future course of events.

Meanwhile the Emperor and the Pope were negotiating their treaty in detail, and Charles's confessor, Pedro a Soto, was trying to disperse a number of doubts which seem to have entered Charles's mind. He pointed out the Schmalkaldians' weakness, and that a war against them would be

[1] Jedin I, 416.
[2] Ibid., 416 f.
[3] Ibid., 422 f.
[4] Ibid., 423 f.; CT X, 170 f.
[5] Jedin I, 426; CT X, 144, 174.
[6] Jedin I, 427; CT X, 213 f.
[7] Jedin I, 430.
[8] Jedin I, 429; CT IV, 435 n. 5; CT X, 226 f., 231 f.
[9] Jedin I, 546 ff.
[10] Ibid., I, 431; II, 11.

for the good of the Church. It was true that the Pope was not altogether reliable, but he was not so 'diabolical' 'that he would destroy the Catholic faith by urging so great an undertaking upon the Emperor and then leave him in the lurch' – though this is precisely what happened. The Schmalkaldians demonstrated their power only once, when they took duke Henry prisoner. And on 3 January the elector of the Palatinate had communion administered in both kinds at Heidelberg and then sought to be admitted to the League.[1] But the attempted reform in Cologne collapsed because the law of the Empire was invoked against it – and the power behind the law as well. On 7 May the Emperor visited Cologne on his way to Worms and he encouraged the city council to resist the elector.[2] In June, at the Imperial Diet, he received their appeal, and put them under his protection. On 10 July the elector made a counter-appeal to the 'free and christian' Council, but this was refuted by his opponents. In the same month the archbishop was summoned to Rome. This gave the Emperor an opportunity of pointing out that Hermann's princely dignity depended upon the archi-episcopal dignity conferred on him by the Pope. The Vice-chancellor, Naves, advised the archbishop to resign in favour of his coadjutor. Hermann was then summoned to Brussels, which meant that proceedings were being taken against him at the Imperial Court. Part of the cathedral chapter made an appeal in support of the archbishop, but both were dismissed by the Emperor. The Schmalkaldians merely expressed their regret and deferred action until their next meeting at Frankfurt in December. When the estates of the territory once again declared their support of the archbishop, the Emperor simply stated that their decisions were invalid.[3]

The members of the League of Schmalkalden met at Frankfurt between 6 December and 7 February. As though there was no threat of war at all, they consulted about prolonging, extending and reforming the League, but decided merely to prolong it for a further six years.[4] The Wittenberg theologians advised this course.[5] The application by the elector of the Palatinate was refused, and the bishop of Münster was told that he would not be allowed to join until he had come to terms with the Evangelicals within his territory. Separate discussions on the Brunswick affair took place among the interested parties, but the outcome was merely that things continued as before. A deputation from Cologne asked the League to support the archbishop's appeal and to send a legation to the

---

[1] A. Hasenclever, *Die kurpfälzische Politik in der Zeit des Schmalk. Kriegs*, 1905.
[2] Varrentrapp, *op. cit.*, 249.
[3] Ibid., 263.
[4] *Mentz* II, 413 ff.; H. Lucke, 'Bremen im Schmalkaldischen Bund 1540–1547', *Veröffentlichungen aus dem Staatsarchiv der Freien Hansestadt Bremen*, 1955, 50 f.
[5] *Ursachen* VIII, 16, p. 1526.

Emperor and to the cathedral chapter. This was agreed on 27 or 31 December, and the next meeting of the League would decide what further assistance might be given, though 'speedy assistance' was promised in the event of an emergency. They even deferred drawing up a protest against the Council.[1] As far as the next meeting of the Imperial Diet was concerned, they were united in feeling that nothing could be expected from the proposed religious conference. After its collapse the theologians were to request a public hearing, but for the rest the efforts to secure 'peace and rights' were to continue.[2] Fighting forces were recruited and paid to be in readiness, but there was only limited armament. The legation which the League sent to the Emperor to support the archbishop of Cologne's appeal reached the Emperor at the end of February, and asked him to treat it in the same way as the cases before the Imperial Cameral Tribunal, i.e. to suspend it. They declared that the League would support the archbishop if force were used against him. They were put off until the next meeting of the Imperial Diet.[3]

6. THE IMPERIAL DIET OF REGENSBURG 1546[4]

The religious discussions began on 27 January. The Emperor had given the conference the task of simply compiling a report which would be presented at the Imperial Diet. This was done in order that the conversations might not seem to be a substitute for the Council or in competition with it. He also appointed the participants. The Catholic side was represented by the Spaniard Malvenda, the Carmelite Billick from Cologne, the Augustinian Johannes Hoffmeister and Cochläus; and the Evangelical side by Bucer (though Saxony did not conceal its reservations about him),[5] Brenz, Schnepf, and, in place of Melanchthon, George Major of Wittenberg. Veit Dietrich also took part after 1 March. Helding and Pflug were in Regensburg, but they took no part in the conversations. The Protestants were concerned that the report and its documentation should be above reproach, and so they insisted on a very cumbersome method of procedure. On 24 February the Emperor indicated his disapproval. On 10 March the Protestants broke off the discussions and departed ten days later. The

---

[1] *Mentz* II, 440.

[2] As n 1

[3] *Mentz* II, 442.

[4] *Ursachen* I, 40 and 41; H. v. Caemmerer, 'Das Regensburger Religionsgespräch im Jahre 1546', *Diss. Berlin*, 1901; W. Friedensburg, *ZKG* 18, 1898, 600 ff.; F. Roth, *ARG* 5, 1907–1908, 1 ff., 375 ff.; V. Schultze, *ARG* 7, 1909–1910, 135 ff., 294 ff.; H. Nebelsieck, *ARG* 32, 1935, 127 ff., 253 ff. The Catholic account: *Actorum colloquii Ratisponensis ultimi . . . verissima narratio*, Inglostadt 1546; Bucer's account in *Ursachen* I, p. 392 ff.

[5] *Mentz* II, 443 f.; J. V. Pollet, *M. Bucer*, 1958, 245 ff.

only discussion of any substance dealt with the doctrine of justification, and both sides presented a summary of their views.

> While the discussions were on, Luther died—'*auriga et currus Israel*'. His death occurred in the early dawn of 18 February at Eisleben, where he had been summoned to settle a dispute between the counts Mansfeld.[1] His last words before retiring the previous evening had been an exhortation to pray 'for our Lord God and his Gospel, that all may go well with it, for the Council at Trent and the accursed Pope are hot with wrath against it'.[2] On the orders of the elector the body was taken to Wittenberg and on 22 February, after a sermon by Bugenhagen and an oration by Melanchthon,[3] it was laid to rest in the church at the castle, 'not far from the pulpit in which, during his lifetime, he had delivered many powerful christian sermons in the presence of the princes of Saxony and the whole church'.[4]

The opening of the Imperial Diet was delayed until 5 June.[5] On the way, the Emperor received in Maastricht the delegation sent by the Schmalkaldians to support the archbishop of Cologne's appeal, and in Speyer he received the new elector of Mainz, the bishop of Speyer, the elector of the Palatinate, and the Landgrave of Hesse, whose obstinate bearing convinced the Emperor that war was necessary.[6] An assembly of the Schmalkaldians had begun at Worms on 12 April, but on 22 April they transferred it to Regensburg. None of the princes was there in person.[7] News had reached them that the Emperor and the Pope were arming—a clear indication of what was to come. In Neuberg a Spanish Lutheran had been brutally murdered by his brother who was a fanatical Catholic. The murderer was not immediately punished by the Emperor, and because he gave the impression that his action was not unrelated to the Council, it was interpreted as an omen.[8] In spite of this, the Protestants still delayed and took no steps to protect themselves. The assembly dealt with its business in as dilatory a fashion as before.

When the Imperial Diet was begun on 5 June, it was stated that the most important matters to be discussed were religion, peace and rights.

---

[1] J. Strieder, 'Authentische Berichte über Luthers letzte Lebensstrunden', *Kleine Texte* 99, 1912, 1930²; cf. *WAR* 54, 478 ff.; C. Schubart, *Die Berichte über Luthers Tod und Begräbnis*, 1917.

[2] *Strieder*, 27, 3 ff.

[3] *Schubart* No. 36 f.

[4] Enders, *Briefwechsel* XVII, 60 ff.; *Jedin* II, 174 and 480 n. 9.

[5] Heidrich, *Karl V*, II, 109 ff.; *Brandi*, 470 f.; *Schl* 28097 ff.

[6] *Mentz* II, 448 f.; minutes of the discussion with Philip in A. v. Druffel, *Beiträge zur Reichsgeschichte (Briefe und Akten III)*, 1882, 1 ff.; A. Hasenclever, *Politik Kaiser Karls V. und Landgraf Philipps v. Hessen*, 1903, 16 ff.

[7] *Mentz* II, 452 ff.

[8] *Jedin* II, 177; F. Roth, *ARG* 7, 1909–1910, 413 ff.; *CR* 6, 112 ff.; Bucer's comment in Bibl. Buceriana, *SVRG* 169, 1952, No. 92.

The Catholics again demanded that 'religion' should be left to the Council. On 13 June the Protestants renewed their demand for a 'free and christian Council' on German soil, a national assembly, an Imperial Diet, or at least a ratification of the existing religious standstills. They refused to discuss anything else until these demands were granted. Their statement, when it was read out, merely made the Emperor laugh.[1] But the discussions at the Diet quickly paled into insignificance, for it became daily more urgent that the Protestants should give their attention to a steadily deteriorating situation. On 12 June they decided to put a question at the Imperial Diet about the evident preparations for war. The reply came on 16 June, when they were informed that the Emperor considered it necessary to take action against 'disobedient princes'. He demanded that the rest remain neutral, and sought to drive a wedge between the cities and their traditional allies.[2] This was the actual declaration of war. Even then the councillors still waited for further explanations, while the Emperor, on that same day, asked a number of ecclesiastical princes for their help against Hesse and Electoral Saxony. On 17 June a mandate was issued against the city of Ravensburg, ordering it to desist from religious reform, and stating that religion did constitute a reason for declaring war.[3] At the Imperial Diet further consultations took place on the Imperial Cameral Tribunal and assistance against the Turks, the Protestants again insisting that religious peace and rights must be decided first. The Emperor made his position clear on 11 July, when he rejected the Protestants' demands, saying that delegates were to be sent to the Council as arranged, and that the membership of the Imperial Cameral Tribunal was to continue as before. The final recess, on 24 July, deferred further discussion until the next Diet. But most of the Protestants had left Regensburg in the early part of July.

The Imperial Diet had in fact merely served to veil the Emperor's final preparations. On 7 June he signed treaties with the Pope and with Bavaria.[4] The house of Wittelsbach made peace with the house of Habsburg, though without promising military assistance. On the same day, England and France signed a peace treaty which was not without significance for German affairs.[5] On 19 June the Emperor made an alliance with

---

[1] Heidrich, *Karl V*, II, 130.

[2] F. Rommel, *Die Reichsstadt Ulm*, 1922, 17; Roth III, 344 f.

[3] K. O. Müller, *Aktenstücke zur Geschichte der Reformation in Ravensburg*, RST 32, 1914.

[4] Jedin II, 178 and 481 n. 15; P. Kannengiesser, 'Die Kapitulation zwischen Karl V. und Paul III. gegen die Protestanten', *Festschrift des prot. Gymnasiums in Strassburg* 2, 1888, 211 ff.; Brieger, *ZKG* 9, 1888, 135; Hortleder, *Rechtmässigkeit* III, 3; Roth III, 355.

[5] The Peace of Guima, 7 June 1546.

duke Moritz,[1] Philip's son-in-law, who in return for a promise that the Emperor would supervise the Council agreed to recognise its decisions. To offset his military costs, Moritz was promised the elector's territory. He was also told that he would be made protector of the bishoprics of Magdeburg and Halberstadt. The Emperor also gained the support of the Margraves of Brandenburg, John of Küstrin and Albert Alcibiades of Brandenburg-Kulmbach. To these he made concessions on religious matters—'which were inconsistent with the object of the war'.[2] The Pope, with the approval of the cardinals, signed the treaty on 26 June, and steps were taken immediately to put it into effect.[3] On 3 July the sentence on Hermann von Wied was published, though it was passed on 16 April. On 20 July the Emperor placed the elector of Saxony and the Landgrave of Hesse under imperial ban.[4] Their attack on the duke of Brunswick provided the pretext for war, on the ground that it was a breach of the peace. What made this pretext a particularly suitable one was that not all the members of the League of Schmalkalden were involved in the Brunswick affair, nor was it directly a religious matter. The Emperor wrote to his sister: 'Although this pretext will not conceal for very long that this war is being fought on account of religion, it will at least serve initially to divide the lapsed.'[5] Only the course of events would uncover and explain his meaning.

The cities and Württemberg replied to the Emperor's declaration of 16 June by recruiting forces, 'in order to be among the first to arm'.[6] As soon as the elector of Saxony was certain of the Emperor's intentions (i.e. from 22 June) he, too, began to recruit and to mobilise the other members of the League. He had hesitated on account of certain reservations among the theologians, but his hesitations did not put him at a disadvantage. The peace treaty between the English and the French indirectly aided the Protestants, for the mercenaries who had been paid off now joined their ranks. At a meeting in Ichtershausen the two heads of the League engaged in rapid diplomatic activity—which on the whole was not very effective—and evolved a plan of campaign which was executed with unusual energy.[7]

---

[1] E. Brandenburg, *Politische Korrespondenz des Herzogs u. Kurfürsten Moritz v. Sachsen* II, 1904, 617 ff.; text, ibid., 662 and *HZ* 80, 1898, 39 ff.

[2] F. Hartung, *Deutsche Geschichte*, 25; L. Mollwo, *Markgraf Hans v. Küstrin*, 1926; E. Opgenoorth, *Die Ballei Brandenburg des Johanniterordens im Zeitalter der Reformation u. Gegenref.*, 1963.

[3] *Jedin* II, 178; Hortleder, *Rechtmässigkeit* III. 9 (text of the Bull).

[4] Hortleder, *Rechtmässigkeit* III, 16.

[5] 9 June. Lanz, *Correspondenz* II, 486 ff.; *Brandi*, 470 f.

[6] Sleidan, *op. cit.*, 480; Rommel, *op. cit.*, 15 f, 19 f.; *Roth* III, 358 ff.

[7] Hortleder, *Rechtmässigkeit* III, 6 and II, 11; H. Baumgarten, *HZ* 36, 1876, 26 ff.

O

At first the Wittenburg theologians had urged the princes to wait. They admitted that it would be right to engage in a preventive war if it were certain that the Emperor intended to wage war on the Evangelicals on account of religion. But if this were not certain, 'we should not make too great haste, for it is a great matter, and a war of this sort will change the face of the German nation for ever'. They thought that the Emperor would wait until the Council ended. 'We do not consider that the Emperor will do anything before then.'[1] On 4 July Bugenhagen issued a letter to all pastors and preachers, urging them to pray, and leaving them in no doubt that it was the duty of every man 'to give loyal service to God by defending the churches, the clergy, christian princes and government, wife and child, honour and discipline', for it was now clear that the war would be a religious one.[2] George Major replied to the imperial ban by issuing a 'Counter-ban'.[3] On 10 July Melanchthon published a new edition of Luther's 'Warning to his beloved German people' and added a preface. Melanchthon considered that in view of the alliance of the Pope with the Emperor the duty of every Christian was now plain.[4] In August Bugenhagen appealed to the people of Bohemia, Silesia and Lausitz not to give assistance to the Emperor.[5] On 20 January he and Melanchthon published a statement which Luther had made on the question of self-defence,[6] and a document entitled 'An Instruction on defence in extremity'[7] appeared in the name of Justus Menius.

During the summer the Protestants published two statements in which they rejected the authority of the Council.[8] The statements which had been submitted to the assembly of the Schmalkaldians at Frankfurt were drawn together by a lawyer called Lamb and were considerably adapted and enlarged. The result was a document in which legal arguments were employed in an attempt to prove that the Council convened by the Pope was not the Council which was promised to the estates. Melanchthon also wrote a paper[9] in which he argued that it was necessary to break with the Pope, and stated that for the sake of doctrine which must never again be suppressed the Council had to be rejected.

Meanwhile, the assembled bishops in Trent had begun their work. First they had to decide on procedure. The Pope had requested decisions on doctrinal issues, and the Emperor had asked that questions of reform be taken first. The bishops took a middle course by deciding to link the two concerns together. Every time a decree on doctrine was published,

---

[1] Hortleder, *Rechtmässigkeit* II, 21, p. 103.
[2] Ibid., II, 22, p. 104 ff.
[3] Ibid., II, 23, p. 122 ff.
[4] CR 6, 190 ff.; Hortleder, *Rechtmässigkeit* II, 24.
[5] Hortleder, *Rechtmässigkeit* II, 27.
[6] Ibid., II, 28.
[7] Ibid., II, 29; Roth III, 352 ff.
[8] *Jedin* II, 175 ff. and 480 n. 12; *Ursachen* I, 43 f. (text).
[9] Stupperich, *Melanchthons Werke* I, 1951, 411 f. (text).

a decree on reform was to be published with it.[1] The actual work was done in the congregations and in the theological commissions which prepared for them. The members of the theological commissions, despite their status as theologians, did not have the right to vote. Only the results of their debates were announced at the 'sessions'. The Emperor was represented by two 'orators', Franzisco de Toledo and Mendoza. His confidants among the clergy were Madruzzo, who was a cardinal and bishop of Trent, and the Spaniard Pedro Pacheco,[2] bishop of Jaën, who in January 1546 was also made a cardinal. The Council set to work on the doctrine of Scripture and of the apostolic tradition, and a reform decree on the study of the Bible was taken with this. The decrees were published at the fourth session on 8 April 1546. The reform decree is a notable attempt to set aside Scholasticism in favour of biblical study. The decree on doctrine met with immediate criticism and Rome decided that it needed to be improved. After this, there was a discussion of the doctrine of original sin, coupled with a decree on the reform of preaching. The doctrinal discussion revealed the enormous range of positions which it was possible to occupy within Catholicism.[3] The Franciscan theologians claimed that hand in hand with the doctrine of original sin went the doctrine of the immaculate conception, and they sought to get a decision on this in their favour.[4] But the Council decided to confine its attention to the doctrines which were in dispute. They felt obliged to condemn the teachings of Erasmus and of Pighius, as well as those of the Protestants.

Then political difficulties arose, for on 22 May Toledo urged that the decrees should not be discussed until an 'instruction' had been received from the Emperor. The legates rightly felt that this was an onslaught on the 'freedom' of the Council and they therefore rejected the application.[5] At the last moment the Emperor told his representatives that they should prevent the decrees on doctrine from being published and urge that the reform decrees be taken instead, 'in order to shut the Protestants' mouths'. The nuncio at the imperial court explained that the Emperor was anxious that nothing should happen which would upset negotiations with the Protestant princes, or which would give the lie to the Emperor's declaration that the war was not a religious one.[6] Despite this, the decrees were published at the fifth session on 17 June.[7] Afterwards, discussions began on the doctrine of justification. At the same time a reform decree was to be taken on the duty of bishops to reside in their dioceses.[8] Both issues were difficult ones in any case, but discussions were interrupted by the

---

[1] *Jedin* II, 23 ff., 104 ff.; *CT* I, 382 ff.; IV, 569 ff. (22 Jan. 1546).
[2] *Jedin* II, 115 f. [3] Ibid., II, 113 ff., 121 ff. [4] Ibid., II, 116 f., 131 f.
[5] Ibid., II, 115. [6] Ibid., II, 133 f.; *CT* XI, 56 f.; X, 525. [7] *Jedin* II, 134 ff.
[8] *Jedin* II, 139 ff.; H.Rückert, *Die Rechfertigungslehre auf dem Tridentinischen Konzil* 1925.

outbreak of war. Schmalkaldian troops penetrated as far as Tirol, which caused such a panic among the fathers that the legates were provided with a welcome excuse to have the Council transferred to a city on Italian soil, in order to escape once and for all from the Emperor's power.[1] The whole of July, including the sixth session on 29 July, was spent discussing this issue. The Emperor would have regarded such a step as highly undesirable, for it would completely destroy his plan. In the general congregations of 28 and 30 July there was a violent collision between Madruzzo, who sympathised with the Emperor, and Del Monte, who wanted to have the Council postponed for an indefinite period.[2] But this could have been interpreted as a new prorogation, which would make the Emperor's demand that the Protestants should attend the Council look ridiculous. However, when the military menace had been removed the debate became a pointless one, and so the Council turned its attention once more to the doctrine of justification.

The Emperor had told the Schmalkaldian delegation that the Cologne affair should be brought up at the next Imperial Diet. But on 16 April, before the Diet had ever begun, the Pope had pronounced his verdict on the archbishop, excommunicating him and stripping him of his office. On 3 July the administration of the archbishopric was transferred to the coadjutor, Adolf von Schaumburg.[3] Hermann did not learn of either decision until September. He refused to take part in the war on the side of the Schmalkaldians, for he still hoped that someone might be able to mediate between him and his opponents, and he justified his stand yet again in a 'True Account', which his opponents answered with an 'Honest Reply'.[4] When told that he had been deposed, he simply renewed his appeal. The Emperor's judgement followed the Pope's. On 21 December a mandate was issued, summoning the estates of Cologne to an assembly in January. Immediately afterwards the coadjutor was instructed to prepare to assume government and in case of necessity to claim assistance from the Emperor's army in the Netherlands. At the meeting of the estates commissaries of the Emperor appointed the coadjutor to the archbishopric. On 31 January 1547 the secular estates submitted—under the threat of force. Hermann gave up further efforts and on 25 February retired to Wied. So before the war had even begun, and without a single sword being drawn, the archbishopric had been saved for the old faith.

---

[1] Jedin II, 179 f.
[2] Jedin II, 184 ff.
[3] Text: Lacomblet, Düsseldorf IV, Archiv für die Geschichte des Niederrheins 4, 1862, 691.
[4] Varrentrapp, op. cit., 270 n. 5.

CHAPTER X

THE COURSE OF THE WAR[1]

I. THE WAR IN SOUTH GERMANY[2]

THE Emperor had intended marching on Saxony and Hesse, but swift action on his opponents' part wrecked his plan. First of all, Schärtlin von Burtenbach, by a bold stroke, reached the hermitage of Ehrenberg on 11 July 1546, thereby bringing the Council into disarray. Then Saxony and Hesse, after a very rapid march, reached the Danube on 4 August. The Emperor withdrew to Landshut, where papal troops joined him on 13 August. The two armies were then equally matched. Troops which had gathered at Aachen joined the imperial army at Ingolstadt on 15 September. This did not affect the balance of the two armies, because the Protestants had left troops behind to cover them. Thereafter, the campaign consisted primarily of strategic marches, each side trying to manoeuvre into a superior position. The armies began to tire, and the Schmalkaldians were soon suffering from a shortage of money.[3] At the end of October the Landgrave got enough from South German supporters to pay the troops the arrears owing to them.[4] During the night of 8/9 November the Emperor was told that duke Moritz and king Ferdinand had decided to invade Electoral Saxony. In spite of this the elector stayed in South Germany. But eventually shortage of money compelled the Protestants to abandon the campaign. On 14 November Philip of Hesse requested an armistice,[5] which was refused five days later.[6] On 15 November a

---

[1] *Schl* 41677–41682; Hortleder, *Handlungen und Ausschreiben*, etc., 1640[2]; *Mentz* III, 1908, 1–112; *Brandi*, 472 ff.; Brandi, *Quellen*, 370 ff.

[2] M. Lenz. *HZ* 49, 1883, 384 ff; A. Schütz, *Der Donaufeldzug*, 1930.

[3] F. W. Schaafhausen, 'Die Geldwirtschaft des Schmalkaldischen Bundes', *Diss.* Göttingen, 1921; Rommel, *op. cit.*, 47 ff. (H. Gerber *ARG* 32–34, 1935–37).

[4] Rommel, *op. cit.*, 56 f.

[5] Rommel, *op. cit.*, 63.

[6] Ibid.

representative of Ulm was negotiating with Granvella,[1] and on 22 November the army withdrew from Giengen to the north, by way of Heidenheim, and its constituent units separated. The cities yielded one after another, their representatives kneeling to beg for pardon. The first was Schwäbisch-Hall (15 December), then Ulm (23 December) and finally Strasbourg, whose representatives appeared in Nördlingen on 21 March.[2] The elector of the Palatinate, Frederick, who had put a small contingent at the disposal of the League, was received in Schwäbisch-Hall in the middle of December and treated with cold disdain. Nevertheless he was allowed to keep the electorate (which had been promised to Bavaria in the event of his being forcibly overrun).[3] Ulrich of Württemberg had to wait even longer to receive pardon. At the end of the year he was received in Heilbronn. His plea had to be read for him, for he was no longer able to kneel, and pardon was granted him on condition that he paid a sum of 300,000 florins. He was allowed to keep his territory, even though it was in feoff to Austria and his part in the war could have been regarded as 'felony'.[4] 'It was difficult to detect much mercy'[5] on the Emperor's part, but he certainly did not wish to create new difficulties before the war had ended. It is for this reason that none of the settlements included instructions on religious matters.

Thus the Emperor was free to continue the war at will. He sent a second army from the Netherlands to march on Minden and Verden, and decided to go himself to give assistance to Ferdinand and Moritz in Saxony, where they were under pressure from the elector. On 4 March he left Ulm, spent fourteen days in Nördlingen and then went through Nuremberg and Eger towards Saxony.

2. THE COUNCIL DURING THE WAR

In January, however, the Emperor had suffered a defeat which counted for more than the victory he had just won. After the Council had once again turned its attention to the doctrine of justification, taking a new draft as the basis for discussion,[6] the Emperor's sympathisers attempted to obstruct the passing of the decree, so as to prevent a decision to which

[1] Ibid.
[2] *Pol. Corr.* IV, I, No. 592; *Roth* III, 440 ff. (on Augsburg); *Pol. Corr.* IV, I, 541, 588, 658; and Rommel, *op. cit.*, 60 ff. (on Ulm); Rommel, *op. cit.*, 85 f. (Biberach, Memmingen, Kempten, Ravensburg, Isny—16 January).
[3] A. Hasenclever, *Die kurpfälzische Politik*, 1905.
[4] Lanz, *Correspondenz* II, 509, 517 f., 523 ff.; Hortleder, *Rechtmässigkeit* III, 56, 61
[5] *Brandi*, 481.
[6] *Jedin* II, 201 ff.; A. v. Druffel, 'Sfondrato', AMA XX/2, 1892, Hist. Klasse, 291 ff.

the Protestants could not submit.[1] This happened in September, and in the following month the Emperor's representatives proposed that the Council should be suspended for six months, simply in order to prevent the decree being published. However, they made this proposal on their own initiative and tried to get an agreement drawn up about it at Trent,[2] but neither the Pope nor the Emperor approved. The legates were convinced that on pastoral grounds alone it was essential that the Catholic definition of the doctrine of justification should be published. They believed that the Council should be brought to a close soon after this decree was published. There was no sympathy in Rome for those who wished to delay publication. So this highly significant decree was published at the sixth session on 13 January 1547, after the theologians had worked on it for a full six months. The doctrine is set out in sixteen chapters, and thirty-three canons list errors which are to be rejected.

No trace remains of the doctrine of twofold justification which had been so widely propounded in the period before the Council began.[3] A Jesuit, Laínez, in a penetrating and pointed speech had proved that it was a novel and un-Catholic idea.[4] The essential points in the decree are that grace requires the co-operation of free will, and that faith is to be understood as readiness to receive sanctifying grace. 'The decree is based on the conclusions of scholastic theology, but it goes beyond them.' The Council 'produced something new' and did not simply reproduce ideas which lay ready to hand.[5] Loofs has pointed out that some of the scholastic antitheses lack clarity, but this is to misunderstand the purpose of the whole decree, which was to draw a line of distinction between the Catholic and the Protestant versions of the doctrine. 'It is the purpose of the 33 canons to draw this distinction',[6] and therefore they are not to be regarded as a mere appendage to the decree. In fact the chapters which contain the exposition of the doctrine are really 'a commentary on the canons, a positive summary of that conscious faith on the basis of which the errors rejected in the canons are condemned'. 'In interpreting the decree, a safe rule is to begin at the place where the distinctions are drawn, i.e. with the canons.' Jedin's second rule for interpreting the decree is worthy of attention: because the Council was not concerned to settle disputed questions within Catholic theology, all appeals—in doubtful instances—to earlier theological positions are entirely permissible.'

The theological decree was accepted unanimously, but the reform

[1] *Jedin* II, 220 ff.
[2] *Jedin* II, 232 ff.; Druffel, *Sfondrato*, 297 ff.
[3] *Jedin* II, 208, 213 ff.
[4] *Jedin* II, 216.
[5] *Jedin* II, 262 (against Loofs and Seeberg). He adopts Harnack's verdict, that it is doubtful whether the Reformation would have come about if this decree had been published at the beginning of the century.
[6] *Jedin* II, 262 f.

decree, simply because it profoundly affected existing practice, caused such dissension that only after further discussions on 25 February was the president able to consider it approved. Even then additions had to be made at the seventh session on 3 March. But that was not the end of the matter, for it had to be taken up again in the third period of the Council. Despite this, the reform decrees passed at the sixth and seventh sessions are a step forward on the road towards Catholic reform. The bishops accepted the key statement 'that of all the rights and obligations conferred in ordination and consecration, the exercise of pastoral care has the pre-eminence'.[1] Those who had enjoyed the delights of the Renaissance period were made to feel the full force of this renunciation. The decree on doctrine which was passed at the seventh session listed the seven sacraments and dealt with baptism and confirmation.

It was not until 6 February that the Emperor was informed officially of the outcome of the sixth session.[2] In the meantime, however, the Pope's policies had changed direction yet again. His nuncio had been excluded from the negotiations which Charles conducted with the defeated South Germans, and the Pope regarded this as a breach of the treaty. He was also angry that the Emperor showed no inclination to be accommodating in Italian affairs.[3] But worse was to come. The death of the duke of Orleans meant that the Peace of Crépy was now unworkable. The French sought new terms, but the Emperor refused, unless the French were prepared to vacate Piedmont. The papal nuncio at the French court gave Francis warning of the Emperor's alleged plans vis-à-vis the Council, and the French again began to prepare for war. So the Pope felt that he had to start another 'peace-initiative'. His approaches were welcomed by France but rejected by the Emperor. The Pope hesitated to renew his treaty with the Emperor, in fact on 2 February in Ulm the nuncio handed Charles a letter dated 22 January, which gave notice that the treaty would be terminated.[4] The Emperor could not contain his indignation. He railed against the Italian troops, said that the Pope was 'neither a pastor nor a man of honour', left the nuncio standing and went off to Mass.[5] The Pope then refused to let church money be used for financing the war.[6] From his point of view the war had been decided and the main work of the Council had already been completed. Now he feared the Emperor's superior power. That is why he pressed for negotiations between France and the Emperor before the Emperor achieved total victory. The Pope

[1] Jedin II, 312.
[2] Jedin II, 348 (justification of the Pope, 347).
[3] Jedin II, 349 f.
[4] Druffel, Sfondrato, 304 f.
[5] Jedin II, 344; Druffel, Sfondrato, 306 f.
[6] Jedin II, 345 f.

had no further interest in consolidating the victories already won. 'In the back of the Pope's mind lurked a profound suspicion of Charles' future intentions. There can be no other convincing explanation of his conduct.'[1]

Relationships were even more strained when it was decided to transfer the Council to Bologna.[2] In Trent, discussions had centred on the eucharist. But at the general congregation of 8 March the president, Del Monte, got up, and without any warning asked the assembled company whether it wished to stay in Trent. He said that sickness had broken out which the Council's doctor considered to be epidemic. Evidently it was typhus, brought in by the soldiers. Since there was no question of dissolving the Council, the only alternative was to transfer it, and because of the problem of finding sufficient accommodation, Bologna seemed to be the only suitable place. This proposal led to a dramatic tussle between the Emperor's sympathisers and the majority, but within two days the legates' proposal was approved, though fourteen bishops protested. The legates appealed to the authority which had been given them two years previously.[3] On 10 March it was officially decided to transfer the Council and the announcement was made on the following day at the eighth session.[4] Sarpi supposed that some secret scheme of the Pope's lay behind the move, but it is not possible to substantiate this, and it is in any case unlikely.[5] So the majority of the fathers betook themselves to Bologna, while the Emperor went to Saxony in order to compel the Protestants to attend the Council. But his plan had now been made impracticable, because even he could not pretend that the Council at Bologna[6] was the kind of Council to which the resolutions of the Imperial Diets had referred. Still less could he demand that the Protestants should submit to it. 'The quarrel which broke out between Pope and Emperor was the salvation of the German Protestants, and came at the moment of their greatest need.'[7]

3. THE CAMPAIGN IN SAXONY[8]

In Saxony Moritz had no difficulty in taking control of the electoral territories. His victory was short lived, for when the elector arrived Moritz was pushed back again. He appealed for help, and the Margrave

[1] *Jedin* II, 352.
[2] *Jedin* II, 353 ff.
[3] *Jedin* II, 367.
[4] *CT* I, 139 ff., V, 1018 ff. and 1025 ff. (cf. *Jedin* II, 365).
[5] *Jedin* II, 372 ff.; *Brandi*, 493 takes a different view; but cf. Brandi, *Quellen*, 384.
[6] *CT* VI, 1960.
[7] *Jedin* II, 376.
[8] *Ursachen* III, p. 567 ff.; Hortleder, *Rechtmässigkeit* III, 68 ff.; *Mentz* III, 97 ff. *HZ* 20, 1868, 53 ff.; *ARG* 5, 1908, 213 ff.; Brandi, *Quellen*, 381.

Albert Alcibiades responded. But while the Margrave was on his way he was surprised at Rochlitz on 2 March and taken prisoner.[1] Moritz subsequently gained time, because the elector Joachim initiated peace negotiations which the estates on both sides accepted.[2]

The elector of Saxony did not attempt to prevent the armies of the Emperor and of the duke of Saxony from combining. On 12 April he went from Meissen up the right bank of the Elbe, hoping to reach Wittenberg or Magdeburg. On Sunday, 24 April, the armies faced one another near Mühlberg, separated only by the river. The elector thought he was safe, but the Emperor's troops found a ford[3] which the Saxons were apparently not aware of, and they attacked the Saxons on the flank. There was no engagement—merely flight and pursuit. The elector tried to reach the forests on the Lochau heath. He joined personally in the last rearguard action which his troops attempted, but he was slightly wounded, taken prisoner, and conducted by Alba to the Emperor. It would still have been possible for Electoral Saxony to continue the resistance. The elector's eldest son, John Frederick (the 'middle' one), had escaped and had reached Gotha, which was well fortified. Wittenberg also was armed for defence. But the matter was decided by the prisoner's trial before the Emperor, who emphasised the seriousness of his intentions by condemning the elector to death. In spite of this, the elector would not yield on the Council issue,[4] though he gave way to the Emperor on all purely political questions, including even the Imperial Cameral Tribunal. He protested only against Moritz's demands. On 19 May Wittenberg signed a capitulation,[5] and on 23 May the town was handed over. On the 30th the elector's son gave in and surrendered Gotha. On 4 June duke Moritz was given possession of the Kurkreis and the status of elector. John Frederick remained the prisoner of the Emperor.

But the attempt by imperial troops to capture Bremen·failed. Cruningen, the commander of the imperial army, fell outside the walls of the city, and the duke of Calenberg, who had entered the Emperor's service, lifted the siege. On 23 May 1547 Christoph of Oldenburg and Albert of Mansfeld defeated his army at Drakenburg an der Weser.[6] That was the salvation of North Germany. Moritz persuaded the Emperor to negotiate with Philip of Hesse[7] and the elector Joachim once again took part. The Emperor conceded that if Philip submitted he would be sentenced neither

---

[1] *Mentz* III, 83 f.; Hortleder, *Rechtmässigkeit* III, 65.
[2] *Mentz* III, 74 ff.
[3] *Mentz* III, 101.
[4] *Mentz* III, 109.
[5] Hortleder, *Rechtmässigkeit* III, 71 f. (text).
[6] *Schl* 36602–36604, 51647; for Bremen cf. H. Lucke, *op. cit.*, esp. p. 72 ff.
[7] *Schl* 30376–30403; Brandi, *Quellen*, 382.

to death nor to life imprisonment. Moritz and Joachim also promised that Philip would keep his freedom and his property—though they had no authority to make such a promise. So Philip came to the Emperor's camp near Halle. On 19 June he went down on his knees before the Emperor while his chancellor read his plea. The only reply he got was a statement by Dr. Seld that he would not be punished with life imprisonment. The Emperor did not give him his hand.[1] He had supper with Granvella, Alba and the two electors, but was not freed afterwards. The elector Moritz made vain efforts on his behalf. The Emperor now regarded the war as ended. Taking his prisoners with him he went to Augsburg for the next Imperial Diet. To get the submission of the North German cities seemed to him to be not worth the trouble, because they were 'strong but poor'. To attempt to conquer them would merely waste time and yield little.[2] On 27 July 1547 the city of Magdeburg was put under the ban.[3] Counts Oldenburg and Mansfield remained in the field until early in 1548.[4] The territorial adjustments in Saxony and the implementation of the Wittenberg agreement gave rise to a lot of friction among the princes of Saxony. The Ernestine princes made no attempt to conceal their views, and Moritz watched suspiciously for the slightest indication that his new dignity and his new possessions were being questioned. The university of Wittenberg was preserved, and Melanchthon remained its loyal devotee, but as early as March in the following year a university was founded in Ernestine Saxony at Jena. It deliberately set itself up in opposition to 'Philipist' Wittenberg, and this was to affect the course of theology in the following period.[5]

[1] Hortleder, *Rechtmässigkeit* IV, 2.
[2] Brandi, *Quellen*, 382 ff.
[3] Hortleder, *Rechtmässigkeit* IV, 2.
[4] *Hartung*, 47.
[5] K. Heussi, *Geschichte der Theologischen Fakultät zu Jena*, 1954.

CHAPTER XI

THE IMPERIAL DIETS AFTER THE WAR, AND THE INTERIM

1. THE 'IRON-CLAD' DIET AND THE INTERIM[1]

ON 1 September 1547 the Emperor opened the 'iron-clad' Imperial Diet in Augsburg. His intention was to take recent events to their logical conclusion. The subjects for discussion were the reform of the Imperial Cameral Tribunal, the reordering of the Empire, and the religious question. The Emperor had long wanted a federal constitution for the Empire, to be achieved by means of territorial alliances which would not only unite the estates but also provide a suitable instrument for putting imperial policies into effect. By such means Charles considered that peace could be established and maintained. He was not a little influenced by the fact that the Swabian League had practically ruled South Germany for fifty years.[2] His alliance plans collapsed completely,[3] so once more the religious question became the principal one.

It was not possible to envisage a simple return to Catholicism. The main reasons for this were that the Emperor had made promises to his Protestant allies on the subject of religion, that relations between Emperor and Pope had gone from bad to worse, and that the Council had been transferred from Trent to Bologna. The Emperor found this last totally unacceptable, and he instructed his representative in Rome to protest against all the decisions reached at Bologna. Then the papal legate Sfondrato, who was received by the Emperor in Bamberg on 4 July, asked for

---

[1] Schl 28100–28106; W. Maurenbrecher, *Karl V. u. die Protestanten 1545–1555,* 1865, 175 ff.; F. Hartung, *Karl V. u. die deutschen Protestanten 1540–1555,* 1910, 36 ff.; F. Roth, *Augsburgische Reformationsgeschichte* IV, 1911, 83 ff. and 111 ff.; Hortleder, *Rechtmässigkeit* III, 84.
[2] *Brandi,* 492 and 498 f.; *Hartung,* 27 ff.
[3] *Hartung,* 40.

help against England, where Henry VIII had died on 28 January. When asked whether the Council would be transferred back from Bologna to Trent, the legate replied that this would only be done if the bishops who supported the Emperor first went to Bologna, and if the Germans submitted to the Council's decisions.[1] The cardinals suggested that the Council should simply be moved back to Trent, but the Pope refused.[2] The Emperor, on the other hand, was considering the possibility of holding a new, imperial Council.[3] So the Pope and the Emperor were no closer. During the Diet the situation was aggravated by the murder of Farnese, who fell victim to a conspiracy, and also by the fact that the imperial governor of Milan occupied Piacenza.[4]

To the Pope it seemed that an alliance with France was the only way out. At the same time, in the Emperor's camp, there were those who argued that the Emperor ought to occupy the Church states. In these circumstances the German religious question could not possibly be referred to the Council. So the Emperor declared at Augsburg on 18 October that he would make efforts to have the Council moved back to Trent, and that he expected the Protestant estates to attend there. At the same time he requested that consultations take place in order that a settlement might be reached 'for the meantime'. The princes gave the required promise, even though at the time it was a purely theoretical one, and the Emperor passed over the reservations voiced by the cities (who once again followed Jakob Sturm's lead) and the brave refusal of the Emperor's prisoner,[5] the elector of Saxony. On the basis of the princes' promise the Emperor made efforts, through the agency of Madruzzo, to persuade Rome to move the Council back to Trent.[6] The Pope, however, referred the decision on this to the Council.[7] On 16 January 1548 the Emperor had protests made in Bologna against the transfer of the Council from Trent, and coupled with them a declaration that he would act personally, as befitted his office. He had the same statements delivered in Rome on 23 January.[8] The Pope replied on 1 February, saying that the Council in Bologna was perfectly valid and he listed reasons in support.[9] For the immediate task with which the Emperor was faced in Germany, the Council was therefore no longer of any use. The only alternative was an interim settlement.[10] The Emperor

---

[1] Druffel, *Sfondrato*, 328 ff.; *Brandi*, 494.
[2] Druffel, *Sfondrato*, 335; *Brandi*, 494.
[3] Druffel, *Sfondrato*, 337 f.; *Brandi*, 494.
[4] *Brandi*, 495.   [5] *Mentz* III, 279 ff.
[6] *CT* VI, 635 and 639 (the instruction and the cardinals' reactions).
[7] *CT* VI, 629.
[8] *CT* VI, 684 ff. (Bologna) and 717 ff. (Rome); *CT* XI, 947 ff.
[9] *CT* VI, 727 ff.
[10] *Schl* 38259a–38330a; G. Wolf, 'Das Augsburger Interim', *Deutsche Zeitschrift für Geschichtswissenschaft* 2, 1898, 39 ff.

had already prepared for this. In August he had invited Catholic scholars
to advise on such a settlement.[1] On 25 October cardinal Sfondrato
reported that three Germans, Helding, Billick and Fannemann, and two
Spaniards, Malvenda and Dominic a Soto, had held consultations about
it,[2] but 'we do not know'[3] what course these consultations took. Meanwhile Pflug had drawn up a *formula sacrorum emendandorum*. On 14
January the Emperor asked the estates to arrange for a few men to discuss
the religious question with those whom he had appointed. He was trying
to get active co-operation from the Diet, but his efforts were thwarted
by the Catholics and by the cities, who referred the task back to him.[4]
He formed a commission himself, but after only three sessions it was
clear that it could not work, because the members could not agree to a
compromise.[5] Thus the Emperor had no other course open to him but
to dictate a settlement himself. Pflug, Helding and Agricola were presented with a draft and told to revise and complete it. Within two weeks
they had done the work. Then the Emperor negotiated with each of the
estates. Bucer, who was brought from Strasbourg, approved the scheme
as a whole, though he thought that the article on justification might have
been better expressed, and he would have preferred the article on the
invocation of saints to be left to the Council. Even though his suggestions for the article on justification were taken up, he later wrote against
it, and nothing would induce him to return to his earlier position.[6] At
this point the electors of the Palatinate and of Brandenburg again undertook to mediate. The electoral dignity had been solemnly conferred upon
Moritz of Saxony on 24 February,[7] but the two mediators were unsuccessful in their efforts to persuade him to take up a position on the proposed
settlement. Even direct representations by the Emperor and the king
failed to move him. John of Küstrin gave a flat rejection both to Agricola
and to the king.[8] Augsburg, Nuremberg and Ulm were disposed to
accept the settlement in principle, but Sturm of Strasbourg declared that
'a Christian might tolerate it, but never approve it'. The Emperor had
written a preface, in which he described the document as a 'recommendation' and asked for it to be approved. This was flatly rejected by Bavaria,
on the grounds that Catholics should simply be ordered to remain loyal

[1] W. Friedensburg, *ARG* 4, 1906–1907, 213 ff.
[2] *NBD* I, 10, 163.
[3] W. Friedensburg, *ARG* 4, 1906–1907, 215.
[4] Wolf, *Interim*, 54 ff.
[5] Ibid., 59.
[6] *Roth* IV, 148 n. 4.
[7] Hortleder, *Rechtmässigkeit* III, 85.
[8] Zittelmann, 'Die Verhandlungen des Markgrafen Joh. v. Küstrin', *Zeitschrift
für preussische Geschichts- und Landeskunde* 4, 1867, 73–84, 151–164, 151–164, 412–426.

to the old faith—the formula was of no interest to them.[1] The ecclesiastical princes decided not to yield on any point without Rome's explicit approval, and they also sought to prevent the formula from being made binding upon Catholics. The Jesuit Bobadilla preached against it and had to be banished. Eventually the Emperor gave in and tried to persuade the electors of the Palatinate and Brandenburg to agree that the formula should be applicable only to Protestants. At about the same time a statement by Melanchthon reached Augsburg, in which he declared that the Canon of the Mass, private Masses, requiem Masses and the invocation of saints were all intolerable. The elector Joachim brushed this aside with the information that Melanchthon was referring to the German, not the standard Latin, text. But the negotiators were so persistent in refusing to restrict the settlement to Protestants that the Emperor decided to enlist the help of the Habsburg theologians in making further changes to the text in order that it might be acceptable to the Catholic theologians also. Joachim and Agricola accepted this version, 'no doubt hoping that it would prevent the Interim from being applied only to the Protestants—which in their view would have been fatal'.[2] They had held discussions with king Ferdinand and a Soto and had been convinced that the Interim was intended for everyone. But when the text was published,[3] it merely put Catholics under obligation to remain loyal to the old faith. The papal legate had arrived in the meantime,[4] and apparently the Emperor feared that the Catholics might seek his help. So in spite of everything the Interim became a law which was applicable to Protestants, though the Emperor took comfort from the fact that several Catholic princes had given him a verbal assurance that the Interim would be upheld in their territories. Moritz at first protested but was later appeased. Margrave John resisted, and Wolfgang of Zweibrücken simply said that he would leave decisions to the bishops within his territory and would not attempt to obstruct them. The Emperor won the support of the cities by making direct representations—by-passing their delegates in Augsburg—and by threatening to billet Italian and Spanish soldiers in them.[5] On 30 June 1548 the new ordinance was published in the final recess of the Diet. It bore little resemblance to the Emperor's original intentions. He had planned a Reformation, but only a special law for Protestants had emerged, which

[1] G. Wolf, Interim, 84 ff. opposes Maurenbrecher, op. cit., 185 and most others on the question whether the Interim was intended as a law for everyone.

[2] Wolf, Interim, 78.

[3] 'Der römisch-kaiserlichen Majestät Erklärung, wie es der Religion halben im Heiligen Reich bis zum Austrag des allgemeinen Konzilii gehalten werden soll.' Text in K. T. Hergang, Das Augsberger Interim, 1855, 20 ff.

[4] CT VI, 767 ff.

[5] Roth IV, 124; M. Simon, Evangelische Kirchengeschichte Bayerns, 1952², 251 f.

no one regarded as the expression of his convictions, and on which even a few Protestants reserved their position. The recess did not include, however, a document drawn up for the catholic estates, entitled *Formula reformationis per Caesaream Maiestatem statibus ecclesiasticis . . . proposita*.[1] The Emperor had put it before the ecclesiastical estates on 14 June, and it was published on 9 July.

The document is in four parts and deals with the reform of the clergy, particularly their training and their courses of study, reform of the Church's life and of the functions of the clergy. Under this heading the importance of preaching is heavily emphasised, and it is laid down that at communion the words of administration are to be in German. Cumulation of benefices is forbidden. Reform is to be implemented by means of visitations and synods, both diocesan and provincial. Visitations were to be undertaken by S. Martin's Day, 1548, and synods were to be held before Lent in the following year. This ordinance, too, was a provisional one, for it lacked papal authority. Many provinces did in fact hold synods, with significant results.[2]

The Interim contains a 'Confession' in twenty-six chapters, which on the whole is modelled on the Augsburg Confession. In addition there are expositions of disputed doctrines, particularly the doctrines of the Mass, of the sacrifice of the Mass, of memorials of the saints and of the dead. Finally there is a statement on ceremonies. Justification is described as the forgiveness of sins, deliverance from guilt, and renewal through the Holy Spirit, by whose power the man who is justified is enabled both 'to desire what is good and right, and to bring that desire to fruition'. The document stresses, however, that this renewal is not total perfection. The doctrine of free will is introduced in language reminiscent of Melanchthon's: God does not drag man towards faith and love as though he were a log, but draws him 'with his own consent'. The exposition of the sacrifice of the Mass stresses the once-for-all aspect of Christ's sacrifice, which is complete and inexhaustible. Nevertheless, the Mass is a sacrifice which serves to remind men of Christ's sacrifice and enables them to appropriate it. The doctrine of the Church is unambiguously Catholic. It states that bishops are essential to the Church, that the Church has the 'power to make canons', to expound Scripture, to inflict punishment. It is ruled over by a chief bishop who is in the succession of S. Peter, 'not to destroy it but to build it up'. In chapter 36 provision is made for the liturgy to be celebrated as before, with all the familiar externals preserved, including the ceremonial for Corpus Christi. However, a sermon is prescribed at the Mass, and the document proposes that the other sacraments be improved liturgically. Images of the saints are not to be venerated in a superstitious fashion, benedictions and blessings are not to be regarded as magical acts. The preface gives the Emperor the right to make changes in the formula. The two most important concessions

[1] Lünig, *Reichsarchiv* II, No. 158, p. 850; *Le Plat* IV, 79 ff.
[2] Lipgens, *Gropper*, 175; on Cologne cf. H. Foerster, *RST* 45–46, 1925; L. Lenhart, 'Die Mainzer Synoden von 1548 u. 1549', *Archiv für mittelrheinische Kirchengeschichte* 10, 1958, 67 ff.

to the Protestants are the administration of the chalice to the laity and the right of priests to marry, both of which are permitted until a decision is reached at the Council, though only in those places where they have already been introduced. But these concessions are granted on condition that no one indulge in further polemics, and that each party recognise and acknowledge in the other's celebration of the Mass the presence of the 'whole Christ'.

After the Imperial Diet the Emperor went to the Netherlands. The garrisons in Augsburg and Ulm were lifted, but 2,000 Spanish soldiers stayed behind in Württemberg.[1] The Emperor returned to Augsburg for another Imperial Diet in June 1550.

2. THE RECEPTION OF THE INTERIM

Rome regarded the Emperor's efforts and the Interim itself as an encroachment on the Church's preserve. Nevertheless on 31 August 1548 the Pope sent three nuncios with authority to grant such dispensations as were necessary for implementing the Interim, though he urged them to tread with great caution and warned them not to be too ready to yield to pressure.[2] The Emperor managed to get the nuncios to agree to transfer the authority which the Pope had given them to the German bishops. But the difficulties did not end there, largely because the Pope's apparent willingness to co-operate was in reality subject to all the vacillations of papal policy, with the result that the Interim 'had no real support from the Pope'.[3]

The way in which the Interim was put into effect varied greatly from one territory to another. It was most strenuously enforced in the territories which had most reason to fear the power of the Emperor. Musculus, a preacher in Augsburg, left the city and went through Constance to Switzerland.[4] The Augsburg city council demanded that choir habit should be worn at services.[5] On 3 August the Emperor altered the city's constitution, and on 12 August the clergy of the city were put on oath to observer the Interim. On 15 August in Ulm the Emperor attended a service which followed the pattern laid down in the Interim, and he received communion in both kinds. After this, the clergy who refused to take the oath were imprisoned, and on 18 August the composition of the local council was changed; the territorial clergy were for the most part dismissed.[6] In Schwäbisch Hall Brenz published his reservations on

[1] *Brandi*, 505.
[2] *Maurenbrecher*, 205 ff., 208; cf. *CT* VI, 767 ff.
[3] *Maurenbrecher*, 210.
[4] *Roth* IV, 134, 139 ff.; cf. M. Simon, *op. cit.*, 250 ff.
[5] *Roth* IV, 146 ff., cf. 159 ff.
[6] Rommel, *op. cit.*, 98 f.; G. Bossert, 'Das Interim in Württemberg', *SVRG* 46–47, 1895.

P

the Interim[1] and on 24 June an imperial commissary was sent to bring him prisoner to Augsburg. However, Brenz escaped and went into hiding in Württemberg. Spanish soldiers occupied Schwäbisch Hall and the town gave in. On 12 September Brenz wrote his letter of resignation to the council, on the grounds that the town now had no use for him. From October until March he lived at Grynäus' house in Basle, where he worked at his commentary on Isaiah and corresponded with Calvin.[2] He then spent eighteen months in hiding in the Black Forest.[3] Bucer wrote *A Summary of the Christian Religion as taught at Strasbourg* and was dismissed on account of it.[4] He went into exile to England and died at Cambridge in 1551.[5] He was bitterly critical of Jakob Sturm's attitude and of others who had complied, 'preferring Mammon to the Son of God'. However, it was Constance which fared worst.[6] The city's delegates at Augsburg struggled hard to get conditions for a religious peace which were acceptable to them, but this led to the city's being placed under the ban on 6 August 1548. Immediately afterwards Spanish soldiers launched an attack on the city. Although this was repelled, the city accepted the Interim on 18 August and on 13 October gave itself up to Austria. It became an Austrian territorial city and returned to Catholicism. Ambrosius Blaurer went to Switzerland. The clergy of Brandenburg-Ansbach[7] rejected the Interim, but on 20 August stated that they were prepared to accept a few modifications in externals. Between 31 October and 3 November an *Auctuarium* was drawn up which they accepted. It was a modification of the Church Ordinance of 1533, various parts of the liturgy of the Mass having been reintroduced. Nuremberg used this as a model in drawing up its own Interim Order on 29 October.[8] Osiander and four other clerics resigned and departed,[9] but Veit Dietrich stayed on and resisted further concessions to the Interim. The city council suspended him from duty on 17 June 1547.[10] The Nuremberg Ordinance was adopted as normative by the surrounding districts, but in Augsburg on 30 September 1549 the Evangelical clergy rejected it. In Brandenburg-Kulmbach, the territory of the Margrave Albert Alcibiades who was bound by treaty

[1] Köhler, *Bibliographie*, No. 162 and 800.
[2] *Hartmann-Jäger* II, 169 ff., 178 f.; *BWKG* 1957–1958, 1; *cR* 41, 57 ff.
[3] Rentschler, *BWKG* 25, 1921, 173 ff.; G. Bossert, *BWKG* 39, 1935, 81 ff.
[4] Bibl. Buceriana No. 96 (*SVRG* 169, 1952); J. V. Pollet, *M. Bucer, Études sur la Correspondance*, 1958.
[5] C. Hope, 'M. Bucer and England', *ZKG* 71, 1960, 822 ff.
[6] E. Issel, *Die Reformation in Konstanz*, 1898.
[7] K. Schornbaum, 'Das Interim im Markgrafentum Brandenburg-Ansbach', *Blätter für brandenburgische Kirchengeschichte* 14, 1907.
[8] G. Bub, *Die Politik des Nürnberger Rats während des Interims*, 1924.
[9] Osiander's letter in P. Tschackert, *Ungedruckte Briefe, etc.*, 1894 (No. 16).
[10] B. Klaus, 'Veit Dietrich, Leben u. Werk', *Einzelarbeiten aus der Kirchengesch Bayerns* 32, 1958.

to the Emperor, the Interim was rejected by everyone.[1] In Württemberg[2] only Molther of Heilbronn and Kaspar Huberinus in Öhringen (who until then had the reputation of being a strict Lutheran) declared themselves in favour of the Interim.[3] The Evangelical clergy of Reutlingen drew up a noteworthy statement against it. The cities submitted for fear of being occupied by Spaniards. Württemberg itself was occupied, and a charge of felony was brought against duke Ulrich, who therefore felt obliged to 'let the devil have his way' and adopted a passive attitude. On the advice of Brenz[4] Ulrich made a distinction between the Interim, which had to be accepted under compulsion, and the Gospel, which was on no account to be surrendered. In other words, he distinguished between what was publicly enforced and what was privately believed by himself and by his subjects. In compliance with an imperial mandate, issued on 24 October 1548, all Evangelical clergy were relieved of their posts as from 11 November, but they were paid compensation. Then clergy had to be found who were prepared to accept the Interim. At Christmas, at least in 'some of the more important cities and districts', preaching clergy were appointed alongside the 'Interim-priests'. But generally it proved difficult to find sufficient men who were willing to put the Interim into effect, either among Catholic priests or former Protestant clergy, and even those who were appointed did not get the support of parishioners. An additional difficulty was that the bishops were not prepared to admit married clergy and also insisted that communion should be administered in one kind only. From May 1549 onwards the duke began to take on the deposed clergy as 'catechists' or 'instructors' and gave them the task of preaching, teaching the young and caring for the sick. The cities followed his example, though in varying degrees. By this means the sting was taken out of the Interim, and it was possible for Evangelical Church order to survive it.

The imprisoned elector of Saxony persistently refused to submit to the authority of a papal Council, and despite threats and chicaneries he would not accept the Interim.[5] The theologians and the territorial estates of Ernestine Saxony declared that the Interim was unacceptable, in fact on 6 August the young dukes said that to accept it would be a sin against the Holy Ghost.[6] The elector Moritz refused to commit himself to the Interim at Augsburg, saying that he would have to have the agreement of the estates of his territory, for both he and the Emperor had given

[1] M. Simon, op. cit., 255 f. (text).
[2] G. Bossert (as n. 34 above).
[3] Bossert, op. cit., 15 f.
[4] C. G. Buder, Zwei Bedenken von J. Brenz über das Interim, 1747, 10ff.
[5] CR 6, 924 ff. and 954; 7, 167; Mentz III, 282 ff.
[6] Mentz III, 286.

them undertakings on the religious question.[1] The Wittenberg theologians, led by Melanchthon, objected particularly to the doctrine of justification given in the Interim. They questioned the statement that 'love is righteousness' and that faith is 'only a preparation' (for justification). They challenged the concept of the Church, the doctrine of the Mass and the invocation of saints. Melanchthon had written on 28 April 1548 to Moritz's adviser, Carlowitz, painfully disavowing Luther's 'contentious disposition' and saying that he had borne Luther's 'yoke' too long and that he was prepared to make concessions.[2] But he rejected the Interim absolutely in the form in which it was actually published. The theologians repeated their reservations before a committee of the estates at Meissen early in July.[3] On the doctrine of justification as presented in the Interim they stated that 'it says much that is good' and 'in better terms than before', but so many 'provisos' and so much 'Pharisaical leaven' had been introduced into it that the doctrine had been obscured; in fact these insertions made the statement the reverse of what the Wittenberg theologians thought must have been intended. However, they drew a distinction between their own private opinion and what the elector would find tolerable. The theologians were then asked to make a positive statement on the question, and so Melanchthon drew up a thorough exposition of the doctrine of justification and of good works.[4] On 31 July he wrote to Margrave John, saying that the Interim's article on justification was 'a piece of deception' and that he personally could not approve it.[5] He recommended that the theologians should stand firm, though without trying to bring pressure to bear upon the politicians.[6] In August a conference was held at Pegau with the bishops of Naumburg and Meissen. At this conference the theologians enlarged their earlier statement at Meissen by means of certain additions which made the document acceptable to the bishops.[7] Even so, the bishops stated that they were not in a position 'to make alterations to the Interim', and that they could grant concessions on the marriage of priests and the administration of the chalice to the laity only if the Pope gave his permission. At an assembly of the estates at Torgau in October the theologians were presented with a draft document which summarised the principal points of Evangelical doctrine and made a list of all the concessions which might possibly be granted. This draft was then worked over, and in this form it became the outline of the *Leipzig Interim*.[8] In November the theologians were summoned to Altencelle and asked to revise the local Church Ordinance of 1539 and

---

[1] Wolf, Interim; S. Issleib, 'Das Interim in Sachsen', *N. Archiv für sächs. Geschichte* 13, 1892, 188 ff. and 15, 1894, 193 ff.
[2] *CR* 6, 879 ff.   [3] *CR* 7, 12 ff.   [4] *CR* 7, 48 ff.
[5] *CR* 7, 85.   [6] *CR* 7, 45, 85, 99.   [7] *CR* 7, 108 ff. and 120 ff.
[8] *CR* 7, 178 f.

to draw up a formula which on matters of little consequence (*adiaphora*) would come as close as possible to the Emperor's Interim.[1] They were ready to make concessions 'in all matters of indifference', 'such as feast days, clerical dress, lectionaries, food, and many other such things', but they would not tolerate 'unsound teaching and obviously idolatrous ceremonies'. Among the latter they included the use of chrism and the canon of the Mass.[2] This formula served as the basis of the Interim of Altencelle, which listed all the points relating to externals on which it had proved possible to reach agreement. This list was compiled and agreed on 19 November,[3] and on 7 December at Jüterbogk it was approved by the elector Joachim. It had not been possible, at Altencelle, to agree about the canon of the Mass.[4] At a meeting of the territorial estates at Leipzig in December the theologians recommended that these 'middle matters' (*adiaphora*) should be accepted,[5] because they did not offend against the principles of the 'right ordering of worship' or of obedience to God's commandments, and also because the true Church 'is at all times *in servitute*', and these agreed details involved merely 'a *servitus* which is outward and carnal'.

As a result of this assembly of the territorial estates the *Leipzig Interim*[6] was published. It included the Pegau formula on justification, recognised the authority of the Church to decide matters of faith, with the proviso that 'it neither ought nor can order anything that is contrary to Holy Scripture'. It requested that 'the principal and other bishops who exercise their episcopal office at God's command and for the purpose of building up the Church and not destroying it' should be respected and obeyed. Confirmation (which Melanchthon thought useful for catechetical purposes) and extreme unction were recognised once more, and ordination was reserved to bishops. Candidates for ordination were to be properly examined. The outward ceremonial of the Mass (including the order for Corpus Christi) and the traditional eucharistic vestments were prescribed again.[7] Pictures and images were allowed as 'reminders', provided that no superstitious practices were associated with them. Also reintroduced were the singing of the daily offices and, at the request of the Emperor, rules of fasting. The theologians managed to overcome the reservations of the estates, and the formula was accepted on 28 December. Only the cities continued to demand changes. The two bishops concerned decided that the formula was consistent 'in general sense' with the Emperor's

---

[1] *CR* 7, 198 ff.
[2] *CR* 7, 210 f.
[3] *CR* 7, 215 ff.
[4] Hortleder, *Rechtmässigkeit* III, 86.
[5] *CR* 7, 255 ff.
[6] *CR* 7, 259 ff.
[7] *CR* 7, 269 ('not merely for the sake of carrying the sacrament about but for preaching about its right use').

ordinance, though 'expressed differently'. They felt that the formula ought to go to the Emperor for his approval.[1] Thus, after six months of toil and under the pressure of political requirements, a compromise had been reached. The dominant theological concern was to stand fast in matters of doctrine, but to make concessions in less fundamental, external matters, provided that no encouragement were given to superstitious practices by so doing. But the *Leipzig Interim* had little or no practical effect, and it was never approved by the Emperor.

In the autumn of 1549 the *Little Interim* was published. It was an excerpt from the Emperor's Interim. This excerpt had been made binding upon all clergy by an imperial mandate of 4 July 1549.[2] The liturgical forms which went with it, however, were not included in the publication. A few clergy were dismissed for refusing to be bound by it. Flacius reports that a few changes were made as a result of it, but the only requirement which had visible effect was that surplices should be worn. The Leipzig Interim was also discussed in the newly constituted Duchy of Saxony on 8 and 9 February, but the theologians there found it unacceptable.[3] In March the territorial estates of Electoral Saxony discussed it, but the results were inconclusive. On 19 May the old elector drew up a statement on the question whether it would be legitimate, if the Emperor should attempt to impose his will by force, to make concessions in inessentials in order to rescue the Gospel and Evangelical faith and practice. But again he came to the conclusion that such a course was not viable—it was necessary to put one's trust in God and not in human reason.[4] Finally, in July 1549 the Thuringians submitted to the Emperor a new confession. We do not know how it was received.[5] The old elector was entirely convinced that passive resistance was the only course to take, and he worked out the principles of such resistance in great detail.[6] Magdeburg and Bremen naturally rejected the Interim and resolved to defend their faith and their privileges to the uttermost.[7] The Leipzig Interim had an explosive effect upon the theologians of Electoral Saxony. Matthias Flacius, a professor at Wittenberg, published at Magdeburg in July 1549 the statement which the theologians had drawn up at Meissen. His intention was to draw public attention to the errors contained in the Interim.[8] Those who had met at Celle had been presented with a docu-

[1] *CR* 7, 279.
[2] *CR* 7, 242 ff.; A. Chalybäus, 'Die Durchführung des Leipziger Interims', *Diss.* Leipzig, 1905; E. Hirsch, Melanchthon u. das Interim, *ARG* 17, 1920, 62 ff.
[3] *Mentz* III, 289 ff.
[4] *Mentz* III, 293.
[5] Ibid, 294 f.
[6] *Mentz* III, 308; F. Herrmann, *Das Interim in Hessen*, 1901.
[7] Hortleder, *Rechtmässigkeit* IV, 3.
[8] W. Preger, *Matthias Flacius Illyricus und seine Zeit* I, 1859, 58.

ment in which he urged that no concessions whatever should be made.[1] At first he attacked the Leipzig Interim anonymously in a volume entitled 'Azariah', in which he criticised the doctrine of justification as expressed in the Interim.[2] At Easter 1549 he left Wittenberg and went to Magdeburg, where with Amsdorf and Gallus he continued his campaign.[3] The controversy over 'adiaphora' seriously undermined Melanchthon's authority. Many of the arguments which Flacius and his friends produced were precisely what Melanchthon himself had said earlier, either in considered statements or in the company of friends. In the end Melanchthon himself admitted that although he would seek to excuse his attitude in this matter he could hardly defend it.[4]

3. THE IMPERIAL DIET OF AUGSBURG 1550 AND THE SECOND PERIOD OF THE COUNCIL

Pope Paul III died on 10 November 1549.[5] On 7 February 1550 cardinal Del Monte was elected to succeed him as Pope Julius III. He had previously been one of the most stalwart defenders of the Council's 'freedom'.[6] Against all expectations his approach to the question of recalling the Council accorded with the Emperor's intentions. As early as April the cardinals agreed that the Council should be reconvened at Trent,[7] and the Emperor and the king of France were told of this in June. The Emperor was requested to see that the Germans attended and that they agreed to be bound by the Council's decisions. It was naturally taken for granted that the decisions which had been taken at the previous sessions should remain in force and that this reconvened Council would be simply a continuation of what had already been begun.[8] The Emperor did not question this, but he insisted that the Germans should at least be given a hearing, and he promised to remain in Germany until the religious question was settled.[9] On 14 November 1550 the Bull was published, summoning a Council at Trent to begin on 1 May 1551.[10]

The Emperor arrived at Augsburg a few weeks before the Imperial Diet was due to begin. His time was fully occupied by discussions with the members of his immediate family circle on the question of arranging

---

[1] Preger, op. cit., 64.   [2] Ibid., 67.

[3] De veris et falsis adiaphoris, Magdeburg, (1 Dec.) 1549—in German, Ein Buch von wahren und falschen Mitteldingen, 1550; N. von Amsdorf, Antwort, Glaub und Bekenntnis auf das schöne und liebliche Interim, 1548; N. Gallus, Eine Disputation von Mitteldingen und von den jetzigen verenderungen in Kirchen die christlich und wolgeordnet sind; cf. O. Ritschl, Dogmengeschichte II/1, 325 ff.

[4] CR 8, 842, 4 Sep. 1556; C. L. Manschreck, 'The Role of Melanchthon in the Adiaphore Controversy', ARG 48, 1957, 165 ff. (he defends Mel.).

[5] v. Pastor V, 674 f.   [6] Ibid. VI, 3 ff.

[7] CT VII, 5 ff.   [8] Druffel, Beiträge I, 423 ff.

[9] v. Pastor VI, 65.   [10] CT VII, 6 ff. and 9 ff.

the succession. His intention was to set the seal upon his life's work by tying the imperial dignity more closely to Spain than had hitherto been planned. Prince Philip, who was heir to the Spanish throne, was to succeed Ferdinand and to take precedence over Ferdinand's son, Maximilian. The negotiations were difficult in the extreme. Mary, the sister of Charles and Ferdinand, had to come from the Netherlands twice in order to mediate. Although agreement was reached in the end, the result of the negotiations was that the brothers were estranged. This had a damaging effect politically.[1]

The subjects for discussion at the Imperial Diet[2] which was opened on 26 July were the Council, the Interim and the establishment of peace within the Empire. Peace had not been completely secured, because Bremen and Magdeburg had not been brought to submission. Negotiations were begun with Bremen,[3] while the elector Moritz was given the task of executing the ban on obstinate Magdeburg. His army was to be paid from imperial funds.[4] But the estates were unwilling to assist the Emperor in implementing the Interim or his own reformation of the Church. The representatives from Württemberg had been instructed to say that the Interim had failed partly because the Pope had not given the necessary dispensations and partly because the Emperor's 'reformation' was in reality no reformation.[5] The estates proposed that the question should be referred to the Council, and in December they agreed to send representatives to the Council.[6] In the final recess of 14 February this decision was reaffirmed, but coupled with it was a demand that the Interim be fully implemented, for the Emperor refused to give way on this, even though the Council was to be reconvened. By a special mandate issued on 8 April[7] the Evangelical princes were required to send their theologians to Trent, in order to give account of their doctrine and to state the reasons for their separation from the Church of Rome.

In the following months the Emperor tried once again to get the Interim put into effect at least in the cities. First he asked for reports. Then the Evangelical clergy and schoolmasters in Augsburg[8] and Memmingen

[1] *Hartung* 53 ff.; *Brandi*, 506 ff., 510; Brandi, *Quellen*, 388 ff.; Druffel, *op. cit.*, 454 f.
[2] Druffel, *op. cit.*, 486 ff.; Brandi, *Quellen*, 389.
[3] *Hartung*, 58.
[4] Druffel, *op. cit.*, 524; Sleidan, *De statu religionis* . . . , Bk. XXII; Brandi, *Quellen*, 389.
[5] G. Bossert, *Interim*, 119.
[6] *Mentz* III, 298 (on John Frederick's position).
[7] Bossert, *Interim*, 149.
[8] On 14 Oct. 1549 Augsburg had sent a legation to Brussels with a detailed report, and on 4 Dec. was instructed to implement the Interim. The entire responsibility for the failure of the Interim was laid at the door of the preachers, whom the Emperor threatened to punish (*Roth* IV, 275, 278). Gerwig von Weingarten's report (April 1550—see *Roth* IV, 280) shows how completely all efforts had failed. On the

were dismissed—an episode which revealed the worst side of the younger Granvella's character. The Regensburg clergy were similarly threatened and immediately fled to Nuremberg.[1] Then began the enormous task of changing the structure of government in the cities of Swabia. This was done by one of the Emperor's officials, Heinrich Has.[2] He went as imperial commissary from one city to the next, suspending their charters and their corporations and installing new burgomasters from among the patricians (Catholics wherever this was possible), new privy councillors and town clerks. Since he sought to impose the Interim, the clergy and other public servants did not escape his attention. It is difficult to know what the reasons were for this action. Presumably the Emperor had given up hoping that the Council would be able to bring the Protestants back into line and therefore sought to hold them at least to the Interim. On 21 October the Emperor went through Munich to Innsbruck, where he could be within easy reach of the Council.

The second period of the Council began, as arranged, on 1 May 1551.[3] The discussions proper did not begin until September, but since much preparatory work had been done at Bologna it was possible to have the decree on the eucharist presented at the 13th session as early as 11 October, though the question of the administration of the chalice to the laity was deferred yet again.[4] At the 14th session on 25 November the decree on penance followed. This emphasised the necessity of auricular confession and the judicial character of absolution. It also stressed the importance of making satisfaction. In the debates on Church reform there were heated arguments, because the bishops felt that the legates were far too lenient in their treatment of the traditional practices of the Curia. When the practice of giving abbotships to men who were not members of the appropriate order was discussed, the archbishop of Cologne was moved to ask whether this was a 'free' Council or not—'which is no evidence that the Council was not in fact "free", but his question reveals how tense the atmosphere was'.[5] It is evidence of the degree to which the Council was subject to the Pope—a subjection which the Protestants found intolerable. But the real crisis occurred when the Protestants appeared at the Council.

'scenes' on account of evangelical preaching during the course of the Diet see *Roth* IV, 305 ff.; and on the implementation of the Interim, *ibid.*, 342 ff. and 377 n. 141.

[1] Gallus, together with Flacius, was one of the most energetic opponents of the Interim. On Regensburg, see M. Simon, *op. cit.*, 251 ff.

[2] Bossert, *Interim*, 133, 196 n. 22. (L. Fürstenwerth, 'Die Verfassungsänderungen in den oberdeutschen Städten', etc. Göttinger Diss., 1893; B. Möller, Reichstadt u. Reformation, 1962 71 ff.)

[3] *CT* VII, 29 ff.

[4] *CT* VII, 200 ff., 343 ff.

[5] H. Jedin, *Kleine Konsiliengeschichte*, 1959, 94.

The representatives of the electorate of Brandenburg stated at the session of 11 October that they were ready to submit to the decisions of the assembly.[1] Electoral Saxony and Württemberg had drawn up their own confessions, the *Confessio Saxonica* and the *Confessio Virtembergica*.[2] A number of other churches (though not the church of the duchy of Saxony) adopted the former as an expression of their convictions, and the Württemberg confession was agreed to by Strasbourg, which in turn represented a number of South German cities. The Württemberg representatives had been waiting almost three months for a hearing. The representatives from Saxony arrived on 7 January, and on 24 January 1552 the Protestants were given a hearing at a general congregation.[3] They asked for better terms of admission, and again expressed in strong terms Protestant wishes with regard to the Council. They demanded that a committee of competent and unbiased experts be set up to settle disputed questions, and that the decrees already decided should be begun afresh. The Württemberg delegation presented their confession and were told that the synod would reply at a future date. They were given improved terms of admission, but were still unsatisfied with these, for although their safety was guaranteed they were not allowed any right to vote.[4] They also received no assurance that Scripture would be the sole criterion on which decisions would be based. Then, in preparation for the session which was due to be held on 19 March, Stuttgart and Strasbourg sent new delegates and a group of theologians led by Brenz who were to challenge the decisions already reached at the Council and to defend their own 'confession'. The session was postponed until 1 May.[5] The official reason given was that more Protestants were expected, but in fact, despite all the efforts by the Emperor's spokesmen at the Council to get the Protestants a hearing, the majority was against allowing them any such opportunity. So on 8 April the delegation departed, for no useful purpose could be served by their remaining. The theologians from Saxony, while they were on their way to the Council, received instructions from the elector that they should return immediately.[6] The Pope had sent instructions that the Council should not receive the heretics unless they submitted in advance to its authority. The papal legate therefore felt that he should suspend the Council rather than agree to admit them.[7] This decision was logical

---

[1] *CT* VII, 197 ff. and XI, 664; Druffel, *Beiträge* I, 782 ff.

[2] *CR* 28, 329 ff.; E. Bizer, *Confessio Virtembergica*, 1952 (text and introduction); on the Conf. Saxonica see R. Stupperich, *ARG* 47, 1956, 54 ff.

[3] *CT* VII, 465 ff.; Bizer, *Conf. Virt.* 50.

[4] *CT* VII, 464 f., 494 ff.

[5] *CT* VII, 512 ff.

[6] *CR* 7, 931.

[7] Bizer, *Conf. Virt.*, 39 ff.

enough, for a Catholic Council cannot conduct disputations with condemned heretics or allow them to challenge decisions already reached, for this would be to deny itself. The Emperor, too, was at a loss to know what to do. He instructed his delegates to do what they could to prevent the Council being suspended, but since he could not suggest anything better it was impossible to do more than discuss ways and means of bringing the matter to a conclusion. Thus all the Emperor's schemes relating to the Council collapsed, for the Council had failed to bring about a unification of the Empire. On 28 April 1552 it was officially announced that the Council was suspended.[1] The Council had learned of the fall of Augsburg on 6 April. Thus the revolt of the German princes released the Council from the necessity of giving an answer to the religious question, and made it unnecessary for the Emperor to admit defeat.

[1] *CT* VII, 529 ff.

CHAPTER XII

THE REVOLT OF THE PRINCES AND THE RELIGIOUS PEACE

I. THE REVOLT OF THE PRINCES[1]

MORITZ of Saxony was dissatisfied with the earlier peace treaty for a number of reasons. He had asked to receive the entire Electorate of Saxony and had been given only a part of it, the *Kurkreis*. He had hoped that the bishoprics of Magdeburg and Halberstadt would become his possessions, but these were denied him. Moreover Philip of Hesse was still the Emperor's prisoner, despite the fact that Moritz had guaranteed his freedom. In view of this—the more so since Philip was his father-in-law—Moritz felt that he had lost his 'princely reputation'. Until 1552 the Emporer had rejected all his pleas that Philip should be set free.[2] When Charles and Ferdinand became estranged as a result of Charles's plans for the succession, the North German Lutheran princes John of Küstrin, Albert of Prussia and John Albert of Mecklenberg made an alliance at Königsberg in 1550 for the defence of Protestantism.[3] Moritz suspected that this alliance was directed against him and that the intention was to invoke French assistance in order to restore the Electorate of Saxony to its earlier form. The Emperor no longer had sufficient power to protect Moritz against such a plan. So Moritz began to negotiate with France through the agency of a councillor from Hesse.[4] He pointed out that because the Imperial Diet had made him responsible for executing the ban against Magdeburg in October 1550, and because in January 1551 he had been

---

[1] Druffel, *Beiträge* I and IV; E. Schlomka, *Kurfürst Moritz und Heinrich II v. Frankreich 1550–1555*, 1884; K. E. Born, *HZ* 191, 1960, 18 ff.
[2] F. Küch, *Politisches Archiv des Landgrafen Philipp* I, 1904, 645 ff.; Lanz, *Staatspapiere*, 485.
[3] H. Kiewning, 'Herzog Albrechts v. Preussen und Markgraf Johanns v. Brandenburg Anteil am Fürstenbund . . . 1547/1550', *Diss. Königsberg* 1889.
[4] Druffel, *Beiträge* I, 800; III, 257 ff.

able to take over an army raised in Verden (originally with the intention of relieving Magdeburg), he had ample proof of his suitability as an ally. Later he managed to make an alliance with the Königsberg signatories and with William of Hesse for the preservation of the Augsburg Confession and for liberating the Landgrave Philip. In return he was promised assistance in protecting the boundary between his territory and Ernestine Saxony. It was expressly stated that no hostilities would be undertaken against king Ferdinand. Thus a powerful group was established with which Henry II of France was glad to make an alliance, especially since he was fighting a war with the Emperor in Italy for the possession of Parma and Piacenza. Negotiations[1] took place at a hunting lodge on the Lochau Heath, and Henry signed the treaty on 15 January 1552 at Chambord.[2] The princes received financial assistance for the purpose of launching an attack upon the Emperor, and Moritz was promised protection against Ernestine Saxony. But the princes promised the French king that he could take possession of the imperial cities of Cambrai, Metz, Toul and Verdun, though he would do so as 'vicar of the Empire' (*Reichsvikar*).[3] The princes made this promise for military reasons, for with Henry in possession of these cities a wedge had been driven between the Emperor's territories in the Netherlands and those in South Germany.[4] John of Küstrin and Albert of Prussia withdrew during the course of the negotiations. Similarly Württemberg and Ernestine Saxony stood aside. The duke of Württemberg warned the Emperor of what was afoot,[5] and the captive elector of Saxony ordered his sons to take no part in the war.[6] Melanchthon on his own initiative issued a statement warning Moritz against the course he had taken.[7] Albert Alcibiades of Kulmbach was not a signatory to the treaty but took part in the war off his own bat.[8] The Emperor paid no heed to the warnings which reached him,[9] and even after the siege of Magdeburg had been lifted in November he was content with the promise of a verbal report from Moritz.[10] When he woke up to the danger it was too late. Even as late as 8 March he offered to let the Landgrave go free and invited Moritz to discuss the matter with him. The natural mediator was Ferdinand, and on 14 March[11] Moritz informed

[1] Ibid. III, 279 ff.
[2] Ibid. III, 340 ff.; *Schl* 33310–33312, 37071.
[3] K. Brandi, *Ausgewählte Aufsätze*, 1938, 386 ff.
[4] *Brandi*, 528 and Brandi, *Quellen*, 396.
[5] V. Ernst, *Briefwechsel des Herzogs Christoph von Wirtemberg* I, 1899, No. 295, 317, 372.
[6] *Mentz* III, 308 ff.
[7] Hortleder, *Rechtmässigkeit* V, 2.
[8] J. Voigt, *Markgraf Albrecht Alcibiades*, 1852; *Hartung*, 127.
[9] Brandi, *Quellen*, 391.
[10] Druffel, *Beiträge* I, 799.
[11] *Brandi*, 519 f. and Brandi, *Quellen*, 392 f.

him of his demands. These were that Philip should be released and that Moritz should have from the princes in the surrounding territories a guarantee of peace. In return Moritz offered to give assistance to king Ferdinand against the Turks, since the Emperor was not at that time in a position to do so. Peace in the immediate territories would have protected him from the Ernestines and also against any attempt at an enforced return to Catholicism. In the second half of March came the spectacular advance of the rebel princes into South Germany.[1] Moritz halted at Linz and stayed there from 19 April until 1 May, for it was a perfect opportunity of negotiating with Ferdinand.[2] This time the Emperor offered to release Philip, though on condition that Moritz's troops should disperse. This condition was totally unacceptable. The Emperor was unwilling to guarantee a permanent peace and suggested instead a 'standstill' until the next Imperial Diet.[3] However, it was agreed that all the electors and a number of the princes should meet on 26 May at Passau for further negotiations. Two days after the negotiations at Linz Moritz terminated the alliance with king Henry of France,[4] who withdrew from his encampment near Speyer but left troops behind in Metz, Toul and Verdun. Meanwhile, Albert Alcibiades pillaged Bamberg and Würzburg and launched an attack on Nuremberg.[5] But the main army went by way of Füssen and the monastery of Ehrenberg (which they reached on 23 May) to Innsbrück.[6] The Emperor fled to Villach, where he began to mobilise his forces. Time was on his side. From a military point of view the princes' advance was pointless, for they could not hope to hold Innsbruck. So the negotiations at Passau[7] between Ferdinand, Moritz and the envoys of the neutral princes[8] were difficult, despite the apparent strength of Moritz's position. The princes were very willing to break off their association with France, but the Emperor still sought to delay Philip's release. Moritz demanded that the religious question should be settled by a national assembly, though not simply by a majority vote. If this

[1] *Schl* 33315–33318, 37098a–37104; Brandi, *Quellen*, 392; Hortleder, *Rechtmässigkeit* V, 3–5; *Roth* IV, 425 ff., 452 ff.

[2] Hortleder, *Rechtmässigkeit* V, 11; H. Barge, *Die Verhandlungen zu Linz und Passau*, 1893; G. Bonwetsch, 'Geschichte des Passauer Vertrags von 1552', *Göttinger Preisschrift*, 1907.

[3] Lanz, *Correspondenz* III, 98 ff.; Druffel, *Beiträge* II, 403 and III, 394 ff.; Bonwetsch, *op. cit.*, 59 n, 1; Hortleder, *Rechtmässigkeit* V, 11.

[4] *Brandi*, 521 f.

[5] Druffel, *Beiträge* II, 591; E. Büttner, 'Der Krieg des Markgrafen Albrecht Alcibiades in Franken 1552–1555', *Archiv für Geschichte u. Altertumskunde von Oberfranken* 23, 1908.

[6] *Schl* 24298, 33315–33318.

[7] Druffel, *op. cit.*, III, 444–569; Lanz, *Correspondenz* III; *Brandi*, 522 f. and Brandi, *Quellen*, 394; *Hartung*, 88 ff.

[8] *Hartung*, 88 ff.

should fail, then a permanent and unconditional peace should be guaranteed. The assembled princes supported him in this, but it was decided that a resolution to this effect should be reserved to the next Imperial Diet. Finally the assembled negotiators asked for an assurance that hostilities should be terminated until the next Diet.[1] On the grievances within the Empire the neutrals supported Moritz. It then remained to them to get the agreement of the princes of the alliance and also the agreement of the Emperor. Moritz managed to persuade the princes to support him—though not without difficulty.[2] But Ferdinand was unable to move the Emperor, who would not guarantee a religious peace beyond the next Imperial Diet and who was determined that decisions about grievances within the Empire rested with him alone. Again the neutrals supported Moritz, and Ferdinand hurried to Villach to see the Emperor, who still refused to change his position. So once again the decision rested with the rebel princes, who laid siege to Frankfurt,[3] where one of the Emperor's colonels had gathered an army. Moritz again assailed the young Landgrave, who acquiesced on 2 August. On 15 August the Emperor ratified a much reduced agreement in which, apart from the liberation of Philip of Hesse, everything still hung in the balance. An incidental matter reveals how completely Moritz was concerned only with his own interests, for shortly before the conclusion of the Passau negotiations Moritz asked Ferdinand to see that the Emperor did not release the aged elector of Saxony.[4] In fact the old elector had been released on 19 May and had remained voluntarily at the imperial court, planning to assist the Emperor against Moritz.[5] This is an aspect of Moritz's behaviour which ill accords with his pose as the defender of German liberty. It demonstrates rather his efforts to secure his booty. It also explains why he was so anxious to be on good terms with Ferdinand, who as king of Bohemia was one of his neighbours. On 3 August he lifted his siege of Frankfurt and took his army to support Ferdinand against the Turks. Margrave Albert Alcibiades, who had not been a party to the alliance with France, now decided to give France a demonstration of 'German loyalty' and went on fighting a war against 'Romish priests' in the style of a robber baron rather than of a field marshal. He pursued a course along the river Main and penetrated Alsace.[6] The Emperor went with fresh troops through Ulm to Strasbourg and thence northwards to continue the war against France. On 24 October the Mar-

[1] Hortleder, *Rechtmässigkeit* V, 14.
[2] *Brandi*, 524.
[3] *Schl* 24509–24512.
[4] Lanz, *Correspondenz* III, 285.
[5] *Mentz* III, 322; Hortleder, *Rechtmässigkeit* III, 87, 88.
[6] Hortleder, *Rechtmässigkeit* VI, 1 ff.

grave came over to his side while he was encamped outside Metz. The
Emperor reluctantly accepted his assistance and recognised his treaties
with the Franconian bishops.[1] The two armies took up their positions
outside Metz and besieged it for many weeks, but were unable to take
the city.[2] At the beginning of January the Emperor was forced to lift
the siege. He returned to the Netherlands, depressed not only by the
failure of this most recent enterprise but also by the Passau agreement
and by his having had to come to terms with Margrave Albert
Alcibiades. He would gladly have declared both agreements invalid.[3]
The Margrave stayed for a time in Franconia and then went to Lower
Saxony. At Sievershausen he was confronted and defeated by Moritz,
who was returning from fighting the Turks. But Moritz was wounded
in the battle and died two days later on 11 July 1553.[4] He was succeeded
by his brother August.[5] Henry of Brunswick continued the fight against
Margrave Albert, who was placed under the ban by the Imperial
Cameral Tribunal[6] and fled to France. He died on 8 January 1557 at
Pforzheim in Baden,[7] given consolation by the theologian Jakob Heer-
brand. An indication of the uncertainty within the Empire is that the
princes once more began to form regional alliances. The Heidelberg
Union had been formed in March 1553 at the instigation of duke Christoph
of Württemberg. It bound Württemberg, the Palatinate, Mainz, Trier,
Bavaria and Cleves to neutrality.[8] On 6 May 1553 Moritz, Ferdinand and
a few other neighbouring princes formed an alliance at Eger against the
Margrave.[9] The Heidelberg Union was of little use from a military point
of view, but it had brought together Protestant and Catholic princes.
Alcibiades' rampages had made everyone aware that establishing peace
within the territories was a matter of urgency. Within the Empire and
also in Austria the Emperor was regarded with suspicion, but he was no
longer an opponent, for he was gradually withdrawing from the affairs
of the Empire. He sent out the notice summoning the estates to the Imperial
Diet, but he did not wish to be present at it himself. His vice-chancellor,
Seld, wrote a memorandum which expressed in detail the Emperor's
views, for the information of his commissaries at the Imperial Diet.

---

[1] *Brandi*, 529 f.; Lanz, *Correspondenz* III, 512.
[2] Brandi, 525 ff.; J. Lestocquoy, 'Le siège de Metz (1552) d'après les dépêches du
nonce apostolique', *Annales de l'Est*, 5e serie VII, 1956, 3 ff.
[3] G. Turba, *AÖG* 90, 1901, 287.
[4] Hortleder, *Rechtmässigkeit* VI, 7 ff.
[5] S. Issleib, *N. Archiv für sächs. Geschichte* 8, 1887, 41 ff.; M. Lenz, *ibid.* 1, 1880, 86 ff.
[6] 1 Dec. 1553—Hortleder, *Rechtmässigkeit* VI, 16 ff.
[7] Ibid., VI, 30.
[8] Ernst, *Briefwechsel* (see n. 9 above); another view: Brandi, *HZ* 95, 1905, 212 ff.;
documents: Druffel, *Beiträge* IV, 72 ff.; Brandi, *Quellen*, 298
[9] Druffel, *op. cit.*, IV, 137, 144–149.

These, however, were barely more than spectators.[1] Responsibility for the conduct of the Diet was placed squarely on king Ferdinand's shoulders (18 June 1554).[2] During the course of the Diet, on 8 April 1555, Charles protested on his own behalf against everything that had been done to offend, insult, weaken or impede the Catholic faith, and he made it clear that no one should expect any guidance or assistance from him on the religious question.[3] No one need doubt that he was bound in conscience to the Catholic faith, as his Evangelical opponents were bound to theirs. For the sake of keeping the peace, Charles had had to renounce an idea which he had spent his whole life pursuing. His renunciation in fact marks the close of the mediaeval Empire.

Meanwhile, the Interim was beginning to lose its force. It was suspended in Augsburg when the rebel princes entered the city. The Protestant preachers were brought back and 'absolved'[4] from the oath which the Emperor had demanded of them. In Württemberg the Mass was forbidden as early as 9 August 1552,[5] and on 10 January 1553 Brenz was appointed as provost of the collegiate church at Stuttgart.[6]

2. THE THEOLOGICAL CRISIS WITHIN PROTESTANTISM

The effect of the Interim was to challenge the Evangelicals to stand by their convictions, but it also caused deep division among the theologians. They had often asserted that the princes and those in authority were custodians of the outward aspects of the Church's life—the so-called 'first table'—but now these very custodians were demanding that the Interim be implemented. This, combined with concern at what was happening in the parishes, caused much uncertainty among the theologians. Former champions of the Protestant cause were subdued by the new situation, and men who had formerly been friends now opposed one another. Not only Flacius, but also Brenz and Aepinus,[7] turned against Melanchthon. The conflict was made more acute by heated polemics and profound personal sensitivity. Flacius' supporters demanded that the Protestant churches should do public penance for having attempted to come to terms over *adiaphora*, or at least publicly recant. As late as

[1] Druffel, *op. cit.*, IV, 411 ff.; *Brandi*, 536.
[2] Lanz, *Correspondenz* III, 622 ff.
[3] Druffel, *op. cit.*, IV, 646 ff.
[4] *Roth* IV, 466 ff.
[5] *Hartmann-Jäger* II, 228 f.; Bossert, *Interim*, 169; *ARG* (suppl.) 5, 1929, 115 ff. Before the revolt of the princes, Lindau had received an assurance from the Emperor that it need not implement the Interim 'provided that it remain loyal to him'; similarly Regensburg—see M. Simon, *op. cit.*, 260.
[6] Kolb, *BWKG* 5, 1901, 70; Pressel, *op. cit.*, No. 209.
[7] *CR* 7, 200 and 367 ff.

Q

January 1557 an attempt was made to reconcile the quarrelling parties at Coswig,[1] but without success.

Out of the controversy about Church government a second controversy developed about the necessity of good works for salvation. Flacius and Gallus, in their edition of the Leipzig Interim, had contested its presentation of the doctrine of justification. Then George Major, replying to a polemical pamphlet by Amsdorf, developed the thesis that 'it is impossible for a man to be saved by evil works, and equally it is impossible that a man be saved without good works'.[2] Amsdorf's reaction was to describe Major as a Pelagian, a Mameluke and a two-faced papist. Major tried to justify his thesis by saying that he had been speaking only of good works after justification, for these were necessary 'in order not to lose again the salvation which has been attained [by faith]'.[3] But this merely added fuel to the fire, for in 1552 Flacius, Amsdorf and Gallus all wrote against Major. Flacius declared that Major's thesis robbed the dying of all comfort.[4] Major then wrote a summary of his position entitled 'A Sermon on S. Paul and on the conversion of all God-fearing men'.[5] By the time that this appeared, Major had already been dismissed from his post as Superintendent by count Mansfeld, who had returned from captivity. Flacius consulted the authorities of various friendly churches and asked them to make comments on Major's thesis.[6] These were published in 1553, but Major was not without supporters. Menius became involved in the controversy in 1554 at Gotha. He had been asked to take part with Schnepf, Stolz and Amsdorf in a visitation. Amsdorf was anxious that this visitation should provide an opportunity for condemning not only Major but also those who had been prepared to make concessions to the Interim. Menius's treatise, 'On preparing for death', contains a proposition which gave offence, namely that it is necessary for salvation that a man should have begun to follow in the way of righteousness. Menius finally accepted the judgement of a synod at Eisenach, but shortly afterwards left the duchy to become superintendent at Leipzig.[7] Major dropped his formula when Melanchthon contested it, but he did not change his view, which was in fact identical with Melanchthon's.

The third great controversy during these years concerned Andreas Osiander and was once again a controversy over the doctrine of justification.[8] Osiander had worked in Nuremberg as a reformer for thirty years

[1] *Preger* II, 32 ff.
[2] G. Major, *Antwort auf des Ehrwirdigen Herrn Niclas v. Amsdorffs schrift*, 1552.
[3] O. Ritschl, *Dogmengeschichte* II, 318 f.; *Preger* I, 384 f.
[4] *Preger* I, 364.   [5] Ibid. I, 364.
[6] K. Schlüsselberg, *Catalogi Haereticum* (13 vols., 1597–1601), 7, 592 ff.; *Preger* I, 374.
[7] O. Ritschl, *op. cit.*, II, 381 f.; *Preger* I, 384 f.
[8] W. Möller, *A. Osianders Leben und ausgewählte Schriften*, 1870; Bizer, *Conf. Virt.*, 95 ff.

and had left on account of the Interim. His patron, Albert of Prussia, gave him a new post as a parish minister and professor at Königsberg. In his first disputation on 5 April 1549 he offended the disciples of Melanchthon at Königsberg, and his second disputation on 24 October made matters worse. He expounded a view of the doctrine of justification which was highly individual and which therefore exposed him to attack from the side of his opponents. Joachim Mörlin, who had come from Göttingen, tried in vain to mediate, but then he had second thoughts himself and brought the controversy into the pulpit. The duke, who sympathised with Osiander,[1] asked for the opinions of theologians throughout the Empire—this happened on 5 October 1551—and so the affair became one which involved the whole of Protestantism. But everyone except Brenz,[2] who had been Osiander's friend for many years, came down against Osiander. Philippists and 'gnesio-Lutherans' were reunited in opposing him.[3] Osiander regarded Melanchthon as the real enemy and replied to him in an extraordinarily coarse pamphlet entitled 'Schmeckbier' and in another personal treatise.[4] He died, however, on 17 October 1552. Brenz wrote two more 'Deliberations'[5] which re-established his theological reputation, but neither they nor a proclamation by the duke[6] were sufficient to still the agitation in Prussia and in the whole Empire. John Frederick of Saxony sent a delegation to mediate, but they had to return home having achieved nothing.[7] Two theologians from Württemberg attempted to persuade the opposition in Prussia to agree to a confession drawn up by duke Albert himself,[8] but in the end the Württemberg theologians demanded that Osiander's supporters should retract. Having made their demand they left Königsberg for home.[9] In December 1554 Brenz issued yet another 'Deliberation',[10] but this met with no more success than its predecessors. Brenz then went to Nuremberg, where many still took Osiander's part, in order to talk with Melanchthon.[11] He departed again, having roused the wrath of the Philippists for venturing to support Osiander's thesis. Stolz, the court preacher at Weimar, became a bitter critic of Brenz's catechism on this account.[12] It was not until 18 April 1558 that duke Albert was able to introduce his Church ordinance in Prussia.

[1] E. Roth, 'Herzog Albrecht von Preussen als Osiandrist', ThLZ 78, 1953, 1 ff.
[2] Köhler, Bibliographie, No. 234; Bizer, Conf. Virt., 97 ff.
[3] Preger I, 217 f.
[4] Widerlegung der ungegründeten undienstlichen Antwort Philippi Melanchthons, 1552.
[5] Bizer, Conf. Virt., 102 and 109. [6] 24 Jan. 1553.
[7] F. Koch, Altpreussiche Monatsschrift 40, 1903, 3 and 4.
[8] E. Roth, ZKG 66, 1955, 272 ff. (the 'original' form).
[9] E. Bizer, Analecta Brentiana, BWKG 1957–1958.
[10] Pressel, op. cit., No. 213.
[11] CR 8, 540, 588; Pressel, op. cit., Nos. 212 and 216.
[12] Bizer (see n. 62) No. 26 f.

Osiander expounded his view of justification in a book which he entitled 'On the only Mediator Jesus Christ and Justification by Faith',[1]
which was published in September 1551.

> The idea which caused such a stir was that the redeeming death of Christ
> and the forgiveness of sins merely create the conditions for justification, so that
> a man is not actually justified until Christ's divinity dwells in him. Osiander
> spoke, not of Christ's righteousness being imputed to men, but of the actual
> righteousness of God dwelling in men. He was not, however, a mystic, but
> a Logos-theologian. The indwelling of Christ is not something which can be
> distinguished as an experience. It occurs simply by believing the Word. But
> it is none the less real for that, and it effects the gradual transformation of
> man until he becomes conformed to the divine image. Thus Osiander can say
> that righteousness is what prompts a man to act rightly. From his point of
> view, righteousness which is only imputed is righteousness in appearance only
> —an 'as if' righteousness—and as such is entirely inadequate to serve as the
> basis on which God is to judge a man. However, it would be wrong to regard
> Osiander's theology as a legitimate development of the original Lutheran
> standpoint, for the 'Word', according to Osiander's use—as also according to
> the use of the Melanchthon school—has lost its character as a word of promise.
> The thinking of the reformers has here become frozen in the ontic categories
> of gnosis.[2]

These controversies were not merely theological. Since the church
authorities were asked to take up positions on them, and since there was
a great deal of mutual recrimination, the unity of the Church was put in
jeopardy. Thus at the very moment when Protestantism was fighting
politically for its right to exist it was politically divided. On the one
hand were the active champions of Protestantism, whose motives were
by no means purely theological; on the other hand were the neutrals
like duke Christoph. Then, in addition, there were those Lutherans (like
John of Küstrin and the former elector of Saxony) who were basically
supporters of the Emperor. Protestantism thus found itself in a theological
crisis which revealed how inadequately the original Lutheran positions
had been developed. There remained much work to be done in the period
which was to follow.

3. THE IMPERIAL DIET OF AUGSBURG 1555 AND THE RELIGIOUS PEACE[3]

Since all previous attempts to re-establish unity within the Empire had
failed, it fell to this Imperial Diet to find a basis on which it would be

[1] Cf. O. Ritschl, *Dogmengeschichte* II, 455 ff.; E. Hirsch, *Die Theologie des Andreas Osiander*, 1919; H. E. Weber, *Ref., Orthodoxie, Rationalismus* I/1, 258 ff.
[2] H. E. Weber, *op. cit.*, 277 f.
[3] G. Wolf, *Der Augsburger Religionsfriede*, 1890; Maurenbrecher, *op. cit.*, 310 ff.;

possible for two religious confessions to live beside each other. A formula for this purpose had been adopted at Passau, namely that a permanent peace should be declared and established. But this raised a host of detailed questions, so that in the nature of the case the Diet was faced with a long and arduous series of negotiations, most of which were conducted in committee. In spite of everything that had gone before, the result was inevitably a compromise.[1] The papal legate, Morone, as a result of the death of Pope Julius III on 23 March 1555 was unable to take as active a part as might otherwise have been the case.[2]

At first king Ferdinand tried to arrange that discussion of a territorial peace should take precedence on the agenda over a religious peace. His 'proposition', delivered on 5 February,[3] disregarded the Passau agreement and dealt with the question of getting a settlement of religious issues, though he was unable to propose anything that had not already been tried. He wanted to have a religious conference which would settle the religious question at the outset of the Diet.[4] But the three secular electors had agreed among themselves beforehand to have a religious peace discussed first, and they were supported by Christoph of Württemberg and Ottheinrich of Neuburg.[5] Discussion about the order of the agenda went on until 11 March, and it was this discussion which really decided everything. The outcome was that the ecclesiastical electors supported the secular electors and the college of princes agreed.[6] So discussion of a religious peace was taken first, on the understanding that it would not be concluded until the question of establishing territorial peace had also been settled. A committee under a councillor of the elector of Mainz produced a draft proposal, which was modelled on the final recess of the Diet of Speyer and the Passau agreement.[7] There was heated argument over details. Was the religious peace to include Calvinists, too? What was the position over property belonging to the churches? Were the bishops to

---

Hartung, 145 ff.; L. Schwabe, 'Kursachsen u. die Verhandlungen über den Augsburger Religionsfrieden', *N. Archiv für sächs. Geschichte* 10, 1889, 216 ff.; W. Friedensburg, *ARG* 34, 1937, 58 ff. Text: K. Brandi, *Der Augsburger Religionsfriede vom 25. Sept. 1955*, 1927²; cf. also Brandi, *HZ* 95, 1905, 256 ff. A Catholic view: H. Tüchle, *Zeitschrift des Hist. Vereins für Schwaben u. Neuburg* 61, 1955, 323 ff. An attractive popular account: M. Simon, *Der Augsburger Religionsfriede*, 1955.

[1] K. Brandi, *HZ* 95, 1905, 206: 'a mood of resignation'.
[2] *v. Pastor* VI, 115; J. Grisar, 'Die Sendung des Kardinals Morone', *Zeitschrift des Historischen Vereins für Schwaben u. Neuburg* 61, 1955, 341 ff.
[3] G. Wolf, *Religionsfriede*, 38.
[4] Ibid., 17.
[5] Ibid., 26 ff., 33 ff.; L. W. Spitz, 'Particularism and Peace, Augsburg 1955', *ChH* 25, 1956, 110 ff. examines the varied political goals of the Protestants.
[6] G. Wolf, *Religionsfriede*, 44 f.
[7] Ibid., 46 ff.

have jurisdiction over the subjects of Protestant princes? Would princes have to allow their subjects or estates within their territories the freedom to practise the religion of their choice? The last of these questions was felt by the elector of the Palatinate to be a particularly important one. Morone, the papal nuncio, reminded the bishops of their obligations towards the Roman seat, and bishop Otto Truchsess spoke in the college of princes against the bishops renouncing their rights and their duties, for they were bound to them on oath.[1] How could the bishops possibly renounce possessions and jurisdiction which they had sworn to preserve and maintain?[2] But on the other hand, if they insisted on maintaining these rights and duties, how could a religious peace be established? The ecclesiastical electors, after hesitating momentarily, decided not to be deterred. This was of decisive significance for the subsequent course of events, and after this it was merely a matter of settling the details. The bishops renounced jurisdiction over Protestant territories, receiving in return the assurance that in cases where cathedral cities had become Protestant, the cathedral chapter would not be driven out. On the question of church property many amendments were made to the draft proposal. Saxony proposed[3] that the religious peace should guarantee to the churches such properties as were in their possession at the time of the Passau agreement. This proposal was carried. The most difficult question of all was the question of granting freedom in religious matters. Württemberg and Brandenburg wanted freedom of conscience and freedom of religious faith for every subject,[4] but king Ferdinand would rather have seen the entire enterprise collapse than grant freedom of this sort.[5] So subjects were merely given the right to emigrate to another territory. The elector of the Palatinate demanded that the religious peace should extend also to any who might in the future adopt the Augsburg Confession, but the elector of Cologne opposed this, urging that no further modifications or changes should be permitted. The college of princes attempted a solution by proposing that no one should be liable to attack merely for adhering to the Augsburg Confession. But this raised the question of the ecclesiastical territories.[6] The ecclesiastical princes urged that only the secular estates should be given the freedom to adopt the religion of their choice, whereas the Protestants were unwilling to see the Reformation ruled out of the ecclesiastical territories. For the future

---

[1] Ibid., 93 f.; *Roth* IV, 678 f.
[2] G. Wolf, *op. cit.*, 61 f., cf. 116 f.
[3] Ibid., 71.
[4] Ibid., 98 f.
[5] Ibid., 99; cf. S. Adler, 'Der Augsburger Religionsfriede und der Protestantismus in Osterreich', *Festschrift für H. Brunner*, 1910, 259 ff.
[6] G. Wolf, *Religionsfriede*, 129 ff.;

shape of the Empire this was a question of the greatest importance, and there was no agreement on it. Then, after lengthy arguments over procedure,[1] the Diet turned its attention to ordering peace among the territories and to passing legislation relating to the Imperial Cameral Tribunal. These matters were quickly settled.[2] Preliminary work on the means of securing territorial peace had been done by a Frankfurt group, whose proposals were accepted without modification. The heads of administrative districts (*Kreisoberste*) were in future to be elected by the estates and given certain executive powers. By this means the responsibility for maintaining territorial peace became a matter for the estates, rather than for the central authority.[3] The regulations relating to the Imperial Cameral Tribunal were changed to allow adherents of the Augsburg Confession to be members of it. Its terms of reference were changed, for it was given the responsibility of upholding common law, territorial peace and also the religious peace which had just been concluded.

But the Diet had yet to win the consent of king Ferdinand. He was out of sympathy with the course which the Diet had followed. Evidence of this is that in July he tried to adjourn the Diet in order that religious conversations might reach a religious settlement before any proposals for a religious peace were enacted.[4] The Diet proposed that even if such conversations failed the religious peace should still be in force, but on 30 August Ferdinand rejected this proposal.[5] To give up the idea of religious unity was as difficult for him as it was for his brother. On the question of the ecclesiastical territories he sided with the ecclesiastical princes and demanded in addition that in the imperial cities where both confessions were represented each confession should be officially recognised. He was not prepared to grant the right of emigration to Habsburg subjects. On 6 September he gave way on the first question, but demanded that the Protestants should recognise the principle of *reservatio ecclesiastica*, i.e. that they should renounce the possibility of introducing the Reformation in ecclesiastical territories,[6] for 'he had sworn on his honour not to give way on this'. The Protestants were divided. After much controversy[7] Saxony proposed to settle the matter by demanding in return that the ecclesiastical princes should allow freedom of religious faith to the Protestant estates in their territories. Ferdinand actually supported this,

[1] Ibid., 139 ff.
[2] Ibid., 152.
[3] See Hartung, *op. cit.* on this question.
[4] G. Wolf, *op. cit.*, 139 ff.
[5] Ibid., 153.
[6] *CR* 8, 478 (Melanchthon's statement).
[7] G. Wolf, *op. cit.*, 161.

but he was unable to persuade the Catholics to allow this concession to be included in the final recess of the Diet. So it was given in a secret document instead, using the device which had been employed during the previous decade, namely a special declaration given by the king on his own authority. Once again the Imperial Cameral Tribunal was not bound by the declaration. The final recess mentioned only that the Protestants were unable to give their consent to the *reservatio ecclesiastica*. The king was asked to deal directly with the imperial cities,[1] who for their part resisted having special regulations applied to them. However, Augsburg and Regensburg—chiefly because they were in fact bi-confessional cities—acceded.[2] The others then accepted the motion that in the free cities and the imperial cities the existence of two confessions side by side should be allowed to continue, and that 'neither party should seek to displace the other's religion, church customs or ceremonies or to compel the other to depart from his faith'. It was also agreed that each confession should retain its own goods and properties. The only city to oppose this was Strasbourg, which sent an envoy with a letter to king Ferdinand even as late as 24 September. The envoy was sent away, however, and on 25 September the Diet was closed, having worked for over seven months.[3]

4. THE SIGNIFICANCE OF THE RELIGIOUS PEACE

The religious peace of Augsburg was a compromise. It was worked out by politicians using the medium of diplomacy. It took account of the political necessities of the hour and it rested on mutual concessions. On both sides there was a strong desire for peace and security, but this desire was not so strong as to cause either party to change its principles or to seek modifications to the laws of the state. Each party was convinced that its position was the only true position, and neither could renounce this claim. All that they were prepared to agree was that force should be excluded from religious politics. No one at Augsburg seriously questioned that legislation for this purpose was within the competence of the Imperial Diet. But because religious differences were not overcome, and because the very structure of the Empire meant that religious considerations inevitably spilled over into political considerations, the religious peace carried within it the seeds of its own destruction. The stronger the religious dynamic, the greater was the danger to peace. But now that there was

---

[1] G. Wolf, *op. cit.* 164.

[2] *Roth* IV, 680 ff. (on Augsburg); cf. G. Pfeiffer, 'Der Augsburger Religionsfriede und die Reichsstädte', *Zeitschrift des hist. Vereins für Schwaben u. Neuburg* 61, 1955, 213 ff.

[3] J. Grisar, *Stimmen der Zeit* 156, 1955, 440 ff. (the positions of the Popes).

parity of representation on the Imperial Cameral Tribunal which was committed to maintaining the peace—both of which measures were incorporated in the terms on which the Emperor was elected—the maintenance of this peace became a fundamental law of the Empire. To this law both sides could appeal from that moment onwards, and for sixty years it made possible a tolerable peace.

The basically Catholic character of the Empire was not changed, for the Emperor continued to be under obligation to defend and protect the Catholic Church. The bishops' jurisdiction over the 'lost' territories was merely suspended. It was not altogether taken away from them. The Empire did not become a state in which both confessions had parity, for the religious peace 'in no way gave explicit or positive recognition to Protestants. It merely stipulated that the right of inquisition be suspended where the religious conflict within the Empire was concerned.'[1] That is why the proposed discussions aimed at achieving religious unity (which the next Imperial Diet was to get under way) formed an integral part of the religious peace. Thus the relationship between the Pope and the Emperor remained, at least in theory, the same as it was before. The Pope continued to make the claims he had made before, though he limited himself, when protesting against the religious peace, to sending notes of protest to the Catholic princes and to the bishops.[2] The Pope's later refusal to recognise the election of Ferdinand as Emperor did not mean that any breach had been made between the papacy and the imperial dignity, though in consequence no Emperor was ever again crowned by the Pope. It was not until the 17th century that 'the dominance of Protestant jurisprudence turned the Augsburg provisions into a permanent regulation by which both confessions enjoyed equal respect and legitimacy'.[3] But such a reinterpretation was only possible when 'the question of theological truth was by-passed'.[4] Thus it was on Protestant soil that a way was prepared for the later law of tolerance, which was to come when the law of Empire was freed from its earlier links with the Church.

As a political instrument the religious peace put the administrative authorities of the Empire under an obligation to remain neutral in religious politics and the struggles associated with them. The law would decide all issues between the parties. But the administrative authorities were thus presented with an impossible task, particularly as it was apparent from the outset that the religious peace was entirely inadequate as a legal instrument. The Protestants, for example, were by no means clear whether the

---

[1] M. Heckel, 'Staat und Kirche nach den Lehren der evangelischen Juristen in der ersten Hälfte des 17. Jahrhunderts', ZSavRG 42, 1956, 133.

[2] Grisar, op. cit., 461; cf. v. Pastor IV, 568 n. 1.

[3] Heckel, op. cit., 135.

[4] Ibid., 136.

law permitted further secularisation or not. The *reservatio ecclesiastica* had to be decreed by the king on his own authority and it was not recognised by the Protestants. At subsequent Imperial Diets they tried persistently and vainly to get it repealed, arguing that it was not permissible to erect barriers against the Gospel. Duke Christoph of Württemberg declared that the *reservatio* made nonsense of all efforts to achieve religious unity, for if the ecclesiastical princes made concessions they would at once forfeit—according to the terms of the *reservatio*—all their rights and possessions. Whether the *reservatio ecclesiastica* was observed or not in practice depended on the relative power which any prince wielded. The elector August of Saxony, who in other respects was completely loyal, managed despite the *reservatio* to secularise the bishoprics of Meissen, Merseburg and Naumburg. The collegiate foundations of North Germany, under varying degrees of pressure, elected Protestant 'administrators' to their chapters and were thus led along the road to Protestantism. Among these were Magdeburg, Halberstadt, Bremen, Lübeck, Verden, Camin. The concession which Ferdinand made to the Protestants to compensate for the *reservatio* (i.e. the *declaratio Ferdinandea*, by which Protestants in Catholic territories were promised protection) gave rise to even greater difficulties. It imposed upon the ecclesiastical princes obligations which as Catholics and as princes they could not keep. Moreover, it had never been published, and the Imperial Cameral Tribunal had never been informed of its existence. Subsidiary declarations of this sort were not included in the final recess of the Diet, and this meant that the declaration had no status whatever in law. On the other hand, the Imperial Cameral Tribunal took no action to prevent the secularisation of monasteries in Württemberg, Baden-Durlach, and Zweibrücken in the Palatinate, which was a bitter pill for the Catholics. The regulations concerning the imperial cities, in which both confessions were to be allowed to exist side by side, were designed to perpetuate the state of affairs which the Interim had produced, and it thereby denied to the imperial cities the right of Reformation which had been conceded to all the other estates. It is hardly surprising that the cities refused to be bound by these regulations and disregarded the Interim. Aachen's attempt to become Protestant admittedly ended in disaster. These three points became the source of innumerable difficulties. Both sides repeatedly found pretexts for listing their grievances and for stirring up agitation about them. Thus mutual suspicion and mistrust were not allayed, and in the end confessional alliances were once again organised, paving the way for a new war, while the administrative authorities within the Empire were unable to implement the law which they were supposed to administer.

Only in one respect was there an open breach of the limitations imposed by the religious peace. Originally the peace was extended only to adherents of the Augsburg Confession. Thus the 'Zwinglians' were expressly excluded from it. But when Frederick III of the Palatinate openly embraced Calvinism, even his most bitter theological opponents could not bring themselves to deny him the protection afforded by the religious peace (1556).[1] The way was now open for further confessional divisions within Protestantism (at Nassau 1578, Bremen 1580, Anhalt 1584) without raising afresh the problem of religious peace in any acute form.[2] The attempts made by the elector of the Palatinate and others to win freedom of conscience and religion for the individual subject met with no success, for they were asked to grant more in return than they felt able to concede. So the basic principle which remained was that the princes were responsible for the religion of their subjects. The only way of achieving freedom of conscience was to emigrate to another territory, and even this right was hotly contested by king Ferdinand at Augsburg and was not recognised in the Emperor's hereditary territories. There was no freedom of religion either in the Protestant territories, for it was the religious peace which made Protestant churches thoroughly territorial churches. They were governed according to an 'episcopal' system devised by church lawyers on a purely legal, not theological, basis. The bishop's rights were simply transferred to the ruler of the territory, who exercised them through his consistory court.[3]

---

[1] B. G. Struve, *Ausführlicher Bericht von der Pfälzischen Kirchenhistorie*, 1721, 168 ff.; A. Kluckhohn, *Briefe Friedrich des Frommen* I, 1686, 610 ff.

[2] Heckel, *op. cit.*, 193 ff.

[3] Ibid., 207 ff., 241 ff.

BIBLIOGRAPHY

I. SOURCES

G. Wolf, *Quellenkunde der deutschen Reformationsgeschichte*, 1915–1923.

F. Schnabel, *Deutschlands Quellen und Darstellungen in der Neuzeit: 1. Das Zeitalter der Reformation 1500–1550*, 1931.

Dahlmann-Waitz, *Quellenkunde der Deutschen Geschichte*, 1931[9].

J. Sleidanus, *De statu religionis et reipublicae Carolo quinto Caesare Commentarii*, 1555. German trans., ed. J. S. Semler, 1771–1773.

W. E. Tentzel and E. S. Cyprian, *Historischer Bericht vom Anfang und Fortgang der Reformation Lutheri*, 1718.

V. E. Löscher, *Vollständige Reformations-Akta und Dokumenta bis 1519*, 1720–1729.

C. G. Neudecker, *Urkunden der Reformations-Zeit*, 1836.

K. E. Förstemann, *Archiv für Geschichte der Reformation*, 1831; and *Neues Urkundenbuch zur Geschichte der evangelischen Reformation*, 1842.

Deutsche Reichstagsakten. Jüngere Reihe (Pub. by the Historical Commission of the Bayerische Akademie der Wissenschaften):

  Vol. 1 (ed. A. Kluckhohn), The Election of the Emperor 1519 (1893);

  Vol. 2 (ed. A. Wrede), The Imperial Diet of Worms 1520–1521 (1896);

  Vol. 3 (ed. A. Wrede), The Imperial Diets of Nuremberg 1522–1523 (1901);

  Vol. 4 (ed. A. Wrede), The Imperial Diet of Nuremberg 1524 (1893–1905);

  Vol. 7 (ed. J. Kühn), The Imperial Diet of Regensburg, 1526–1527, the Diets of the Swabian League 1527–1528, and the Imperial Diet of Speyer 1529 (1935).

Die Bekenntnisschriften der ev.-lutherischen Kirche, 1954[4] (*BSLK*).

A. L. Richter, *Die evangelischen Kirchenordnungen des 16. Jahrhunderts*, 1846.

E. Sehling, *Die evangelischen Kirchenordnungen des 16. Jahrhunderts*, vols. 1–5, 1902–1913; vols. 6–7 (Lower Saxony), 1955–1963; vol. 11 (Franconia), 1961; vol. 12 (Swabia), 1963.

P. Börger, *Quellen zur Geschichte der Reformation*, 1953.

B. Bendfeld, *Quellen zur Geschichte des späten Mittelalters. Europa im Zeitalter der Reformation*, 1957.

J. Greving (ed.), *Reformationsgeschichtliche Studien und Texte*, 1908 ff.

K. Kaulfuss-Diesch, *Das Buch der Reformation, geschrieben von Mitlebenden*, 1927.

W. Köhler (ed.), *Das Buch der Reformation Huldrych Zwinglis von ihm selbst und gleichzeitigen Quellen erzogen*, 1926.

II. BIBLIOGRAPHIES, LEXIKONS, ETC.

W. Maurer, *Namenliste zur deutschen Geschichte des 16. Jahrhunderts*, 1941.

R. H. Bainton, *Bibliography of the Continental Reformation*, Chicago 1935.

J. Dag, *Bibliographie chronologique de la Littérature de Spiritualité et de ses sources (1501–1610)*, Paris 1952; and by the same author, *Bibliographie de la Réforme* (4 vols.), 1958–1963.

H. Rössler and G. Franz, (1) *Biographisches Wörterbuch zur Deutschen Geschichte*, 1952; (2) *Sachwörterbuch zur Deutschen Geschichte*, 1958.

Mennonitisches Lexikon, 1913 ff.

Mennonite Encyclopaedia, 1956–1959.

III. OTHER LITERATURE

J. von Pflugk-Hartung (ed.), *Im Morgenrot der Reformation*, 1912.

J. Huizinga, *Herbst des Mittelalters*, 1953[7].

R. Stadelmann, *Vom Geist des ausgehenden Mittelalters*, 1929.

W. Andreas, *Deutschland vor der Reformation*, 1948[5].

W. E. Peuckert, *Die grosse Wende*, 1948.

L. von Ranke, *Deutsche Geschichte im Zeitalter der Reformation*, ed. Duncker and Humblot, 1924.

G. Kawerau, *Reformation und Gegenreformation*, 1907.

T. Brieger, *Die Reformation*, 1914.

K. Kaser, *Das Zeitalter der Reformation und Gegenreformation*, 1922.

H. Hermelink and W. Maurer, *Reformation und Gegenreformation*, 1931.

R. Huch, *Deutsche Geschichte II: Das Zeitalter der Glaubensspaltung*, 1954[2].

K. Brandi, *Deutsche Geschichte im Zeitalter der Reformation u. Gegenreformation*, 1960[3].

G. Ritter, *Die Neugestaltung Europas im 16. Jahrhundert*, 1950.

E. G. Schwiebert, *Luther and his Times. The Reformation from a new perspective*, 1950.

P. Joachimsen, *Die Reformation als Epoche der deutschen Geschichte*, 1951.

F. Hartung, *Deutsche Geschichte im Zeitalter der Reformation, der Gegenreformation und des 30 jährigen Krieges*, 1951.

K. D. Schmidt, *Geschichte der Kirche im Zeitalter der Ref. u. Gegenref.*, 1952.

F. H. K. Green, *Renaissance and Reformation*, 1952.

R. H. Bainton, *The Reformation of the 16th Century*, 1952.

P. Rassow, *Das Zeitalter Luthers und Karls V.*, 1953.

H. J. Grimm, *The Reformation Era (1500–1650)*, 1954.

H. Rössler, *Europa im Zeitalter von Renaissance, Ref. u. Gegenref.*, 1956.

L. von Muralt, 'Die Reformation', *Historia Mundi* VII (1957), 39–113.

J. G. Clark, *Early Modern Europe, ca. 1450 to 1720*, 1957.

E. Hassinger, *Das Werden des neuzeitlichen Europa 1300 bis 1600*, 1959.

H. Holborn, *A History of Modern Germany, I: The Reformation*, 1958.

J. Jansen, *Geschichte des deutschen Volkes seit dem Ausgang des Mittelalters*, 8 vols., 1876 ff.

Hinneberg, *Die Kultur der Gegenwart*, 1922[2] (essay by A. Ehrhard, 'Katholische Christenheit und Kirche in der Neuzeit').

J. Lortz, *Die Reformation in Deutschland*, 1949[3]; and *Wie kam es zur Reformation?*, 1955.

H. Bornkamm, *Das Jahrhundert der Reformation*, 1961.

W. Köhler, *Luther und das Luthertum in ihrer weltgeschichtlichen Auswirkung*, 1933.

W. Maurer, 'Was verstand Luther unter der Reformation der Kirche?' *Luther*, 1957, 49–62.

INDEX

R